Encyclopedia of Transcendentalism

ENCYCLOPEDIA
OF
TRANSCENDENTALISM

Edited by
Wesley T. Mott

Greenwood Press
Westport, Connecticut • London

Library of Congress Cataloging-in-Publication Data

Encyclopedia of transcendentalism / edited by Wesley T. Mott.
    p.   cm.
    Includes bibliographical references (p.) and index.
    ISBN 0–313–29924–2 (alk. paper)
    1. American literature—History and criticism—Encyclopedias.
    2. Transcendentalism (New England)—Encyclopedias.
    3. Transcendentalism in literature—Encyclopedias. I. Mott, Wesley
    T.
    PS217.T7E53   1996
    810.9'384—dc20   95–40030

British Library Cataloguing in Publication Data is available.

Library of Congress Catalog Card Number: 95–40030
ISBN: 0–313–29924–2

First published in 1996

Greenwood Press, 88 Post Road West, Westport, CT 06881
An imprint of Greenwood Publishing Group, Inc.

Printed in the United States of America

The paper used in this book complies with the
Permanent Paper Standard issued by the National
Information Standards Organization (Z39.48–1984).

10 9 8 7 6 5 4 3 2

Copyright Acknowledgments

The editor and publisher gratefully acknowledge permission to reprint the following material:

Excerpts reprinted by permission of the publishers from *The Collected Works of Ralph Waldo
Emerson*, Vols. 1–5 edited by Alfred R. Ferguson, Jean Ferguson Carr, et al., Cambridge, Mass.:
The Belknap Press of Harvard University Press, Copyright © 1971– by the President and
Fellows of Harvard College.

Excerpts reprinted by permission of the publishers from *The Journals and Miscellaneous
Notebooks of Ralph Waldo Emerson*, Vols. 1–16 edited by William H. Gilman, Ralph H. Orth, et
al., Cambridge, Mass.: The Belknap Press of Harvard University Press, Copyright © 1960–1982
by the President and Fellows of Harvard College.

For
Norman Pettit

Contents

Preface

The *Encyclopedia of Transcendentalism* is a comprehensive guide to the major philosophical concepts, antecedents, genres, institutions, organizations, movements, periodicals, events, and places associated with Transcendentalism in the United States.

The 145 alphabetically arranged entries focus on the New England Renaissance but include classical, European, Oriental, and native sources and influences. A history-of-ideas approach governs the book, embracing religious, philosophical, literary, artistic, educational, political, scientific, and reform aspects. American Transcendentalism was not a monolithic "movement": Its manifestations included compelling ideas, a specific cultural moment in U.S. history, popular conceptions and misconceptions, and extraordinary diversity of expression. The definitions, assumptions, and scope of the book are explained in the entry "Transcendentalism."

The first historian of the movement, Octavius Brooks Frothingham, exaggerated when he suggested that "there never was such a thing as Transcendentalism out of New England." This book takes the "vantage ground" (to use Emerson's phrase) of Transcendentalism in New England but encompasses a broader national scope, including important developments out of New England. Moreover, though Transcendentalism arose in the 1830s and peaked by the Civil War, the book includes important foreground as well as later transformations and influences of the movement. The Chronology affords an overview of events and publications significant to the emerging, flourishing, and memorializing of American Transcendentalism, with selected historical events included as benchmarks; the juxtapositions offer several revealing parallels as well as ironies.

With its history-of-ideas emphasis, the *Encyclopedia* is designed as a companion volume to the *Biographical Dictionary of Transcendentalism* (Greenwood, 1996), which has entries on persons who lived until at least 1830, including those who shaped, criticized, and memorialized the movement. Cross-references to the *Dictionary* in this *Encyclopedia* are indicated by a double asterisk (**). Significant philosophical, theological, and literary antecedents who died before 1830 appear in this volume. Entries on persons are not comprehensive biographies but—like entries on other types of topics—emphasize the subjects' *significance* to American Transcendentalism.

Individual literary works, such as Emerson's *Nature* (1836) and Thoreau's *Walden* (1854), can be accessed through the index. Separate entries are provided for major periodicals that affected or were published by Transcendentalists.

Entries on sources and influences, including selected important background texts, attempt to establish the nature and extent of the impact: Which Transcendentalists were most importantly affected, when, and through what channels? Was the source known personally? by reputation? in original language? through European periodicals? through translations? Inclusion of such entries has been necessarily selective. Most Transcendentalists were remarkably eclectic readers—an attempt to compile all sources and influences on Emerson alone would be futile. Nevertheless, Transcendentalism in the United States was woven from important strands derived from many times and many cultures. Individually, Virgil or Shakespeare may hardly seem ''Transcendental.'' But Transcendentalists took what they needed from their reading, whether classics of Western culture or surprising and exotic items. From these influences—international and native, ancient and contemporary—the Transcendentalists shaped on these shores a complex and dynamic movement noted for its ''newness.''

Cross-references to other entries in the *Encyclopedia* are indicated by an asterisk (*). Each entry concludes with selected references to significant modern, and historically important, scholarship. Reference items are chosen that specifically link the topic to Transcendentalism. For major world figures, on whom new studies are published each year, standard editions and general guides may also be listed. For many other topics, little modern scholarship is available, and older studies or sources may still be indispensable. The index will help locate topics not covered by separate entries and cross-referencing.

Seventy scholars from a wide range of fields and backgrounds have contributed to this volume. Within common purpose and scope, freedom of interpretation and expression has been encouraged in keeping with the rich diversity of Transcendentalism. I am grateful to the authors not only for their own research but also for responding to countless queries. I especially thank Joel Myerson for reviewing the project at its early stages; Ronald A. Bosco, Robert E. Burkholder, James Duban, Benjamin F. Fisher, Philip F. Gura, and Kent P. Ljungquist for recommending several contributors; Sterling F. Delano, David M. Robinson, and Edmund A. Schofield for reviewing specific items; and the Concord Free Public Library (Marcia Moss, curator), the American Antiquarian Society, and the libraries of Boston University and Worcester Polytechnic Institute for their indispensable help with research. Thanks also to my daughter, Sarah T. Mott, for her help with the manuscript; to production editor Desirée

Bermani and copyeditor Susan E. Badger for their professionalism; and to Dr. George F. Butler of Greenwood Press for his guidance.

"In the right state," Emerson declared in his 1837 Phi Beta Kappa oration, the scholar "is, *Man Thinking.*" Moreover, he asked, "is not the true scholar the only true master?" This volume is dedicated to Norman Pettit, of Boston University—mentor, friend, and "true" American Scholar.

Wesley T. Mott

Guide to Abbreviations and References

An asterisk (*) denotes cross-reference to an entry in this volume. A double asterisk (**) denotes cross-reference to an entry in *Biographical Dictionary of Transcendentalism* (Greenwood, 1996). Terms may be cross-referenced to a different form of the term or different part of speech (e.g., "Swedenborgianism" may be cross-referenced to "Swedenborg, Emanuel," or the adjective "Unitarian" to the noun "Unitarianism"). And a word highly charged in the Transcendentalist setting may be cross-referenced to an entry with a slightly different turn of phrase (e.g., "miracles" to "Miracles Controversy"). In biographical entries, the subject's full name is given at the beginning. Thereafter in the entry, the person's surname is given by initial only, without period (e.g., Immanuel Kant is "K").

STANDARD REFERENCE SOURCES

B&M	Robert E. Burkholder and Joel Myerson. *Emerson: An Annotated Secondary Bibliography* [1816–1979]. Pittsburgh: Univ. of Pittsburgh Press, 1985.
Buell	Lawrence Buell. *Literary Transcendentalism: Style and Vision in the American Renaissance.* Ithaca: Cornell Univ. Press, 1973.
Chielens	Edward E. Chielens, ed. *American Literary Magazines: The Eighteenth and Nineteenth Centuries.* Westport, Conn.: Greenwood Press, 1986.
Cooke	George Willis Cooke. *An Historical and Biographical Introduction to Accompany* The Dial. 2 vols. Cleveland: Rowfant Club, 1902.

CW   *The Collected Works of Ralph Waldo Emerson.* Edited by Alfred R. Ferguson et al. 5 vols. to date. Cambridge: Harvard Univ. Press, 1971– .

Dahlstrand   Frederick C. Dahlstrand. *Amos Bronson Alcott: An Intellectual Biography.* Rutherford, N.J.: Fairleigh Dickinson Univ. Press, 1982.

DLB   *Dictionary of Literary Biography.* Detroit: Gale.

EEM   Henry D. Thoreau. *Early Essays and Miscellanies.* Edited by Joseph J. Moldenhauer and Edwin Moser, with Alexander Kern. Princeton: Princeton Univ. Press, 1975.

EL   *The Early Lectures of Ralph Waldo Emerson.* Edited by Stephen E. Whicher, Robert E. Spiller, and Wallace E. Williams. 3 vols. Cambridge: Harvard Univ. Press, 1959–72.

EP   *The Encyclopedia of Philosophy.* Paul Edwards, Editor in Chief. 8 vols. New York and London: Macmillan, 1967.

Frothingham   Octavius Brooks Frothingham. *Transcendentalism in New England: A History.* New York: G. P. Putnam's Sons, 1876; rpt. Univ. of Pennsylvania Press, 1972.

Gohdes   Clarence L. F. Gohdes. *The Periodicals of American Transcendentalism.* Durham: Duke Univ. Press, 1931.

Gougeon   Len Gougeon. *Virtue's Hero: Emerson, Antislavery, and Reform.* Athens: Univ. of Georgia Press, 1990.

Harding   Walter Harding. *The Days of Henry Thoreau.* New York: Knopf, 1965. Enl. ed., New York: Dover, 1982.

Howe   Daniel Walker Howe. *The Unitarian Conscience: Harvard Moral Philosophy, 1805–1861.* Cambridge: Harvard Univ. Press, 1970.

Hutchison   William R. Hutchison. *The Transcendentalist Ministers: Church Reform in the New England Renaissance.* New Haven: Yale Univ. Press, 1959.

JMN   *The Journals and Miscellaneous Notebooks of Ralph Waldo Emerson.* Edited by William H. Gilman et al. 16 vols. Cambridge: Harvard Univ. Press, 1960–82.

L   *The Letters of Ralph Waldo Emerson.* Vols. 1–6 edited by Ralph L. Rusk; vols. 7–10 edited by Eleanor M. Tilton. New York: Columbia Univ. Press, 1939, 1990–95.

Matthiessen   F. O. Matthiessen. *American Renaissance: Art and Expression in the Age of Emerson and Whitman.* New York: Oxford Univ. Press, 1941.

Miller	Perry Miller. *The Transcendentalists: An Anthology.* Cambridge: Harvard Univ. Press, 1950.
Mott	Frank Luther Mott. *A History of American Magazines.* 4 vols. Cambridge: Harvard Univ. Press, 1938–57.
Myerson	*The Transcendentalists: A Review of Research and Criticism.* Edited by Joel Myerson. New York: Modern Language Association of America, 1984.
*NET*Dial	Joel Myerson. *The New England Transcendentalists and the* Dial: *A History of the Magazine and Its Contributors.* Rutherford, N.J.: Fairleigh Dickinson Univ. Press, 1980.
PJ	Henry D. Thoreau. *Journal.* General Editor Robert Sattelmeyer. In THE WRITINGS OF HENRY D. THOREAU. 4 vols. to date. Princeton, N.J.: Princeton Univ. Press, 1981–.
PN	*The Poetry Notebooks of Ralph Waldo Emerson.* Edited by Ralph H. Orth et al. Columbia: Univ. of Missouri Press, 1986.
Pochmann	Henry A. Pochmann. *German Culture in America: Philosophical and Literary Influences, 1600–1900.* Madison: Univ. of Wisconsin Press, 1957.
Richardson	Robert D. Richardson, Jr. *Myth and Literature in the American Renaissance.* Bloomington: Indiana Univ. Press, 1978.
Robinson	David M. Robinson. *The Unitarians and the Universalists.* Westport, Conn.: Greenwood Press, 1985.
RP	Henry D. Thoreau. *Reform Papers.* Edited by Wendell Glick. Princeton: Princeton Univ. Press, 1973.
Rusk	Ralph L. Rusk. *The Life of Ralph Waldo Emerson.* New York: Scribners, 1949.
Sermons	*The Complete Sermons of Ralph Waldo Emerson.* Edited by Albert J. von Frank et al. 4 vols. Columbia: Univ. of Missouri Press, 1989–92.
TN	*The Topical Notebooks of Ralph Waldo Emerson.* Edited by Susan Sutton Smith, Ronald A. Bosco, and Glen M. Johnson. 3 vols. Columbia: Univ. of Missouri Press, 1990–94.
W	*The Complete Works of Ralph Waldo Emerson.* Edited by Edward Waldo Emerson. 12 vols. Centenary Edition. Boston: Houghton Mifflin, 1903–04.

JOURNALS AND PERIODICALS

AHR	American Historical Review
AL	American Literature
AmLH	American Literary History
AQ	American Quarterly
ARLR	American Renaissance Literary Report: An Annual
ArQ	Arizona Quarterly
Atl	Atlantic Monthly
ATQ	American Transcendental Quarterly
BoQR	Boston Quarterly Review
BRPR	Biblical Repertory and Princeton Review
ChEx	Christian Examiner
ChH	Church History
CRevAS	Canadian Review of American Studies
CS	Concord Saunterer (Thoreau Society)
EdR	The Edinburgh Review
EIHC	Essex Institute Historical Collections
ELN	English Language Notes
ESP	Emerson Society Papers
ESQ	Emerson Society Quarterly (1955–71); ESQ: A Journal of the American Renaissance (1972–)
FoR	Foreign Review
FrM	Fraser's Magazine
HLQ	Huntington Library Quarterly
HTR	Harvard Theological Review
HuLB	Huntington Library Bulletin
JAH	Journal of American History
JAmS	Journal of American Studies
JAMS	Journal of the American Musicological Society
JHI	Journal of the History of Ideas
MassQR	Massachusetts Quarterly Review
MLN	Modern Language Notes
MP	Modern Philology
NAR	North American Review
NCF	Nineteenth-Century Fiction
NCL	Nineteenth-Century Literature
NCM	New-Church Messenger

NCS	*Nineteenth-Century Studies*
NEMag	*New England Magazine*
NEQ	*New England Quarterly*
NJM	*New Jerusalem Magazine*
NYH	*New York History*
PMLA	*PMLA: Publications of the Modern Language Association of America*
PQ	*Philological Quarterly*
PRIHS	*Publications of the Rhode Island Historical Society*
PUHS	*Proceedings of the Unitarian Historical Society*
RALS	*Resources for American Literary Study*
SAR	*Studies in the American Renaissance: An Annual,* ed. Joel Myerson (Boston: Twayne, 1977–82; Charlottesville: Univ. Press of Virginia, 1983–96)
SchS	*School and Society*
SIR	*Studies in Romanticism*
SP	*Studies in Philology*
SSF	*Studies in Short Fiction*
TSB	*Thoreau Society Bulletin*
UCPMP	*University of California Publications in Modern Philology*
WM	*Western Messenger*

Chronology

1803	Ralph Waldo Emerson born in Boston (25 May)
	Monthly Anthology established
1805	Henry Ware elected Hollis Professor of Divinity at Harvard
1807	Boston Athenaeum founded
1810	Sarah Margaret Fuller born in Cambridgeport (23 May)
	Madame de Staël, *De l'Allemagne*
1811	J. S. Buckminster appointed first Dexter Lecturer of Biblical Criticism at Harvard
	Informal beginnings of Divinity School at Harvard
1812	War of 1812 begins
1813	*Christian Disciple* (later *Christian Examiner*) founded by liberal Christians
	Robert Owen, *A New View of Society*
1815	*North American Review* (*NAR*) commences
1817	Henry D. Thoreau born in Concord (12 July)
	Edward Everett first American granted the Ph.D. by the University of Göttingen
	Samuel Taylor Coleridge, *Biographia Literaria*
1818	Harvard sophomore Ralph Waldo Emerson reads Hugh Blair's *Rhetoric*
1819	William Ellery Channing preaches "Unitarian Christianity" in Baltimore
	Faculty of Divinity organized at Harvard
	Andrews Norton named Dexter Professor at Harvard

Emerson studies Dugald Stewart, *Elements of the Philosophy of the Human Mind*

1820   Missouri Compromise postpones crisis over slavery

William Ellery Channing, "The Moral Argument Against Calvinism"

Rammohan Roy, *The Precepts of Jesus*

1821   "The Present State of Ethical Philosophy," Emerson's Bowdoin Prize essay, acknowledges Reid, Paley, Stewart

Emerson hears Channing's Dudleian Lecture, "The Evidences of Revealed Religion," at Harvard

Sampson Reed, "Oration on Genius"

1822   Dugald Stewart's *A General View of the Progress of Metaphysical, Ethical, and Political Philosophy* published in Boston

John and William Langhorne's edition of Plutarch's *Lives* published in New York

1823   George Bancroft on Schiller in *NAR* (October)

William Sewel's *The History of the . . . Quakers,* 3d ed.

1824   William Emerson studies theology at University of Göttingen

Goethe's *Wilhelm Meister's Apprenticeship* translated by Thomas Carlyle

George Bancroft on Goethe in *NAR* (October)

Lydia Maria Child, *Hobomok, a Tale of the Times*

Benjamin Constant, *De la Religion, Considérée dans sa Source, ses Formes et Ses Developpements* (5 vols., 1824–31)

1825   George Bancroft on Herder in *NAR* (January)

Thomas Carlyle, *Life of Schiller*

S. T. Coleridge, *Aids to Reflection*

Henry Ware, Jr., *The Faith Once Delivered to the Saints*

1826   First American lyceum established at Millbury, Massachusetts

Sampson Reed, *Observations on the Growth of the Mind*

Lyman Beecher, *Six Lectures on Intemperance*

1827   Carlyle's "State of German Literature" published anonymously in *Edinburgh Review*

New Jerusalem Magazine founded

1828   William Ellery Channing preaches "Likeness to God"

Bronson Alcott writes for *American Journal of Education*

1829   Emerson ordained as junior pastor of Second Church in Boston (11 March)

James Marsh's American edition of S. T. Coleridge's *Aids to Reflection* (1825) published

[Carlyle,] "Signs of the Times," *The Edinburgh Review*

[Carlyle,] essay on Novalis, *Foreign Review*

George Combe, *The Constitution of Man*

Guillaume Oegger, *La Vrai Messie*

1830   Henry Ware, Jr., appointed Professor of Pulpit Eloquence and the Pastoral Care at Harvard Divinity School

Emerson begins reading Gérando, *Histoire comparée des systèmes de philosophie*

Emily Dickinson born

First volume of Charles Lyell's *Principles of Geology* published in London

Letters of Pestalozzi on the Education of Infancy, translated by J. P. Greaves, published in Boston

Elizabeth Palmer Peabody, *First Lessons in Grammar, on the Plan of Pestalozzi*

Gérando, *Self-Education: or, The Means and Art of Moral Progress,* translated by E. P. Peabody

1831   William Lloyd Garrison founds *The Liberator* in Boston   —

Nat Turner leads slave revolt in Virginia

[Carlyle,] "Characteristics," *The Edinburgh Review*

Henry Ware, Jr., *The Formation of the Christian Character*

1832   New England Anti-Slavery Society founded

Emerson resigns Second Church ministry (28 October)

Victor Cousin's *Introduction to the History of Philosophy* (translated by Henning G. Linberg) published in Boston

Phrenologist Johann Spurzheim lectures in Boston

Gérando, *The Visitor of the Poor,* translated by E. P. Peabody

Rammohan Roy, *Translation of Several Principal Books, Passages and Texts of the Veds*

Spurzheim, *Outlines of Phrenology*

Lydia Maria Child, *Biographies of Madame de Staël and Madame Roland*

1833   Alcott reads Plato and Francis Okeley's *Life of Jacob Behmen*

Father Taylor preaches at new Seamen's Bethel in Boston

Thomas Carlyle's *Sartor Resartus* appears serially in *Fraser's Magazine* (1833–34)

Emerson visits Jardin des Plantes in Paris

Emerson meets Carlyle at Craigenputtock

F. H. Hedge reviews Coleridge and Swedenborg in *Christian Examiner*

1837	Panic of 1837
	M. L. Hurlbut attacks W. H. Furness in March *Christian Examiner*
	Emerson delivers Phi Beta Kappa address ("The American Scholar") at Harvard (31 August)
	Thoreau visits cabin of C. S. Wheeler on shores of Flint's (Sandy) Pond
	Massachusetts Board of Education formed
	Andrews Norton, *Evidences of the Genuineness of the Gospels* (3 vols., 1837–44)
	Harriet Martineau, *Society in America*
1838	Cherokees embark on Trail of Tears
	Abner Kneeland imprisoned for blasphemy
	W. E. Channing lectures on "Self-Culture"
	Emerson delivers "An Address" (the Divinity School Address) to seniors in Divinity College (15 July)
	Orestes Brownson starts *Boston Quarterly Review* (attacks "Francis Bowen")
	Alcott closes Temple School
	New England Non-Resistance Society formed
	Frederick Douglass escapes from slavery
	Bronson Alcott hears George Combe lecture
	George Ripley inaugurates *Specimens of Foreign Standard Literature* (14 vols., 1838–42)
	First English translation (Francis Haywood) of Kant's *Critique of Pure Reason* published in London
	Alcott House established in Surrey, England
	Andrews Norton, "The New School in Literature and Religion" (Boston *Daily Advertiser,* 27 August)
	George Bancroft, *On the Progress of Civilization*
	Henry Ware, Jr., *The Personality of the Deity*
	Isaac Ray, *Treatise on the Medical Jurisprudence of Insanity*
	Harriet Martineau, *Retrospect of Western Travel*
1839	James Walker named Alford Professor of Natural Religion and Moral Philosophy at Harvard
	Emerson elected to the Social Circle of Concord
	Brownson attacks "Norton's Evidence" in *BoQR*
	J. P. Eckermann, *Conversations with Goethe,* translated by Margaret Fuller
	Andrews Norton, *A Discourse on the Latest Form of Infidelity*

George Ripley, *"The Latest Form of Infidelity" Examined*

Jones Very, *Essays and Poems* (ed. R. W. Emerson)

N. P. Willis, *Loiterings of Travel*

1840　*The Dial* commences

Elizabeth Peabody opens bookshop on West Street in Boston

The Alcotts move to Concord

Millerites and Come-Outers hold convention in Groton, Massachusetts

First Chardon Street Convention

　　Bronson Alcott, 50 "Orphic Sayings," *The Dial* (July)

　　Richard Hildreth, *A Letter to Andrews Norton on Miracles as the Foundation of Religious Faith*

　　Orestes Brownson, *The Laboring Classes*

　　"Levi Blodgett" [Theodore Parker], *The Previous Question Between Mr. Andrews Norton and His Alumni*

　　George Ripley, *Defence of "The Latest Form of Infidelity Examined." A Second Letter to Mr. Andrews Norton*

　　George Ripley, *Defence of "The Latest Form of Infidelity Examined." A Third Letter to Mr. Andrews Norton*

　　Edward Palmer, *A Letter to Those Who Think*

1841　Brook Farm established

Emerson lectures on "The Transcendentalist" at Masonic Temple in Boston

Horace Greeley founds New York *Tribune*

New Englanders among audience as Schelling lectures in Berlin

Ezra Ripley, D.D., dies

　　Ralph Waldo Emerson, *Essays* (First Series)

　　Theodore Parker, *The Transient and Permanent in Christianity*

1842　John Thoreau dies from lockjaw

Five-year-old Waldo Emerson dies from scarlet fever

Convers Francis appointed to faculty of Harvard Divinity School

Newlyweds Nathaniel and Sophia Hawthorne take up residence at the Old Manse

Emerson and Hawthorne visit Shaker community at Harvard

　　[Charles Mayo Ellis,] *An Essay on Transcendentalism*

　　Orestes Brownson, *The Mediatorial Life of Jesus*

　　J. F. Clarke, *A Sermon Preached in Amory Hall*

　　Charles Caldwell, *Facts in Mesmerism and Thoughts on Its Causes & Uses*

	Theodore Parker, *A Discourse of Matters Pertaining to Religion*
	G. Oegger, *The True Messiah,* translated by E. P. Peabody
1843	Bronson Alcott arrested in January for refusing to pay poll tax
	Fruitlands experiment begins (1 June)
	The Present founded in New York by W. H. Channing
	Ellery Channing, *Poems*
	Parke Godwin, *Democracy. Constructive and Pacific*
	L. M. Child, *Letters from New-York*
	Charles Lane, *The Law and Method of Spirit-Culture, An Interpretation of Bronson Alcott's Idea and Practice at the Masonic Temple*
1844	Fruitlands experiment ends (January)
	Millerites' "Great Disappointment" as Christ fails to appear
	Thoreau reviews N. P. Rogers's *Herald of Freedom* in April *Dial*
	Emerson purchases Wyman field in Walden Woods—site of Thoreau's Walden house
	Ralph Waldo Emerson, *Essays: Second Series*
	Margaret Fuller, *Summer on the Lakes, in 1843*
	Parke Godwin, *Popular View of the Doctrines of Fourier*
1845	*The Harbinger* commences
	Thoreau moves into his Walden "house" (4 July)
	Emerson lectures in Boston on "Representative Men" (winter 1845–46)
	Margaret Fuller, *Woman in the Nineteenth Century*
	Sylvester Judd, *Margaret*
	William Goodell, *Come-Outerism: The Duty of Secession from a Corrupt Church*
	Frederick Douglass, *Narrative of the Life of Frederick Douglass*
	L. M. Child, *Letters from New-York. Second Series*
	Robert Owen, *Book of the New Moral World*
1846	Mexican War (1846–48)
	Henry Thoreau jailed for refusing to pay poll tax
	Potato famine in Ireland
	Ralph Waldo Emerson, *Poems*
	Margaret Fuller, *Papers on Literature and Art*
	Nathaniel Hawthorne, *Mosses from an Old Manse*
	Charles Kraitsir (with Elizabeth Peabody), *The Significance of the Alphabet*

Adin Ballou, *Christian Non-Resistance, in All Its Important Bearings, Illustrated and Defended*

Henry C. Wright, *Defensive War Proved to Be a Denial of Christianity and of the Government of God*

Samuel Johnson and Samuel Longfellow, comp., *A Book of Hymns for Public and Private Devotion*

Josiah Warren, *Equitable Commerce*

Charles Grandison Finney, *Memoirs*

1847   Brook Farm closes

Thoreau leaves Walden (6 September)

Theodore Parker founds *Massachusetts Quarterly Review*

E. A. Poe attacks Transcendentalism in review of Hawthorne in *Godey's Lady's Book* (November)

Women's Associative Union founded in Boston

Ellery Channing, *Poems, Second Series*

Ellery Channing, *Conversations in Rome Between an Artist, a Catholic, and a Critic*

Parker Pillsbury, *The Church as It Is; or, The Forlorn Hope of Slavery*

Asa Mahan, *A System of Intellectual Philosophy*

Francis Wayland, *The Duty of Obedience to the Civil Magistrate*

1848   First Women's Rights Convention, Seneca Falls, New York

Marx and Engels, *The Communist Manifesto*

W. H. Channing, *Memoir of William Ellery Channing*

F. H. Hedge, *The Prose Writers of Germany*

J. R. Lowell, *A Fable for Critics*

1849   Sole issue of *Aesthetic Papers* (May), includes H. D. Thoreau, "Resistance to Civil Government"

California Gold Rush

Spirit of the Age founded in New York

Town and Country Club organized by Alcott with Emerson

Emerson and Alcott read Lorenz Oken

Herman Melville hears Emerson lecture

Henry D. Thoreau, *A Week on the Concord and Merrimack Rivers*

Ralph Waldo Emerson, *Nature; Addresses, and Lectures*

Ellery Channing, *The Woodman*

William B. Greene, *Transcendentalism*

1850	Compromise of 1850 (including the Fugitive Slave Law) enacted into law
	Margaret Fuller perishes in shipwreck off Fire Island
	Thoreau reads Alexander von Humboldt (c. 1850)
	Ralph Waldo Emerson, *Representative Men*
	Nathaniel Hawthorne, *The Scarlet Letter*
	Cyrus Bartol, *Discourse on the Christian Spirit and Life*
	Henry James, Sr., *Moralism and Christianity*
1851	Emerson delivers "Fugitive Slave Law Address"
	Herman Melville, *Moby-Dick*
	Charles Beecher, *The Duty of Disobedience to Wicked Laws*
	Nathaniel Halls, *The Limits of Civil Obedience*
1852	*Dwight's Journal of Music* established
	Nathaniel Hawthorne, *The Blithedale Romance*
	Memoirs of Margaret Fuller Ossoli, edited by Ralph Waldo Emerson, William Henry Channing, and James Freeman Clarke
	Theodore Parker, *Discourse* on Webster
	Harriet Beecher Stowe, *Uncle Tom's Cabin*
	Charles Kraitsir, *Glossology: Being a Treatise on the Nature of Language and the Language of Nature*
	William Hosmer, *The Higher Law, in Its Relations to Civil Government*
	Marx Edgeworth Lazarus, *Love vs. Marriage*
	Herman Melville, *Pierre*
1853	*Putnam's Monthly Magazine* founded
	Stephen Pearl Andrews, *Love, Marriage, and Divorce, and the Sovereignty of the Individual*
1854	Rendition of fugitive slave Anthony Burns protested
	Saturday Club takes form
	Henry D. Thoreau, *Walden; or, Life in the Woods*
	Orestes Brownson, *The Spirit-Rapper: An Autobiography*
	T. T. Stone, *Sermons*
	N. P. Willis, *Outdoors at Idlewild*
	Timothy Shay Arthur, *Ten Nights in a Bar-room*
1855	Sleepy Hollow Cemetery consecrated in Concord
	Walt Whitman, *Leaves of Grass*
	Henry C. Wright, *Marriage and Parentage*
	Henry James, Sr., *The Nature of Evil*

Theodore Parker, *The Collected Works* (14 vols., published in London, 1863–71)

Josiah Warren, *True Civilization: An Immediate Necessity*

1864   Henry D. Thoreau, *The Maine Woods* (ed. Sophia Thoreau)

J. F. Clarke, *Natural and Artificial Methods in Education*

John Weiss, Jr., *The Life and Correspondence of Theodore Parker*

Louisa May Alcott, *Moods*

Samuel Johnson and Samuel Longfellow, comp., *Hymns of the Spirit*

1865   Lincoln is assassinated

J. R. Lowell debunks Thoreau as nature-loving hermit in *North American Review*

The Radical founded

Henry D. Thoreau, *Letters to Various Persons* (ed. R. W. Emerson)

Henry D. Thoreau, *Cape Cod* (ed. Sophia Thoreau)

F. H. Hedge, *Reason in Religion*

Orestes Brownson, *The American Republic: Its Constitution, Tendencies, and Destiny*

David A. Wasson, *The Radical Creed*

1866   St. Louis Philosophical Society founded

Henry D. Thoreau, *A Yankee in Canada* (ed. Sophia Thoreau)

1867   Free Religious Association formed

Radical Club formed by Cyrus Bartol

C. A. Dana acquires New York *Sun*

Ralph Waldo Emerson, *May-Day and Other Pieces*

John Burroughs, *Notes on Walt Whitman as Poet and Person*

1868   Louisa May Alcott, *Little Women* (2 vols., 1868–69)

Bronson Alcott, *Tablets*

1869   Samuel J. May, *Some Recollections of Our Antislavery Conflict*

Henry James, Sr., *The Secret of Swedenborg*

Josiah Warren, *True Civilization: A Subject of Vital and Serious Interest to All People*

1870   Ralph Waldo Emerson, *Society and Solitude*

Emerson, introduction to *Plutarch's Morals* (ed. William W. Goodwin)

M. D. Conway, *The Earthward Pilgrimage*

John Humphrey Noyes, *History of American Socialisms*

Elizabeth Peabody, *Kindergarten Culture*

1871   Emerson visits John Muir at Yosemite

Ellery Channing, *The Wanderer*

J. F. Clarke, *Ten Great Religions*

John Weiss, Jr., *American Religion*

Louisa May Alcott, *Little Men*

1872   Cairn started by pilgrims to site of Thoreau's Walden house

Bronson Alcott, *Concord Days*

Cyrus Bartol, *Radical Problems*

Samuel Johnson, *Oriental Religions and Their Relation to Universal Religion: India*

S. P. Andrews, *The Basic Outline of Universology*

1873   Elizabeth Peabody establishes *The Kindergarten Messenger*

Ellery Channing, *Thoreau, the Poet-Naturalist*

Louisa May Alcott, "Transcendental Wild Oats"

L. M. Alcott, *Work: A Story of Experience*

1874   *Parnassus,* favorite poems collected by Emerson

Cyrus Bartol, *The Rising Faith*

J. F. Clarke, *Common-Sense in Religion*

M. D. Conway, *Sacred Anthology*

1875   C. P. Cranch, *The Bird and the Bell with Other Poems*

Henry James, *Roderick Hudson*

1876   Ralph Waldo Emerson, *Letters and Social Aims*

Octavius Brooks Frothingham, *Transcendentalism in New England: A History*

John Weiss, Jr., *Wit, Humor, and Shakespeare. Twelve Essays*

1877   Bronson Alcott, *Table-Talk*

Samuel Johnson, *Oriental Religions . . . : China*

Harriet Martineau, *Autobiography*

1878   J. F. Clarke, *Memorial and Biographical Sketches*

Henry James, *The Europeans*

1879   First session of the Concord School of Philosophy

Henry James, Sr., *Society the Redeemed Form of Man*

1880   C. T. Brooks, *William Ellery Channing: A Centennial Memory*

Elizabeth Peabody, *Reminiscences of Rev. Wm. Ellery Channing, D.D.*

John Weiss, Jr., *The Immortal Life*

1881   Bronson Alcott, *New Connecticut: An Autobiographical Poem*

G. W. Cooke, *Ralph Waldo Emerson: His Life, Writings, and Philosophy*

1891	J. F. Clarke, *Autobiography, Diary and Correspondence* (ed. E. E. Hale)
	F. H. Hedge, *Sermons*
	O. B. Frothingham, *Recollections and Impressions*
1892	John Muir becomes first president of the Sierra Club
	H. D. Thoreau, *Autumn* (ed. H.G.O. Blake)
1893	F. B. Sanborn and W. T. Harris, *A. Bronson Alcott: His Life and Philosophy*
1894	*The Familiar Letters of Henry David Thoreau* (ed. F. B. Sanborn)
	J. T. Codman, *Brook Farm: Historic and Personal Memoirs*
	John Muir, *The Mountains of California*
1895	Caroline Dall, *Margaret [Fuller] and Her Friends*
	W. H. Furness, *Recollections of Seventy Years*
1896	John Tyndall, *Fragments of Science*
1897	Caroline Dall, *Transcendentalism in New England*
1898	Spanish-American War
	T. W. Higginson, *Cheerful Yesterdays*
1899	T. W. Higginson, *Contemporaries*
	Julia Ward Howe, *Reminiscences, 1819–1899*
	Charles Eliot Norton, *Letters from Ralph Waldo Emerson to a Friend, 1838–1853*
1901	F. B. Sanborn, *The Personality of Thoreau*
	F. B. Sanborn, *Ralph Waldo Emerson*
	John Muir, *Our National Parks*
1902	Ednah Cheney, *Reminiscences*
1903	Emerson Centennial observed
	F. B. Sanborn, *The Personality of Emerson*
1903–04	*The Complete Works of Ralph Waldo Emerson,* Centenary Edition, edited by Edward Waldo Emerson
1904	M. D. Conway, *Autobiography, Memories and Experiences*
	Henry James, *The Golden Bowl*
1906	*The Writings of Henry David Thoreau,* Walden Edition, edited by Bradford Torrey and Francis H. Allen
1907	Theodore Parker, [*The Centenary Edition of the Works* (15 vols., 1907–12)]
	William James, *Pragmatism*
1908	F. B. Sanborn, *Bronson Alcott at Alcott House, England, and Fruitlands, New England (1842–1844)*

1909	F. B. Sanborn, *Recollections of Seventy Years*
1911	William James, *Some Problems of Philosophy*
1915	Clara Endicott Sears, *Bronson Alcott's Fruitlands*
1917	United States enters World War I
	F. B. Sanborn, *The Life of Henry D. Thoreau*
	Edward Waldo Emerson, *Henry Thoreau as Remembered by a Young Friend*

A

ABOLITIONISM, though there has been much disagreement on the specific definition of the term, here is taken to mean an organized effort to abolish slavery in the United States, either immediately or gradually, through moral suasion, agitation, or political action. An abolitionist is one who belonged to, or who substantially supported, such an organization. Opposition to slavery in America appeared as early as the Puritan* Samuel Sewell's *The Selling of Joseph* (1700). The first secular abolitionist organization, the Society for the Relief of Free Negroes Held in Bondage, was established in Philadelphia in 1775. However, the movement took a major step forward on 1 January 1831 when W. L. Garrison** founded *The Liberator* in Boston. Soon after, in 1832, Garrison, along with E. G. Loring** and others, founded the New England Anti-Slavery Society. Garrison was eventually joined by W. Phillips,** who was soon recognized as the movement's most gifted orator. Many women joined the movement early on, including R. W. Emerson's** wife Lidian** and H. Thoreau's** mother and sisters.

Most Transcendentalists were decidedly opposed to slavery. Dr. W. E. Channing** published a famous, and controversial, attack on the system and its supporters in *Slavery* (1835). Despite the considerable public criticism visited upon Channing by wealthy conservatives in Boston's commercial class in response, Emerson admired the study and referred to it as one of the "perfectly genuine works of the times." Despite this strong antislavery feeling among Transcendentalists, however, there was considerable ambivalence regarding abolition and its proponents. This ambivalence had many sources. Generally, Transcendentalists emphasized self-reliance and therefore eschewed organized efforts at reform that were believed to diminish the independence of individuals. Additionally, they opposed one-issue reformers as myopic. Reform, they felt, should be universal. Also, Transcendentalists generally believed that social reform properly began with individual moral reform and that reform could not be imposed from without upon either individuals or society. Finally, in addition to these concerns, many Transcendentalists were also put off by the personalities of some abolitionists who were seen as egocentric, pompous, and crude. Emerson expressed his early views on the matter in lectures such as "Man the Reformer" (1841 [CW, 1:141–60]), "New England Reformers" (1844 [CW, 3:147–67]), and the famous essay "Self-Reliance" (1841 [CW, 2:25–51]). Thoreau criticized organized reform in "Reform and the Reformers" (1844 [RP, 181–97]) and "self-styled reformers" in Walden (1854, 153–54). M. Fuller** expressed her concerns about the abolitionists in a letter to Maria Weston Chapman in 1840. Despite these early reservations, many Transcendentalists eventually openly supported the abolition movement. Among the provocative events that encouraged this development were the emancipation of slaves in the British empire in 1834, frequent and virulent attacks upon free speech and abolitionists, the admission of Texas to the Union as a slave state in 1845, the passage of the Fugitive Slave Law in 1850, and J. Brown's** dramatic attack upon Harpers Ferry in 1859. The most prominent abolitionists among the Transcendentalists were Emerson, Thoreau, Fuller, T. Parker,** W. H. Furness,** B. Alcott,** and W. H. Channing.** Other Transcendentalists, for various reasons, did not actively support the abolition movement. These included G. W. Curtis,** G. Ripley,** F. H. Hedge,** and O. A. Brownson.**

For their part, Garrison and his followers were often critical of the Transcendentalists. They found their stated opposition to slavery incongruous with their opposition to associated efforts at reform. Thus, Garrison once referred to Channing's attacks on slavery as "moral plagiarisms from the writings of abolitionists." Similarly, the Eighth Annual Report of the Boston Female Antislavery Society (1841) pointed out defensively that "our experience confutes the assertion of Dr. Channing, that organization weakens individual energy, cramps the freedom of the individual mind, and confines it to the contemplation of one idea, till its judgment of the relative importance of things is impaired." It is indicative that when Parker announced his commitment to the abolition cause in 1841 Edmund Quincy commented, in a letter to a friend, that Parker made his commitment "without any Emersonian or Channingian qualifications."

Eventually, Emerson became an outspoken supporter of abolition. He gave his first antislavery address in Concord* in November 1837, following the murder of Elijah Lovejoy, an abolition publisher, in Alton, Illinois. Throughout the 1840s, and up to the Civil War, he, as well as Thoreau, Parker, Alcott, T. W. Higginson,** M. D. Conway,** and others, attacked the institution of slavery in a variety of public ways, often joining with Garrison, Phillips, and their supporters in the process. After the passage of the Compromise of 1850* this activity became, at times, almost frenetic. It would continue through the Civil War, during which time Emerson and other Transcendentalists became regular proponents of emancipation and equal rights.

REFERENCES: Among the most useful works on abolition are Gerald Sorin, Abolitionism: A New Perspective (1972); Merton L. Dillon, The Abolitionists: The Growth of a Dis-

senting Majority (1974); and Martin Duberman, ed., *The Antislavery Vanguard: New Essays on the Abolitionists* (1965). For Emerson and the relationship of abolition and Transcendentalism, see Gougeon (1990). For Transcendentalism and reform, see Anne C. Rose, *Transcendentalism as a Social Movement, 1830–1850* (1981), and Taylor Stoehr, *Nay-Saying in Concord: Emerson, Alcott, and Thoreau* (1979). On abolitionism in the context of the general sweep of reform at the time, see Alice Felt Tyler, *Freedom's Ferment* (1944, 1962). For a comprehensive, annotated collection of Emerson's antislavery writings, see Len Gougeon and Joel Myerson, eds., *Emerson's Antislavery Writings* (1995).

Len Gougeon

The **ADIRONDACK CLUB**, an outgrowth of the Saturday Club,* was created by the journalist and painter William J. Stillman to provide members of the Boston and Cambridge cultural elite with a wilderness experience. Its most memorable outing, its second, occurred in August 1858, when Stillman induced R. W. Emerson,** J. R. Lowell,** L. Agassiz,** Ebenezer Rockwood Hoar, and several others to spend two weeks roughing it on then-untouched Follensby Pond in one of the remotest sections of the northern Adirondacks. Because of the intellectual attainments of the party, the camp became known, half-jocularly, as "Philosophers' Camp." The members slept in spruce-bark shelters, fished, hunted, swam, took canoe trips, botanized, listened to the tales of the local guides, and marveled at the grandeur and stillness of the wilderness. Stillman commemorated the outing with a painting, *Philosophers' Camp,* now in the Concord Free Public Library. Encouraged by the success of the expedition, Stillman purchased 22,500 acres surrounding nearby Lake Ampersand for $600, and for several years thereafter, various club members (but not including Emerson) returned for further visits. The Civil War soon put an end to the excursions, the land was sold for unpaid taxes, and in a few years the area around both lakes was cut over for timber, obliterating all traces of Philosophers' Camp. In recent years efforts have been made by New York State to buy the land around Follensby Pond, partly because of its literary associations.

Besides the painting by Stillman, Philosopher's Camp is memorialized in Emerson's poem "The Adirondacs," first published in *May-Day* (1867). In 343 lines, Emerson describes the trip down the Raquette River and through a marsh to the pond, the setting up of the camp, the activities undertaken (including a deer hunt in which Emerson "shot at a mist"), and the philosophical implications of the wilderness experience. Long used to the domesticated environs of Walden Pond,* Emerson saw that primordial nature* was of a different order altogether: It seemed to hold a great mystery waiting to be unraveled, a "mystic hint" of "spiritual lessons . . . Inviting to new knowledge." At the end of the poem, the campers learn of the completion of the transatlantic telegraph cable, a symbol of man's dominance over nature. Humanity's destiny, it seems, is not to linger in the past, which the wilderness represents, but to fulfill itself through science, commerce, and culture.

REFERENCES: The main sources for information about the Adirondack Club are Stillman, *The Old Rome and the New and Other Studies* (1898), 265–96, and his *Autobiography of a Journalist*, 2 vols. (1901), 1:239–56; E. W. Emerson,** *The Early Years of the Saturday Club 1855–1870* (1918), 169–76; Emerson's record of the 1858 trip in *JMN*, 13:34–35, 55–57, and his poem "The Adirondacs," *W*, 9:182–94. See also Paul F. Jamieson, "Emerson in the Adirondacks," *NYH* 39 (1958): 215–37.

                                                                    Ralph H. Orth

AESTHETIC PAPERS (May 1849), edited and published by E. P. Peabody** from her bookshop at 13 West Street, Boston, was a single-issue periodical.

By the late 1840s, only the *Spirit of the Age** and *The Massachusetts Quarterly Review** continued to provide periodical outlets for Transcendentalist thought and expression. In 1848 Peabody began soliciting contributions from what she hoped would be differing views of "Philosophy, of Individual and Social Culture . . . and of the Scientific and Literary World" (*Aesthetic Papers*, iii). Peabody pressed her brother-in-law N. Hawthorne** for an entry. Julian Hawthorne writes that his father originally sent "Ethan Brand" but judged that "too lurid for Miss Peabody's aestheticism" and substituted "Main-street." From R. W. Emerson** Peabody extracted an essay on "War," delivered as a lecture in Boston in 1838. She contributed three essays, including the introduction, and seven other contributors, including H. Thoreau,** rounded out the issue's essays. The poems, by Peabody, E. S. Hooper,** T. W. Higginson,** and Louisa Higginson, are unremarkable.

In the "Prospectus," Peabody announced that successive issues would be released when enough material had been collected and enough subscribers located. This cautious approach may have suited the times, when many readers found themselves distracted by political events like the escalating argument over slavery and the western territories; readers might also have been deterred by the ponderous nature of the essays. In any event, Peabody's caution was well founded; the first issue proved to be the last.

In her introductory essay, "The Word 'Aesthetic,' " Peabody distinguishes between the idiosyncratic element in art, championed by French criticism, and the German approach emphasizing the universal and "disinterested" qualities in art. In its stress on idea rather than on taste, Peabody thought, German criticism deserved the term "aesthetic," and it was this version of the aesthetic that she sought to explore in her journal.

The majority of essays in *Aesthetic Papers* follow and develop this broad approach to art and to ideas, seeking the cosmic, universal, and divine principles behind phenomena. The essays and authors in agreement with this approach include S. G. Ward's** "Criticism," S. Reed's** "Genius," Samuel Perkins's "Abuse of Representative Government," J. S. Dwight's** "Music," Emerson's "War," Peabody's "Language," P. Godwin's** "Organization," and James J. G. Wilkinson's "Correspondence.*"

Ironically, the essays in *Aesthetic Papers* that deviate from the journal's stated purpose are the most distinguished, vigorous, and complex in the collection.

Indeed, two of them, Hawthorne's "Main-street" and Thoreau's "Resistance to Civil Government," undermine the very assumptions of the periodical.

Hawthorne's sketch is ostensibly a history of the social and moral progress of Salem, but that theme is challenged by a critic who ridicules the pasteboard cut-out figures who move across the stage. The whole demonstration breaks down when the wire breaks, suggesting the fragility and artifice of the notion of progress and cultural unity.

Perhaps the most famous essay in this collection is Thoreau's "Resistance to Civil Government," later known as "Civil Disobedience.*" In striking contrast to Godwin's essay, which celebrates social and political organization, Thoreau disdains government and civil authority, preferring the moral majority of one.

Peabody's essay on "The Dorian Measure, with a modern application," is original in its call for instruction in gymnastics, dance, music, and art in the public schools, following the model of the ancient Greeks. As for the cost, she writes, "it is plain, that, if we can spend a hundred millions of dollars in a year for so questionable a purpose as the late war of Mexico, we have resources on which we might draw for public education*" (109–10).

Finally, "Vegetation about Salem," by an anonymous English resident, is a remarkable intertwining of botanical and social history, revealing a deep Thoreauvian love of nature* and its particularities.

REFERENCES: *Aesthetic Papers* is available in a modern edition, ed., with a fine introduction, by Joseph Jones (1957). The fullest treatment of the periodical is in Gohdes (1931). Brief mention is in Cooke** (1902), in Edward Chielens, *The Literary Journal in America to 1900* (1975), and in Joel Myerson, ed., *The American Renaissance in New England (DLB*, 1978). Julian Hawthorne's recollection of his father's involvement, together with some family letters, is in *Nathaniel Hawthorne and His Wife*, 2 vols. (1884), 1: 330–32.

Bruce A. Ronda

AGRICULTURE, the theory and practice of farming, was an important source of the Transcendental concept of culture. The Transcendentalists understood culture as a process, not a product. Self-cultivation was for them a major purpose of life, and their ideas about culture and self-cultivation owe at least as much to their knowledge of agriculture as they do to Goethean** or Arnoldian or anthropological conceptions of culture.

The Transcendentalists knew agriculture at first hand. H. Thoreau** raised beans and corn at Walden Pond.* He knew how to graft fruit trees. He had a garden at home for many years where he grew spectacular squashes (one weighed 123 ½ pounds) and gave a popular annual melon party. He read current agricultural reports as well as the Roman agricultural writers, he took an ever-increasing interest in fruits and seeds of all kinds, and he delivered his important contribution to the science of ecology ("On the Succession of Forest Trees") at the Middlesex Agricultural Society's Cattle Show in September 1860.

Brook Farm,* the Transcendentalist utopian community, was set up on a milk farm in West Roxbury, Massachusetts, and its founder, G. Ripley,** assumed that the perfect life would be grounded in both farming and education.*

R. W. Emerson** and B. Alcott** were more interested in arboriculture than agriculture (technically speaking), in orchards rather than field crops. Alcott's Fruitlands* community was set up to put into practice the ideas of Alcott and his friends about the reform of farming. They intended to eliminate exploitation of animals (no meat, no leather, no wool, no draft animals) and to eliminate as well any dependence, however remote, on slavery (no cotton). Fruitlands placed a heavy dependence on "aspiring" vegetables (no root crops; nothing that grew downward, seeking darkness) and fruit trees. Emerson also took a keen interest in orchards, planting many varieties of apple and pear, as well as quince for grafting stock. He kept an orchard book. One of his apple trees was a "Thoreau," either named after or developed by his young friend. "Apples," said Emerson, "are the national fruit." In the mid-19th century, there were more than 1,400 distinct sorts of apples being grown. Emerson was also fascinated by the theories of Van Mons about the artificial improvement of varieties of fruit.

From agriculture and arboriculture, the Transcendentalists acquired an organic* view of life that harmonized well with German and English Romantic ideas about self-cultivation and the organic concept of art. Growth and development were important for people as well as for plants, and the Transcendental emphasis on self-cultivation was in the end more than metaphor, expressing as it did their conviction that humans are inescapably part of nature,* are formed by natural processes, and prosper best when they are closest to what T. S. Eliot would later call the "life of significant soil."

REFERENCES: Important articles are Robert A. Gross, "Culture and Cultivation: Agriculture and Society in Thoreau's Concord,"* *JAH* 69 (June 1982): 42–61 (rpt. in Robert St. George, *Material Life in America* [1988]); and David M. Robinson, " 'Unchronicled Nations': Agrarian Purpose and Thoreau's Ecological Knowing," *NCL* 48 (December 1993): 326–40.

Robert D. Richardson, Jr.

The major **AMERICAN MAGAZINES** of the post–Civil War era (1865–1900) provide two divergent perspectives on the Transcendental movement of the previous generation. One view looked fondly backward to an age when American literature and culture were being shaped by the vibrant idealism* and optimistic humanism of R. W. Emerson** and his followers. The opposite view looked backward with bemused condescension at the mysticism of an eccentric generation. From the former group G. W. Curtis** and other Transcendental sympathizers had long since entered the American mainstream and were dispersed among the prominent literati after the war. They played a significant role in establishing Emerson's entrance into the small pantheon of American writers of genius and continued throughout the remainder of the century to find in Transcendental writings insight and inspiration. While few of those of the latter (and smaller) group would deign to criticize the sainted Emerson, some, led by

J. R. Lowell,** often referred to the Transcendental movement and its members with scorn.

Of course, the most important factor in shaping later judgments of the Transcendental movement was the war itself. After the war, few remembered what had made Emerson and Transcendentalism once so threatening. The movements of armies instilled fear; an intellectual movement led by a New England Platonist* did not. In any case, Emerson had proven his loyalty by his strong support for the Union cause and was now embraced by most of the magazines and their readers as an example of the type of healing model that the postwar decades needed.

The most consistent and ardent celebrator of all things Transcendental was Curtis, who occupied an influential seat as writer of *Harper's* "Editor's Easy Chair" column. While throughout the 1850s *Harper's* viewed Transcendentalism as a movement of "modern skepticism" that "would have astonished the old infidels of the eighteenth century" (6: 554–58), by 1871 it saw Transcendentalism as nothing less than the center of "the moral, intellectual, social, and political renaissance of American life" (43: 929–33), a judgment that *Harper's* would maintain into the 20th century. The *Atlantic** shared *Harper's* praise for the fructifying influence of Transcendentalism and allowed O. B. Frothingham,** like Curtis a former disciple of the Concord* School, to present in its pages in 1883 his general tribute to Transcendentalism's intellectual, historical, and philosophical importance (52: 13–23). The *North American Review,** while speaking kindly about Emerson, published at the end of the Civil War a disparaging essay on H. Thoreau** (101: 597–608) by Lowell and a decade later a scornfully dismissive piece on the entire Transcendental movement (123: 468–74) by Henry Adams. The approach of the *Century Magazine* was similar: general praise for Emerson as man and writer but mocking scorn for everything and everyone else associated with the Transcendental school (see, e.g., 3: 637 and 5: 515). For the *Century,* even the hallowed Emerson had his faults. At his death Emerson was eulogized by E. C. Stedman as one of "the true founders of American literature," an inspirer, but not its "true poet."

The weekly *Critic,* consistent with the aims of editor J. Gilder's attempts to promote all things American, embraced the chief figures of the Transcendental movement despite philosophical misgivings, provided a balanced forum for articles measuring Thoreau's greatness, and opened its pages to W. Whitman's** prose. *Scribner's Magazine* found numerous occasions to insert brief respectful allusions to Emerson as introductory to the discussion of an important issue or to buttress an argument.

The magazines most surprising in their response to Transcendentalism were the *Overland Monthly* and *Galaxy,* one the literary voice of the new West, the other the literary voice of New York. The *Overland* reflected the same admiration for Emerson found in the other magazines, offering frequent allusions to his works, especially when discussing nature,* philosophy, and good writing. It judged him to be "the most original and independent thinker of America" (13:

90) and referred to Thoreau as the model by which nature writers should be measured. The *Galaxy* praised Emerson and Thoreau for their radical protests against dilettantism and formalism, especially in a series of articles by artist and social critic Eugene Benson, who lauded the Transcendental era as a healthy counterpoint to the current age's materialism and mechanism.

REFERENCES: For readers interested in a broader examination of the contents of these and other magazines of the post–Civil War era, Mott (1938–57) is invaluable. Specific citations to Transcendentalists and their works in these and other magazines can be found in *The Literary Index to American Magazines, 1815–1865* (1980) and *The Literary Index to American Magazines, 1865–1900* (1995) by Daniel A. Wells.

Daniel A. Wells

AMERICAN UNION OF ASSOCIATIONISTS, formed in 1846 in New York City, was devoted to the principles of C. Fourier** and their implementation in the United States. After studying with Fourier abroad, A. Brisbane** returned to the United States and encouraged a number of Fourierist communities through his column in H. Greeley's** New York *Tribune*. In addition, a number of clubs, or "unions," were formed in many cities and towns to discuss Fourier's ideas. Many Transcendentalists, including C. A. Dana** and G. Ripley,** became interested in Fourierism, prompting the conversion of Ripley's Brook Farm* community to a Phalanx. Brook Farm became one of the centers of the Fourierist movement in the United States with its publication of the weekly newspaper *The Harbinger,* and it was Ripley's wish to unite the many unions under one organization. The American Union of Associationists first met in May 1846. W. H. Channing** wrote the announcement of its formation for *The Harbinger,* claiming that the society was based on a system of "Joint-Stock Property; Co-operative Labor; Association of Families; Equitable Distribution of Profits; Mutual Guarantees; Honors According to Usefulness; Integral Education; (and) Unity of Interests." Officers, including Greeley, Channing, P. Godwin,** Ripley, Dana, Brisbane, and J. S. Dwight,** decided policy from West Roxbury and New York. They were committed to spreading Associationist ideas in the United States, often through lectures to the "unconverted." By 1848, however, the movement was in peril. The demise of *The Harbinger* in 1849, due to financial problems, foreshadowed the American Union's demise. The last meeting of the American Union, by then largely symbolic, occurred in 1851.

REFERENCES: The best source on the rise of Fourierism in the United States and the American Union of Associationists is Carl J. Guarneri, *The Utopian Alternative: Fourierism in Nineteenth Century America* (1991). O. B. Frothingham,** *George Ripley* (1882), and Charles Crowe, *George Ripley, Transcendentalist and Utopian Socialist* (1967), describe Ripley's role in the American Union. Studies on Brook Farm and collections of letters from the community, including Lindsay Swift, *Brook Farm* (1900), and Henry W. Sams, *Autobiography of Brook Farm* (1958), are good starting points for research on the connection between the Transcendentalist movement and the American Union of Associationists.

Julie M. Norko

ATLANTIC MONTHLY, founded in 1857 and still in publication, was initially conceived as an outlet for Boston-area writers, served as an organ of New England cultural and political interests, and was directed toward a predominantly Yankee readership; this sectional character predominated into the 20th century. Transcendentalists whose essays, poems, and reviews were printed in the first 46 volumes (through December 1880) included R. W. Emerson,** H. Thoreau,** A. B. Alcott,** Ellery Channing,** T. Parker,** G. Ripley,** C. A. Bartol,** J. F. Clarke,** M. D. Conway,** C. P. Cranch,** J. S. Dwight,** O. B. Frothingham,** F. H. Hedge,** T. W. Higginson,** S. Judd,** E. P. Peabody,** F. B. Sanborn,** and J. Weiss.** Many other contributors during this period were associated with the Transcendental movement by virtue of friendship, family ties, and intellectual or political affinities or antagonisms: L. M. Alcott,** the Unitarian* clergyman and journalist Henry Whitney Bellows, J. Burroughs,** J. E. Cabot,** L. M. Child,** G. W. Curtis,** C. W. Dall,** J. T. Fields (the *Atl*'s second editor and publisher, owner of Ticknor and Fields,* America's premier publishing house in the 1850s and 1860s), his wife Annie, P. Godwin,** N. Hawthorne,** O. W. Holmes,** J. W. Howe** (whose "Battle Hymn of the Republic" was first published in one of the wartime issues), William Dean Howells, who succeeded Fields as editor, the Swedenborgian* H. James, Sr.,** and both his famous sons,** J. R. Lowell,** H. Martineau,** the communitarian and educator R. D. Owen, Horace E. Scudder (himself to become, in the 1890s, editor of the *Atl* and of the first collected edition of Thoreau), Senator C. Sumner,** D. A. Wasson,** Thoreau's friend Mary Russell Watson, E. P. Whipple,** W. Whitman,** J. G. Whittier,** and Francis Henry Underwood.

It was Underwood who conceived of the magazine in the early 1850s, planning it with John P. Jewett, publisher of *Uncle Tom's Cabin.* In 1853 he was canvassing the reform-minded New England literati for contributions, but Jewett's failure quashed the scheme. Four years later, having taken counsel with such intellectual luminaries as Emerson, Holmes, John Lothrop Motley, H. W. Longfellow,** Lowell, and E. E. Hale,** Underwood persuaded the Boston house of Phillips, Sampson, and Company (then Emerson's publisher) to undertake the magazine. Holmes, a lavish and popular contributor, devised the monthly's name; its first editor (November 1857–June 1861) was the urbane and prolific Lowell. He was assisted by Underwood, who also supplied a great deal of copy before 1860. At the end of 1859, Fields' senior partner, William D. Ticknor, unenthusiastically purchased the *Atl* from the bankrupt Phillips, Sampson firm, and Fields soon replaced Lowell as editor. Ticknor and Fields authors understandably were often featured in the columns of the *Atl,* where works like Hawthorne's English sketches appeared before being issued in book form. The editors also printed reviews of newly published or immediately forthcoming Ticknor and Fields volumes.

For the first dozen years, contributions were (with rare exceptions) printed anonymously, but their authorship was public knowledge, and starting in 1862 the indexes of the semiannual volumes included attributions. However parochial the *Atl*'s contributor list may have been, its content was catholic; the original subtitle was *A Magazine of Literature, Art, and Politics.* Science was added to the list in October 1865. Many of its pieces concerned biography and history; travel and geography; science and natural history* (by L. Agassiz** and Higginson, among others); religion; foreign affairs; economics and finance (the *Atl* was inaugurated in the Panic year 1857, when many magazines failed); music and the visual arts. There was poetry and abundant fiction—serialized novels by H. B. Stowe** and local color stories by Rose Terry Cooke, for instance. Its politics were, predictably, antislavery, Republican, and during the war, Unionist.

To the inaugural volume Emerson contributed several poems and essays: "The Rommany Girl," "The Chartist's Complaint," "Days," "Brahma," "Illusions," "Solitude and Society," "Two Rivers," "Books," and "Persian Poetry." He continued in the same vein until the 1870s, with such pieces as an essay on Saadi* in July 1864, "Terminus" in January 1867, and his renowned biographical sketch of Thoreau, based on his funeral oration for his friend, in August 1862. (The invaluable "Historic Notes of Life and Letters in Massachusetts" [changed to "in New England" in the 1883–84 Riverside Edition] was printed posthumously in October 1883.) "The Forester," B. Alcott's article in praise of Thoreau, appeared in the April 1862 issue, as its subject lay dying in Concord.* L. M. Alcott commemorated him in verse, "Thoreau's Flute," September 1863—one of five poems and short stories she gave to the *Atl.* Thoreau's own experience as a contributor to the magazine began badly. He had sent an unidentified 57-page manuscript to Underwood on 2 December 1853. Before the end of January 1858, Lowell solicited a Maine paper from Thoreau for the infant *Atl;* Thoreau offered "Chesuncook" and sent manuscript copy of the first half on 5 March. The narrative appeared in three installments, June, July, and August 1858. Thoreau had requested proofsheets, a precaution inspired by his disappointments with *Putnam's.** In the proofs of the July segment, he found that a pantheistic* sentiment was blue-penciled for cancellation: "It [the pine tree] is as immortal as I am, and perchance will go to as high a heaven, there to tower above me still." Against the stricken matter he wrote "Stet" to indicate that it should be retained, but on 22 June, when the July issue reached him, he was astonished to find the sentence lacking. His coldly furious letter of protest to Lowell "should be framed in every editorial office," wrote Henry S. Canby. It was not until 1862, when Fields had assumed the editor's chair, that Thoreau again submitted copy to the *Atl,* evidently at Fields' invitation. From his deathbed he dispatched "Autumnal Tints" to Ticknor and Fields on 20 February, "The Higher Law"* ("Life without Principle") eight days later, and "Walking" on 11 March. The manuscript of "Wild Apples" followed on 2 April accompanied by Thoreau's last dated letter, dictated to his sister Sophia. "Walking" was the first of the late natural history essays to see print, a fortnight after Thoreau's death on 6 May; "Autumnal Tints" and "Wild Apples" appeared in October and November, suitably to their seasonal subjects; "Life without Principle" came out in October 1863; and "Night and Moonlight"—drawn from a lecture manuscript—was reprinted from the just-published *Excursions* volume in November. The following year, previewing *Cape Cod,* Fields printed two chapters, "The Wellfleet Oysterman" (October 1864) and "The Highland Light" (December). In 1878 and 1885 the *Atl* printed four sets of seasonal passages from Thoreau's manuscript journal,* extracted by H.G.O. Blake.** In addition to the printings of Thoreau textual materials and commemorations already mentioned, there were published in the *Atl* before 1880 reviews of Thoreau's *The Maine Woods, Cape Cod,* and *Letters to Various Persons* (all by Higginson), of the Englishman Alexander H. Japp's pseudonymous ("H. A. Page") biography of Thoreau, and of Channing's *Thoreau: the Poet-Naturalist* by Sanborn.

REFERENCES: Mott (1938–57) contains an authoritative chapter on the magazine, 2:493–515. James C. Austin, *Fields of the Atlantic Monthly* (1953), draws upon the vast archival resources of the Huntington Library's Fields Collection in recounting the editor's relations with his contributors. See also Bliss Perry, *Park Street Papers* (1908), 205–77, and H. E. Scudder, *James Russell Lowell: A Biography* (1901), 1:408–55. A recent study of the magazine's "literary, social, and political ideology" as a force in New England intellectual culture is Ellery Sedgwick, *The Atlantic Monthly 1857–1909: Yankee Humanism at High Tide and Ebb* (1994).

Joseph J. Moldenhauer

B

BERKELEY, GEORGE (1685–1753), was an Irish-born English bishop and philosopher whose contributions to the philosophy of idealism* influenced R. W. Emerson** and other Transcendentalists. B is best known for the "immaterial hypothesis," in which he asserted that "only persons exist; all other things are not so much existences as the manners of the existence of persons." In denying the independent existence of matter, B maintained that "to be is to be perceived" (*esse est percepi*). Proceeding from the premise that material objects exist only as we conceive them to exist, B argued for the existence of God. Since ordinary objects are but "collections of ideas," B held, they are "necessarily perceived by an infinite mind, therefore there is an infinite mind, or God." Accordingly, B rejected the scientific theories of his time on the basis that the phenomena they purported to deal with did not exist. Like much Transcendentalist thought, his belief that "ideas are things" bears the imprint of Plato.*

Emerson is known to have borrowed B's books from the Boston Library Society and makes several references to him in his journals.* In 1853, he wrote of English intellectuals, "They make a great ado about a truth. . . . There is poorsmell, & learned trifling, & Locke* instead of B." O. A. Brownson** calls attention to B's influence on the "Idealism" chapter of Emerson's *Nature* in a contemporary review of that book. Of Emerson, Brownson wrote, "He all but worships what his senses seem to present to him, and yet is not certain that all that which his senses place out of him, is not after all the mere subjective laws of his own being, existing only to the eye, not of a necessary, but of an irresistible Faith" (*Boston Reformer*, 10 September 1836, 2). Echoing B, Emerson himself wrote in "Idealism": "Idealism sees the world in God. It beholds the whole circle of persons and things, of actions and events, of country and religion, not as painfully accumulated, atom after atom, act after act, in an aged creeping Past, but as one vast picture, which God paints on the instant eternity, for the contemplation of the soul." An early draft of Emerson's sermon XLIII refers directly to "the pious Bishop B." In an 1827 letter to his brother Charles,** Emerson acknowledged that the "warp" of his idealism was from the skeptic philosopher Pyrrho, the "woof" from B. In 1841, he wrote to M. Fuller** of "the joy with which in my boyhood I caught the first hint of the Berkleian philosophy, and which I certainly never lost sight of afterwards."

REFERENCES: Kenneth Walter Cameron, *Emerson the Essayist* (1945), proposes that B had a significant influence on Emerson, as does Blakeney J. Richard, "Emerson and Berkeleian Idealism," *ESQ* 58 (1st Q 1970): 90–97. Stephen Whicher dismisses this claim in *Freedom and Fate* (1953). A. A. Luce, *B's Immaterialism* (1945), is a seminal commentary on B's "Treatise Concerning the Principles of Human Knowledge." A. C. Grayling, *B: The Central Arguments* (1986), presents a modern-day defense of B's main philosophical arguments. Margaret Atherton interprets B's first major work, *An Essay towards a New Theory of Vision* (1709), in *B's Revolution in Vision* (1990).

Mark J. Madigan

BHAGAVADGĪTĀ (Song of the Blessed One) is the most universally revered scripture of the world's Hindus and a text coveted and held in highest regard by several of the Transcendentalists. Conceived by traditional commentators as the quintessence of the Veda, or absolute knowledge, "the *Gītā*" consists of an interlude of 18 chapters from the sixth book of India's longest national epic, the *Mahābhārata*. Though complex in form, the *Mahābhārata* essentially relates the story of a catastrophic war, together with its antecedents and consequences, which occurs between two sides of an ancient royal family. Set in a no-man's land between the two armies drawn up for battle, the *Gītā* recounts the dialogue between Arjuna, the greatest archer of his time, and Kṛṣṇa, his kinsman and teacher, who as a noncombatant in the war agreed to serve as Arjuna's charioteer. Though Arjuna is renowned for his courage, when faced with the near prospect of destroying an enemy consisting in large part of his own family, he falters in his resolve and appeals to Kṛṣṇa for help.

While framed as a counsel of war, Kṛṣṇa's subsequent teachings encompass such perennial issues as the nature of life and death; the purpose of human life; the value of spiritual discernment (*jñāna*), devotion to God (*bhakti*), and action (*karman*); liberation; and the importance of *dharma* (social duty). They climax in the *Gītā's* famous theophany—the revelation to Arjuna of Kṛṣṇa's cosmic status as Viṣṇu, the supreme Lord of the universe. So encyclopedic are Kṛṣṇa's teachings that Arjuna's personal dilemma comes to be seen as a microcosm* of the human condition generally. Composed in Sanskrit verse around the beginning of the Common Era (c. 200 B.C.E.–200 C.E.), the *Gītā* has been the subject of much subsequent commentary and interpretation, its nearly universal appeal over the centuries owing in part to the synthetic and syncretistic character of its teachings.

Since the mid-19th century, the *Gītā* has also appeared in numerous translations in English and other European languages. Of these, the first was Charles

Wilkins's *Bhagvat-geeta, or Dialogues of Kreeshna and Arjoon* (1785). Published under the sponsorship of Warren Hastings, then governor-general of British India, this was the first major effort to translate a classical Hindu text directly from the Sanskrit, and it remained Europe's principal access to the *Gītā* for the next 60 years.

Though celebrated in Europe, Wilkins's translation was not available in America for several decades. When the first copies began making their way to Boston in the mid-1840s, the *Gītā* was known to American Orientalists* only vaguely and mainly by reputation or through summaries presented in shorter works. In a piece of late correspondence to the eminent Indologist F. Max Müller, R. W. Emerson** dated his first encounter with the *Gītā* to his reading of a sketch offered in V. Cousin's** *Cours de philosophie* in 1831.

Such previews notwithstanding, when Emerson finally procured a copy of Wilkins's complete translation from his friend J. E. Cabot** in 1845, he was charged with enthusiasm, later recalling in his journal:* "I owed . . . a magnificent day to the Bhagavat Geeta.—It was the first of books; it was as if an empire spoke to us, nothing small or unworthy, but large, serene, consistent, the voice of an old intelligence which in another age and climate had pondered and thus disposed of the same questions which exercise us." Although Emerson's direct knowledge of the *Gītā* came too late to inform his early essays and addresses, he extolled it frequently in his letters and journals after 1845. Upon acquiring his own copy, he passed it on to several friends and neighbors, including H. Thoreau,** B. Alcott,** and J. G. Whittier,** thus becoming for a time the *Gītā*'s leading American advocate and sponsor.

Hardly less fervent was Thoreau's own reception of Wilkins's *Gītā*, which he had probably encountered in Emerson's library by the time he moved to Walden Pond* in the summer of 1845. But unlike Emerson, Thoreau's immersion in the *Bhagavadgītā* occurred at a time when all his major work was still before him. Large sections of the "Sunday" and "Monday" sections of *A Week on the Concord and Merrimack Rivers* are devoted to Thoreau's reflections on his Oriental researches, "Monday" in particular providing a showcase for an extended presentation with commentary of Kṛṣṇa's dialogue with Arjuna. *Walden* itself draws deeply on the *Gītā* and Thoreau's Oriental readings, as its various depictions of the author as a kind of Hindu anchorite suggest: "In the morning I bathe my intellect in the stupendous and cosmogonal philosophy of the Bhagvat-Geeta, since whose composition years of the gods have elapsed, and in comparison with which our modern world and its literature seem puny and trivial; and I doubt if that philosophy is not to be referred to a previous state of existence, so remote is its sublimity from our conceptions." Together with the *Laws of Manu** and Colebrooke's translation of the *Sāṃkhya-Kārikas,* the *Bhagavadgītā* was the main source of Thoreau's understanding of the principles and practice of yoga and of Hindu religious life generally.

Though Alcott never read the Eastern texts as widely as Emerson and Thoreau did, he shared fully in their admiration of the *Gītā*, declaring it in his journal the "best of books—containing a wisdom blander and more sane than that of the Hebrews, whether in the mind of Moses or of Him of Nazareth.'' After such a debut, the *Gītā* thus achieved a canonical status among Transcendentalists and served as a key text for such later Transcendentalist expositors of Indian traditions as W. H. Channing,** S. Johnson,** J. F. Clarke,** and M. D. Conway.**

REFERENCES: Of modern English translations, the most literal is Franklin Edgerton, *The Bhagavad Gītā* (1944), but Edgerton's fidelity to Sanskrit syntax makes his translation at times difficult to read. His accompanying essay, "Interpretation of the Bhagavad Gītā,'' 105–94, however, is still one of the best presentations of the context and content of the *Gītā* available. For a more readable translation, see Barbara Stoler Miller, *The Bhagavad Gītā: Krishna's Counsel in Time of War* (1986). On the *Gītā* in the context of the *Mahābhārata,* see J.A.B. van Buitenen, *The Bhagavadgītā in the Mahābhārata* (1981). On the place of the *Bhagavadgītā* in Transcendentalist thought, see Arthur Christy, *The Orient in American Transcendentalism: A Study of Emerson, Thoreau, and Alcott* (1932), 23–29.

Alan D. Hodder

BLAIR, HUGH (1718–1800), the Scottish Presbyterian minister, rhetorician, and litterateur, published his lectures in Edinburgh as the enormously popular and practical textbook *Lectures on Rhetoric and Belles-Lettres* (1783). This textbook was then imported to America, became a fixture in American education until the Civil War, and figured prominently in the Harvard curriculum during R. W. Emerson's** and H. Thoreau's** education there. Since the Harvard Unitarians* employed polite letters no less than pulpit oratory as a means of moral persuasion, B's text, written for the clerical students of Edinburgh University, suited their purposes: B asserted that literature was capable of refining the sensibilities and joining judgment with feeling. As the Unitarians lost potential members to the dramatic conversion practices of evangelical Calvinists, the Harvard elite turned increasingly to literature as a way of both enlightening the understanding and rendering vividly their religious and moral values: "Sentiment and affection must be brought to the aid of reason,'' insisted B in his sermon "On Devotion.'' Indeed, B's *Rhetoric,* prescriptive in its methods and confident in its assurance of objective standards of taste (see his lecture "Taste''), helped the Harvard educators maintain the moral and social influence of their own cultivated class through the endorsement of certain kinds of aesthetic tastes and preferences. Moreover, as belles lettres critics on the editorial boards of such important periodicals as the *North American Review** and *The Christian Examiner,** these Harvard Unitarians were in a position to enforce B's values when they reviewed new English and American literary works.

B's *Rhetoric* was based strongly on classical models and neoclassical examples: Quintilian's *Institutio Oratoria* (first century A.D.) was one of B's favorite Roman sources—particularly since it emphasized the moral as well as intellectual development of students of rhetoric. B drew heavily upon the writings of such 18th-century authors as Joseph Addison, Jonathan Swift, and Alexander Pope; four additional lectures were entirely given over to analyzing the stylistic felicities of the 18th-century English *Spectator Papers*. B's rhetorical preferences, moreover, harmonized well with the practical and empirical values of such Scottish Common Sense* philosophers as T. Reid* and D. Stewart* (who were also part of the Harvard training). B preferred above all an elegant transparent style—a style that "frees us from all fatigue of searching for his meaning," "flows always like a limpid stream, where we see to the bottom," is "easy, agreeable . . . carrying a character of smoothness more than strength . . . [a] character of modesty, and politeness." These suggest that self-discipline and social consensus within an unambiguously structured and stable society were the "natural" order to be desired. B's emphasis on "correctness," "strict unity," "refinement," decorum, and propriety harmonized well with his, and the Harvard Unitarians', significant esteem for rationality and social decorum. Yet B occasionally accommodated Romantic elements in his rhetorical discussions: He demonstrated a regard for genius and suggested that rhetorical rules cannot compare with genius as an aid to inventive ability. He also revealed an appreciation of the sublime as capable of evoking powerful emotions, citing (in "Sublimity in Writing") Milton's* depiction of the majestical Satan in the first two books of *Paradise Lost*. These Romantic elements corresponded to B's willingness to engage the human emotions. On the whole, however, reason was to superintend feelings. B's social and aesthetic tastes tended most often toward conservatism: He discouraged writers from attempting certain innovations of style "except [those] whose established reputations gives them some degree of dictatorial power over Language."

B's *Rhetoric* was Emerson's required reading in his sophomore year (1818–19) at Harvard, and indeed the diligent student emulated in some of his early writings the hallmarks of B—lucidity, reason, and simple elegance. Although some modern critics have attempted to date precisely Emerson's turn away from the neoclassical values B endorsed, Emerson's journals* suggest a mercurial young author who from the beginning of his journal enthusiastically experimented with a variety of styles—English Renaissance,* neoclassical, Romantic, as well as American vernacular.

The Transcendentalists' unappreciative response to B's *Rhetoric* is well documented and suggests that at least as taught by Harvard professors, B's prescriptive practices were overemphasized while his Romantic accommodations were either dismissed or disregarded. In his autobiographical memoirs of his training at Harvard, J. F. Clarke** (Class of 1829) confessed that "while our English professors were teaching us out of B's 'Rhetoric,' we were forming our taste by making copious extracts from Sir Thomas Browne or Ben Jonson. Our real professors of rhetoric were Charles Lamb and Coleridge,** Walter Scott and Wordsworth."** Similarly, Emerson asked in "On the Best Mode of Inspiring a Correct Taste in English Literature": "[W]ill you not save [the young scholar] wholly that barren season of discipline which young men spend with the Aikins and Ketts and Drakes and Blairs acquiring the false doctrine that there is something arbitrary or conventional in letters?" (*EL*, 1:215). This latter comment was probably in direct response to B's observation that "the connection between words and ideas may . . . be considered as arbitrary and conventional, owing to the agreement of men among themselves" ("Of Language").

Yet the Emerson of *Nature* did learn from B to think about the metaphoric origins of language in relation to "primitive" peoples. According to B's *Critical Dissertation on the Poems of Ossian,* "Men never have used so many figures of style as in those rude ages, when besides the power of a warm imagination to suggest lively images, the want of proper and precise terms for the ideas they would express, obliged them to have recourse to circumlocution, metaphor, comparison, and all those substituted forms of expression, which give a poetical air to language." These notions about the characteristics of "primitive" expression led B to lend his considerable authority in support of the authenticity of the Ossian poems purportedly written by a third-century Irish bard and "translated" in 1760 but later revealed as a hoax. Emerson admired the Ossian poems and subscribed to B's ideas about the origins of poetical language. In the "Language" chapter of *Nature* Emerson avows, "Because of this radical correspondence* between visible things and human thoughts, savages, who have only what is necessary, converse in figures. As we go back in history, language becomes more picturesque, until its infancy, when it is all poetry." However, whereas B declares that "[s]tyle becomes more chaste, but less animated" as a nation's civilization advances, Emerson instead, creating an analogy between language and devalued paper money, detects a profound "corruption" in the language of civilized man.

REFERENCES: The standard edition of B's *Lectures on Rhetoric and Belles-Lettres* is ed. Harold F. Harding, 2 vols. (1965). The implications of B's aesthetics for American belles lettres are traced by William Charvat, *The Origins of American Critical Thought: 1810–1835* (1936), ch. 3. A detailed evaluation of Emerson's use of B is Sheldon W. Liebman, "The Development of Emerson's Theory of Rhetoric, 1821–1836," *AL* 41 (May 1969): 178–206.

Robin Sandra Grey

BÖHME, JAKOB (c. 1575–1624), religious reformer and mystic, was born in Altseidenberg, Saxony, and later moved to nearby Görlitz to practice his trade as a shoemaker, living there with brief interruptions until his death. In 1600 he had a mystical experience lasting a quarter of an hour, and subsequent reflection and inquiries into its theological, philosophical, and alchemical significance led to his first book, the *Aurora* (1612). Attacked by the Lutheran rector of Görlitz, B kept his silence for several years before publishing a number of other significant works in the four years before his death. In the volume translated under the title of *The Way to Christ* (1622), he included nine treatises on the spiritual life written, among other reasons, to defend himself against charges of Calvinism, chiliasm, and sectarianism even as he criticized the growing formalism of his own Lutheran Church. The *Mysterium Magnum* (1623) and the *De Signatura Rerum* (1623) explained the creation by advancing a nature* mysticism based on traditional German mystic teachings, Paracelsan speculative alchemy, and Reformation concerns about freedom and the relationship between good and evil. B offered an allegorical reading of the "sign and signification of the severall forms and shapes in the creation, and what the beginning, ruin, and cure of every thing is" and asserted a dialectical principle of reality to explain it as a process. His theory of signs anticipated Swedenborg* in some regards—R. W. Emerson** typically linked the two—and the notion of the dialectic of creation was later taken up in a Romantic context by F. Schelling.**

Translated into English in the 17th century by John Sparrow and John Elliston, B's works were readily available in William Law's four-volume 18th-century edition, which B. Alcott** purchased in 1842. The apparent center of B enthusiasm among the Transcendentalists, Alcott had first encountered him in 1833 when he read Francis Okeley's *Life of Jacob Behmen.* This began a life-long interest; in 1867 he called B "the master mind of these last centuries," and at the Concord School of Philosophy* he drew upon B and other mystics in order to attack Darwinism** from a "Christian theist" position. In December 1839, he noted in his journal,* "Emerson passed the afternoon with me. We had desultory conversation on Swedenborg, Bruno,* Behmen, and others of this sublime school." Emerson had first read B in 1835, starting with *Aurora,* and seems to have come back to him at various times over the next 25 years. When E. Peabody** borrowed his copy of *The Way to Christ,* he told her, "This is my 'vade mecum.' " In "Swedenborg; or, The Mystic" he criticized both Swedenborg and B for "attaching themselves to the Christian symbol, instead of to the moral sentiment, which carries innumerable christianities, humanities, divinities in its bosom." But he went on to contrast the "strange, scholastic, didactic, passionless, bloodless" Swedenborg to a "healthily and beautifully wise" B, "tremulous with emotion [whose] heart beats so high that the thumping against his leathern coat is audible across the centuries." The German mystic's reliance on divine communion was the focus for many of Emerson's notations on him in his journals, but he was also attracted to B's stance as a reformer within his Lutheran communion. In "New England Reformers" he said, "Behmen . . . is not irritated by wanting the sanction of the church, but the church feels the accusation of his presence and belief."

REFERENCES: Translated versions of B's writings were most readily available to 19th-century readers in the four volumes of the "Law's edition," *The Works of Jacob Boehmen, the Teutonic Theosopher . . . with figures, Illustrating his Principles, Left by William Law* (1764–81). Useful studies of B include Alexandre Koyré, *La philosophie de Jacob Boehme* (1929; rpt. 1971), and John Joseph Stoudt, *Jacob Boehme: His Life and Thought* (1968). Elisabeth Hurth, "The Uses of a Mystic Prophet: Emerson and Boehme," *PQ* 70 (1991): 219–36, and Arthur Versluis, "Bronson Alcott and Jacob B," *SAR* 1993: 153–59, are useful studies of specific Transcendentalist response to B.

Frank Shuffelton

The **BOSTON ATHENAEUM** was a cultural center and library frequented by many of the Transcendentalists. Founded in 1807 by a group of elite Boston gentlemen who belonged to the Anthology Society, the Athenaeum aimed to raise the intellectual and cultural level of Boston and provide subscribers with access to the best the literary, scientific, and art world could offer. The Athenaeum consisted of a reading room, which was stocked with current American and foreign periodicals ranging from literary topics to politics and science, and a library, composed of what Josiah Quincy called "the great works of learning and science in all languages; particularly such rare and expensive publications, as are not generally to be obtained in this country . . . the works of all the best authors, ancient and modern." The library also offered general reference books, dictionaries, and encyclopedias in French and English. The Athenaeum also contained a lecture room, a room for scientific experiments, a museum of natural artifacts, and an art museum. One aim of the Athenaeum was to encourage native talent; consequently, the center exhibited the works of American painters and sculptors such as W. Allston,** Thomas Doughty, Gilbert Stuart, and H. Greenough.**

Although the Boston Athenaeum was generally accessible only to the elite, it served as a resource for many New England intellectuals, including the Transcendentalists. R. W. Emerson,** whose father was one of the original founders, was a life subscriber to the Athenaeum and occasionally borrowed books that he lent to H. Thoreau.** Beginning in 1823 and continuing into 1869, he introduced guests—including Thoreau, N. Hawthorne,** H. James,** and W. Whitman**—to the Athenaeum, who, as his guests, had library privileges. Other Transcendentalists, such as T. Parker,** G. Ripley,** B. Alcott,** and J. F. Clarke,** visited the Athenaeum and charged out books.

The Boston Athenaeum still exists today, mainly as a members and research library, and is no longer restricted to the elite. Yet during the early decades of the 19th century it was a meeting place for New England intellectuals and literati and played a role in the cultural development of the new nation.

REFERENCES: A good history, by one of the earliest subscribers and former president of the Athenaeum, is Josiah Quincy, *The History of the Boston Athenaeum, with Biographical Notices of Its Deceased Founders* (1851). Sources stressing the Athenaeum's connection to intellectual and literary circles are *The Federalist Literary Mind,* ed. Lewis P. Simpson (1962), and *The Influence and History of the Boston Athenaeum,* ed. Charles K. Bolton (1907). Histories focusing on the development of its art collections are Mabel Munson Swan, *The Athenaeum Gallery, 1827–1873* (1940), and Pamela Hoyle, et al., *A Climate for Art* (1980). For a list of Transcendentalists who visited the Athenaeum and the books they borrowed, see Kenneth Walter Cameron, *Transcendental Reading Patterns* (1971). See also Cameron's *Ralph Waldo Emerson's Reading* (1962) and "Emerson at the Boston Athenaeum: New Evidence," *ESQ* 3 (1956): 12–13. A provocative work examining social aspects is Ronald Story, "Class and Culture in Boston: The Athenaeum, 1807–1860," *AQ* 27 (May 1975): 178–99.

Kathleen M. Healey

BOSTON QUARTERLY REVIEW, published between 1838 and 1842 by O. A. Brownson,** was created to "say to those who may choose to listen . . . just what I wish to say" (*BoQR* 1 [January 1838]: 4). While the review contained essays by other Transcendentalists, most of its pages were filled by Brownson himself, including his defenses of Transcendentalism against the attacks of F. Bowen** and A. Norton.** After the first issue, H. Thoreau** wrote that now "we [know] where to look for the expression of *American* thoughts." B. Alcott** felt in 1839 that the *BoQR* was "the best journal now current on this side of the Atlantic." In the first issue of *The Dial,** G. Ripley** called it "the best indication of the culture of philosophy in this country" (1 [July 1840]: 31). However, Brownson's increasing disillusionment with Transcendentalism after 1840, caused partly by the appearance of *The Dial*, led him in the final volume to also write some of the harshest criticism of the movement.

The *BoQR* covered a wide range of topics, including literature, politics (particularly democracy in America), currency debates, education,* and religion and philosophy. Reviews of philosophical treatises were the most prevalent. With *The Christian Examiner** no longer available to the advocates of the "New School," the *BoQR* gave the Transcendentalists a vehicle in which to discuss important works and to comment on their colleagues and attackers. Among the reviews in the first issue are E. P. Peabody's** on J. G. Whittier's** abolitionist* poems and W. H. Channing's** on R. W. Emerson's** "Phi Beta Kappa" speech, in which he praised Emerson for his "many traits befitting an American, that is, a Christian, free writer" (1: 108). Also in the first issue, Brownson refuted Bowen's "Locke* and the Transcendentalists," claiming that Bowen "does not discern clearly . . . the difference there is between knowledge and philosophy" (88). Other Transcendental contributors were M. Fuller,** who in her "Chat in Boston Bookstores, No. II" attacked Norton, whose "first publication seemed to me to annihilate the basis of religious faith" (3 [October 1840]: 328), and Alcott, who contributed selections of his Orphic Sayings to this journal rather than to *The Dial*. One Transcendentalist who never wrote for Brownson's journal, however, was Emerson.

The *BoQR* also contained articles by those not closely connected with Transcendentalism, including G. Bancroft** "On the Progress of Civilization," A. H. Everett** on the currency debate, and Henry S. Patterson on "Shelley's Poetical Works." Most issues also contained brief literary notices on works such as William Alcott's *Young Housekeeper*, A. Brisbane's** Fourierist** *Social Destiny of Man*, and H. Martineau's** *Deerbrook*. One writer Brownson praised highly was N. Hawthorne,** a "true genius" (4 [January 1841]: 133), whom Brownson, in his review of *Twice-Told Tales*, asked "to attempt a higher and a bolder strain than he has thus far done" (5 [April 1842]: 252).

Although Brownson published the strongest defense of the movement in his review of *Two Articles from the Princeton Review* (July 1840), other Transcendentalists began to shun the *BoQR* because of his publication of "The Laboring Classes," in the same issue, and because of his domineering personality. With the desertion of his former colleagues, Brownson often resorted to publishing old sermons. His later reviews of Transcendentalist works reveal a distance. While seeing "a mystic divinity" in Emerson's *Essays,* he also felt that Emerson was a pantheist,* and "we regard Pantheism as an error of no less magnitude than Atheism itself" (4 [July 1841]: 298, 304). Brownson devoted the final issue (October 1842) to rejecting T. Parker's** argument in *A Discourse of Matters Pertaining to Religion.*

Beginning in 1843, Brownson merged his review with *The United States Magazine and Democratic Review,* but feeling the restraint of an editor, he established *Brownson's Quarterly Review* in 1844. Reaction to his new journal was mixed. W. H. Channing's *The Present** anticipated a periodical similar to the *BoQR* because "take it all in all, it was the best journal this country has ever produced, at once the most American, practical and awakening" (1 [15 October 1843]: 72). Parker speculated, however, that "he will devote it to the overturn of the principles established in the first series" (*Life and Correspondence,* 1: 229). Parker was right; by 1844, Brownson was converting to Catholicism, and he attacked his former friends vituperatively, especially Parker.

REFERENCES: Hard copies of the *BoQR* are rare, but it is available on microfilm. Many of Brownson's contributions are published in [Henry F. Brownson, ed.,] *The Works of Orestes Augustus Brownson,* 20 vols. (1882–1907). See Mott (1938–57) and Gohdes (1931). See also Leonard Gilhooley's entry "Orestes Augustus Brownson," in Myerson (1984).

John P. Samonds

BROOK FARM (1841–47) was established by G.** and Sophia Ripley** in April 1841 on a nearly 200-acre tract of land in West Roxbury, Massachusetts, approximately nine miles west of Boston. Chief among the purposes of the community, as Ripley described it to R. W. Emerson,** was "to insure a more natural union between intellectual and manual labor than now exists; to combine the thinker and the worker . . . in the same individual."

To Emerson, Ripley's scheme seemed like "arithmetic and comfort"; he had no "wish to remove from my present prison to a prison a little larger." His refusal of Ripley's invitation to join the community—arrived at "slowly and I may almost say penitentially"—proved to be one of the great, if quiet, crises in Emerson's philosophical life.

N. Hawthorne,** perhaps surprisingly, did not share the misgivings of the Concord* Sage—at least at first. He was one of the original members and shareholders of Brook Farm. S. Ripley described him early on as "our prince—yet despising no labour and very athletic and able-bodied in the barnyard and field." Hawthorne's own journal* entries during this period describe Brook Farm with warmth, enthusiasm, and affectionate good humor. Nevertheless, Hawthorne quickly lost his enchantment for utopian life. His permanent departure in November 1841—just six months after his arrival—occurred just as the community was issuing its first "Articles of Association" and identifying itself as the "Brook Farm Institute of Agriculture and Education."

Students of Brook Farm typically divide the community into two distinct phases of development: the so-called Transcendental period (1841–44) and the Fourierist period (1844–47). This oversimplification fails to underscore the complexity of Brook Farm's evolution, but it does serve as a useful reminder that the community underwent a decisive shift in focus after January 1844, at which time its name was changed and a new "Constitution of the Brook Farm Association, for Industry and Education" was published.

By the end of 1843, Ripley and his colleagues had become convinced that the social and economic doctrines of French social scientist C. Fourier** were compelling enough that they ought to be given a practical trial in New England. Brook Farm, already then in existence for more than two years, boasted many advantages for such an experiment, and that is what prompted the revised Constitution published in January 1844, which organized and announced the principles upon which Brook Farm would henceforth operate. From that time forward, Brook Farm moved steadily toward the moment when it would formally declare itself a Fourierist Phalanx in May 1845.

The vision, however, proved grander than the reality, and the remaining years were marked by constant financial difficulties, by a rigidity in many aspects of community life imposed by the Fourierist system, and by the fracturing of any unified plan among the community's leaders and its external supporters with respect to Brook Farm's role in the larger Fourierist movement. Operations at Brook Farm were abandoned in summer 1847. The causes of its demise are complex, but three obvious factors may be cited: the unsuitable location of Brook Farm (for farming and commerce); lack of practical experience among community leaders in business and commercial matters; and the devastating financial loss caused by the complete destruction by fire in March 1846 of the "Phalanstery," an uninsured "unitary dwelling" that was near completion when it was destroyed.

At no time does there seem to have been more than 100 people in residence at the community. Many of these—G. and S. Ripley, of course, but such others as J. S. Dwight,** C. A. Dana,** I. Hecker,** and G. W. Curtis,** to mention just a few prominent names—brought an impressive array of abilities to the community. Of visitors, there was certainly no shortage. One Brook Farm resident reported years later that a logbook listed the names of 4,000 visitors in one year. No doubt one of the attractions was the quality of life at the West Roxbury community; invariably it has been recollected in the most positive, and even glowing, terms. "Enjoyment," one commentator noted, "was almost from the first a serious pursuit of the community." The community could even boast a "mistress of the revels," who, as chief of the Amusement Group, regularly organized plays, games, and dances.

Among the regular diversions at Brook Farm, dramatic improvisations, singing, dancing, musical recitals, and coffee parties in the rooms of residents were commonplace. With Dwight on the premises, moving renditions of classical pieces composed by Beethoven and others occurred often. In spring and summer there were picnics, walking, and boating on the Charles River; in winter there were skating and sledding. Reading clubs and literary societies flourished, and there were not infrequent lectures by the many different visitors to the community. Emerson and M. Fuller** came often, and so did T. Parker,** W. H. Channing,** A. Brisbane,** and B. Alcott.** Not surprisingly, conversation*— according to one commentator—was the substance of Brook Farm life. In any event, of the 84 utopian communities in existence in America in the 1840s, none could boast a more varied and stimulating quality of life than that provided at Brook Farm.

During the years of its existence, C. Lane**—Alcott's colleague at Fruit-lands* (1843) and no supporter of Brook Farm—would complain that the Brook Farmers were "playing away their youth and day-time in a miserably joyous frivolous manner," but still he had to acknowledge that the West Roxbury community "is the best which exists here, and perhaps we shall have to say it is the best which *can* exist." And Emerson, long after Brook Farm's demise, recalled with good-natured humor (if mistakenly) that clothespins dropped plentifully from the pockets of the men as they danced. Yet his final comment in "Historic Notes of Life and Letters in New England" (1883) was to express the hope that those who participated in the utopian experiment did not consider it a failure. "It was a close union," he stated, "like that in a ship's cabin, of clergymen, young collegians, merchants, mechanics, farmers' sons and daughters, with men and women of rare opportunities and delicate culture, yet assembled there by a sentiment which all shared . . . of the honesty of a life of labor and of the beauty of a life of humanity." It is qualities such as these that explain why—more than a century and a half later—popular and scholarly interest in Brook Farm continues to be undiminished.

REFERENCES: The best place to begin sorting through the more than 300 articles and 13 books devoted to Brook Farm over the years is Joel Myerson, *Brook Farm: An Annotated Bibliography and Resources Guide* (1978). See also Carol Johnston, "Transcendentalist Communities," in Myerson (1984), 56–68. For first-hand accounts of Brook Farm, Marianne Dwight, *Letters from Brook Farm, 1844–1847,* ed. Amy L. Reed (1928), is essential reading. Also of interest is Myerson's *The Brook Farm Book: A Collection of First-Hand Accounts of the Community* (1987). Perhaps surprisingly, the most reliable book-length study of the utopian community continues to be Lindsay Swift, *Brook Farm: Its Members, Scholars, and Visitors* (1900). One of the best articles is Richard Francis, "The Ideology of Brook Farm," *SAR* 1977: 1–48.

Sterling F. Delano

BRUNO, GIORDANO (1548–1600), was an Italian Dominican monk who challenged Catholic scholasticism through various beliefs in pantheism* and materialism, eventually burning at the stake in Rome for his beliefs. B's mystic pantheism and Neoplatonism* synchronized with many Transcendentalist beliefs. R. W. Emerson** notes B's debt to Plato* in "Plato, or the Philosopher" in *Representative Men* (1850). Transcendentalists were also exposed to B through the writings of S. T. Coleridge.** O. B. Frothingham** (1876), quoting from *Biographia Literaria* (1817), includes Coleridge's observation that he and Schelling** "had both equal obligations to the polar logic and dynamic philosophy of GB," a dynamic system later used by Kant.*

Philosophers define B's Neoplatonism as "consistently identifying infinite deity with nature*" and "maintaining the infinity of nature itself" while admitting "the existence of a universal soul . . . understood as the principle of life, as a spiritual substance permeating all things and constituting their motive principle." Rejecting the notion of a finite universe, B posited that God was synonymous with the universe and that divinity was in nature. As Frances A. Yates explains, B assumed that "there is no death in nature, only change," and B's religious experiences were achieved in the universe itself, not through divine mediation. For B, God was defined as a world of soul encompassing all nature in an infinite and ever-changing universe.

REFERENCES: Important works include *Dialogues Concerning Cause, Principle, and One* (1584). Dorothea Singer, *GB: His Life and Thought* (1950), explores his ideas of a universe in continuous motion and his leanings toward both theism and pantheism in different stages of his life. See also Frances A. Yates, *GB and the Hermetic Tradition* (1964), for a discussion of B's use of hieroglyphs and occultism, and her entry in *EP*, 1:405–8. The quotation on B's Neoplatonism is in *Dictionary of Philosophy*, ed. I. Frolov (1967, 1984), 50–51. See also Sidney Greenberg, *The Infinite in GB* (1950), and Paul O. Kristeller's chapter 8 in *Eight Philosophers of the Italian Renaissance* (1964). Various references to B are in *The Cambridge History of Renaissance Philosophy*, ed. Charles B. Schmitt and Quentin Skinner (1988).

Doni M. Wilson

BUCKMINSTER, JOSEPH STEVENS (1784–1812), was a Unitarian* minister, biblical scholar, and man of letters. The son of clergyman Joseph Buckminster, the younger B caused a rift with his father when, under the influence of James Freeman, Unitarian minister of King's Chapel, Boston, he moved away from the orthodox Calvinism of his father. Attracted to Unitarianism's liberal assessment of human nature and its emphasis on a rational approach to scripture, B quickly became one of its strongest proponents and a leader in establishing the critical methods of the higher criticism* in American exegetical practices.

Ordained on 30 January 1805 as the minister of the socially exclusive Brattle Street Church, where he served for eight years, B was a popular minister, admired for his rhetorical gifts and the intensity of emotion he brought with him to the pulpit. He influenced at least two generations of ministers who, like him, moved away from the traditional sermon form and infused their sermons with eloquence and imaginative polish. B's sermons are also marked by their emphasis on moral development and self-cultivation. His central belief was "that the great moral design of the gospel is, to produce a moral influence on the human character."

Delighting in the joys of literature and concerned with what he found to be the decline of American letters, B was instrumental in organizing *The Monthly Anthology and Boston Review,** for which he contributed a number of essays, and The Anthology Club and in founding the Boston Athenaeum,* to which he donated some 3,000 volumes. His own library, the largest in New England at the time, was dispersed through auction after his death, extending in this way his influence on biblical scholarship. One result of his unrelenting literary and scholarly activity was to ensure Boston's place as the center of cultural and literary activity in the decades following his death.

The other primary result of his scholarly interests consisted in helping to bring German exegetical methods to America. In addition to writing articles and sermons that argued for and demonstrated a more rational approach to establishing and interpreting biblical texts, he was instrumental in securing the 1809 publication of J. J. Griesbach's critical edition of the Greek New Testament, the first such edition to be published in America and one that would serve as a textbook for several decades. The impact of higher criticism on American theology was evidenced when Harvard appointed B its first Dexter Lecturer of Biblical Criticism in 1811. Unfortunately, he died before he could fill the post. Nonetheless, his efforts to inaugurate a more rational approach to biblical study influenced such people as E. T. Channing,** W. E. Channing,** A. Norton,** and R. W. Emerson,** whose journal* notes reading Griesbach and "B's 1st Sermon On evidences" in 1825.

REFERENCES: The Boston Athenaeum is the major repository of B's papers. For early accounts of his life and work, see *The Works of JSB with Memoirs of His Life,* 2 vols. (1830), and Eliza Buckminster Lee, *Memoirs of Rev. Joseph Buckminster, D.D., and of His Son, Rev. JSB* (1849). More recent studies include Lewis P. Simpson, *The Man of Letters in New England and the South* (1973), and Lawrence Buell, "JSB: The Making of a New England Saint," *CRevAS* 10 (1979): 1–29.

Susan L. Roberson

BUFFON, GEORGES-LOUIS LECLERC, COMTE DE (1707–1788), the
French natural historian,* was born at Montbard and studied law, medicine, and botany in nearby Dijon and in Angers. His early scientific interests were encouraged by his friendship with the duke of Kingston, who had met him while traveling in France, and he entered the Académie Royale des Sciences in 1733. In 1739 he became keeper of the Jardin du Roi, where he responded to a request to catalog the royal collections by projecting a 50-volume work that would account for all of nature.* Appearing between 1749 and 1804 (the final 8 volumes posthumously), the *Histoire naturelle, générale et particulière* was one of the great works of 18th-century science, especially notable for his theory of natural causation acting over immense periods of time and his theory of successive geological epochs. B was elected to the Académie Française in 1753. His inaugural address, the *Discours sur le style,* was widely admired, and its claim "Le style c'est l'homme même" became a commonplace, quoted by R. W. Emerson,** among others (see *TN,* 2:166).

When Emerson visited the Jardin des Plantes in 1833, he was encountering the Buffonian scene as modified by successors, and this distanced experience perhaps typified B's significance for the first Transcendentalist generation. He was more often referred to than carefully read by those like Emerson and H. Thoreau** who found their science in more up-to-date and more convenient texts than B's, reading B through Cuvier and Agassiz** in effect. Emerson's interest in science in the early 1830s typically produced two references in early lectures that contradicted each other: In "The Uses of Natural History" of November 1833, Linnaeus,* B, Cuvier, and Humboldt** are cited as men who can walk into a "dull dumb unprofitable world" and make it "break forth into singing." Two years later, however, in the introductory lecture to his series on English literature, he could dismiss "all Linnaeus' and B's volumes" as "dry catalogues of facts." Each comment is probably true, because B offered both intelligible catalogs of natural facts and sometimes passionate commentary, speculation, and philosophizing, but Emerson's casual treatment does not suggest that he had read B closely. The only apparent reference to B in Thoreau's journals* comes by way of another source. B's real impact on Thoreau and others, however, derived from his theories about the degeneration of life forms in the New World. Describing the American continents as colder and damper than the Old World, he argued that plants and animals, including human beings, would be smaller and weaker there. Thomas Jefferson in his *Notes on the State of Virginia* (1785) was one of the first Americans to try to refute this, and B's ideas helped provoke a distinct nativist strain in American natural historical writing. As John Hildebidle has observed, "[T]he notion that the most blessed spot on earth might be a small pond in the vicinity of Concord* rests in part on the prevailing tendency of science."

REFERENCES: B's great work is the *Histoire naturelle, générale et particulière avec la description du Cabinet du Roi.* For bibliographic information as well as for a good, concise account of his career, see Otis E. Fellows and Stephen F. Milliken, *B* (1972). For Thoreau's involvement in the discourse of natural history, see John Hildebidle, *Thoreau, a Naturalist's Liberty* (1983).

Frank Shuffelton

C

The **CHARDON STREET AND BIBLE CONVENTIONS** were a series of four gatherings called to examine contemporary religious institutions, "to ascertain whether their claims to a Divine ordination be indeed valid, or whether they be but inventions and traditions of men" (*The Liberator,* 16 October 1840). Inspired by the widespread but unfocused desire to mold the "Church of the Future,"* the Conventions epitomized—for supporters and detractors alike—the reform impulse of the age. W. L. Garrison** was generally regarded as the force behind the Conventions, though he seems not to have had a direct hand: The five-person planning committee included B. Alcott;** Boston Brahmin Edmund Quincy was chairman and Maria W. Chapman secretary; and the "Call" was signed by 24 "Friends of Universal Reform" including Henry C. Wright, W. H. Channing,** A. Kelley,** and T. Parker.**

The original three installments, the Chardon Street Convention, met at the Chardon Street Chapel as three-day events (Tuesdays through Thursdays): The Sabbath was discussed on 17–19 November 1840; the Ministry on 30 March–1 April 1841; and the Church on 26–28 October 1841. A one-day installment on the Bible was held at the Masonic Temple on 29 March 1842. Despite their overtly religious purpose, the Conventions attracted reformers of every stamp, including Garrison, W. E. Channing,** G. Ripley,** C. P. Cranch,** S. J. May,** J. Very,** and even H. Thoreau.** Some orthodox ministers, such as "Father" E. T. Taylor,** came out of curiosity or to rebut heresy; the Methodist *Zion's Herald* warned against sweeping away divine institutions as imagined obstacles to legitimate abolitionist* aims, labeling "Universal Reform" "this new-fangled infidelity." The Chardon Street Chapel itself was associated with all manner of radicalism. Its minister, Joshua V. Himes (1805–1895), was a temperance* and woman's rights* activist and Garrisonian who had helped organize and served as first director of the Non-Resistance* Society. He was also a leading advocate of Millerism,* and his Second Christian Church (1837–42) was Adventist in emphasis.

The press both ridiculed the Conventions as an assortment of oddballs and praised their rich freedom of debate. Contrary to expectations, the Conventions published no proceedings and thus have been known primarily through R. W. Emerson's** *Dial** essay, a shrewd account noting both absurdities and flashes of "eloquence" and "character." Chardon Street echoed in Emerson's "New England Reformers" (1844) as the embodiment of the admirable idealism* and individualism, and the foolish impracticality and "piecemeal" approach to virtue, inherent in reform movements. Even though 200 to 300 attended the final Bible Convention, momentum could not be sustained, and with no "formal resolutions" passed, the legacy of the Conventions was indeterminate. Parker had private misgivings from the outset, and Garrison denied having had any formal role in calling them; his subsequent abolition activities suffered in some quarters from the stigma that infidelity pervaded the Conventions. Even Alcott, whose presence dominated the sessions, was disillusioned with the rigors of coordinating crowds: He had hoped to conduct debate at the Bible Convention as a Conversation!* Still, a Rhode Island contingent, inspired by Alcott and supported by the wealthy Thomas Davis, formed the "Providence movement," which published *The Plain Speaker* and tried unsuccessfully to coax Alcott to their utopian farm, Holly Home. And the spirit of Chardon Street did persist in countless meetings, lecture series, and specific church reforms.

REFERENCES: Emerson's account (unreliable as to dates and sequence of topics) is "Chardon Street and Bible Conventions," *The Dial* 3 (July 1842): 100–12; rpt. as "The Chardon Street Convention," *W,* 10:373–77. A reactionary reminiscence by temperance preacher Thomas Poage Hunt is presented in Wesley T. Mott, " 'All Kinds of Error and Extravagant Isms': An Orthodox View of the Chardon Street Convention," *CS* 19 (December 1987): 17–25. John McAleer places Chardon Street in the context of the Groton Convention of August 1840, in *Ralph Waldo Emerson: Days of Encounter* (1984), 295–303. Linck C. Johnson examines the related Amory Hall reform lectures of 1844 in "Reforming the Reformers: Emerson, Thoreau, and the Sunday Lectures at Amory Hall, Boston," *ESQ* 37 (4th Q 1991): 235–89. See, too, David T. Arthur, "Joshua V. Himes and the Cause of Adventism," in *The Disappointed: Millerism and Millenarianism in the Nineteenth Century,* ed. Ronald L. Numbers and Jonathan M. Butler (1987), 36–58.

Wesley T. Mott

THE CHRISTIAN EXAMINER was, according to Mott (1938–57), "one of the most important of American religious reviews" and "the most distinguished Unitarian* journal." Begun in 1813 as the *Christian Disciple,* its founders (W. E. Channing,** Charles Lowell, Samuel Cooper Thacher, and Joseph Tuckerman) organized the new periodical intending the work to be more evangelical and less sectarian than other liberal Christian publications of the period. Initially, under its first two editors, Noah Worcester and H. Ware, Jr.,** the work served largely as a communications link between the dispersed liberal clergy in New

England and thereby brought about a greater unity and cohesiveness among those who would, by the time of the founding of the American Unitarian Association in 1825, consider themselves part of a more formally established Unitarian denomination.

By the 1820s, however, Orthodox attacks in Calvinist journals such as *The Spirit of the Pilgrims* led its editors to adopt a more polemical position and a new name, *The Christian Examiner and Theological Review*. The work soon became the grand bulwark for Unitarianism in America and the chief organ through which "the Unitarian position" was propagated. Many of the most prominent Unitarians of the era (Channing, A. Norton,** J. G. Palfrey,** Ware, to name but a few) were affiliated with the work's editorial board or "Society" and frequently published essays and reviews in the magazine. When the Examiner Society chose J. Walker** as the work's new editor in 1831, they little realized that Walker and his associate editor F.W.P. Greenwood would lead the magazine in a new direction. Unlike Palfrey and Norton, Walker saw the *ChEx* as an open forum for the presentation of all ostensibly liberal Christian views. He accepted essays from conservatives and radicals alike and was particularly receptive to submissions from individuals such as G. Ripley,** O. A. Brownson,** T. Parker,** F. H. Hedge,** and others affiliated with the nascent Transcendentalist movement. During Walker's tenure as editor (1831–39), some of the most important works associated with the Transcendentalist movement were published in the *ChEx,* including Hedge's essay on "Coleridge,"** Brownson's "Progress of Society," F. Bowen's** "Locke* and the Transcendentalists," Ripley's essay on "Martineau,"** and many others. Walker's new policy may have given Transcendentalists a forum for their thoughts, but the change in the magazine's direction was not without controversy. The publication of Ripley's works in particular so infuriated Norton that he threatened to break his ties with the magazine and excoriated Ripley and the Transcendentalists over the question of miracles.*

The editors who followed Walker throughout the 1840s and the early 1850s either were hostile toward Transcendentalism or were so fearful of the adverse effect that any controversy might have on subscriptions that they effectually "shut out" most Transcendentalist writers. Ezra Stiles Gannett's hostility throughout his editorship (1843–49) to the "subversive" influence of Parker led him to publicly denounce the latter in the pages of the *ChEx.* But George E. Ellis and George Putnam (his successors) were averse to publishing works by such radicals, not so much on philosophical as on economic grounds, with the result that very little was printed about Parker or R. W. Emerson** either in praise or in condemnation during their tenure (1849–57).

When Hedge took control of the magazine in 1857, Parker claimed that, in Mott's words, he "recognized the more liberal character of the *Christian Examiner* under its new management." Hedge, who had been given his first opportunities to publish pieces for the magazine while Walker was editor, wished to see the *ChEx* become the sort of arena of free inquiry that Walker had envisioned. And while increasing denominational divisions and financial difficulties during the war years led eventually to the demise of the *ChEx* in 1869, in its final years a younger generation of writers such as J. Weiss,** D. A. Wasson,** Joseph Henry Allen, and O. B. Frothingham** published articles on H. Thoreau,** Parker, Emerson, and other Transcendentalists, praising their works and reclaiming them as important figures in the history of the Unitarian movement.

REFERENCES: The most complete history is Alfred G. Litton, " 'Speaking the Truth in Love': A History of the *Christian Examiner* and Its Relation to New England Transcendentalism'' (Diss., Univ. of South Carolina, 1993). Frances Pedigo, ''Critical Opinions of Poetry, Drama, and Fiction, in the *Christian Examiner,* 1824–1869'' (Diss., Univ. of North Carolina, 1953), analyzes the reviews in the magazine largely from a ''New Critical'' perspective but does not consult the Examiner Society Records or any of the manuscript material available. Mott, 1:284–92, is a reprint of his article of 30 years earlier (*NEQ* 1 [April 1928]: 197–207) and contains a number of errors. The best modern ''thumbnail'' sketch of the magazine's history is in Edward Chielens, *The Literary Journal in America to 1900* (1975), 103–7, though it, too, contains errors esp. regarding the magazine's publication. Both Hutchison (1959), 52–97, and Wilson Smith, *Professors & Public Ethics* (1956), 149–85, offer interesting discussions of Walker's and Norton's involvement with the magazine.

Alfred G. Litton

CHURCH OF THE FUTURE was one of a number of names used to denote diverse and sometimes vague conceptions of an ideal church infused with Transcendentalist principles. Although a number of Transcendentalist ministers including R. W. Emerson** and G. Ripley** abandoned the church, many male Transcendentalists spent their lives in the ministry attempting to refashion the church in ways that would promote individual spiritual growth. Two consecutive meetings of the Transcendental Club* were devoted to a ''new church,'' and various Transcendentalists participated in the Chardon Street Convention* and other meetings and debates about church reform that were part of the extraordinary religious and social ferment of the period. O. Brownson,** J. F. Clarke,** and F. H. Hedge** all wrote extensively about the ideal church and its role in society. Among the more conspicuous Transcendentalist experiments in church reform were Brownson's Society for Christian Union and Progress (founded 1836), Clarke's Church of the Disciples (1841), W. H. Channing's** Christian Union (1843) and Religious Union of Associationists (1846), and T. Parker's** Twenty-Eighth Congregational Society (1845).

While the main contribution of the Transcendentalists to church reform came in their creative use of the sermon and their opposition to formalism, a number of Transcendentalists introduced innovations in church organization or services intended to decrease the distance between clergy and laity, to stimulate individual spiritual development, or to encourage participation in social reforms. These mostly unoriginal innovations included abolishing pew rent, augmenting traditional services with religious conversations,* developing study groups devoted to particular social reform issues, and having members of the congregation lead religious services and even preach sermons. Transcendentalists also showed their eclecticism and eccentricity by accommodating individual preferences such as baptism by total immersion (Clarke), by modifying traditional rites (Channing used bread, water, and fruit in his communion service), and by reading from the sacred books of other religions (Parker and others). Although Clarke's Church of the Disciples survived well into the 20th century, other churches founded by Transcendentalist ministers were relatively short-lived. The Transcendentalists' developments in preaching and their flexible attitudes toward historical religion and religious tradition, however, were increasingly accepted by later generations of Unitarians.*

REFERENCES: Brownson's *New Views of Christianity, Society, and the Church* (1836) is the most ambitious, and most idiosyncratic, published statement on church reform by a Transcendentalist. Additional material can be found in the writings of Clarke, Emerson, Hedge, Parker, and others. The only modern discussion of Transcendentalist attempts to reform the church is Hutchison (1959), esp. 137–89. On preaching, see Buell (1973), 102–39.

Gary L. Collison

CIVIL DISOBEDIENCE is a form of dissent that has had a long history in America. In the broadest sense, the term describes decisions to disobey the law in the name of conscience. But *civil disobedience* is usually used in a somewhat narrower sense, to describe acts of passive resistance, nonviolent protests undertaken by those willing to accept punishment for breaking the law. Such protests were common in the Massachusetts Bay Colony, where Quakers* and Baptists opposed violations of religious liberty, especially the legal requirement that they pay taxes in support of Congregational ministers and the orthodox Standing Order. During the 19th century, a number of Unitarian* ministers taught that civil disobedience might be necessary in the face of other unjust acts of government. In his 1838 "Lecture on War," for example, W. E. Channing** insisted that a Christian was duty bound to "bear witness against unholy wars," adding: "If called to take part in them, let him deliberately refuse. If martial law seize on him, let him submit. If hurried to prison, let him submit. If brought thence to be shot, let him submit. There must be martyrs to peace as truly as to other principles of our religion."

Many of the Transcendentalists also preached or practiced civil disobedience. As early as 1843, B. Alcott** was arrested for refusing to pay his poll tax, a tax levied on all adult males in Massachusetts. H. Thoreau** also refused to pay his poll tax, initially as a protest against slavery and later in opposition to the Mexican War. After he was arrested and briefly imprisoned in 1846, Thoreau vigorously defended his stand in a lecture, "The Rights and Duties of the Individual in Relation to the State," delivered at the Concord* Lyceum* in 1848 and published the following year as "Resistance to Civil Government." Appealing to the authority of conscience, Thoreau argued that if unjust laws required one "to be the agent of injustice to another," then the individual must "break the law." During the 1840s, few agreed that American laws required them to be the agents of injustice; but as part of the Compromise of 1850* Congress passed a new and far more aggressive Fugitive Slave Law, which in effect required all citizens to aid the federal commissioners responsible for enforcing the law. The passage of the law drove even some of the more moderate Transcendentalists to embrace the logic of civil disobedience. "We shall never feel well again until that detestable law is nullified in Massachusetts & until the Government is assured that once for all it cannot & shall not be executed here," R. W. Emerson** exclaimed in his journal* early in 1851. After the law was executed in the case of Thomas Sims, a fugitive slave returned from Boston to a Georgia plantation, Emerson publicly urged others to assume the same unyielding stand. "The law is suicidal, and cannot be obeyed," Emerson declared in the first of his addresses on the Fugitive Slave Law, delivered in 1851.

During the 1850s, however, some of those who had formerly urged civil disobedience moved to far more militant positions. As a Free Soil candidate for Congress in 1850, T. W. Higginson** insisted that those required to aid in the enforcement of the Fugitive Slave Law must "DISOBEY IT," demonstrating their "good citizenship by taking the legal consequences." But Higginson and others later sought to take the law into their own hands. In 1854, he thus led an attack on the Boston Courthouse during which a deputy was killed as Higginson and his followers sought to free a fugitive slave named Anthony Burns before he could be sent back into slavery. Significantly, Alcott participated in that abortive attack, which Thoreau in "Slavery in Massachusetts" described as "braver and more disinterestedly heroic" than the Boston Tea Party. Moreover, in 1859, Thoreau eloquently defended J. Brown,** whose armed raid on the Federal Arsenal at Harpers Ferry, Virginia, was far removed from the kind of civil disobedience Thoreau had urged ten years earlier in "Resistance to Civil Government."

Despite the arguments made on behalf of various forms of resistance to government during the antebellum period, the term *civil disobedience* apparently did not appear in print until after the Civil War. The term was probably suggested by various broadsides in the ongoing debate over the limits of governmental authority. In 1847, several months before Thoreau delivered his lecture on the rights and duties of the individual in relation to the State, Francis Wayland published *The Duty of Obedience to the Civil Magistrate,* in which he in fact emphasized the limits of that duty when government engaged in immoral actions like the Mexican War. After 1850 that theme was developed in innumerable texts, including Charles Beecher's *The Duty of Disobedience to Wicked Laws* (1851) and Nathaniel Halls's *The Limits of Civil Obedience* (1851). But the term *civil disobedience* was apparently coined by Thoreau, who used it as the title of the essay earlier published as "Resistance to Civil Government."

Since that essay was first published as ''Civil Disobedience'' in *A Yankee in Canada, with Anti-Slavery and Reform Papers* (1866), four years after Thoreau's death, one of the editors of the volume may have substituted the new title for ''Resistance to Civil Government.'' But evidence suggests that Thoreau himself had made the substantive revisions incorporated in the 1866 printing of the essay, including the alteration of the title to ''Civil Disobedience.''

In any case—and despite the fact that Thoreau had strongly endorsed the use of militant force in ''Slavery in Massachusetts'' and his addresses on Brown— ''Civil Disobedience'' profoundly influenced those who later sought to make nonviolent resistance the basis of mass political movements. In 1907, when he was fighting for the civil rights of Indians in South Africa, Mahatma Gandhi printed extracts from ''Civil Disobedience'' in his newspaper, *Indian Opinion*, and later reprinted them in pamphlet form for distribution among his followers. As he later remarked, Gandhi subsequently took the name of his movement from ''Civil Disobedience,'' which he used as the English translation of his Indian word *Satyagraha*. The essay was also adopted as a handbook of political action during the early years of the British Labor Party and used as a manual of arms by the leaders of the Danish resistance during World War II. After the war, ''Civil Disobedience'' became equally influential in the United States, where it helped shape both the civil rights movement—Martin Luther King, Jr., frequently cited it as a primary source of inspiration—and the widespread resistance to the Vietnam War. Indeed, the fame of Thoreau's essay has created the impression that he invented the concept of civil disobedience, whereas he simply gave eloquent expression to ideas deeply rooted both in Protestant traditions and in antebellum American culture.

REFERENCES: The various traditions of civil disobedience are discussed in the introduction to *Civil Disobedience in America: A Documentary History*, ed. David R. Weber (1978), a wide-ranging anthology of writings from the 17th century to the 1970s. Assessments of the Transcendentalists' attitudes toward law and government include Edward Madden, *Civil Disobedience and Moral Law in Nineteenth-Century American Philosophy* (1968); and A. Robert Componigri, ''Individual, Civil Society, and the State in American Transcendentalism,'' in *American Philosophy from Edwards to Quine*, ed. Robert W. Shahan and Kenneth R. Merrill (1977), 49–77. Emerson's response to the passage of the Fugitive Slave Law is discussed in Gougeon (1990), 138ff. Higginson's campaign speech, published as *Address to the Voters of the Third Congressional District* (1850), is discussed in Tilden G. Edelstein, *Strange Enthusiasm: A Life of Thomas Wentworth Higginson* (1968), 103–5. Thoreau's famous essay is printed as ''Resistance to Civil Government'' in *RP*; Wendell Glick in the ''Textual Introduction'' argued that others may have been responsible for the substantive changes made in the 1866 printing of the essay, including the change in the title to ''Civil Disobedience'' (313–21). Glick's position has been challenged by Thomas Woodson, ''The Title and Text of Thoreau's 'Civil Disobedience,' '' *Bulletin of Research in the Humanities* 81 (1978): 103–12; and Fritz Oehlschlaeger, ''Another Look at the Text and Title of 'Civil Disobedience,' '' *ESQ* 36 (1990): 239–54. Scholars have also devoted a good deal of attention to the influences upon the essay, its relation to Thoreau's later antislavery addresses, and the impact of "Civil Disobedience." A useful survey of the scholarship is Walter Harding and Michael Meyer, *The New Thoreau Handbook* (1980), 80–81, 156–57, and 210–11.

Linck C. Johnson

COME-OUTERS was a term frequently used to describe Transcendentalists and other religious dissidents during the antebellum period—"a name then as familiar and distinctive as is that of the Salvation Army to-day," T. W. Higginson** recalled in a memoir published at the end of the century. Part of the language of revivals, the term was derived from biblical texts like the angel's prophesy of the fall of Babylon: "Come out of her, my people, that ye be not partakers of her sins, and that ye receive not of her plagues" (Rev. 18:4). As such, the term initially referred to those inspired during evangelical revivals to offer a public profession of faith, after which the converts entered into a new relation with the sinful world. The term was also adopted by or applied to various enthusiastic sects, including the "Cape Codders," as Higginson called them, who seceded from various churches in order to establish a more perfect society based on the absolute freedom of each individual. Numbering 200 or 300 persons, the Cape Codders had neither a church building nor an organization, rejecting all religious creeds, forms of governance, and membership requirements. Viewed as an ideal of harmonious self-government by some reformers, the Cape Codders were also known for their anarchic tendencies: They were reported to stand in front of churches during Sunday services, shouting, "Come out!"; they enthusiastically harassed clergymen; and their disorderliness at reform meetings was legendary.

As exemplified by the Cape Codders, come-outerism was closely associated with various reform movements, especially religious reform and radical abolitionism.* The beliefs of the Cape Codders were closely akin to the principles of nonresistance,* which also sharply distinguished between the rule of God and human governments and which was embraced by anticlerical abolitionists like W. L. Garrison,** P. Pillsbury,** and N. P. Rogers.** Despite sharp differences in class, education, and religious temperament, the Cape Codders also shared some common ground with the Transcendentalists. In their insistence that the primary source of truth was not the Bible but the voice of God speaking directly to each individual, for example, the Cape Codders were not far distant from R. W. Emerson** and other leaders of the revolt within Unitarianism.* Emerson, of course, would never have stood bellowing in front of a church, but at least some believed that he had caused even greater disruption in his 1838 address at the Chapel of the Harvard Divinity School,* where he had vigorously challenged the creeds and cold formalism of the Unitarian Church, much as the Cape Codders challenged other Protestant churches. Their withdrawal from those churches was echoed by H. Thoreau,** who in 1840 signed off from the First Parish Church in Concord,* declaring "that I, Henry Thoreau, do not wish to be regarded as a member of any incorporated society which I have not joined."

The Cape Codders and other come-outers had an even more direct impact on other Transcendentalists. During the summer of 1840 B. Alcott,** C. P. Cranch,** T. Parker,** and G. Ripley** attended a joint convention in Groton, Massachusetts, of the Millerites* and the Come-outers. At once amused and excited by the proceedings, the Transcendentalists experienced a liberating shock of recognition as they listened to those unlettered men and women express many of their own deepest religious convictions. Shortly after the convention, Parker and several other Transcendentalists helped organize and participated in the Chardon Street Convention,* which met in Boston three times during 1840–41 to examine the validity of the Sabbath and to inquire into the authority of the institutions of the Ministry and the Church. At the same time, Ripley resigned from his Boston ministry in order to establish Brook Farm,* which was itself a manifestation of come-outerism, a kind of religious society designed to ensure the freedom and equality of its members. The term *come-outers* was also extended to the members of religious societies formed by ministers like Parker and J. F. Clarke.** As Arthur S. Bolster, Jr., has remarked, Clarke's innovative Church of the Disciples was viewed by the conservative clergy of Boston as "a collection of transcendentalists, radical reformers, and come-outers of every breed." In fact, Clarke's highly educated congregation bore little resemblance to come-outers like the enthusiastic Cape Codders. But what connected the two groups was their common desire for greater spiritual freedom and a more meaningful religious experience, a desire that many men and women of the antebellum period believed could not be fulfilled within the narrow confines of established churches. Certainly that connection seemed clear to Higginson, who observed that "the so-called Transcendentalist body" had actually been a combination of two different elements, "more refined votaries" like Clarke, Emerson, and Parker, and "a less educated contingent, known popularly as 'Come-Outers.' "

REFERENCES: The fullest exposition of the doctrine of come-outerism was William Goodell, *Come-Outerism: The Duty of Secession from a Corrupt Church* (1845). A brief contemporary account of various groups of come-outers was included in Rev. P. Douglass Gorrie, *The Churches and Sects of the United States* (1850), 223–25. Parker's account of the convention in Groton, which includes a detailed description of the religious views of the come-outers from Cape Cod, was printed in J. Weiss,** *Life and Correspondence of Theodore Parker,* 2 vols. (1864), 1:125–29. Clarke's innovations in the Church of the Disciples are discussed in Bolster, *James Freeman Clarke: Disciple to Advancing Truth* (1954), 127–56. Higginson made the connection between the come-outers and the Transcendentalists in *Cheerful Yesterdays* (1899), 114–16. That connection is explored in greater detail in an excellent scholarly discussion of the Cape Codders and other come-outers: Lewis Perry, *Radical Abolitionism: Anarchy and the Government of God in Antislavery Thought* (1973), esp. ch. 4.

Linck C. Johnson

COMMON SENSE PHILOSOPHY, although at least as old as Aristotle, insofar as American Transcendentalism is concerned, deals with Scottish Common

Sense, or Scottish Realism, which dominated American academic philosophy between 1768 and 1850 and had, therefore, a significant formative influence on the students who would become the New England Transcendentalists. We use the term *common sense* most often to mean ordinary understanding or practical sense; to the Common Sense philosopher, the term had another meaning, which the *Oxford English Dictionary* calls the "faculty of primary truths" and "the general sense, feeling, or judgement of mankind."

As promulgated by T. Reid* and his followers, the Scottish Common Sense school originated in reaction to the skeptical philosophy of D. Hume's* *A Treatise of Human Nature* (1739–40), which suggested that things are the contents of the mind and, conversely, the mind is its contents. Convinced that Hume's philosophy undermined morality and religion, the Scottish school's first intention was to answer him, but it became much more than a mere refutation of Hume.

Scottish Common Sense philosophy has two poles, empiricism and intuition. James McCosh, an American Common Sense philosopher of the 19th century, concentrated on the first when he said that the three principal features of the philosophy are that it is based on observation; self-consciousness is the instrument of observation; and by observation of consciousness, principles prior to and independent of experience are attained. The other pole, intuition, is based on three elements: By introspection one is able to abstract general concepts and principles not derived from experience; through the study of languages it is obvious that common principles of thought and perception operate in all people; and judgments based on these common principles affirm their reality to individuals without having to be proved—indeed, without being able to be proved. The Common Sense philosophers wanted to learn how the human mind was constructed, to find exactly what the principles of Common Sense are and how they operate so that from that base empirical experimentation about mental activity could proceed.

As Common Sense philosophy became entrenched in academia in America, it dominated the Harvard curriculum and played an important role in the Unitarian* movement; nearly all the New England Transcendentalists received a long and thorough indoctrination in Scottish Common Sense. Even as they broke from Unitarian tradition and rebelled against the conservative branch of Scottish Common Sense that had allied itself with matters of morality and religion, they carried into Transcendentalism ideas from the Common Sense philosophy such as intuitive perception of truth. Furthermore, the Scottish school had a tremendous influence on German and French philosophy, which in turn made direct contributions to the ideas of American Transcendentalism. Both R. W. Emerson** and H. Thoreau** were thoroughly grounded in the tenets of the Scottish school but moved beyond the rationalistic version taught at Harvard to the intuitive principles of Transcendentalism.

REFERENCES: Excerpts from the writings of nine Scottish philosophers are in Daniel Sommer Robinson, *The Story of Scottish Philosophy* (1961). Richard J. Petersen, "Scottish Common Sense in America, 1768–1850: An Evaluation of Its Influence'' (Diss., American Univ., 1964), devotes a chapter to the influence of the philosophy on New England Transcendentalism. See also Howe (1970). Manfred Kuehn, *Scottish Common Sense in Germany, 1768–1800: A Contribution to the History of Critical Philosophy* (1987), demonstrates the relationships between the German and Scottish philosophers who were important influences on the concepts of New England Transcendentalism.

Mariane Wurst Schaum

COMPENSATION, the title of the most optimistic (and most frequently criticized, by 20th-century readers) of R. W. Emerson's** essays, is the doctrine that posits a divine system of balance in the universe. Emerson sees the traditional view of compensation as flawed: In this world the wicked succeed while the good are miserable, so one's ''compensation,'' to be received in the afterlife, is seen as ''revenge.'' But in every part of nature,* he argues, we meet ''[p]olarity, or action and reaction''; and as the world ''is thus dual, so is every one of its parts.'' Emerson sees the same dualism underlying the nature and condition of humans, creating an inherent system of checks and balances in *this* world: For every evil there is good; every excess causes a defect; every crime is punished; every virtue rewarded—if not by society, then by the self, by the conscience. Thus, all things are moral, illustrating the maxim ''The dice of God are always loaded.'' Emerson proceeds to find in nature and human behavior a multitude of illustrations of this simple philosophy, enumerating them not only in the essay but throughout his journals.*

This philosophy has its potency, illustrated by its application in the works of such Transcendentalists as H. Thoreau** and B. Alcott**—the only two people besides himself, Emerson once noted, who seem ''fully to see this law''—and of such explorers of the human psyche as E. A. Poe,** N. Hawthorne,** and Dostoevski. The assertion that ''[c]rime and punishment grow out of one stem,'' or that every crime is redressed by one's conscience, would certainly appeal to those thinkers. But when Emerson describes vice as an ''absence or departure'' of ''real Being,'' and asserts that the soul ''always affirms an Optimism, never a Pessimism,'' he parts company with such darker artists and opens the philosophy to the criticism that it too cavalierly dismisses what more cynical intellects would consider integral and powerful aspects of human nature. The philosophy in general has been seen to illustrate amorality, or at least moral ambivalence: If all wrong is redressed, or seen as unreal, there is no real need for morality. Emerson explains that the soul's own nature is deeper than compensation, since it is ''not a compensation, but a life.'' Simply being human compels us to choose and act along moral lines.

REFERENCES: The essay is found in *CW*, 2: 53–73. Among those critics who have discussed flaws in the doctrine of compensation are Stephen Whicher, *Freedom and Fate* (1953), 34–39, and Gertrude Reif Hughes, *Emerson's Demanding Optimism* (1984), 95–100. Early versions of the doctrine may be found throughout *JMN* and in Joseph Slater, ed., *The Correspondence of Emerson and Carlyle*** (1964), 107, 121. See also Donald Yannella, *Ralph Waldo Emerson* (1978), 44–47.

David Hicks

THE COMPROMISE OF 1850 was the name given collectively to five pieces of legislation enacted into law in the fall of 1850. The purpose of the Compromise was to settle sectional tensions that developed over territorial accessions that resulted largely from the American victory in the Mexican War (1846–48). The original resolutions were introduced in the Senate by Henry Clay of Kentucky on 29 January 1850. In its final form the Compromise provided for the admission of California to the Union as a Free State, the organization of New Mexico as a territory without restriction on slavery, the organization of Utah on the same basis, the abolition of slavery in the District of Columbia, and a Fugitive Slave Law, which amended the original law of 1793 and provided a legal mechanism for the return of fugitive slaves from the Free States.

The debate over these measures was protracted, acrimonious, and historic. William H. Seward, senator from New York, vigorously opposed the Compromise. In his address, he appealed to a "higher law"* than the Constitution, which sanctioned the abominable institution of slavery. John Calhoun and Henry Clay eloquently defended the Compromise as a means of preserving the Union. A major turning point in the debate occurred on 7 March 1850 when D. Webster,** the distinguished senior senator from Massachusetts, rose to declare his support for the measure in a speech that began, "I wish to speak today, not as a Massachusetts man, nor as a Northern man, but as an American. . . . I speak today for the preservation of the Union." Abolitionists* and their supporters were shocked by this apparent perfidy and expressed outrage at Webster, the Compromise generally, and the Fugitive Slave Law in particular. By 1850 several Transcendentalists had openly supported the antislavery cause. Among the most prominent in this regard were R. W. Emerson,** H. Thoreau,** B. Alcott,** T. Parker,** M. Fuller,** W. H. Furness,** and W. H. Channing.** Emerson was the most outspoken in his opposition to the Fugitive Slave Law. In his journal* he expressed his amazement that "this filthy enactment was made in the 19th Century, by people who could read & write," and he vowed, "I will not obey it, by God." He would later repeat this sentiment in his "Fugitive Slave Law Address" (1851 [*W*, 11:177–214]), which also contains a virulent attack on Webster and his "treachery" in the matter. Emerson repeated this speech as a stump oration on numerous occasions in his Middlesex District of Massachusetts in an unsuccessful effort to get J. G. Palfrey,** a Free Soil candidate, elected to Congress in the spring of 1851. Emerson was prompted to take this unusual step, in part, by the rendition of Thomas Sims, a fugitive slave living in Boston, in April of that year. The rendition of fugitive slaves, though few in number because of widespread opposition to the law throughout the Free States, served to throw fuel on the fires of resistance. Thoreau, whose "Resistance to Civil Government" (*RP*, 63–90) was published in 1849, was moved to deliver his most acerbic address, "Slavery in Massachusetts" (*RP*, 91–109), in July 1854, largely in response to the rendition of Anthony Burns, who was also arrested in Boston. In this speech, Thoreau was absolutely defiant of the Fugitive Slave Law, which he suggested trampling under foot—and "Webster, its maker, with it, like the dirt-bug and its ball." Emerson observed the fourth anniversary of Webster's speech by delivering his second "Fugitive Slave Law Address" (1854 [*W*, 11:215–44]) on 7 March in New York City. Less acerbic than the first, this address also indicted Webster for his perfidy and examined the increasingly pernicious effects of slavery on American character generally. Both Emerson and Thoreau were frequent participants in the activities of the Underground Railroad, which was very active in Concord.*

Some Transcendentalists expressed their reaction to the situation more directly. When Anthony Burns was first captured, Parker joined W. Phillips,** T. W. Higginson,** and others in developing a plan to rescue Burns by force. Alcott joined the mob that eventually attacked the courthouse where Burns was held. The attack was unsuccessful, and Phillips, Parker, and Higginson were later arrested for treason. The case was eventually dismissed on a technicality.

Overall, the Compromise of 1850, and especially the Fugitive Slave Law, polarized opinions on the slavery question and pushed many Transcendentalists to a high level of engagement in the most dynamic reform effort of their age, the abolition movement.

REFERENCES: On the Fugitive Slave Law and the reactions of Transcendentalists, see Gougeon (1990); for a discussion of reactions to the Fugitive Slave Law generally, see Merton L. Dillon, *The Abolitionists: The Growth of a Dissenting Majority* (1974), and Alice Felt Tyler, *Freedom's Ferment* (1944; rpt. 1962).

Len Gougeon

CONCORD, MASSACHUSETTS, has had an important place in the American imagination nearly from the beginning of New England's existence as a social, cultural, and political entity, first as the earliest established inland town in the Massachusetts Bay Colony (1635). It was named for the desire of its founders, John Jones and Peter Bulkeley, to live in peace away from the controversies raging in the seacoast settlements in the 1630s. Then in April 1775 it was the site of the now-legendary "shot heard round the world," as the Concord Minutemen, aroused by Paul Revere, William Dawes, and Samuel Prescott, met and stood their ground against the British regulars under the command of General Gage. It was R. W. Emerson** who so famously characterized that first shot at Concord's North Bridge, and it is perhaps to Emerson and H. Thoreau** that Concord owes its present place in the American consciousness.

When Emerson, a seventh-generation descendant of Bulkeley, moved to Concord permanently in October 1834, it is safe to say that in spite of its glorious past it did not have the metaphorical importance assigned to it today. But as early as the 1835 *Historical Discourse, . . .* , Emerson used Concord's history to transform the village into a symbol of the power of the virtuous private citizen.

As Emerson's reputation as writer and sage grew, Concord became identified with him and with New England Transcendentalism, and that association drew a number of distinguished visitors and new residents to the town, including W. Ellery Channing,** F. B. Sanborn,** and A. B. Alcott,** the latter of whom moved to Concord with his family in 1840. L. M. Alcott,** who grew up in Concord, made the village the setting for some of her most famous work, including *Little Women* (1868–69). Between 1842 and 1845, N. Hawthorne** and his wife, Sophia,** lived in Concord in the Old Manse,* where Emerson himself had lived and where he wrote much of *Nature*. Hawthorne wrote about his first residence in the village and his reservations about Emerson's philosophy in "The Old Manse," the autobiographical sketch that introduces *Mosses from an Old Manse* (1846), a collection of writing he did while living in Concord. The Hawthornes returned to Concord in 1852 and purchased a house that Hawthorne named the Wayside. Thoreau, who was born and lived most of his life in Concord, is perhaps most responsible for linking Concord to environmental causes. In his meditative book *Walden* (1854), Thoreau associates observation of the natural environment around his hometown with self-discovery. Because of this association, Walden Pond,* less than two miles from the center of Concord, and recently Walden Woods* have become symbols for preservationists and environmentalists of the pressing need to protect all locations of particular natural beauty or cultural significance from the encroachment of developers.

Like Walden Pond, Concord, too, has served as a microcosm* for a larger world. It has been a source of symbolism and a model for the making of American civilization. Emerson's study of, observation of, and frequent walks into Concord's surrounding woods and countryside caused him to consider the value of the natural environment to any community. In participating in the establishment of Sleepy Hollow Cemetery* in 1855, Emerson sought to preserve the essential qualities of that landscape* ("the lay and look of the land") for future generations. In his "Address to the Inhabitants of Concord at the Consecration of Sleepy Hollow" he pointed out that the Sleepy Hollow landscape was actually a park for contemplation and recreation. It was also part of a system of public open space. Emerson wrote that the cemetery "lies adjoining the Agricultural Society's ground, to the New Burial Ground, to the Court House and Town House, making together a large block of public ground, permanent property of town and country—all the ornaments of either adding so much value to all." The idea of a town-country continuum provided a pattern for the making of cities more creatively connected to the landscape. Emerson wished that all cities might be intimately related to their natural hinterlands and that they should be more internally "natural" or "organic."* Horace Cleveland, designer of Sleepy Hollow, was inspired by Emerson's ideas and the Concord pattern, and he developed the concept of a town-country continuum in planning a park system for Minneapolis and other burgeoning western cities.

Concord continues to have important meaning for the American public. It is a popular tourist destination, where people seek to connect with the historic events that led to the founding of the nation, and it is a literary mecca, an inspirational destination for scholars, writers, and environmentalists. Annually thousands of people visit the battlefield and North Bridge; the Old Manse; and the houses of Emerson, Hawthorne, and Alcott; and they follow in the footsteps of the Transcendentalists through Walden Woods and along the paths of Walden Pond and Sleepy Hollow. Concord is today as Emerson predicted it would be in 1855: "full of history," for "the good, the wise, and the great . . . have made the air tuneable and articulate."

REFERENCES: See Lemuel Shattuck, *A History of the Town of Concord* (1835); E. W. Emerson,** *Emerson in Concord: A Memoir* (1889); R. W. Emerson, "The Young American" (*CW*, 1:217–44), "Historical Discourse" (*W*, 11:27–86), and "Address to the Inhabitants of Concord at the Consecration of Sleepy Hollow" (*W*, 11:427–36); Townsend Scudder, *Concord: American Town* (1947); Ruth R. Wheeler, *Concord: Climate for Freedom* (1967); Michael Cowan, *City of the West: Emerson, America, and Urban Metaphor* (1967); Robert A. Gross, *The Minutemen and Their World* (1976); Leonard Neufeldt, " 'The Fields of My Fathers' and Emerson's Literary Vocation," *ATQ*, no. 31 suppl. (summer 1976): 3–9; Robert E. Burkholder, "Emerson and the West: Concord, the *Historical Discourse*, and Beyond," *NCS* 4 (1990): 93–103; Daniel Joseph Nadenicek, "Sleepy Hollow Cemetery: Transcendental Garden and Community Park," *Journal of the New England Garden History Society* 3 (fall 1993): 8–14, and "Sleepy Hollow Cemetery: Philosophy Made Substance," *ESP* 5 (spring 1994): 1–2, 8.

Daniel Joseph Nadenicek and Robert E. Burkholder

CONCORD SCHOOL OF PHILOSOPHY was the last flowering of the Transcendentalist movement. It was, in some ways, a return to the "Conversations"* that A. B. Alcott** and M. Fuller** had given in the 1830s and 1840s (and, like the earlier series, the School's sessions were attended by more women than men). When W. T. Harris** of St. Louis, editor of the *Journal of Speculative Philosophy*, came east in 1879 to visit Concord,* he acted as the catalyst for starting a conversational series whose beginnings were modest: A five-week session (15 July–18 August) took place at Alcott's home, usually in his parlor, with F. B. Sanborn** serving as secretary. At the second session (12 July–14 August 1880), the Hillside Chapel (which still stands) was built next to the Orchard House, the Alcotts' home. Also in this year, the audience reached its normal size of between 30 and 100. The third session (11 July–13 August 1881) was uneventful, but the fourth (17 July–12 August 1882) was not. R. W. Emerson** had died in April, and this was the last session at which Alcott lectured, for he would suffer a paralytic stroke in October. The lectures for this year were published as *Concord Lectures on Philosophy* (ed. Raymond L. Bridgman [1883]). Following the fifth session (18 July–10 August 1883), two major changes came about with the sixth session (23 July–1 August 1884): The length was shortened, and rather than have presentations on miscellaneous topics, the sessions were structured around two topics. The subjects for this year's session were immortality and Emerson (the papers on the latter were edited by Sanborn

as *The Genius and Character of Emerson* [1885]). The topics at the seventh
session (16 July–1 August 1885) were "Is Pantheism* the Legitimate Outcome
of Modern Science?" and "Goethe's** Genius and Work," with the latter resulting in another book, also edited by Sanborn, *The Life and Genius of Goethe*
(1886). The eighth session (14–29 July 1886) discussed Plato* and Dante,* and
the ninth session (July 1887) was devoted to Aristotle and dramatic poetry.
Alcott died on 4 March 1888, and the only meeting of the School that summer
was a memorial service for him on 16 June. This was the final meeting of the
School. It was not revived because some speakers had died, while other speakers
were old and infirm, and because its leaders, Harris and Sanborn, had moved
on to other interests.

REFERENCES: See Austin Warren, "The Concord School of Philosophy," *NEQ* 2 (April
1929): 199–233; Kenneth Walter Cameron, *Concord Harvest* (1970); Cameron, *Responses to Transcendental Concord* (1974).

                                                                    Joel Myerson

CONVERSATION, R. W. Emerson** claimed in "Circles," "is a game of
circles. In conversation we pluck up the *termini* which bound the common of
silence on every side." The Transcendentalist movement itself might be thought
of as bounded by conversation, beginning with as much organization as it ever
attained in the conversations of the Transcendental Club* that first met in September 1836 and evanescing with the Conversations that B. Alcott** staged
around the country in the later years of his life and in the proceedings at his
Concord School of Philosophy.* Conversation was a recurrent theme for many
Transcendentalists as well as, upon occasion, an organized event that was part
oral improvisation, part discussion group, and part seminar. It was also an ideal
form toward which many of the Transcendentalists aimed their writing; Emerson, for instance, admired Carlyle** for drawing "strength and motherwit out
of a poetic use of the *spoken* vocabulary, so that his paragraphs are all a sort
of splendid conversation." Indeed, as Lawrence Buell has pointed out, much
Transcendentalist writing "is largely oral literature, in the sense of having been
composed originally for the pulpit and the lyceum."*

One source for Transcendentalist admiration of conversational forms is the
Wordsworthian** injunction to use the real language of men, particularly understood as oral practice. Exemplars of the art of conversation included Madame
de Staël,* Coleridge,** and Goethe.** In addition to her own reputation as a
brilliant talker, de Staël's comments on conversation in *Germany* attracted wide
notice, and her Romantic heroine Corinne, an Italian *improvisatrice,* was a vir-
tuoso of inspired conversation. Coleridge's *Table Talk* (1835) was published
just as the Transcendental movement began, and M. Fuller's** translation of J.
Eckermann's** *Conversations with Goethe* (1839) placed the authority of the
great German Romantic intellectual and artist behind conversational art. Conversation was attractive for a number of reasons, not the least being its inherently
democratic assumptions. In a postrevolutionary world, valuing orality leveled

the distinctions made by earlier privileging of literacy and led to the recognition of common voices. Shepherds who spoke with the diction and sentiments of learned poets were displaced by Michaels who surprised Wordsworths with native depths of feeling and linguistic resource. Conversation for Transcendentalists brought into the circle of thought and feeling those who had traditionally been excluded. Alcott at the Temple School* encouraged children to express their views on the Gospels as "the testimony of unspoiled natures," and Fuller's Conversations with women urged them to find and develop their own powers. H. Thoreau,** typically suspicious of frivolous socializing, claimed that "speech is for the convenience of the hard of hearing" and complained of "the difficulty of getting to a sufficient distance from my guest when we began to utter the big thoughts in big words." Nevertheless, when he came to write of his visitors at Walden,* he focused on the conversation of the Canadian woodchopper A. Therien,** who "suggested that there might be men of genius in the lowest grades of life, however permanently humble and illiterate, who take their own view always, or do not pretend to see at all; who are as bottomless even as Walden Pond was thought to be, though they may be dark and muddy."

For the Transcendentalists, conversation offered supposed spontaneity, a proximate relationship between thought or feeling and expression. When Emerson praised Montaigne's* writing as "the language of conversation transferred to a book," he thought as if it were a living presence: "Cut these words, and they would bleed; they are vascular and alive." "Spontaneous Me" W. Whitman** called himself and claimed his words were able to inseminate generations to come. Conversational spontaneity was regarded sometimes as personally liberating, sometimes as opening a nearly direct communication with the minds of others. Discussing the personal empowerment offered by conversational freedom, Emerson claimed that the "best success in conversation puts the world, like a ball, in our hands. . . . [E]motion communicates to the intellect the power to sap and upheave nature.*" Dreaming of a utopian communal inspiration, on the other hand, Alcott thought of the perfect conversation as "a pentecost of tongues, touching the chords of melody in all minds."

The spontaneity of conversation at times almost seemed to make thought transparent to itself. "The Beatitude of Conversation," said Emerson, was that "[h]ere I come down to the shore of the Sea & dip my hands in its miraculous waves. Here I am assured of the eternity, & can spare all omens, all prophecies, all religions, for I see & know that which they obscurely announce." Conversation's freedom could occasion inspiration, the moment when the seer became the sayer, and it could also unlock voices that were unspoiled because of their exclusion from the material concerns of the world or because they were not yet fully self-conscious, voices of children, women, geniuses "from the lowest grades of life." Alcott announced that his *Conversations with Children on the Gospels* (1836–37) were "the Record of an attempt to unfold the Idea of Spirit from the Consciousness of Childhood."

These were severely criticized, however, for having too much of the flesh mixed into their search for spirit, and Emerson complained, "All conversation among literary men is muddy." Transparency was too rare, but that did not prevent some Transcendentalists from institutionalizing conversation, although the results tended to support Emerson's warnings against the dangers of all institutionalized forms. In November 1839, Fuller initiated a series of Conversations for "well-educated and thinking women," meeting once a week at noon in the West Street rooms of E. Peabody,** who had earlier recorded Alcott's Conversations with his students. The participants discussed topics like Greek mythology, the focus of Fuller's earliest series, and at one time or another included L. Emerson,** Almira Barlow, C. S. [Tappan]**, E. S. Hooper,** Elizabeth Bliss Bancroft, Eliza Farrar, L. M. Child,** Peabody, and her sisters, Mary and Sophia [Hawthorne].** Fuller continued to hold her Conversations until she moved to New York in 1844, eventually opening them on a selective basis to men as well. Alcott offered his own Conversations, beginning in the autumn of 1848 in Peabody's rooms where Fuller had begun hers. Alcott eventually took his Conversations on the road from Boston to St. Louis and conducted them for the rest of his life on typically grandiose topics such as "Man— His Parentage, Planet, Talents, Temptations, Culture and Tendencies" or, apparently with no sense of irony whatsoever, "Silence."

The contents of these Conversations are not easy to piece together, depending upon the memories of participants with often only fragmentary impressions. What survives, however, justifies Buell's description of them as "amateurish, stilted, and slightly bizarre." There was less spontaneity than pretended, since some participants insisted on making predetermined points, strove self-consciously after sublimity and wit, and let vapid idealism* pass for seriousness. Nevertheless, they were also, as Buell points out, harbingers of the adult education* movement and an art form that "came as close to a truly transcendental utterance as the movement ever attained."

REFERENCES: Alcott's *Conversations with Children on the Gospels* (1836–37) are not typical of the Transcendentalist Conversations because of their pedagogic intent, but they do attest to the enhanced regard for spontaneous oral expression. C. H. Dall** gives the best account of Fuller's Conversations in *Margaret and Her Friends* (1895). The chapter "From Conversation to Essay" in Buell (1973), 77–101, is the best account of the role of conversation in Transcendentalist life. Bell Gale Chevigny, *The Woman and the Myth: Margaret Fuller's Life and Writings* (1994), 210–23, relates Fuller's Conversations to her composition of *Woman in the Nineteenth Century*. Madelon Bedell describes Alcott's later Conversations in *The Alcotts: Biography of a Family* (1980), 312–27. Less accessible but more important is E. Cheney's** "Reminiscences of Mr. Alcott's Conversations," *Open Court* 2 (1888): 1131–32, 1142–44. Useful accounts of specific Conversations led by Alcott are given by Clarence Gohdes, "Alcott's 'Conversation' on the Transcendental Club and the *Dial*,"* *AL* 3 (1931): 14–27, and by Helen R. Deese, "Alcott's Conversations on the Transcendentalists: The Record of Caroline Dall," *AL* 60 (1988): 17–25.

Frank Shuffelton

CORRESPONDENCE, for Perry Miller, provided Transcendentalism with "the final confirmation of the link between mind and nature,"* revealing the organic* relationship between the spiritual and the material, the natural and the man-made, the object and the idea As a theory of language, a theory of art, and a theory of morals, correspondence grew out of a fundamental set of principles: The natural, material world is a direct expression of the mind of the Creator; creative productions of the human mind are reflections of these natural forms; the purest forms of human endeavor thus provide insight into the divine spirit. Language, then, in its purest form is a system built upon natural images (rather than mere words), which in turn correspond to spiritual truths; similarly, sculpture, painting, and architecture owe their beauty to the natural forms upon which they are modeled; finally, natural laws provide the proper model for human morality because such laws are true revelations of the divine will. As Sherman Paul observed, "[C]orrespondence covered all the ways by which man came into relation with the world *outside* of himself, transformed the world *into* himself, and expressed the insight of the *experience* in words and character."

The idea of correspondence animated the work of a number of Transcendentalist figures, including S. Reed,** B. Alcott,** G. Ripley,** and C. P. Cranch.** Most important, however, was R. W. Emerson,** whose *Nature* (1836) defined the relationship between correspondence and Transcendentalism. Seeking to establish the "radical correspondence between visible things and human thoughts," Emerson used the doctrine of correspondence as a lens through which to better understand the "mystery of humanity." Thus, a "work of art is an abstract or epitome of the world. It is the result or expression of nature, in miniature." Language, too, could be understood as a function of correspondence: "Words are signs of natural facts. . . . Particular natural facts are symbols of particular spiritual facts. . . . Nature is the symbol of spirit." Indeed, Emerson urged, "the whole of nature is a metaphor of the human mind." Emerson would return to this idea throughout his subsequent work, notably in "Spiritual Laws," "Nominalist* and Realist,*" "The Poet," and *Representative Men* (1850).

Thomas Aquinas (1225–1274) was one of the first to use "correspondence" as a means of denoting the relation between thought and reality, though the idea itself may be traced to Plato* and Plotinus.* It was also a significant force in the work of Coleridge** and Goethe,** both of whom enjoyed a wide influence among the Transcendentalists. E. Swedenborg,* however, was the most immediate source. Reed was profoundly affected by his reading of Swedenborg, and this influence was reflected in his "Oration on Genius" (1821) and *Observations on the Growth of the Mind* (1826), both of which, in turn, deeply moved Emerson. Drawing on Swedenborg, Reed argued that language, particularly poetic language, served as an illustration of truth to the degree that it made use of natural imagery, since such imagery was an immediate reflection of the Creator. In *Representative Men* Emerson saw in Swedenborg the very embodiment of correspondence, for he blended in his person—as metaphysician, mathematician, and geologist—the world of science and the world of spirit.

REFERENCES: For correspondence and the "organic principle," see Matthiessen (1941), 133–66. The influence of correspondence on Transcendentalist literary style is discussed by Buell (1973). Sherman Paul examines Emerson's understanding of correspondence in *Emerson's Angle of Vision* (1952). For a discussion of the wide-ranging significance of correspondence for the Transcendentalists, see Catherine L. Albanese, *Corresponding Motion* (1977).

                                                                    Charles Mitchell

CUDWORTH, RALPH (1617–1688), who spent most of his life at Cambridge as a scholar and religious philosopher, was the leading 17th-century Cambridge Platonist.* His writings are often considered, in Clarence Gohdes's phrase, the "background of New England thought." His two most important works, *The True Intellectual System of the Universe* (1678) and *A Treatise Concerning Eternal and Immutable Morality* (1731, published posthumously), attempt to refute Hobbesian materialism and argue for the acceptance of Descartes's* rationalism, by welding together the new science of the 1600s with the Platonic tradition of metaphysics and theology. According to C, God did not create the universe only to set it in motion and expect it to self-regulate; nor did He intend to divinely intervene in earth's business. C did not believe in materialistic metaphysics but stressed the dynamic workings of the mind.

R. W. Emerson's** belief in the infallibility of intuition owes much to the writings of C. Vivian Hopkins argues that Emerson found "philosophical sanction for art's value in the analysis presented by C in his *True Intellectual System of the Universe* of 'plastic nature,'* which acts as a deputy of Divine wisdom in shaping the material world. Emerson assigns to human art a similar energizing and fashioning power, placing art on a level with C's 'plastic nature' as an executor of Divine commands. Thus art and nature have different functions within an integral relationship and art no less than nature bears a responsibility to Divine power."

C was born at Aller, Somerset, and educated at Cambridge. He became master of Clare Hall and Regius Professor of Hebrew at Cambridge in 1645. His sympathies with both the Puritan* cause and the Restoration movement as well as his sermons given in Parliament on church government made him exceedingly unpopular with his colleagues; he left Clare Hall, having made many enemies with his politics and his difficult personality, but went on to become master of Christ's College in 1654 and prebendary of Gloucester in 1678. He remained at Christ's College until his death.

REFERENCES: See esp. John Arthur Passmore, *RC: An Interpretation* (1951), and Vivian C. Hopkins, *Spires of Form: A Study of Emerson's Aesthetic Theory* (1951); also Gohdes (1931); Harold C. Goddard, *Studies in New England Transcendentalism* (1908); Donald N. Koster, *Transcendentalism in America* (1975); Philip L. Nicoloff, *Emerson on Race and History* (1961); and *EP*.

                                                                    Suzanne D. Green

D

DANTE ALIGHIERI (1265–1321), epic poet whose universal moral message appealed to 19th-century Americans, was born in Florence, a city that remained of central importance to him throughout his life. As a member of the papist Guelf family, he took part in the political power struggle begun generations earlier with the imperialist Ghibelline family. Exiled from Florence when the Ghibellines gained control, D presented himself in his early work, the *Vita nuova,* not only as a cavalryman fighting the imperialists but also as the inheritor of a distinguished family history and culture. For example, D dated his immediate family back to his great-great-grandfather, Cacciaguida, whom he reverently describes as a crusader. In addition, D presents primary influences on his thinking in terms of mentors who fought with their pens on behalf of society. These mentors included his teacher, the leading Florentine intellectual Brunetto Latini; his friend Guido Cavalcanti; and the poet Guido Guinizelli.

While much of D's famous epic poem, *La divina commedia* (*The Divine Comedy*), derives from his bitter reactions to exile from his beloved city and contains statements applicable only to the political climate of medieval Italy, the poem's appeal to later centuries is founded on its central structure as an allegorical journey through the metaphysical realms of hell, purgatory, and paradise. God's will appoints the narrator, generally assumed to be D, two guides on his journey, the Roman epic writer Virgil* and the heavenly woman of D's desires, Beatrice. Supposedly based on Bice Portinari, a young Florentine woman whose affections D was unable to win, and who was placed further out of his reach by her death in 1290, Beatrice developed in D's works, originally appearing in a more human form in the *Vita nuova*. Beatrice's more abstract role in Paradise is to turn D's eyes from herself to the greater glory of God, the universal mover of which she is merely the instrument.

Using his native Tuscan dialect rather than Latin as the vehicle for his most famous work, D's use of a common language in the exalted epic genre encouraged literary development of the lay languages in western Europe. However, while D's work was quite popular during his own time, it experienced a bleak reception during the Renaissance. Renaissance humanists reviving Greek and Latin texts associated D with a medieval culture they strove to reject and brushed his works aside with the excuse that they were difficult to understand. D's reputation rebounded from oblivion in the 17th century. A growing curiosity about D led to the first attempts at English translation of his works, culminating in Henry Francis Cary's complete blank-verse translation of 1814. Coleridge's** praise of this edition in his lecture "On the Meaning and Importance of D's Works" sparked the renewal of D's popularity in both England and America. Moreover, Cary's translation stimulated interest in D's original text. In America this interest encouraged serious study of the Italian language, taught by immigrants from Italy such as Lorenzo Da Ponte, who ran a school in Manhattan and later taught at Columbia College and who centralized in his curriculum reading and memorization of passages from the Italian *Commedia.*

The D revival was a significant milestone in the thinking of the American Transcendentalists, who valued D aesthetically and philosophically. While H. W. Longfellow** was teaching his popular course on D at Harvard, which encouraged students to discuss the *Commedia* critically rather than merely to translate it mechanically, M. Fuller** condemned the general tendency to popularize D studies as casting pearls before swine. While R. W. Emerson** may have shared this elitist view, he also shared the increasing interest in D of his time. This interest is evident in Emerson's writing the first nearly complete English translation of D's *Vita nuova,* which was discovered in manuscript form in 1941. Carlyle's** reverence toward D, as expressed in his lecture "The Hero as Poet" (1840), epitomized the 19th century's new perception of this distant voice from a bygone era. Carlyle lauds *The Divine Comedy* as "at bottom, the *sincerest* of all Poems . . . it goes deep, and through long generations, into ours."

REFERENCES: On D's 19th-century revival, see Angelina La Pina, *D's American Pilgrimage: A Historical Survey of D Studies in the U.S. 1800–1944* (1948); and William J. De Sua, *D into English: A Study of the Translation of the Divine Comedy in Britain and America* (1964). Carl L. Johnson's *Professor Longfellow of Harvard* (1944) describes Longfellow's D course. See R. W. Emerson, trans., *D's "Vita Nuova,"* ed. J. Chesley Matthews (1960); and Ernest S. Sandeen, "Emerson's Knowledge of D," *Studies in English* 22 (1942): 171–98. Carlyle's praise of D is in Lecture III, "The Hero as Poet," *On Heroes, Hero-Worship, and the Heroic in History,* ed. Michael K. Goldberg (1993). See Rachel Jacoff, *The Cambridge Companion to D* (1993), for details on his life and works.

Elisa E. Beshero

DESCARTES, RENÉ (1596–1650), was a French mathematician and philosopher whose renouncement of tradition and arguments defending the integrity of individual reason appealed to the Transcendentalists. D's philosophy began from the proposition that one must suspend all beliefs founded upon evidence of the senses, which he held to be unreliable. While sensory evidence in itself is never conclusive and the existence of physical matter is uncertain, D argued, the reality of one's mind is irrefutable. D's most renowned axiom, "I think; therefore I am," reflects his belief that one could not, finally, doubt that one was thinking. Thus, it was not through one's senses but by the exercise of reason that one could confirm one's existence as a thinking being.

Above all else, D argued that sensory impressions must be subjected to rational analysis and that the basis for evaluating any belief should be logical as opposed to perceptual. From this position, D argued for the existence of God. D reasoned that since human beings are cognizant of their own imperfection, they must necessarily hold an idea of perfection of which they fall short. This notion could not have arisen from experience, which is by its very nature imperfect, so it must be "innate," implanted in the human mind by a perfect being or creator. God, the perfect being who created human beings, must then exist, according to D.

R. W. Emerson's** father's library included works by D, and Emerson's journals* contain several references to the philosopher. In one entry, Emerson quotes D: "Essence of mind consists in thinking, and that of matter in extension." O. A. Brownson,** in a review of Emerson's *Essays,* calls D a "transcendentalist" in that he believed in God and the existence of a spiritual world (*BoQR* [4 July 1841]: 291–308). The Cartesian questioning of the existence of physical objects underlies much of Emerson's and other Transcendentalists' work, including such central essays as "Experience" and the "Idealism"* chapter of *Nature,* in which Emerson writes, "A noble doubt perpetually suggests itself . . . whether nature* outwardly exists."

REFERENCES: *Essays on the Philosophy and Science of RD* (1993), ed. Stephen Voss, is a collection on Cartesian philosophy, metaphysics, and science. John Cottingham, ed., *The Cambridge Companion to D* (1992), is a compendium of essays on D's life and work. *RD: A Biography* (1970) by Jack R. Vrooman provides an account of D's life and career.

Mark J. Madigan

THE DIAL was a quarterly journal published between July 1840 and April 1844. It grew out of a meeting of the Transcendental Club* on 18 September 1839 at which it was proposed that a journal "designed as the organ of views more in accordance with the soul" be started. B. Alcott** suggested the title, named after the heading he had given his thoughts that he had been assembling from his journals* over the past few years. M. Fuller** volunteered to be editor and tried for two years to fairly present "all kinds of people" in her magazine. *The Dial*'s contributors indeed had, in Fuller's words, "freedom to say their say, for better, for worse," but the reviewers, choosing *The Dial* (and especially Alcott's "Orphic Sayings") as a convenient scapegoat for the unpopular aspects of Transcendentalism, heaped abuse on the new journal, and the public, unable to understand the varied contents, declined to buy *The Dial,* whose subscription list never rose above 300. In March 1842, beset by ill health and having never been paid, Fuller resigned. Despite R. W. Emerson's** assuming the editorship, the journal failed in 1844. The first eight numbers were edited by Fuller and the last eight by Emerson; G. Ripley,** the founder of Brook Farm,* served as business manager (mostly a titular position) through the October 1841 number, and H. D. Thoreau** oversaw the editing of the April 1843 issue in Emerson's absence. Among its important contributors, the magazine counted, in addition to its editors, Alcott, J. E. Cabot,** W. Ellery Channing,** L. M. Child,** J. F. Clarke,** C. P. Cranch,** G. W. Curtis,** J. S. Dwight,** F. H. Hedge,** J. R. Lowell,** T. Parker,** E. P. Peabody,** and J. Very.** *The Dial* was important to many of its contributors: It was where Fuller and Thoreau first published works that they revised and incorporated into their later writings; it provided Parker and Ripley with a place to publish their religious works once the conservative Unitarian* journals had refused their pages to them; and it presented some of Emerson's best poetry, sketches, and lectures. *The Dial* was the most visible focal point for the Transcendentalist movement in America.

REFERENCE: See *NET*Dial.

Joel Myerson

E

ECKHART, JOHANNES (c. 1260–1327/8), called Meister E, was a German mystic and theologian whose name was probably unknown to the New England Transcendentalists he influenced. (In 1882, John Orr, explaining the debt of Transcendentalism to mysticism, referred to an "Erckhart . . . without [whose] previous existence probably Transcendentalism could not have been.") A Dominican friar, E held teaching posts in Paris (including the chair once held by Thomas Aquinas), Strassburg, and Cologne. He had an enormous influence on the Rhenish mystics and, eventually, on Martin Luther, who knew his work only anonymously because it had been condemned by the pope. E spent the last years of his life trying to free himself from charges of heresy. In 1329 John XXII declared 11 of E's propositions rash and 17 heretical but stated that E had recanted before his death.

In the 19th century Franz von Baader rehabilitated the work of Meister E and J. Böhme,* both of whom influenced the thought of G.W.F. Hegel** and F. Schelling.** Schelling's influence on S. T. Coleridge** is well documented, as is Coleridge's contribution to American Transcendentalism. Other lines of continuity from E to the New England Transcendentalists are less direct but nevertheless discernible: E's ideas played roles in the development of the thought of J. G. Fichte* and F. Schleiermacher.**

Like his philosophical heir R. W. Emerson,** E was not always consistent. At times he asserted that God is essentially *intelligere,* Mind or Intellect, rather than *esse,* Being. On other occasions, although he never approved of thinking of God anthropomorphically, as *a being,* he referred to God as Being; indeed, he said Being is the essence of God and that God's creatures exist only because they are related to God, who alone is. Because they are God's creations, God's creatures participate in the divine Being. E was always careful to distinguish between God as God *is* and God as God *is known,* expressing the distinction in such arresting lines as "God does not exist but I exist" and "I give God existence."

For E, God is perfect Oneness, ineffable and indescribable. He called this Oneness the Godhead; it reveals itself as the Persons of the Trinity. We must not, he insisted, confuse the revelation of God, the God that we can know, with the perfection of unity, the God that is but that cannot be known. In creation, E taught, God bestowed itself upon its creatures. Although E's metaphorical language has led some of his interpreters to call him a pantheist,* it is likely he meant only that we can never fully know the ways in which we live and move and have our being in God.

E made careful distinctions between the faculties of the soul, such as memory, and the *Grund,* or ground of the soul. At the core of every human personality, E said, resides a divine spark that is uncreated and eternal. Through contemplation, therefore, it is possible to transcend ordinary activities of the mind and consciousness of the self and to gain unity with the Godhead.

E taught that the soul operates at five levels. At the lowest level, it operates through the body, next through the emotions and lower intellect (which he called *sensus communis* or common sense, the faculty that combines what is given through the senses into objects of perception). At the third level the soul operates through memory, will, and higher intellect; at the fourth it knows abstractions or pure forms as they exist in the mind of God. Finally, the divine spark in the soul can know God directly as God is.

E believed that in each person a true self is being born, the true self being a word of God just as Christ was the Word. He taught that creation is ongoing and that the Incarnation of the historical Christ reflected in time the eternal birth of God in the individual human soul. While E's theology was influenced by the teachings of both Thomas Aquinas and St. Augustine, it is also in some respects kin to the Eastern mystical tradition.

REFERENCES: See Thomas O'Meara, "E," *The Encyclopedia of Religion,* vol. 4, ed. Mircea Eliade (1987); E. J. Tinsley, "E," *A Dictionary of Christian Theology,* ed. Alan Richardson (1969); Ninian Smart, "Meister E," *EP;* Matthew Fox, *Breakthrough: Meister E's Creation Spirituality* (1980); and Edmund Colledge and Bernard McGinn, *Meister E: The Essential Sermons, Commentaries, Treatises and Defenses* (1981). Orr's reference to "Erckhart" is in Philip F. Gura and Joel Myerson, *Critical Essays on American Transcendentalism* (1982), 184.

Mariane Wurst Schaum

THE EDINBURGH REVIEW shines as one of the many gems among British periodicals. Inaugurated in 1802, it was the brainchild of Francis Jeffrey, Sidney Smith, Francis Horner, John Allen, and Henry Brougham. *EdR* delighted its readers with a pleasing mix of literary, political, social, and scientific essays. Its genteel reformism had wide appeal on both sides of the Atlantic.

Scholars have overwhelming evidence that the British periodicals were devoured by the literati of the United States. And *EdR* did not escape the attention of Transcendentalists. B. Alcott,** for example, credited the periodical with introducing him to the writings of Jeremy Bentham. R. W. Emerson** likewise recognized its importance. His journals* are replete with references to articles he discovered between its covers. Emerson believed the magazine an influential force; there he perused articles by Carlyle** and essays on Goethe** and other facets of German literature, as well as a variety of social and reform issues. Scarcely a hotbed of radical social change, *EdR* ran such articles as "Law Reform—District Courts" (July 1830), "American Slavery" (April 1836), and "Rights and Conditions of Women" (April 1841). Such themes form the marrow of Transcendentalist social concerns.

EdR also covered the gamut of 19th-century religious topics with articles concerning biblical criticism, fanaticism, preaching, and miracles.* Many of these entries appeared in the 1830s and 1840s, adding fuel to the Transcendental dialogues on inspiration, skepticism, and the like. With material also on U.S. and European culture, *EdR* truly became an international force. Glancing at the table of contents of any issue, one cannot help but imagine members of the Transcendental Club* poring over the latest number and gathering for discussions on their readings.

REFERENCES: Few scholars have assessed critically at length *EdR*. Brief mentions of it and its relation to various Transcendentalists appear in such works as Dahlstrand (1982). In 1902 A. R. D. Elliot published a fairly detailed history of the magazine—*"The EdR [1802–1902]"*—in the periodical itself. *The Wellesley Index* remains the most complete consideration.

E. Kate Stewart

EDUCATION REFORM arose from a general cry, beginning in the 1820s, for improved teacher training, curriculum consistency, school discipline, teachers' salaries and working conditions, and public commitment to pedagogical innovations, especially those coming from Europe. The 1837 formation of the Massachusetts Board of Education responded to such demands. On other fronts, B. Alcott** and E. Peabody** devoted themselves to teaching and pedagogical theory; Alcott's ideas in turn influenced M. Fuller's** teaching of both children and adult women; and Brook Farm* housed a progressive boarding school.

Both the Massachusetts Board of Education and Transcendentalist reformers believed that urbanization and industrialization had weakened the ability of the church and the family to influence the moral development of youths and that educators should claim this role. "If internal and moral restraints be not substituted for the external and arbitrary ones that are removed," warned an educator in the *Common School Journal,* "the people, instead of being conquerors and sovereigns over their passions, will be their victims and slaves" (12 August 1850, 236). Peabody, too, argued that treating moral goodness as intrinsic to students helped them overcome modern susceptibility to "bodily ease and enjoyment." Using her favorite metaphor for the teacher/pupil relationship, she suggested the educator/gardener supplies the nourishment that surrounds the student/plant, "feeding it on beauty and good" and "admitting nothing that it cannot assimilate unto itself." If educators assist students in assimilating "moral restraints" or "goodness and beauty," then they learn to control base passions let loose by a materialistic and secular society.

Mainstream and Transcendentalist reformers differed, however, in their relative emphasis on the ability of the individual to cultivate her own moral nature. H. Mann,** Secretary of the Massachusetts Board of Education, agreed with his friend Peabody that humans have a natural will to goodness but had little faith in what Transcendentalists came to call self-culture—the ability to develop one's own spiritual and moral senses without organized and systematic outside influence. Even Transcendentalists didn't agree on the proper pedagogy for developing the student's inner spirituality.

Peabody admired German educator Friedrich Froebel (1782–1852) for his invention of activities that seemed to lead children to spontaneously discover religious and moral truths. Gathering children from different families into a "Child Garden," explained Peabody in one of her many accounts of the Froebelian Kindergarten, he would have them act out "movement plays" rehearsing "moral sentiments" and "intellectual exercise." Peabody also promoted Froebel's organized system of games, songs, symbolic dances, marches, finger plays, block building, drawing, sewing, and nature* experiences. Respect for children and their ability to "learn by doing" has the religious function, she believed, of making both child and teacher aware "that there is a mysterious third Being present, who is neither the teacher nor the child, but in whom they meet, through whom they communicate."

In emphasizing activities, Peabody contradicted the prevailing practice that began children's education with reading. When children do begin to read, Peabody advised that they not memorize facts by rote but rather learn simultaneously to write and follow the German "philosophical method" of concentrating on the meaning of a text through discussion. She believed active uses of language, such as writing and speaking, develop children's spirituality: Instead of religious authorities revealing truth, children engage in "naming," or in the conceptual activity whereby they reach, through language, an understanding of God. To support her assertions about the conceptual power of language, she cited the case of Laura, blind and deaf since the age of two, who learned to read but had never read the word *God.* Laura suddenly came across the word *God* in her reading and wondered if this might be the power that makes rain. For Peabody, reading the word *God* corresponds simultaneously with the conceptual ability to imagine God.

Peabody's efforts to pioneer the kindergarten in America spanned over 50 years. She raised funds to establish Froebelian kindergartens and training schools for teachers, recruited and trained teachers, and wrote over 70 books and articles. Her Froebelian journal, *The Kindergarten Messenger,* established in 1873, eventually became a department of the *New England Journal of Education.*

By the time Peabody agreed in 1834 to help Alcott gather and teach children at his Temple School,* she had already observed her mother instruct for many years, taught her own infant school, and published an article on Pestalozzi's* teaching methods. What Alcott retained from Pestalozzi, Peabody enthusiastically approved: the effort to educate moral, physical, and intellectual aspects of the child, the use of the mother-child relationship as a model for educator-pupil relationships, and reliance on conscience rather than the ferule to encourage good behavior. But Peabody realized that Alcott also abandoned Pestalozzi's emphasis on children's natural propensity for artistic expression and play. He had used his "personal power" to "tear the rosebud open," wrote Peabody. By 1874, after she had studied Froebel and begun to pioneer the kindergarten movement, she was more explicit in her dissatisfaction with Alcott's methods: "Froebel's method of cultivating children through artistic production, in the childish sphere of affection and fancy, is a healthier and more effective way than self-inspection, for at least those years of a child's life before the age of seven."

Alcott at the Temple School stressed introspection and the Conversation.* The purpose of children's education was "contemplation of Spirit as it unveils itself within themselves"; the primary means of this contemplation, "self-analysis." To facilitate self-analysis, Alcott sat with the children in a circle and read and discussed with them moral fables, parables, allegories, and passages from the Bible. He then questioned them on abstract topics like freedom, war, love, and their own spiritual nature, all the while looking for evidence to confirm his theories about children's intrinsic knowledge of spiritual and religious truths.

Pestalozzi, and not religious beliefs, motivated Alcott's efforts at education reform during his first years as a teacher in a small school in Cheshire, Connecticut, when he titled his journal* for 1825 "The Cheshire Pestalozzian School." Dissatisfied with conventional emphasis on rote learning, Alcott taught by association and analogy, building on what his students already knew, in a step-by-step fashion. He responded to the stark physical conditions of the classroom by making individual desks and seats for students, buying them writing slates and a library of 100 books, and decorating the room with pictures, engravings, and Cyprus branches to suggest the beauty of nature. Feeling that sitting postures confined children, he arranged desks along outer walls to make room in the center for marching, dancing, and other physical activities and used walks, games, storytelling, and exercises instead of traditional textbooks and recitation.

From these early years until Alcott published accounts of his Temple School, supporters called him an "American Pestalozzi" because he emphasized organic* teaching methods, a pleasant learning environment, and moral regeneration through education. But unlike Peabody, Alcott did not share Pestalozzi's emphasis on learning through activity. It was perhaps easier to find evidence of the Spirit in conversations with children that he led and controlled than in games they played or in pictures they drew.

Alcott continued to use the Conversation as a pedagogical strategy in his later years, though he no longer emphasized this technique to the exclusion of more active kinds of learning. As superintendent of Concord* schools in 1859, he gave teachers examples of the Conversation but also began using the community and neighborhood of Concord as a microcosm* of the world and of the spirit-world. Students learned about geography Thoreau**-style, by studying the geography of their own town. They learned history by examining the lives of local people, information Alcott collected and intended for a textbook called "Concord Book," though he never finished it. Composition instruction included letter writing, diary keeping, and a student-run newspaper. While Alcott still saw the classroom as a place to culture the soul, he left more room for individual expression, introducing marching, dancing, singing, and recreation to an otherwise monotonous curriculum. Henry Barnard, editor of *Barnard's American Journal of Education*, thought Alcott's report for 1859–60 the best he had ever seen and encouraged Alcott to publish it as a book.

Though Alcott had limited influence on early childhood education, the Conversation remained important as a means to self-culture for adults. In 1848 Alcott began to host Conversations, seven weekly sessions on "Man: His History, Resources, and Expectations." He held eight more series between 1848 and 1853 in small towns throughout Massachusetts, discussing human potential, the way to self-culture, the family, the church, reform and reformers, childhood, diet, and regimen. Alcott would introduce a theme and read from a classic author, and participants would provide variations on the topic. He believed his "parlor awakening" a method for sparking the spirit of the individual. Peabody led a Conversation group for women to discuss history, believing that "in women's education history should take the place that law, medicine, or theology takes in the liberal education of men."

Fuller, too, led Conversations on "History" as well as on "Mythology" and "The Arts." Her audience included Sophia Ripley,** Lydia Parker, S. Hawthorne,** Mary Mann, many wives of Harvard professors, and their husbands on occasion. Fuller believed that the Conversation had the potential to rectify the lack of rigor in women's education, for it required active student participation rather than rote recitation or lecturing. At the Greene Street School, where she taught from 1837 to 1838, Fuller insisted that her female students participate orally, even though official school policy restricted oral declamations to male students. Nonetheless, "it must not be our object to hear her talk," a student reported in the journal Fuller asked her to keep. These journals contained students' reactions to readings and lessons, which Fuller read and corrected regularly. For Fuller, acknowledging that women "have intellect which needs developing" topped the agenda for education reform. There was no hope for accomplishing this without a pedagogy that encouraged women to speak and write their ideas freely.

Students also took an active role in their education at Brook Farm, which housed a college-preparatory and an alternative school with an elective curriculum. Without mandated study hours, students set their own. Without servants, they labored manually in the fields or in the kitchen. Taking responsibility for one's education also meant questioning traditional religious and moral authorities. Fuller's father hoped his son "would learn, for the first time, perhaps, that all these matters of creeds and morals are not quite so well settled as to make thinking nowadays a piece of supererogation."

Transcendentalists had long resisted teaching Christian ideals with creeds and morals. Better to place values in the conscience, which had direct access to God. But by the end of the century, people questioned even the sanctity of the soul. In response Alcott established in 1879 the Concord School of Philosophy,* his final attempt to defend the values of idealism* and Christianity against an encroaching skepticism and materialism made worse by Darwinism** and naturalism. Over five weeks during the summer, he and other well-known literary critics, educators, artists, and professors of philosophy, theology, astronomy, and classical civilizations lectured, demonstrating, Alcott hoped, the timeless truth of man's connection to the universal spirit. But some of these teachers felt that ignoring advances in sciences only replaced a dogmatic materialism with a dogmatic spiritualism. When Alcott suffered a stroke, they revised the curriculum to include scientific theories antithetical to Christianity, signaling a waning of the ideology that had previously spurred calls for education reform.

REFERENCES: Ruth M. Baylor, *Elizabeth Palmer Peabody: Kindergarten Pioneer* (1968), describes the sources and development of Peabody's ideas on education. Peabody evaluated Alcott's system and discussed her own in her preface and conclusion to *Record of a School* (1836) and in the preface to *Record of Mr. Alcott's School* (1874). C. Lane** compares Alcott's educational philosophy with that of Pestalozzi in *The Law and Method of Spirit-Culture, An Interpretation of Bronson Alcott's Idea and Practice at the Masonic Temple* (1843). Dahlstrand (1982) details the progression of Alcott's ideas on education as he developed them through reading and teaching. Henry L. Greene presents Fuller's years as a teacher: "The Greene-St. School, of Providence, and Its Teachers," in *PRIHS* 6 (January 1899): 199–219. Laraine R. Fergenson transcribes journals of Fuller's students: "Margaret Fuller as a Teacher in Providence: The School Journal of Ann Brown," *SAR* 1991: 59–118; and "Margaret Fuller in the Classroom: The Providence Period," *SAR* 1987: 131–42. Lindsay Swift recounts education at Brook Farm in *Brook Farm: Its Members, Scholars, and Visitors* (1900).

D'Ann Pletcher-George

EICHHORN, JOHANN GOTTFRIED (1752–1827), biblical professor at Jena and Göttingen, was one of the first scholars to analyze the Bible scientifically and to question its authorship. His outlines of the Old and New Testaments and lectures shocked and influenced many of his students, among them E. Everett,** who in his translations of these works states that he is glad E's ideas are safely locked in the German tongue where they will affect few Americans, and later W. Emerson** (R. W.'s** brother), who after reading E could no longer pursue the ministry.

E distinguished the documentary and cultural sources of the Old Testament Law. He questioned the Pauline authorship of the New Testament letters to Timothy and Titus and suggested a single Aramic text as the source of the four

Gospels. One of E's leading tenets was his view of the Pentateuch. Questioning Mosaic authorship, he believed that Moses gathered and collated the first five books of the Bible but that they actually derived from two sources because they refer to God by two different names, *El-Elohim* and *Jah-veh* (pronounced Jehovah). Hence, he questioned that the Bible was the word of God, given directly to chosen individuals who wrote down what God dictated. The compilation of the Bible was a far more complicated matter. His outlines of the Old and New Testaments (*Einleitung ins das Alte Testament* and *Einleitung ins das Neue Testament*)—a collection of sketches recounting biblical stories but lacking in thorough investigation—explain miracles* through natural phenomena. A violent thunderstorm sanctions Moses' declaration of the Ten Commandments and his smashing the golden idol. The shallowness of the water and a subsequent wind explain the parting of the Red Sea. The conversion of the Apostle Paul is attributed to a dream or an active imagination on Paul's part. Christ is well intentioned, but his miracles become more a matter of perception on the part of those who followed and admired him. Furthermore, E sought historical proof that prophecies were written after rather than before the events that they presumably foretold, which accounted for their historical accuracy. While E offered no absolute proof for his teachings, he did lead the way for questioning and examining in a historical, scientific context what had once been considered sacred and unquestionable.

E also claimed that the Greek word *logos* translated as *word* in John 1:1 originally referred not exclusively to Christ but to God's immanence* in his creation, his working through his creation, and only later took on its limited connotation referring only to Christ. E believed that God united his spirit with Christ and worked through him as he worked through all his creation. Thus, while God may have used and worked through Christ to a greater degree than he did through most men, Christ is still not essentially different from other men. Christ differed only in degrees, not in kind, from other men—an idea that R. W. Emerson expressed in his Divinity School Address.

REFERENCES: Everett translated but never published at least major portions of E's *Einleitung in das Alte Testament* (1803) and *Einleitung in das Neue Testament* (1804). E's *Treatise on the Authority and Canonical Authority of the Scriptures of the Old Testament* was trans. and published by John Frederick Schroeder in 1892. Also see Paul G. Buchloh and Walter T. Rix, *American Colony of Göttingen: Historical and Other Data Collected Between the Years 1855 and 1888* (1976).

Karen L. Kalinevitch

ENGLISH RENAISSANCE culture of the 16th and 17th centuries represented to the Transcendentalists the felicitous conjunction of a religious sensibility, vital humanist art, the enterprise of exploration, and the dawn of empirical science heralded by Francis Bacon. More particularly, 17th-century English culture represented an age of appealing heterodoxy to these American apostles of "the Newness" who would themselves challenge many of the prevailing orthodoxies in their culture: "When Orthodoxy reigns unquestioned, and all is reduced to uniformity of opinion, literature cannot flourish," observed O. Brownson** in his 1840 article on "American Literature." "The richest portion of English literature belongs to the seventeenth century; and what is that century in England but an epoch of political and religious revolutions, defeated, effected, or adjourned?" As Brownson's comment suggests, and as W. E. Channing's** essay "Remarks on a National Literature" confirms, 19th-century writers were deeply concerned with the relation between political democracies and the aesthetic production of vital national literatures. The hours spent in the private reading of English Renaissance authors—introduced to these Americans in the writings of S. T. Coleridge,** Charles Lamb, and W. Wordsworth**—enabled Transcendentalists to garner an alternative canon of literature that they used to challenge, complicate, or displace those Augustan texts, Addisonian prose styles, and conservative values taught in the Harvard classroom. "While our English professors were teaching us out of Blair's* 'Rhetoric,' we were forming our taste by making copious extracts from Sir Thomas Browne or Ben Jonson," commented J. F. Clarke** in his memoirs of his Harvard days. The Transcendentalists, however, did not themselves formulate a shared idiom as an alternative to the neoclassicism promulgated in American universities and enforced by criticism in contemporary periodicals. Instead, they relied on their own individual inventiveness both in seeking out the writings of the earlier period and in appropriating its various strategies.

In addition to the prominent place the ever-varied Shakespeare* holds in R. W. Emerson's** *Nature* and *Representative Men,* Emerson identified strongly with the inspired language and apocalyptic ferocity of Milton's* antiprelatical prose tracts of the 1640s (*Of Reformation* [1641], *The Reason of Church-Government* [1642], *An Apology Against a Pamphlet* [1642], and *Areopagitica* [1644]). Emerson's unorthodox insistence that "[t]he Reason of Ch.[urch] Gov[ernment] & Areopagitica are better poems than whole books of P[aradise] L[ost]" attested to his belief in the power of varied and vehement prophetic eloquence to guide a nation toward spiritual renovation and ecclesiastical reform. Emerson sensed that the Whig Unitarian* promulgation of a uniform aesthetic in oratory checked or restrained the prophetic eloquence he sought to employ. In crucial periods of his own self-fashioning, Emerson turned to Milton's apocalyptic prose writings, as much for their displays of polemical agility or "manly" ad hominem ferocity as for the occasions they offered to explore and conceptualize inspired, efficacious language.

Emerson also lectured on Francis Bacon, "the Restorer of science," praising his *Essays* (1625) as "clothed in a style of such splendor" and commenting on the *Novum Organum* (1620) that he "condenses an unrivaled degree of matter in one paragraph." However much he was troubled by Bacon's ethics and morals, Emerson continued to admire Bacon's genius for reforming the methods of science: "[H]e would put his Atlantean hands to heave the whole globe of the Sciences from their rest, expose all the gulfs and continents of error, and with creative hand remodel and reform the whole." In fact, the structure both of Emerson's American Scholar "Address" and of "Self-Reliance" may owe much to Bacon's method (in the *Advancement of Learning* and the *Novum Organum*) of identifying the "Idols" of belief that masquerade as knowledge that must be swept away before true inquiry may proceed. Yet in his lecture, Emerson is disappointed by the substantive result of the empiricist's data. In the end it discloses no broad axioms or natural laws but merely "lies along the ground, a vast unfinished city. . . . The fire has hardly passed over it and given it fusion and a new order from his own mind."

While Bacon's writings offered a model of the reformer of knowledge, the Cambridge Platonists' writings—R. Cudworth's* *True Intellectual System of the Universe* (1678) and Henry More's *Philosophical Poems* (1647) and metaphysical prose writings (1653–71)—provided Emerson with appealing interpretations of Platonism.* Emerson also relished the sonorous cadences, elegant prose rhythms, and pious convictions of Sir Thomas Browne's *Religio Medici* (1643) and *Hydriotaphia* (1658) and Jeremy Taylor's *Holy Living* (1650) and *Holy Dying* (1651).

After graduating from Harvard, H. Thoreau** embarked upon an anthology project—an homage to English literature suggested by Emerson. For the next three years (1841–44) Thoreau immersed himself in English Renaissance literature, reading everything from religious meditations to Jacobean and Caroline court masques, and from the Cavalier poets to pastoral idylls and georgics to Renaissance epics. Although his anthology remained unfinished, Thoreau's *A Week on the Concord and Merrimack Rivers* and *Walden* reveal his significant use of such texts as Thomas Carew's masque *Coelum Britannicum* (1634), Izaak Walton's *The Compleat Angler* (1653), Abraham Cowley's *Essays* (1668), as well as the ethos presented in Sir Thomas Browne's meditative prose. By quoting, revising, and emulating these texts, Thoreau was able to present a natural world mediated by the artifice of the 17th-century literary pastoral and georgic. In this way, Thoreau sought to prevent his audience from indulging in un-self-conscious, nostalgic longing for an American pastoral landscape.* He urged them instead to discern the limits of their illusions about the American landscape and the basis of American national identity, exhorting them to be more alert to the potential for change rather than to be vigilant against it. Moreover, by emulating the stylization and theatricality of courtly masques (Carew's *Coelum Britannicum,* Jonson's *Masque of Queens*), and by assuming the dramatic guises of distinctive characters (Carew's Momus and Mercury, Walton's Piscator, and Browne's extravagant persona in *Religio Medici*), Thoreau portrayed an America gracious in its magnanimity, unflinching in its confidence, and worldly in its sophistication as an alternative to a dispirited and conforming America that could imagine for itself only the role of rustic simplicity.

As M. Fuller's** former mentor and one of her posthumous editors, Emerson boasted that he "had the pleasure of making her acquainted with Chaucer, with Ben Jonson, with Herbert, Chapman, Ford, Beaumont and Fletcher, with Bacon, and Sir Thomas Browne.'' While Fuller admired Milton's poetry, and was struck by his remarkable elaboration of companionate marriage in his divorce tracts, her deepest imaginative sympathies were invested in George Herbert and Lord Herbert of Cherbury. Fuller's artful imaginary dialogue between the "Two Herberts" (1844)—George Herbert, the religious poet, and his elder brother Lord Herbert, the courtier, diplomat, poet, and proponent of natural religion*—dramatized the argument that in America "the figure we most need to see before us now is not that of a saint, martyr, sage, poet, artist, or preacher, or any other who vocation leads to a seclusion and partial use of faculty, but 'a spiritual man of the world.' '' Impersonating Lord Herbert in her imaginary dialogue, she challenges the "partial" nature of her society, which makes the female the repository of moral virtue and spiritual refinement, yet does so at the cost of her worldly engagement. Fuller, moreover, adapts Lord Herbert's controversial treatise *De Veritate* to expose the "partial" nature of revealed religion, whereby God favors "one race and nation, and not another.'' In doing so, she challenges the exclusions and prerogatives of Christianity. Fuller's Lord Herbert effectually eliminates dependency ("prayers") upon the will of a partial God for favors ("gifts of grace"), wresting the power to gain knowledge and immediate experience of the divine ("aspirations") instead for all individuals through an inborn faculty. Yet in those moments in personal letters when Fuller does allow herself to identify with the reclusive George Herbert, it is to speak of the pain of her quotidian burdens. Herbert's "Affliction (I)'' comes to mind when in 1842 she expresses her frustration with outward circumstances, even as she is proffered compensations:* "My inward life has been rich and deep. . . . It seems to me that Heaven, whose course has ever been to 'cross-bias me,' as Herbert hath it, is no niggard in its compensations . . . [and yet] the pen has been snatched from my hand just as I longed to give myself to it.'' In an 1845 letter to her lover James Nathan, who had abandoned her, Fuller used lines from Herbert's poem "The Temper'' in a desperate attempt to mitigate the discord in their relationship by describing it as "but the tuning of the breast / To make the music better.'' Her moments of identification with George Herbert, then, are those when she was most chastened by circumstances.

REFERENCES: A seminal discussion of the English Renaissance in relation to American authors is Matthiessen (1941). For more recent work, see my *The Complicity of Imagination: The American Renaissance, Contests of Authority, and Seventeenth-Century English Culture* (1995), and Kevin P. Van Anglen, *The New England Milton: Literary Reception and Cultural Authority in the Early Republic* (1993). See also Michael J. Colacurcio's fine essay " 'The Corn and the Wine': Emerson and the Example of Herbert,'' *NCL* 42 (June 1987): 1–28.

Robin Sandra Grey

EPICTETUS (c. 50–c. 130) was an influential figure in the development of the Stoic* school of Greek philosophy. Born a slave in Phrygia, Asia Minor, he was manumitted by his owner, a government official, around 68. E's philosophy stresses submissiveness to the inexorable, simplicity of living, and a stance of principled moral and religious tension, all of which should lead to a life of tranquillity. Not to be construed as fatalism, E's position emphasizes the improvement of the world through individual effort, while viewing the universe as essentially benign.

E's accent on individualism and his lack of political involvement appealed to the Transcendentalists, especially R. W. Emerson,** who saw the betterment of society as essentially a matter of individual effort. Emerson's Stoic propensities have been remarked by his biographers, and his early reading of E and other Stoic philosophers (like Marcus Aurelius) undoubtedly strengthened an already ascetically inclined personality.

A Stoic tendency can be seen in several of the Transcendentalists, manifested by attempts to regiment their lives through collective discipline. The Brook Farm* and Fruitlands* experiments are examples of the unsuccessful implementation of ascetic principles in the lives of the movement's members. Their inability to balance austerity with practicality shows an otherworldly predilection that was congenial to Stoicism, particularly manifested in B. Alcott,** who subjected his family to undue privation while attempting to put his ascetic ideas into practice.

REFERENCES: Scattered references to E appear throughout Emerson's *JMN*, illustrating his admiration for the Stoic philosopher's ideas. Good short sketches of E's life and main concepts are in *EP;* and *Encyclopaedia of Religion and Ethics*, ed. James Hastings (1928).

                                                                    John D. Cloy

F

FÉNELON, FRANÇOIS DE SALIGNAC DE LA MOTHE- (1651–1715), educator, theologian, mystic, and archbishop of Cambrai, was for a time a favorite at the court of King Louis XIV. However, his relationship with and strange attachment to the devout widow and mystic Madame Guyon, whose advocation of the mystical doctrine of Quietism disturbed staid orthodox churchmen, caused him to lose the favors of both Court and Church. The bitter controversy with the bishop of Meaux, Jacques Bénigne Bossuet, led to F's papal condemnation and permanent exile to his archdiocese of Cambrai.

F's connection with American Transcendentalism lies in his influence on R. W. Emerson** and B. Alcott.** Kenneth W. Cameron in *Young Emerson's Transcendental Vision* (1971) prints passages from Emerson's sermons that are parallel in thought with passages from F's writings found in Mrs. E.L.C. Follen's** 1831 edition of *Selections from the Writings of F* . . . (3d rcv. ed.), most strikingly passages on listening to the voice of God in the soul, mysterious but pervasive. Emerson, who mentions F from time to time in his journals,* had begun to read F's *Les aventures de Télémaque* (1699), a takeoff of a heroic poem on Homer and Virgil,* as early as November 1816. This fantastic narrative included lessons designed to shape the moral character of a prince who likely was destined to occupy the throne. F had been appointed preceptor of Louis XIV's grandson, the Duc de Bourgogne, and heir presumptive to the throne.

Alcott's philosophy of education,* conception of mysticism, and view of the relationship of God to nature* appear indebted to F. No two men could have been so different and yet so much the same: F, an aristocrat of ancient lineage, college and seminary educated, tutor to royalty, constitutional monarchist who detested autocracy, and priest and Church official; Alcott, the son of a poor farmer, entirely self-educated, pedlar and teacher of the common people, and democratic-republican who sought to abolish slavery. Yet both were pure minded and high principled, natural-born teachers who pioneered in educational theory; both upheld the dignity of women; both were dedicated men of letters; both felt that one could achieve communion with God through contemplation and divine love outside of the ordinary understanding; and both respected the intelligence and creativity of the young. Compare Alcott's "Orphic Saying" VIII. *Mysticism:* "Because the soul is herself mysterious, the saint is a mystic to the worldling. He lives to the soul; he partakes of her properties, he dwells amidst the dust and vapors of his own lusts, which dim his vision, and obscure the heavens wherein the saint beholds the face of God"; with F, in his *The Maxims of the Saints Explained, Concerning the Interior Life* (1698): "It is by a continual and unreserved acquiescence in all that you know and even in all that you do not know that you become capable of receiving that interior light which gradually develops the ground of the soul and makes it visible, and teaches the soul from moment to moment what God wants of her; all other lights show only the outer surface of the heart." Six F titles, one in French and five in English, were in Alcott's library at Fruitlands.*

When Mrs. Follen's *Selections* appeared in 1829, W. E. Channing** reviewed it and declared F "an original thinker" and "though a Catholic, he was essentially free. He wrote from his own mind, and seldom has a purer mind been tabernacled in flesh." In 1836 Emerson thought F one of his "wise devout men" who knew "the cyclus of Orphic words," a spirit vibrating in the same mode as such stalwarts as King David, St. Paul, Thomas à Kempis, Henry Scougal, George Herbert, Jeremy Taylor, Marcus Aurelius, Robert Leighton, and Confucius.

Alcott, more a mystic and more like F than Emerson, had perhaps a deeper appreciation of F. Like Emerson, however, Alcott thought of F in terms of Orpheus, the Thracian bard who had received the lyre from Apollo. Given instruction by the Muses, he charmed not only wild beasts but also rocks and trees; and he became a famous seer and prophet. Alcott considered his own utterances no less inspired than the Bible or other "sacred scriptures"; hence, he labeled his own diary *Scriptures* and his own utterances "Orphic Sayings." Alcott became the preeminent Transcendentalist saint; but like F he was later ridiculed and disparaged as one who was senseless and could be dismissed. It is gratifying, therefore, to note that Thomas Merton has observed how astonishing it is that "one so brilliant" as F "should remain so obscure."

REFERENCES: English translations of separate works by F, in order of original French publication, include *Dialogues on Eloquence,* trans. Wilbur Samuel Howell (1951); *F on Education,* trans. H. C. Barnard (1966); *Dialogues of the Dead* (1797); *Adventures of Telemachus,* trans. Dr. Hawkesworth (1859); and *F: Letters of Love and Counsel,* with "Reflections on the Character and Genius of F," by Thomas Merton, ed. John McEwen (1964). Biographical studies of F and Madame Guyon are Ella Katharine Sanders, *F: His Friends and His Enemies, 1651–1715* (1901); Katherine Day Little, *F de F: A Study of Personality* (1951); T. C. Upham, *Life and Religious Opinions and Experience of Madame de la Mothe Guyon,* 2 vols. (1955); and Michael De La Bedoyere, *The Archbishop and the Lady* (1956). General studies of F's writings are James Lewis May, *F, a*

Study (1938), and James Herbert Davis, Jr., *F* (1979). Special studies touching on Transcendentalists are Cameron, "Homiletical Background of Emerson's Poem 'Gnothi Seauton' (1831)," in *Young Emerson's Transcendental Vision* (1971), 386–405; Cameron, "The Genesis and Meaning of Emerson's 'Gnothi Seauton'," *ARLR* 3 (1989): 85–120; Frederic I. Carpenter, "Bronson Alcott: Genteel Transcendentalist—An Essay in Definition," *NEQ* 13 (1940): 34–48; and Cameron, *Transcendental Curriculum; or, Bronson Alcott's Library* (1984).

Richard P. Benton

FICHTE, JOHANN GOTTLIEB (1762–1814), was a German philosopher who studied theology and philosophy at Jena. He made a living as a tutor in Saxony, Zürich, Warsaw, and Königsberg, where he became a disciple of I. Kant.* F's first publication, *Versuch einer Kritik aller Offenbarung* (1792), earned the praise of Kant, and in 1794, F took a position as a professor at Jena. He presented his modification of Kant's system in the *Wissenschaftslehre* (1795) with his view of the science of knowledge in which the *ich,* or the ego, substitutes for the Kantian notion of the "thing-in-itself," and the *nicht-ich,* the non-ego, for the objective world. Generally perceived as one of the bases of modern existentialism, F's philosophy was further elaborated in his later publications: *Grundlage des Naturrechts* (1796), *Grundzüge des gegenwärtigen Zeitalters* (1806), and *Anweisung zum seligen Leben und Religionslehre* (1806). Along with Schelling** and Hegel,** F was one of a group of new philosophers in Germany whose works were discussed by the Transcendentalist circle. R. W. Emerson,** whose early definition of nature* is clearly based on F's philosophy, knew F's work mainly through his reading of the commentaries of Coleridge** and especially Carlyle,** who provided a long analysis of F's dichotomy between nature and soul in "Novalis."*

In the 1830s, M. Fuller** and J. F. Clarke** exchanged a series of letters about their reading in German literature and philosophy, including F. Struggling to understand post-Kantian philosophy as a necessary background to the "Life of Goethe"** that she was planning to write, Fuller told Clarke that she wanted a philosophic system "which shall suffice to my character, and in whose applications I shall have faith. I do not wish to *reflect* always, if reflecting must be always about one's identity, whether '*ich*' am the true '*ich*' &c. I wish to arrive at that point where I can trust myself, and leave off saying, 'It seems to me,' and boldly feel, It *is* so to me." On 9 July 1846, Fuller reviewed William Smith's *Memoir of JGF* for the *New-York Daily Tribune.*

REFERENCES: For the relation of F's thought to Emerson's work, see Kenneth Marc Harris, "Emerson's Second Nature," in Joel Porte, ed., *Emerson: Prospect and Retrospect* (1982), 33–48. For general treatments of German sources of Transcendentalism, see Stanley M. Vogel, *German Literary Influences on the American Transcendentalists* (1955), and Pochmann (1957).

Susan Belasco Smith

FOREIGN REVIEW, based in London and also known as the *Foreign Review and Continental Miscellany,* was significant to the Transcendentalist movement for its anonymous publication of T. Carlyle's** essays on Novalis* in 1829, on Goethe** and Goethe's *Helena* in 1828, and on Voltaire in 1830. Additional Carlyle essays dealing with German playwrights and J. P. F. Richter* appeared in *FoR* as well. R. W. Emerson** was a reader of *FoR;* his journals* comment on his making payment for an installment of the journal to G. P. Bradford** in December 1834. Emerson also enumerates Carlyle's works published in *FoR* in several places in his journals.

The scope of the publication consisted of five volumes, the first appearing in 1828, the last in 1830. The first volume of the serial appeared six months after the inauguration of the *Foreign Quarterly Review and Continental Literary Miscellany.* An extended feud existed between the editors of the two journals apparently based on the similarity of the titles and the less-than-ethical practices of the *FoR* editors. The editors of the *FoR* were not satisfied to closely copy the name of the *Foreign Quarterly Review* but also introduced themselves as the former editors of that periodical when trying to sell their magazine on the Continent. The second number of the *FoR* contains in the front matter a disclaimer directed to the *Foreign Quarterly Review* editors, claiming that their readers do not expect them to carry on an "idle controversy"; accordingly, they defer to the editors of the *Foreign Quarterly Review* as "masters of the field, so far as silly invective, couched in the language of vulgar impertinence, can confer that honour upon them" (vol. 1, no. 2). The *FoR* editors then attempt to take the moral high ground, refusing to engage in any further rejoinders on the subject.

Carlyle relied heavily on little magazines like *FoR* for serial publication of his otherwise unpublished work; he returned to this venue after the 1831 rejection of *Sartor Resartus* in London, all the while bemoaning what J. Don Vann called the "triumph of journalism over literature." Appearing in volume 4, number 7 of *FoR* in 1829, Carlyle's essay on Novalis presents the idiosyncrasies of the new metaphysics that were "regenerating the German mind" (54) and praises Novalis for creating a complete philosophy of reason.

FoR published essays on a variety of topics, ranging from descriptions of wars, literary histories, and religion to book reviews and discussions of economic issues on the Continent. The magazine included three continuing columns: "Short Review of Books"; "Continental Literary Intelligence," consisting largely of publication announcements, travel reports, and similar topics, all reported in a gossip-column style; and "List of Foreign Books Just Published," which gave publication data for what the editors considered the most important books published in the prior three to six months in most major fields of study.

REFERENCES: See *JMN,* vols. 4, 5, 6, 8, 14; Frothingham** (1876), 52, 55; *A Guide to the Early British Periodicals Collection on Microfilm,* ed. Jean Hoornstra and Grace Purvas (1980); *Union List of Victorian Serials: A Union List of Selected Nineteenth-Century British Serials Available in United States and Canadian Libraries,* ed. Richard D. Fulton and C. M. Colee (1985); *The Waterloo Directory of Victorian Periodicals:*

1824–1900, ed. Michael Wolff, John S. North, and Dorothy Deering (1981); *The Welles-ley Index to Victorian Periodicals, 1824–1900,* ed. Walter E. Houghton (1966); and *Victorian Periodicals: A Guide to Research,* ed. J. Don Vann and Rosemary T. Van-Arsdel (1978).

Suzanne D. Green

FRASER'S MAGAZINE was founded in London by William Maginn in February 1830. Taking the cue from the founder, editor John William Parker envisioned a periodical of "progressive thought" that bordered on "open revolt." Enjoying a run from 1830 to 1882, *FrM* existed largely as a vehicle to express views on politics, religion, and social conditions. *FrM*'s overt attempt at social revolution, reform, and free thought had special appeal for the Transcendentalists, and its most fruitful period coincided with the finest hour for the Transcendentalists. R. W. Emerson** lists numerous articles in his journals.*

To carry out its editorial philosophy, *FrM* contained several unconventional entries: J. A. Heraud's "On Human Perfectibility" (March 1830); J. A. Carlyle's "Animal Magnetism" (July 1830); D. M. Moir's "Occult Science" (July 1840); and "Woman and the Social System in Socialism and Free Love*" (June 1840). These articles demonstrate perhaps best the gutsiness of Parker's open revolt. Although not a literary magazine per se, *FrM* presented offerings by W. M. Thackeray, James Hogg, Mrs. Hemans, and Charles Dickens. With a combination of radical articles and literature, *FrM* enjoyed a degree of success. Its editors fashioned *FrM* after the vastly popular *Blackwood's.* Although it did not achieve the renown of its model, it did offer much to the public. And like other Victorian periodicals, it exerted influence on American life and letters.

REFERENCES: Critics generally view the 1830s as *FrM*'s heyday. See Miriam M. H. Thrall, *Rebellious Fraser's: Nol Yorke's Magazine in the Days of Maginn, Thackeray, and Carlyle* (1934). *The Wellesley Index* is key to the study of *FrM.*

E. Kate Stewart

FREE LOVE began as a term of opprobrium and was appropriated by reformers who sought to solve society's problems by abolishing or redefining the institution of marriage. Free lovers argued that lifelong marriage conflicted with the transience of human affections and that the state should not regulate those affections. Though few Transcendentalists were actively involved in the free love movement, many were interested in it. Moreover, because Fourierism** influenced the free love movement and was identified with it, members of the Brook Farm* community were often accused of being free lovers.

Strictly construed, free lovers advocated the abolition of marriage and all institutions restricting sexuality. But many social and religious movements advocated marriage reform, some associating marriage with unjust property relations. In 1826, R. Owen** declared that marriage "founded on individual property" was a "monstrous evil" and that natural marriages could only be contracted under conditions of material and educational equality (*Selected*

Works, 2:51, 53). Such marriages, he argued, would be "more permanent than they have ever yet been"; meanwhile, since affections could not be controlled, it should be possible to terminate a marriage if affections subsided (2:53). His son, Robert Dale Owen, worked with reformer Frances Wright and campaigned legislatively for married women's property rights. Wright and the Owens were falsely labeled free lovers by conservative critics, but their ideas laid the foundation for the free love movement.

This movement matured in the early 1850s, boosted by reformers influenced by Fourier's view of "passional attraction" and his rejection of the individual household. H. James, Sr.,** published his translation of Victor Hennequin's *Love in the Phalanstery* in 1849, and in 1852, Marx Edgeworth Lazarus published *Love vs. Marriage,* the first American free love tract. Free lovers also drew inspiration from spiritualism,* mesmerism,* harmonialism, and Swedenborg's* ideas of spiritual union.

Several free love leagues flourished in this period, but many free lovers had fluid affiliations. Thomas and Mary S. Gove Nichols, for example, advocated various forms of free love and associated with several communities. Like many free lovers, they advocated free love but never unbridled sex. Before renouncing free love for Catholicism, they promoted "Progression in Harmony," allowing multiple sexual partners and rejecting external constraints but permitting intercourse only for procreation.

Utopian communities also shaped free love theory and practice. At Modern Times, J. Warren** advocated a cost principle and individual sovereignty. Though Warren condemned free love, his system of finite relationships privately agreed upon by individual couples was, as John Spurlock has said, "free love in everything but name." Those who founded Berlin Heights also believed in individual sovereignty, emphasizing free love and attraction.

The community at Oneida, founded by John Humphrey Noyes, practiced a different kind of marriage reform, which Noyes initially called "free love" but later renamed "Bible communism" or "complex marriage." All members of the community were married to each other; exclusive relationships and all particular attachments were discouraged. Moreover, Noyes advocated "male continence" as a contraceptive and as a social force, justifying it in accordance with the phrenological* separation of "amative" and "propagative" functions of intercourse.

The first generation of the free love movement, and popular interest in it, began to wane as the Civil War approached, though individuals and communities continued to practice and preach free love. By 1879, the Oneida community had abandoned complex marriage, and several prominent free lovers had become quietly respectable. A new generation of marriage reformers, including Victoria Woodhull, Ezra Heywood, Moses Hull, and Moses Harman, was emerging. Postwar free lovers were more marginal than their predecessors and were more vigorously and effectively opposed by conservative institutions. Nevertheless, free love ideas resurfaced continually through the 20th century.

Many Transcendentalists considered marriage reform and had contact with prominent free lovers, though few were active in the free love movement. Lazarus had friends at Brook Farm, and Mary Gove Nichols visited Brook Farm after she had upset the community at Fruitlands* by having an affair with Henry Gardiner Wright, who had come to America with C. Lane.** After Wright's defection, concerns about marriage and family structure continued to divide Fruitlands. Though Lane and B. Alcott** envisioned an ascetic rather than a sensual paradise, their disagreement about the role of the marital family contributed to the community's failure.

Brook Farmers' Associationist ideas aroused suspicions that they were free lovers as well, especially after the community's embrace of Fourierism. In 1846, when J. S. Dwight** translated portions of Fourier's *The New Industrial World* in *The Harbinger,** he added a detailed defensive note on the phrase "liberty in love," emphasizing that Fourier advocated neither "unbridled freedom" nor "rash abolition of marriage" (3:137). Moreover, he emphasized, Fourier deferred experiments about the nature of marriage until other aspects of society had already been reformed (3:137). And Dwight distanced the Brook Farmers even from this position, asserting that they had "for the most part evinced little curiosity about [Fourier's] speculations upon love and marriage," and that Swedenborg's ideal of love as "the meeting of two souls inwardly and from forever destined to be the complement of each other's being" was "quite as commonly the cherished and congenial view among believers in the social unity of man, as [was] the view of Fourier" (3:138). Though Swedenborg's ideas on love and marriage were themselves radical, Dwight's assertions about the relative conservatism of Brook Farm are validated by Lane's disappointed report that Brook Farm was neither a "community" nor an "association" but "merely an aggregation of persons" and thus could not "bring to issue the great question of whether the existence of the marital family is compatible with that of the universal family, which the term 'Community' signifies" ("Brook Farm," *The Dial** 4 [January 1844]: 354, 355). In fact, he found "the moral atmosphere so far pure" (352).

R. W. Emerson,** who accepted Lane's "Brook Farm" piece for *The Dial,* ruminated extensively about marriage in his journals,* even describing a dream in which "a congregation assembled . . . to debate the Institution of Marriage" and in which those objecting to the institution were doused by a spouting hose, leaving Emerson to awaken "relieved to find [himself] quite dry, and well convinced that the Institution of Marriage was safe for tonight." Emerson found Fourier's ideas about women "ridiculous" but faulted Swedenborg for believing that true marriages can exist in heaven. Instead, he insisted, in "Swedenborg," "of progressive souls, all loves and friendships are momentary" and declared in his journals that "marriage should be a temporary relation. . . . When each of two souls had exhausted the other of that good which each held for the other, they should part in the same peace in which they met, not parting from each other, but drawn to new society." Nevertheless, because the "natural eye" of mankind "is not fixed into coincidence with their spiritual eye," he regretfully conceded that "it will not do to abrogate the laws which make Marriage a relation for life, fit or unfit"; indeed, he explained, "now we could not trust even saints & sages with a boundless liberty."

M. Fuller's** pronouncements on love and marriage were less radical. In *Woman in the Nineteenth Century,* she advocated not the abolition of marriage but a reformed and egalitarian marital relationship. And in an October 1841 letter to Emerson, Fuller expressed her commitment to lifelong marriage and to "the chivalric idea of love through disease, dungeons and death, mutilation on the battle field, and the odious changes effected by the enchanter's hate."

H. D. Thoreau** published a poem entitled "Free Love" in the October 1842 issue of *The Dial* (3). Though the poem idealized love as "the favoring gale / That bears me on" and not "the fowler's net / Which stays my flight," Thoreau's interest in free love seems to have remained largely theoretical and abstract. W. Whitman's** poetry also seemed to embrace the ideals of the free love movement, but his journalistic writings were more conservative. In the *Brooklyn Daily Times* of 2 September 1857, Whitman deplored the prevalence of "conjugal infidelity" and blamed the "influence of a loose popular literature" for "debauching the public mind." He asserted, moreover, "The sacredness, the divine institution of the marriage tie lies at the root of the welfare, the safety, the very existence of every Christian nation." However, in 1859, he cautiously conceded that unmarried women might understandably choose to have "one taste of substantial joys and sorrows that shall wake all the pulses of womanhood; even though the experience be brief and dearly bought." He also revealed his interest in free love by reading, marking, and keeping an issue of *The Social Revolutionist* that was especially rich in essays on free love.

REFERENCES: Recent books considering the free love movement and providing useful bibliographic material include Spurlock, *Free Love: Marriage and Middle-Class Radicalism in America, 1825–1860* (1988); Taylor Stoehr, *Free Love in America: A Documentary History* (1979); Louis J. Kern, *An Ordered Love: Sex Roles and Sexuality in Victorian Utopias—the Shakers, the Mormons, and the Oneida Community* (1981); Martin Henry Blatt, *Free Love and Anarchism: The Biography of Ezra Heywood* (1989); and Hal D. Sears, *The Sex Radicals: Free Love in High Victorian America* (1977). For Whitman's remarks, see *I Sit and Look Out: Editorials from the Brooklyn Daily Times,* ed. Emory Holloway and Vernolian Schwarz (1932), 113, 122; and Kenneth M. Price, "Walt Whitman, Free Love, and *The Social Revolutionist,*" *American Periodicals* 1, no. 1 (fall 1991): 73.

Important mid-19th-century texts on sex and marriage include John Humphrey Noyes, *The Bible Argument* (1848); Marx Edgeworth Lazarus, *Love vs. Marriage* (1852); Andrew Jackson Davis, *The Great Harmonia,* vol. 4 (1855); S. P. Andrews,** *Love, Marriage, and Divorce, and the Sovereignty of the Individual* (1853); Thomas L. Nichols, *Esoteric Anthropology* (1853); Thomas and Mary Nichols, *Marriage* (1854); George Drysdale, *The Elements of Social Science* (1854); Austin Kent, *Free Love or, A Philosophical Demonstration of the Non-Exclusive Nature of Connubial Love* (1857); Henry C. Wright, *Marriage and Parentage* (1855); James Clay, *A Voice from Prison* (1856);

and John B. Ellis, *Free Love and Its Votaries; Or, American Socialism Unmasked* (1870). Nineteenth-century journals publishing articles on marriage reform and free love include *The Christian Socialist, Una, Vanguard,* the *Nichols Journal,* the *Social Revolutionist,* the *Age of Freedom,* and *Good Time Coming.*

Lisa M. Gordis

The **FREE RELIGIOUS ASSOCIATION** (FRA) was formed in 1867 by a group of disaffected Unitarians* in reaction to Henry W. Bellows's organization of the National Conference of Unitarian Churches in 1865. The FRA was an important movement of protest within Unitarianism and represents a second phase in the evolution of the Transcendentalist movement, led by a younger generation of ministers who extended the tradition of R. W. Emerson** and T. Parker.** Important figures in the Free Religion movement include Francis Ellingwood Abbot (1836–1903), C. Bartol,** John White Chadwick (1840–1904), O. B. Frothingham,** William Channing Gannett (1840–1923), William J. Potter (1829–1893), and J. Weiss.**

The Free Religion movement shared with the Transcendentalist movement an originating desire to broaden the doctrinal perspective of the Unitarian denomination and to reinvigorate its theology. In his address at the organizational meeting of the FRA in 1867, Emerson noted "the feeling that the churches are outgrown; that the creeds are outgrown; that a technical theology no longer suits us."

But while the first generation of Transcendentalists may have set the original tone of the group, a new theological atmosphere began to emerge among some of the younger FRA members, who were influenced by developments in scientific thinking and dedicated to the establishment of a theology on more empirical grounds. Abbot, who became the leading voice in the FRA through his editorship of the *Index,* argued in 1871 that there were two forms of theology within the Free Religion movement, which could be distinguished on epistemological grounds. One of the movement's theological positions grounded religious knowledge in intuition, a position that began earlier in the century with Emerson and his followers' rebellion against Lockean* epistemology. A newer position that had arisen within the FRA grounded religious knowledge in science. An advocate of the "scientific" view, Abbot found the paradigm of modern science essential to a meaningful reformulation of modern theology and expressed confidence that science would ultimately be found to enlarge and confirm the most important religious ideas. Yet Emerson's belief that intuitive knowledge was the ultimate grounding of religion remained influential also. This Emersonian position was articulated most importantly in the work of Frothingham and Bartol, who, like Emerson, found in human nature and human perception the key to religious certitude.

The FRA members were emphatic advocates of theological individualism and accordingly somewhat suspicious of the growth of religious institutions, although many of them were excellent ministers and churchmen. They objected to Bellows's organization of the National Conference because they feared the possibility of a creed and doctrinal conformity from such a structure. The FRA exerted its influence primarily through their preaching, their writings in periodicals such as *The Radical** and the *Index,* and through books such as Bartol's *Radical Problems* (1872), Frothingham's *The Religion of Humanity* (1873), Chadwick's *The Faith of Reason* (1879), and Abbot's *Scientific Theism* (1885). The antisupernatural, evolutionary theology that characterized these works came to represent the best in Unitarian theology and formed the basis of modern liberal theology in America. The positions of the FRA, of many Western Unitarian ministers who held similarly radical theological views, and of more moderate Unitarians were reconciled at an 1894 meeting of the National Conference, which affirmed Unitarian noncreedalism and stressed the ethical applications of religious principles.

REFERENCES: The standard history of the FRA is Stow Persons, *Free Religion: An American Faith* (1947). For the impact of the Free Religion movement on American Unitarianism, see Conrad Wright, " 'Salute the Arriving Moment': Denominational Growth and the Quest for Consensus, 1865–1895," in *A Stream of Light: A Sesquicentennial History of American Unitarianism* (1975), 62–94; and Robinson (1985), 107–17. Valuable information on the developing views within the Free Religion movement can be found in two periodicals, *The Radical* (Boston, 1865–72) and the *Index* (Toledo, Ohio, 1870–80; and Boston, 1881–86). For Emerson's address to the FRA, see *W,* 11:475–81. An important account of Abbot's role in the movement is Sydney E. Ahlstrom, "Francis Ellingwood Abbot and the Free Religious Association," *PUHS* 17, pt. 2 (1973–75): 1–21. Abbot's work and career are treated at full length in W. Creighton Peden, *The Philosopher of Free Religion: Francis Ellingwood Abbot, 1836–1903* (1992).

David M. Robinson

FRUITLANDS, a communitarian experiment at Harvard, Massachusetts, that lasted from June 1843 to January 1844, was operated by A. B. Alcott** and C. Lane.** Next to Brook Farm* this was the second most significant such venture undertaken by the Transcendentalists. The idea for launching a utopian community began when Alcott visited England in 1842 and met a number of English reformers, including Lane, Henry G. Wright, and others who conducted the Alcott House, which founder J. P. Greaves** modeled directly on Alcott's Temple School* in Boston.

In the fall of 1842 Alcott, Lane, his son, and Wright returned to America to search for an appropriate site, the Lanes and Wright living with the Alcotts in Concord.* At Lane's urging, they agreed that their community would be a consociate family, a union of like-minded people living harmoniously under the same roof. During this eight-month planning period, however, in what proved to be a foreshadowing of events to come, serious problems occurred among the principals. Wright complained of Alcott's despotic manner in enforcing a strict vegetarian diet and regimen, which included early morning cold water baths even in the winter; and Mrs. Alcott and Lane had sharp personality differences, the former regarding Lane as self-centered and overbearing, the latter seeing her as only partially committed to the enterprise. Despite Wright's quitting the Alcott household and the tensions between Lane and Mrs. Alcott, plans for what Lane called their "love colony" went forward.

In the spring of 1843, having paid his ever-improvident partner's debts, Lane purchased the 90-acre Wyman farm at Harvard for $1,800, receiving the house and barn rent free for a year. Alcott's brother-in-law S. J. May** cosigned a mortgage note for $300 of the purchase price, a transaction that later played a role in the dissolution of the community. On 1 June, the Alcotts and their four daughters, the Lanes, and a few others moved to the farm.

From the outset the New Eden had problems, not the least of which was that neither Alcott nor Lane was good at farming. The soil was poor, the crops were not planted early enough for a sufficient harvest, and the use of animals to work the land was incompatible with their philosophy. In addition, as short-term resident I. Hecker** noted with irony, Fruitlands did not even have any fruit trees, which were to provide the basis of their diet. What little money was available was spent on linen tunics and bloomers—leather, wool, and cotton being unacceptable because they necessitated the exploitation of animals and slaves. The most practical person associated with Fruitlands, J. Palmer,** was more a visitor than a resident. He supplied Lane and Alcott with useful advice and volunteered his own labor as well as the use of his plow animals when it became clear that "spade work" could not sustain agriculture.*

Recruiting efforts failed; probably at no time did the community ever have more than a dozen or so people living there. People came and went with little advance notice, prompting Mrs. Alcott to complain that she felt as if she were running a hotel with ungrateful guests. Included among the odd assortment of drifters, social misfits, eccentrics, and seekers who participated in Fruitlands were Samuel Bower, a nudist; Wood Abram, whose individualist personality was expressed by the reversal of his name from Abram Wood; and Samuel Larned, recently from Brook Farm, where he is said to have lived one year on crackers, the next on apples.

Years later L. M. Alcott** recalled Fruitlands in a gentle satire entitled "Transcendental Wild Oats" (*Independent* 25 [18 December 1873]: 1569–71). Ten at the time, she saw her father somewhat unrealistically as playing meek Abel Lamb to the mean Timon Lion of Lane. Other records, however, suggest that Alcott himself may have been responsible for driving away many of the residents or would-be residents. Bower and Hecker, for instance, both singled out Alcott rather than Lane as causing their departure; Alcott, they felt, was standoffish and simply too inflexible in his demands for perfectionism.

Added to all these difficulties was the growing conflict between Mrs. Alcott and Lane, which reached a crisis in early fall when it appeared that Lane was about to make Bronson a convert to celibacy. Having become ill on the strict vegetarian diet of fruit, potatoes, bread, water, and nuts and worried that her husband would leave with Lane to join a nearby Shaker* group, Mrs. Alcott threatened to take the children and leave and told her brother not to make the next mortgage payment. Lane realized that the experiment could not continue and at the end of the year departed and took up residence with the Shakers. Physically and mentally exhausted, if not in fact suicidal, Alcott abandoned Fruitlands in mid-January 1844 and after a few months of recuperation returned with his family to Concord.

No single reason satisfactorily explains why this ultraistic attempt at plain living and high thinking failed and failed so quickly. It was fraught with debilitating contradictions from the start. Both Lane and Alcott hated property holding yet had to buy property to start the community. Both opposed exploiting animals but found fieldwork impossible to perform without oxen and horses. Both deserted the farm at harvest time to go on lecturing and (unsuccessful) recruiting missions. More problematical was the question of individual freedom. They despised forms, creeds, and customs, yet daily life at Fruitlands was distinguished by regimen, conformity, and a rigid asceticism that few found liberating or spiritually uplifting. And as Mrs. Alcott and Ann Page, the only other adult female to live there, painfully discovered, there was nothing radically different about the role assigned to women: Domestic drudgery was the order of the day. Finally, Lane's vision of a consociate family (completely dedicated to celibacy) was not ultimately capable of being realized by the Alcotts because of their deep commitment to the sacredness of the conjugal family.

REFERENCES: Nineteenth-century references include Alcott and Lane, "Fruitlands," *The Dial** 4 (July 1843): 135–36, and E. D. Cheney,** *Louisa May Alcott: Her Life, Letters, and Journals* (1889), which prints part of Louisa's Fruitlands journal.* Her journal notes are also available in *The Journals of Louisa May Alcott,* ed. Joel Myerson, Daniel Shealy, and Madeleine B. Stern (1989). Bronson's journals for the Fruitlands period were lost, but those of Mrs. Alcott have survived: The manuscripts are at Harvard; part of them are printed in *The Journals of Bronson Alcott,* ed. Odell Shepard (1938). Bronson's letters for the period are in *The Letters of Bronson Alcott,* ed. Richard L. Herrnstadt (1969). Valuable are Annie M. L. Clark, *The Alcotts in Harvard* (1902), F. B. Sanborn,** *Bronson Alcott at Alcott House, England, and Fruitlands, New England (1842–1844)* (1908), and Clara Endicott Sears, *Bronson Alcott's Fruitlands* (1915). Modern references include Odell Shepard, *Pedlar's Progress: The Life of Bronson Alcott* (1938); David Palmer Edgell, "The New Eden: A Study of Bronson Alcott's Fruitlands" (M.A. thesis, Wesleyan Univ., 1939); Roger William Cummins, "The Second Eden: Charles Lane and American Transcendentalism" (Diss., Univ. of Minnesota, 1967); Robert Howard Walker, "Charles Lane and the Fruitlands Utopia" (Diss., Univ. of Texas, 1967); Richard Francis, "Circumstances and Salvation: The Ideology of the Fruitlands Utopia," *AQ* 25 (May 1973): 202–34; Joel Myerson, "William Harry Harland's 'Bronson Alcott's English Friends,' " *RALS* 8 (spring 1978): 24–60; Madelon Bedell, *The Alcotts: Biography of a Family* (1980); and Dahlstrand (1982). Harvard Common Press published Louisa May's *Transcendental Wild Oats* (1975), intro. William Henry Harrison, director of Fruitlands Museums.

The original buildings at Fruitlands have been restored and are open to the public. In 1993, Fruitlands Museums sponsored a sesquicentennial conference on the utopian community.

Larry A. Carlson

G

GILPIN, WILLIAM (1724–1804), educator and founder of the English picturesque school, was a favorite author of H. Thoreau,** who refers to G frequently in his journals.* G is best known for *Remarks on Forest Scenery and Other Woodland Views (relating chiefly to picturesque beauty), illustrated in the scenes of the New Forest* (1790), which Thoreau called "pleasing." G based his theory of the picturesque on the premise that "all objects are best as nature* made them. Art cannot mend them." The theory found its way to New England by the late 18th century. By the 19th century, authors such as R. W. Emerson,** N. Hawthorne,** and E. A. Poe** were acknowledging aspects of the picturesque in their writings. In the essay "Nature," for example, Emerson declares, "[O]ur hunting of the picturesque is inseparable from our protest against false society."

Two years before publication of *Walden*, Thoreau quarrels with G in his journal for 6 August 1852 after reading "Lakes of Cumberland": "I wish he would look at scenery sometimes not with the eye of an artist. . . . [H]e never ascends to the top of a mountain, and if he gets up higher than usual, he merely says that the view is grand and amusing, as if because it was not easy to paint, or *picturesque*, it was not . . . deserving of serious attention." More positively, G's continuing influence appears in an 1854 letter to D. Ricketson:** " '[T]his is my thunder' lately—WG's long series of books on the Picturesque with their illustrations." In 1855 Thoreau inquired for G's works at several Boston bookstores, discovering that Little, Brown & Company had ordered an incomplete set of G's writings five years earlier but the set had already been sold.

REFERENCES: William D. Templeman treats G's influence in "Thoreau, Moralist of the Picturesque," *PMLA* 47 (September 1932): 864–89. On G's role in developing and popularizing the concept of "picturesque beauty," see Templeman, "Theory of the Picturesque," in *The Life and Work of WG (1724–1804), Master of the Picturesque and Vicar of Boldre,* in *Illinois Studies in Language and Literature* (1939). See also Carl Paul

Barbier's biography, *WG. His Drawings, Teaching, and Theory of the Picturesque* (1963).

Heidi M. Schultz

GRAHAMISM, GRAHAMITE was the umbrella term given the 19th-century health and diet reform movement and those who put its teachings into practice. Named for S. Graham,** a popular lecturer, the movement was too nebulous and eclectic to be confined to his set of credos. It was most powerful in the 1830s and 1840s, often leagued with progressive concerns such as abolition,* temperance,* and woman's rights.* Its effects lingered throughout the century in hydrotherapies, prominent spas, interest in what we have learned to call "whole foods," and the Kellogg cereal empire.

In Jacksonian* America, the term *Grahamite,* usually intended as a half-mocking slur, indicated a person who ate only vegetable foods, often at a "Graham boardinghouse." Connotations extended to the Grahamite's sexual practices, use of tobacco and alcohol, and thoughts on personal hygiene.

REFERENCE: See "Sylvester Graham" in *Biographical Dictionary of Transcendentalism* (1996).

Barbara Ryan

H

HAFIZ, MOHAMMED SHAMS OD-DIN (1325/26–1389/90), was a Persian lyric poet whose writings were of great interest to R. W. Emerson.** Born in Shiraz, where he spent nearly all of his life, H gained the patronage of the local princes through his ghazals, lyric poems of six to 15 couplets, which were collected into a work called the *Divan*. The poems, written in simple but musical language and full of colorful images, puns, and proverbial expressions, celebrate nature,* love, wine, Allah, the local rulers, and the joy of living. They are influenced by the mystical tradition of Sufism and have often been interpreted in the Islamic world as religious allegories.

European scholars became interested in the poetry of H as early as the 17th century, but it was not until the *Divan* was translated into German, French, and English in the 19th century that H began to be fully appreciated. Emerson purchased Joseph von Hammer-Purgstall's two-volume German verse translation of the *Divan* (Stuttgart and Tübingen, 1812–13) in April 1846 and for many years thereafter periodically entered his own translations from the German version into his journals* and notebooks, especially the notebook he called Orientalist.* Among the published poems of Emerson that were directly drawn from H are "Epitaph," "Friendship" ("Thou foolish H!"), "From H," "From the Persian of H," "Ghaselle: From the Persian of H," "The Phoenix," and "To Himself." The influence of H is also noticeable in such H-like poems as "Bacchus." H figures prominently in Emerson's essay "Persian Poetry," published in the *Atlantic Monthly** in 1858.

Emerson was attracted by the gnomic character of H's poetry, by his playful wit, freewheeling images, and "facility of allusion." He rejected the idea that H's "erotic and bacchanalian songs" reflected a mere "vulgar debauch" and instead spoke of his "hardihood and self-equality" and his "complete intellectual emancipation," which allowed him to make the freest use of the cultural and religious materials of his conservative age in the interest of "heroic sentiment.'' Moreover, H was the sort of bard that Emerson himself awaited in America: ''The muleteers and camel-drivers, on their way through the desert, sing snatches of his songs, . . . and the cultivated Persians know his poems by heart.''

REFERENCES: English translations of the *Divan* are by H. Wilberforce Clarke in prose (1891) and John Payne in verse (1901). For Emerson's translations of H from the German, see notebook Orientalist in *TN*, 2: 37–141; see also *PN* and *W*, vol. 9 (poetry). Emerson's essay ''Persian Poetry'' is in *W*, 8: 235–65. See also J. D. Yohannan, ''Emerson's Translations of Persian Poetry from German Sources,'' *AL* 14 (January 1943): 407–20, and Arthur Christy, *The Orient in American Transcendentalism* (1932), esp. 137–54.

Ralph H. Orth

THE HARBINGER (1845–49), one of the periodicals of American Transcendentalism, was a weekly newspaper whose chief aim was the dissemination of the utopian-socialist theories of French social scientist C. Fourier.** The first number was published on 14 June 1845 at G. Ripley's** utopian Brook Farm* community (1841–47), which itself had recently converted to a Fourierist Phalanx. There it continued to be published under the direction of Ripley, J. S. Dwight,** and C. A. Dana** until June 1847, when, due to the imminent collapse of the community, the paper was transferred to New York City, where it was edited by P. Godwin** and published by the American Union of Associationists* until its demise in February 1849. (The student of Brook Farm will be quite disappointed by the mere handful of brief references to the community scattered throughout the paper.)

The Harbinger was the immediate successor to A. Brisbane's** *The Phalanx* (1843–45), though W. H. Channing's** *The Present** (1843–44) may also be said to have been its predecessor. It should be noted, too, that 11 of the paper's contributors had earlier written for *The Dial** (1840–44), although the character of that journal was entirely different from that of *The Harbinger.*

Though the pages of *The Harbinger* are filled with detailed explanations and discussions of all manner of matter having to do with Fourier's utopian vision—frequently supplemented by lengthy translations of the master himself, as well as the works of other leading French Associationists—Ripley and his associates from the start recognized the need to offset the often tedious nature of their materials with reviews of books and music, a column of poetry, and even a series of daring translations of two works of fiction by the controversial French writer George Sand. The aim was to produce a paper of notable literary merit while advancing the doctrines of Fourierism and Associationism.

Among the most interesting of the more than 350 literary reviews in *The Harbinger* are those of the ''disciples of the newness in Boston and its vicinity,'' which included, among others, R. W. Emerson,** T. Parker,** C. P. Cranch,** Ellery Channing,** and M. Fuller.** Of particular note is the treatment of Emerson, who, it would not be forgotten, had refused Dwight's request in 1845 for a line or two for the new paper (''I will not promise a line to any which has chosen a patron''), just as a few years earlier, in 1840, he had refused Ripley's request to join Brook Farm (''It seems to me a circuitous & operose way of relieving myself of any irksome circumstances''). But even *The Harbinger* had to acknowledge Emerson's ''infallible originality'' and his ''majesty of thought.'' And while the paper recognized that Emerson was ''a consummate artist'' and ''a true poet,'' it was noted on more than one occasion that his poems were like the man: ''cold and distant; they counsel loneliness, and call that true life.'' This was hardly surprising, of course, for a man whose life had been ''one ever-lasting non-committal.''

The poetry column was unquestionably one of the most difficult to supply. The vast majority of poems published in the paper were reprinted from a wide variety of sources. J. G. Whittier** was persuaded to contribute one original poem, and J. R. Lowell** sent along two. Most of the original poetry, however, came from friends. T. W. Higginson**—perhaps best remembered today as E. Dickinson's** literary ''adviser''—supplied nine poems, while Cranch and G. W. Curtis** contributed six and five poems, respectively.

Much more successful were the reviews of music. This feature of *The Harbinger,* in fact, is arguably the paper's most distinguished one. At a time when there was little serious criticism of music, *The Harbinger* presented more than 100 musical reviews during the four years of its existence. The bulk of these were written by Dwight, though Curtis, W. W. Story,** and Cranch also contributed to the column. Though Dwight later established *Dwight's Journal of Music* (1852–81), it was in *The Harbinger* that he made important contributions to the development of America's emerging cultural life.

Of all the periodicals associated with American Transcendentalism, *The Harbinger* was the most highly regarded by its journalistic competitors. *Hunt's Merchants' Magazine* (New York), for example, thought it ''one of the most ably conducted and most readable weekly journals that comes to our office.'' *Nineteenth Century* magazine (Philadelphia) stated that the paper was ''distinguished by its critical character, its elevated and serious tone, and its deep faith in the future perfection of the race.'' The Chicago *Daily Tribune* remarked that ''there is not a single newspaper in the Union which maintains so high a standard of literary taste.'' And the Cincinnati *Herald* said that ''there is no periodical which we read with more pleasure or profit.''

REFERENCES: The only book-length study of *The Harbinger* is Sterling F. Delano, The Harbinger *and New England Transcendentalism* (1983). A brief but valuable discussion is in Gohdes (1931). Donald F. Warders, ''Transcendentalist Periodicals,'' in Myerson (1984), 69–83, provides useful bibliographical references for *The Harbinger.* Also helpful is Sterling F. Delano and Rita Colanzi, ''An Index to Volume VIII of *The Harbinger,*'' *RALS* 10 (autumn 1980): 173–86.

Sterling F. Delano

HARVARD DIVINITY SCHOOL, the Unitarian* seminary in Cambridge, directly and indirectly promoted the spread of Transcendental idealism.* Although severely criticized at various times by T. Parker,** R. W. Emerson,** and others, the school nevertheless influenced the many Transcendentalist ministers who attended. These included Emerson and Parker as well as J. F. Clarke,** G. Ripley,** other first-generation Transcendentalists, and nearly all of the second-generation Transcendentalists such as S. Johnson** and T. W. Higginson.** From its informal beginnings in 1811, the school helped undermine historical Christianity by introducing students to higher criticism* and serving as a forum for other new ideas. Following the appointment of C. Francis** in 1842, students had a faculty link to the Transcendentalist circle. In the 1850s F. H. Hedge** and Clarke became associated with the school as adjunct professors.

Students themselves also fostered the spread of Transcendentalism. By 1838, when the senior class invited Emerson to deliver his famous Divinity School Address, strong Transcendentalist sympathies at Divinity Hall were evident. Afterwards, the school became a magnet for young men already infected with Transcendental idealism. These students and new converts turned Divinity Hall into an almost continuous Transcendentalist breeding ground. Students also had firsthand access to Transcendentalism through *The Dial,** Emerson's winter lectures, Parker's Sunday services, and many other sources.

REFERENCES: The history of the school is ably recounted in George Huntston Williams, ed., *The Harvard Divinity School: Its Place in Harvard University and American Culture* (1954). See also Gary L. Collison, " 'A True Toleration': Harvard Divinity School Students and Unitarianism, 1830–1859," in *American Unitarianism, 1805–1865,* ed. Conrad Edick Wright (1989), 209–37.

Gary L. Collison

HERDER, JOHANN GOTTFRIED VON (1744–1803), German critic, theologian, philosopher, and a leading figure of the Sturm und Drang literary movement, helped usher in the Romantic era. In a 27 August 1824 letter to R. W. Emerson,** his older brother, William,** wrote from Göttingen, Germany, "[G]et all of H that you can."

H anticipated the spiritual concepts of Darwin's** theory of evolution. Similar to Schleiermacher** and Goethe** in his outlook, he felt that nature* was a history of the earth, whereby species moved to a greater and greater perfection. The highest product, man, became capable of creating his own order of a new and higher nature, a world of culture, freedom, and civilization. God works in and through all creation but is not limited by persona or personality. Man is limited and hence has personality, identity. God is like a root and a fountain in man working through man's inmost nature. God possesses infinite power of action and thought. Man possesses reason, which has its ground in itself and knows itself; Supreme Reason (or God) has in itself the ground of the connection of all things and knows that it has.

According to H's theology, God is Noumenon in all phenomena. Religion is nothing more than reason's practical reception and organization of the Supreme Reason, the awareness of the Noumenon's entering and working through man.

H maintained that biblical stories and miracles,* like Greek mythology, while perhaps untrue or unprovable from a historic standpoint, were poetically true in that they conveyed natural and sensible images of higher thoughts. The moral ideas were the kernel of the narrative; the historical served as an excellent illustration and context. Revelation was always given to man from within, present in his reason and conscience often as the feeling that underlies ideas. Prophets came about because God occasionally uses people for specific purposes. Inspiration is the arousing of the noblest powers of the mind—good cheerful thoughts and acts.

H characterized Christianity as man's awareness that God is the Father, that man is weak, and that his weakness is the object of God's patience and effort. H also, however, emphasized the divine in man and his capacity for strong, pure, and noble acts and the love of man uniting with other men, enabling him to erect God's Kingdom among men. H did not adhere to supernatural interpretations of Christ, believing that Christ himself maintained that God was not his father but the father of all men and that all men were brothers. This concept is the very one expressed by other German philosophers and theologians of the time and one of the major points of Emerson's Divinity School Address.

REFERENCES: Primary sources of H's works in translation include *God: Some Conversations,* trans. Frederick H. Burkhardt (1949), and *Outline of a Philosophy of the History of Man,* trans. T. Churchill (1800). For explanations of H's philosophy, see J. Mace Andress, *JGH as an Educator* (1916), and F. McEachran, *The Life and Philosophy of JGH* (1939).

Karen L. Kalinevitch

HIGHER CRITICISM, also known as historical criticism, was an outgrowth of the European Enlightenment that helped undermine conservative Unitarian* beliefs and stimulated the growth of Transcendentalism. Although this criticism took various forms and had varying emphases, the unifying assumption was that all texts, including sacred Scriptures, reflected the historical circumstances in which they were created. Consequently, before the meaning of any text could be understood, rigorous historical study was required. Archeology, anthropology, sociology, linguistics, and textual scholarship all became essential adjuncts to this study. Applied to the Bible in the late 18th and early 19th centuries by scholars like J. G. Eichhorn,* J. G. Herder,* and D. F. Strauss,** higher criticism aimed to put Christianity on a more scientific basis but had the unintended effect of increasingly undermining traditional religious sources of authority. First generation Unitarians such as J. S. Buckminster,* A. Norton,** and W. E. Channing** enlisted higher criticism to assert that key Calvinist doctrines were unscriptural and that many biblical ideas were merely limited Jewish conceptions rather than eternal truths. Higher criticism became permanently embedded in denominational thinking when Norton and other professors brought it into the Harvard Divinity School* curriculum. However, Norton and other first-generation Unitarians did not agree with the more radical German higher critics and continued to regard the Bible and the figure of Jesus as the uniquely authoritative centers of their faith.

The Transcendentalist-Unitarian ministers most familiar with higher criticism were F. H. Hedge,** C. Francis,** and T. Parker,** but R. W. Emerson,** G. Ripley,** O. Brownson,** J. F. Clarke,** and many lesser figures also took an interest in or were influenced by these developments. Although the direct and indirect effects of higher criticism on the Transcendentalists varied considerably and have been only partially charted by scholars, two main results are clear. First, higher criticism allowed many Transcendentalists to complete the shift of religious authority from the Bible to the individual consciousness and to intuition. Second, by blurring or erasing the boundary between literature and sacred Scripture, higher criticism fed into Romantic notions of inspiration and genius to give an extraordinary spiritual and cultural status both to authorship and to myth. The effects of higher criticism can be seen in works ranging from Parker's rationalistic accounts of the development of religion to the scripture-like productions of Emerson, H. Thoreau,** B. Alcott,** and J. Very.**

REFERENCES: A useful general survey of the development of higher criticism is Hans Frei, *The Eclipse of Biblical Narrative: A Study in Eighteenth and Nineteenth Century Hermeneutics* (1974). Jerry Wayne Brown, *The Rise of Biblical Criticism in America, 1800–1870: The New England Scholars* (1969), devotes separate brief chapters to Parker and a few other Unitarians. The first three chapters of Hutchison (1959) are also helpful. Richardson (1978) separates out the various Transcendentalist responses to higher criticism and myth. See also Richard Grusin, *Transcendentalist Hermeneutics: Institutional Authority and the Higher Criticism of the Bible* (1991); Philip Gura, *The Wisdom of Words: Language, Theology, and Literature in the New England Renaissance* (1981); and Barbara Packer, "Origin and Authority: Emerson and Higher Criticism," in *Reconstructing American Literary History,* ed. Sacvan Bercovitch (1986), 67–92.

Gary L. Collison

HIGHER LAW was a term denoting a supreme moral law, which the Transcendentalists and many others believed nullified any civil statutes that conflicted with it. In *Slavery* (1835), W. E. Channing** thus insisted that no law of government could make the institution any less evil, since there was a "higher law, even Virtue, Rectitude, the Voice of Conscience, the Will of God." The term *higher law* was later popularized by William Seward, a Whig senator from New York. Speaking on the floor of the Senate on 11 March 1850, four days after Webster** had delivered his famous speech in favor of the Compromise of 1850,* Seward argued that the terms of the Compromise, especially the Fugitive Slave Act, involved "the surrender of the exercise of judgment and conscience." Rehearsing the familiar argument that human laws drew their sanction from the law of God, he declared that "there is a higher law than the Constitution." Although the speech was denounced in the South, as well as by many supporters of the Compromise in the North, it received extravagant praise from antislavery forces. The American Anti-Slavery Society distributed 10,000 copies of the address, which was also reprinted by H. Greeley** in his influential New York *Tribune*. Moreover, Seward himself sent out 50,000 copies of what quickly became known as his "Higher Law Speech," which immediately made him the leading antislavery spokesman in Congress.

Whereas Seward appealed to the higher law in an effort to defeat the Compromise, others later invoked the term to justify breaking the Fugitive Slave Law. In his first address on that law, R. W. Emerson** in 1851 described his "dismay at hearing that the Higher Law was reckoned a good joke in the courts," arguing "that it was a principle in law that immoral laws are void." Similarly, in his later address on the same topic, delivered on the fourth anniversary of Webster's Seventh of March Address, Emerson cited a gibe the senator had made about the higher law as a sign of his "wretched atheism." A few months later, H. Thoreau** delivered "Slavery in Massachusetts" at an antislavery meeting during which W. L. Garrison** burned a copy of the Constitution. Thoreau's address was a kind of verbal equivalent of that act, since he called upon the inhabitants of Massachusetts to dissolve their ties to the state until the state dissolved its ties to the Union. "What is wanted is men, not of policy, but of probity—who recognize a higher law than the Constitution," he proclaimed. In an editorial that accompanied the text of Thoreau's address in the 2 August 1854 issue of the *Tribune*, Greeley described it as "a *genuine* Higher Law Speech," adding: "No one can read this speech without realizing that the claims of Messrs. Sumner,** Seward and Chase to be recognized as Higher-Law champions are of very questionable validity. Mr. Thoreau is the Simon-Pure article."

Among the Transcendentalists, however, the most steadfast champion of the higher law was not Thoreau but T. Parker.** Taking up the argument "that the Constitution of the United States is the supreme law of the land, and that sanctions slavery," Parker in his "Sermon on Slavery," preached in 1841, responded: "There is no supreme law but that made by God; if our laws contradict that, the sooner they end or the sooner they are broken, why, the better." During the remaining 18 years of his life, Parker consistently measured the acts and enactments of men against that absolute moral standard. In the "Function of Conscience in Relation to the Laws of Men," for example, he demanded nullification of the Fugitive Slave Law, since the "law of God has eminent domain everywhere." In effect, for Parker, like Emerson, belief in the higher law was equivalent to religious belief. "No man has done so much to debauch the conscience of the nation," Parker observed in his *Discourse* on Webster, published shortly after the senator's death in 1852. "There is no Higher Law, quoth he, and how much of the pulpit, the press, the forum and the bar, denies its God."

During the 1850s, Parker and others increasingly used the higher law to sanction violence. Appealing to both the higher law and the example of the American Revolution—his grandfather had led the Minutemen on Lexington Green—Parker urged forceful resistance to the enforcement of the Fugitive Slave Law. He subsequently rallied support for the Free Soil settlers in Kansas, where his disciple T. W. Higginson** became the first Transcendentalist actually to take up arms against slavery. Parker and Higginson were also members of "The Six," the secret group that raised money for J. Brown,** another man who claimed to be acting in accordance with the higher law. In his final statement to the court, Brown appealed to "the law of God" and insisted that he had done no more than follow the teachings of the Bible. Comparing his actions with the charge of the Light Brigade, Thoreau in "A Plea for Captain John Brown" affirmed that Brown's steady charge "against the legions of Slavery, in obedience to an infinitely higher command, is as much more memorable than that, as an intelligent and conscientious man is superior to a machine." The higher law had thus become a command given, not simply by the supreme maker of law but by the kind of militant God whose coming J. W. Howe** later celebrated in "The Battle Hymn of the Republic." Indeed, the higher law was finally transmuted into what Howe read as "a fiery gospel, writ in burnished rows of steel"—that is, in the rifles of Union soldiers marching in the army of the Lord.

REFERENCES: A useful discussion of the wide range of figures who affirmed the higher law is Ferenc M. Szasz, "Antebellum Appeals to the 'Higher Law,' 1830–1860," *EIHC* 110 (1974): 33–48. One of the fullest expositions of the concept was William Hosmer, *The Higher Law, in Its Relations to Civil Government* (1852). Hosmer's book was dedicated to Seward, whose famous speech is at least briefly discussed in virtually all of the histories of the period, as well as in biographies like Glyndon G. Van Deusen, *William Henry Seward* (1967), 121–28. Among works on the Transcendentalists, one of the most useful discussions of the higher law is the chapter "Slavery and the Higher Law" in Henry Steele Commager, *Theodore Parker: Yankee Crusader* (1936), 197–213. Commager observed that there was "no satisfactory study of Parker's contribution to the Higher Law doctrine in American politics" (326). Unfortunately, that is still the case, though the numerous quotations in Commager's biography suggest just how significant that contribution was.

Linck C. Johnson

HUME, DAVID (1711–1776), Scottish empiricist or skeptic, a touchstone of philosophical thought for the Transcendentalists, was born in Edinburgh. After leaving the university there at 15, he pursued individual study in philosophy, history, and politics. His first philosophical work, *A Treatise of Human Nature* (1739), was not well received. He revised this work under the title *An Enquiry Concerning Human Understanding,* and it, along with *Principles of Morals* and *Political Discourses,* made a great reputation for him on the Continent. Despite these successes, he was turned down for professorships at Edinburgh and Glasgow. He traveled to France as the secretary to the British ambassador in 1763, where he met one of his staunchest supporters, Rousseau.* In 1767 he was appointed under-secretary of state. In 1769 he returned to Edinburgh, where he died of cancer. Besides his philosophical works, he is also known for work in history, most especially his *The History of England* (1754–62).

H's desire was to build a science of human understanding. Standing on the shoulders of Leibniz,* Descartes,* and Spinoza,* he both borrowed from and dismantled Locke* and Berkeley* in his work. His method of analysis allowed him to place all the contents of the mind into two categories: "impressions," which are nonreducible phenomena, and "ideas," which are generated by impressions. His radical skepticism caused him to doubt the persistence of impressions of things outside the mind—and indeed causality itself. Because all proofs for the existence of God can be reduced to arguments from causal analogies, he denied this also. Many of H's early critics considered only this pessimistic stance and therefore regarded H as a threat to civil society. R. W. Emerson** himself suggested, in a letter to Aunt Mary** in 1823, that he was disturbed by the atheistic implications of H's writings, calling him the "Scottish Goliath" and decrying the absence of a "stripling who can cut off his most metaphysical head."

H's ethical stance takes a more optimistic turn. He bases his ethics on sentiment, specifically the feeling of sympathy, or fellow-feeling. He avoids a subjectivist turn here by claiming that sympathy binds humanity together, for it is a "principle in human nature beyond which we cannot hope to find any principle more general."

H's influence on the Transcendentalists underwent a shift as the movement progressed and different thinkers moved to the foreground. Both A. Everett** and I. Ray** spurned his views. Later, O. Brownson** was to turn aside from H's skepticism. (However, Brownson also rejected the writings of Hegel** and Kant,* two important influences on the movement.) H's argument that reason cannot tell us how to live, and his recognition that we must then follow our natural inclinations (among which he includes mathematical and empirical reasoning) in a "common life," bears a striking resemblance to H. Thoreau's** work in *Walden* and Emerson's critiques of the emerging American industrialization. Emerson's thoughts on self-consciousness point to H's epistemological concern that we can never objectify the self because we will always end up with some particular perception of the self. Finally, H's reliance upon a common feeling of sympathy as a basis for all actions may be a minor source for Emerson's thoughts on the community of humanity in the Over-Soul.

REFERENCES: The standard source is *The Philosophical Works,* first printed in London in 1886, rpt. Scientia Verlag (1964). Judiciously chosen selections and acute commentaries on his work can be found in Terence Penelhum, *DH: An Introduction to His Philosophical System* (1991), and Antony Flew, ed., *An Enquiry Concerning Human Understanding* (1988). References to H throughout the Transcendentalist corpus are noted in Miller (1950).

Joe Pellegrino

I

IDEALISM is generally thought to be the philosophical foundation of New England Transcendentalism. Many of the latter's leading figures borrowed routinely from two major sources: Platonism* and Neoplatonism,* and German idealist philosophers such as Kant,* Fichte,* and Jacobi* and their adapters such as the English poet S. T. Coleridge.** The New England Transcendentalists also established their positions in part by opposing the influence of "Lockean"* empiricism and Scottish "Common Sense"* philosophy in Anglo-American thought. They particularly disliked the "empiricist" idea that the mind draws its impressions and thoughts entirely from the world of sense. And they associated empiricism with the excessive power of conventional wisdom, politics, and business to define the meaning of life in America.

Idealism can be regarded as a variable mixture of at least four related doctrines—epistemological, metaphysical, psychological, and political. The first is concerned with the status of knowledge. It often contrasted itself with "materialism" or empiricism in holding that no impressions could be attributed to the senses that were not found first in the mind. Reality resides in the ideas of consciousness, while the physical world is an "appearance." Once the "despotism of the senses" is relaxed, as R. W. Emerson** put it, we can understand that the mind's most important knowledge derives not from empirical experience but from preexisting intellectual structures or the absolute laws of being.

Second, idealism often posited the existence of a realm of ideas, intelligence, laws, forms, or spirit that lay beyond the realm of the senses. The variety of idealisms that influenced U.S. thinkers produced a variety of interpretations. Those interested in Swedenborg,* Plato,* or the Neoplatonist Plotinus* stressed the real existence of other planes of being. Those closer to Kant focused on the nonsensuous preconditions of consciousness. Still others stressed certain principles of being that preexist and control physical life: Emerson, in his midcareer assessment of Plato, downplayed the other world and featured Plato's belief in the Oneness of all things. All agreed that thought or law preceded the natural world.

Third, New England idealism asserted the divinity of the human mind. Idealism offered not only epistemological doubts about the world's reality but also a direct correspondence* between God's order and human reason. Through consciousness the individual becomes "a partaker of the divine nature," as G. Ripley** put it. Individual reason sees the "inward spirit" of things and "gives us an immediate perception of Truth." Idealism was thought to grant unusual intellectual, moral, spiritual, and even practical power to individuals.

Fourth, idealism also drew on the more colloquial meaning of the term, referring to a belief that the world can be made a better place. Transcendentalist idealism often affirmed that individual abilities and social arrangements were crippled by a "materialism" that put business, affluence, and economic efficiency at the center of American culture. Many Transcendentalists were committed social reformers and felt that American life unduly stifled its citizens' innate potential. Emerson expresses the link between idealist views of reason and of material change when he says, "The sensual man conforms thoughts to things; the poet conforms things to his thoughts." Many Transcendentalists went much further than he in supporting reforms in education,* economics, and family life; most supported the abolition* of slavery.

REFERENCES: Fundamental statements of New England idealism include S. Reed,** *Observations on the Growth of the Mind* (1826); B. Alcott,** *Conversations* with Children on the Gospels* (1836); Emerson, *Nature* (1836); E. P. Peabody,** *Record of a School* (1836); Ripley, *Discourses on the Philosophy of Religion* (1836); G. Bancroft,** *On the Progress of Civilization* (1838); T. Parker,** *A Discourse of the Transient and Permanent in Christianity* (1841); and Emerson, "The Transcendentalist" (1841) and "Plato; or, the Philosopher," in *Representative Men* (1850). Many of these and other important pieces are collected in the still-indispensable Miller (1950). Coleridge's most influential works in New England were *Biographia Literaria* and *Aids to Reflection.* An excellent overview of Transcendentalism as idealism is Michael J. Colacurcio, "Idealism and Independence: The Mind of a Renaissance," *Columbia Encyclopedia of American Literature* (1988), 207–26. On political idealism, see Anne C. Rose, *Transcendentalism as a Social Movement, 1830–1850* (1981) and, reading a related current of reform, Carl J. Guarneri, *The Utopian Alternative: Fourierism** in Nineteenth-Century America* (1991).

Christopher Newfield

IMMANENCE derives from the late Latin *immanere,* to dwell or remain in. Generally, this term means the state of being immanent, present, or indwelling. In metaphysics or theology, immanence signifies the ubiquitous presence of essence, being, power, divinity. In Transcendentalism, the concept of immanence is related closely to a pantheism* akin to the Hindu thought that the animate as well as the inanimate are part of the cosmic scheme operated by an overseeing God.

The term *Transcendentalism* is misleading, for *transcendental* could be understood to imply God's transcendence, rather than humanity's transcendence via a deity who is intimately manifested in all of nature* as the Supreme Spirit of the Universe, or Over-Soul. The Transcendentalists believed that through an immanent, intuitive reception of knowledge, humans could transcend the limits of logic and sense. Intertwining Kant's* philosophy with Hindu cosmology, the Transcendentalists staged an epistemological revolt against Locke's* empiricism, materialism, and sensationalism.* This sensationalism had dominated the American philosophical scene for more than a century and was also propagated through Unitarian* philosophy.

The *immanence* in Transcendentalism was part of the idealist reaction to Locke's empiricism, which did not reflect belief in innate and a priori capacities of the human mind. Instead, the Transcendentalists maintained that "man has ideas, that come not through the five senses, or the powers of reasoning; but are either the result of direct revelation from God, his immediate inspiration, or his immanent presence in the spiritual world" (*An Essay on Transcendentalism* [1842], probably written by C. M. Ellis**).

The following quotations are examples of how the concept of immanence manifested itself in the writings and thoughts of Transcendentalists. Note the aspects of universality of being, the nonreliance upon traditional rationality, and the spiritual, as well as physical, intimacy with nature, wherein is God's spirit.

R. W. Emerson** wrote in *Nature:* "In the woods, we return to reason and faith. . . . —all mean egotism vanishes. I become a transparent eye-ball. I am nothing. I see all. The currents of the Universal Being circulate through me; I am part or particle of God. . . . I am the lover of uncontained and immortal beauty." W. H. Furness** wrote in his *Remarks on the Four Gospels:* "God, who was afar off, is brought near and enthroned in Nature." Finally, W. Whitman** wrote in *Song of Myself:*

> Swiftly arose and spread around me the peace and knowledge that pass all the
>   argument of the earth,
> And I know that the hand of God is the promise of my own,
> And I know that the spirit of God is the brother of my own,
> And that all the men ever born are also my brothers, and the women my sisters
>   and lovers,
> And that a kelson of the creation is love,
> And limitless are leaves stiff or drooping in the fields. (5, lines 91–96)

REFERENCES: See Wilbur Long, "Immanence," *Dictionary of Philosophy,* ed. Dagobert D. Runes (1983); and Umesa Patri, *Hindu Scriptures and American Transcendentalists* (1987).

Moumin Manzoor Quazi

J

JACKSONIAN DEMOCRACY, the term used to describe the political ideology of the Democratic Party in the three decades before the Civil War, formed the political context in which the Transcendentalists thought and wrote. Spurred by the election of Andrew Jackson to the presidency in 1828, Democrats built upon their Jeffersonian heritage and fostered an ideology similar in many ways to the views put forth by R. W. Emerson** and H. D. Thoreau.** Both the Jacksonian Democrats and the Transcendentalists advocated individualism, limited government, and the virtues of the common man while denouncing collectivism, privilege, and the materialism of the new commercial capitalism.

Emerson, however, repeatedly denounced the partisanship of the Jacksonians because he deemed party spirit detrimental to America's intellectual development. Particularly in the 1830s Emerson spoke out strongly against the populist politics aroused by the Jacksonians. He believed that vital intellectual and emotional energy was being wasted on the pursuit of politics rather than encouraging the cultural and intellectual growth of the country. Despite such views, a brief comparison of Transcendental and Jacksonian ideologies reveals that the two movements were not so different as Emerson might have claimed.

While historians debate the extent to which the lower and middle classes supported the Jacksonian Democrats, the rhetoric espoused by the party vigorously opposed wealth and privilege. Just as Emerson in "The American Scholar" and "Self-Reliance" criticized society's acquisitiveness, Jacksonians such as the New York writer and politician James Kirke Paulding denounced the greed and materialism of the rich new entrepreneurs. Banks, internal improvements, and tariffs were viewed not only as tools of the wealthy but also as unconstitutional extensions of governmental authority. The individual was left to better himself without the aid of government-sanctioned banks or monopolies. Thus, the Jacksonian Democrats and the Transcendentalists shared the belief that individual liberty flourished only under limited government. Although

Emerson and other leading Transcendentalists rarely aligned themselves publicly with the Democrats, they nonetheless shared an ideological outlook with the Jacksonians that gave meaning both to the social and economic changes of antebellum America and to the future course of the young nation.

REFERENCES: Of the hundreds of books and essays on the politics of Jacksonian America, only a few of the most important are mentioned here. The leading historian who contends that the Jacksonian Democrats represented the interests of and drew support from the lower classes is Arthur Schlesinger, *The Age of Jackson* (1945). In the past 30 years, numerous scholars have challenged Schlesinger's thesis and maintained instead that Jacksonian Democrats failed to represent the common man. For an explanation of this thesis, see esp. Lee Benson, *The Concept of Jacksonian Democracy: New York as a Test Case* (1961), and Edward Pessen, ed., *The Many-faceted Jacksonian Era* (1977). Ronald P. Formisano, "The New Political History," *International Journal of Social Education,* 1 (autumn 1986): 5–21, and "The Invention of the Ethnocultural Interpretation," *AHR* 90 (April 1994): 453–77, analyze the main currents of scholarship on Jacksonian politics over the last three decades.

Jonathan Wells

JACOBI, FRIEDRICH HEINRICH (1743–1819), was a German businessman whose interest in philosophy prompted him to study the works of Helvétius, Rousseau,* Spinoza,* and Kant.* In 1804 he was appointed president of the Academy of Sciences in Munich, where he was in contact with such prominent contemporary thinkers as Mendelssohn and Goethe.** Noted especially for his criticisms of earlier philosophers such as Descartes,* Spinoza, Kant, and Hume,* J coined the term "Nihilismus" (nihilism) when rejecting Kantian idealism* and the followers of Kant, beginning with J. G. Fichte.* Rousseau's *Émile* prompted J to formulate his philosophy of religion: The limits of human understanding of God force us to accept God by faith, assuring us of the existence of a reality outside the mind. He refutes Hume's idea that knowledge is belief, subjective and uncertain, in *David Hume über den Glauben* (David Hume on faith [1787]). J wrote only occasional essays, and his philosophy, according to Crawford, was "only a living power of the soul, and not a system of doctrine." New Englanders encountered J's philosophy primarily through the writings of B. Alcott,** T. Parker,** and M. Fuller.** All three had J's volumes in their libraries, and they studied his writings. Alcott mentions J in *Concord Days* (1872), and Fuller writes of him in *Memoirs of Margaret Fuller Ossoli* (1852): "When I was in Cambridge, I got Fichte and J. . . . Fichte I could not understand at all. . . . J I could understand in details, but not in system. It seemed to me that his mind must have been moulded by some other mind, with which I ought to be acquainted in order to know him well,—perhaps Spinoza."

REFERENCES: See Alexander Crawford, *The Philosophy of F. H. J* (1905); Samuel Atlas's entry in *EP;* Harold C. Goddard, *Studies in New England Transcendentalism* (1908); Wulf Koepke, "FHJ," *DLB,* vol. 94, ed. James Hardin and Christopher Schweitzer (1990); and Norman Wilde, *FHJ: A Study in the Origin of German Realism* (1894).

David J. Sorrells

JOURNALS were the most favored and widely practiced written form among the Transcendentalists, a fact that in part accounts for their relative lack of conventional literary productions. At the same time, journals have been traditionally regarded by scholars and critics as mainly preparatory or supplemental to writing for publication and have themselves remained relatively unstudied as literary artifacts. Among the most widely known men and women associated with the movement, R. W. Emerson,** H. Thoreau,** B. Alcott,** Ellery Channing,** M. Fuller,** E. P. Peabody,** T. Parker,** C. K. Newcomb,** and C. S. Wheeler** all kept journals with greater or lesser degrees of fidelity.

In part this focus on private writing was a trait they shared with the populace at large, especially in New England, with its long tradition of religiously motivated self-examination. Many people in all walks of life kept journals and used them for a variety of purposes ranging from keeping family and farm records to looking for evidence of salvation. The vast bulk of this writing has disappeared, of course, and virtually all that survives is unknown, stored in family papers and library and historical society archives. A thorough understanding of the more literary Transcendentalist journals will require not only that good editions of them be published (at present, only Emerson's and Thoreau's journals are available in modern scholarly editions) but also that they be set in the context of the wide range of other private writing practiced in antebellum America.

Although the Transcendentalists never produced a formal theoretical justification for their preference for journals, Emerson's introduction to selections from Channing's poems in *The Dial** in 1840 makes a case on both political and aesthetic grounds for valuing what he called a literature of the "portfolio" over traditional published forms. First, such private writing was a democratic phenomenon that reflected, along with increasing literacy and availability of printed material, an opportunity to everyone for self-culture: "Only one man in a thousand may print a book, but one in ten or one in five may inscribe his thoughts, or at least with short commentary his favorite readings in a private journal" (*The Dial,* 2: 220).

More important, the apparently artless, spontaneous, and unconstrained nature of private writing made it potentially the best medium for capturing those promptings of genius and "untaught sallies of the spirit" that the Transcendentalists valued above all else. The unpolished journal might provide the most immediate and authentic transcription of moments of inspiration. Conversely, highly finished and elegant literary works were likely to be the products of writers of talent but not genius.

In practice, however, the Transcendentalists were ambivalent about the literary value of their journals. While such titles as "Notes from the Journal of a Scholar" or "Musings of a Recluse" were not uncommon in *The Dial,* there was little effort to find a public venue for the dissemination of the literature of the portfolio. Many of the writers shared portions of their manuscript journals with their friends, so that the form was not uniquely personal but had a socially constituted dimension as well and was governed in part by well-understood if unstated conventions. Yet this limited circulation also meant that the form could have no very wide influence on the literary culture of the time.

The outcome of the only project to publish selections from the journals of some of the major Transcendentalists during their lifetimes illustrates the way in which their literary ideals were thwarted by convention. In 1853 Channing proposed to select and edit portions of his, Emerson's, and Thoreau's journals and publish them under the rubric of "Country Walking." Both Emerson and Thoreau gave Channing access to their manuscript journals (and Emerson advanced him money as well), but although Channing did a great deal of work, no publication followed. Channing finally published a version of this work 20 years later, inserting it to lengthen his 1873 biography, *Thoreau, the Poet-Naturalist.* But the product bears little resemblance to the originals, for Channing felt obliged to recast the material as a series of highly stylized and often stilted literary dialogues in which the speakers often address one another by reciting long poems.

Among these writers, only Thoreau seems to have contemplated the advantages of printing a journal in its original form. Although he had mined his early journal for essays, *A Week,* and early drafts of *Walden,* he gradually abandoned this practice after 1850. In 1852 he observed, "I do not know but thoughts written down thus in a journal might be printed in the same form with greater advantage—than if the related ones were brought together in separate essays. They are now allied to life—& are seen by the reader not to be far fetched—". This reference to "the reader" also reveals that his journal was more consciously composed with an audience in mind than journals ordinarily are, perhaps even with a view toward a posthumous readership. In fact, it could be argued that his journal was the principal imaginative work of Thoreau's career, consciously adopted in preference to writing primarily for publication. Even the nominal "dailiness" of Thoreau's journal is in part a literary device, for he typically composed several days' entries at one time from notes he wrote in the field, while individual entries are written as though they were composed on the day in question. Assessing Thoreau's journal is further complicated by the fact that its nature changed radically over the course of his career, starting out as an extension of the commonplace books he kept in college, evolving into a writer's note and draft book during the 1840s, and eventually becoming a register of scientific observation during the last decade of his life.

Emerson, on the other hand, consistently considered his journals to be a "savings bank," whose contents he drew upon for lectures and essays. His notebooks are carefully indexed and cross-referenced to facilitate this process and contain, in addition to original thoughts and quotations from his reading, much information about his career as a professional man of letters. The most voluminous and as yet mostly unpublished journal among the Transcendentalists belongs to Alcott. Oddly, the journal of this most unworldly and speculative member of the movement, often ridiculed for his "Orphic Sayings," contains the highest proportion of information about daily life, social contacts, and characterizations of other people. Like Thoreau, though, Alcott eventually came to regard his journal as an important text in its own right rather than as pre-text for more conventional published work.

During most of the first three quarters of the 20th century, when varieties of historicism and formalism dominated literary studies, the journals of the Transcendentalists were bound to be devalued except as source or background material. Being able to appreciate and understand them as multivalent texts requires a more catholic and flexible critical practice, as well as sound scholarship in the construction of good editions of these documents. As critical attention spreads to other kinds of private and noncanonical writing, as autobiographical theory becomes more sophisticated, and as the social dimensions of these texts are probed, the journal may eventually acquire the privileged status that the Transcendentalists wished to claim for it.

REFERENCES: No critical survey of the journal as a Transcendentalist form exists at present; nor have most of the Transcendentalists' journals been edited according to modern scholarly practice or even printed. For Emerson, *JMN* is standard. See also Lawrence Rosenwald, *Emerson and the Art of the Diary* (1988). The 14-volume edition of Thoreau's Journal published in the 1906 Houghton Mifflin Walden Edition has served readers and scholars alike for most of the 20th century, but it is both incomplete and misleading with respect to the text itself. It is gradually being superseded by a scholarly edition, *PJ;* 16 volumes are projected. Critical works that treat Thoreau's journal in detail include William L. Howarth, *The Book of Concord:* * *Thoreau's Life as a Writer* (1982), Sharon Cameron, *Writing Nature: Henry Thoreau's Journal* (1985), and H. Daniel Peck, *Thoreau's Morning Work: Memory and Perception in* A Week on the Concord and Merrimack Rivers, *the Journal, and* Walden (1990).

Robert Sattelmeyer

K

KANT, IMMANUEL (1724–1804), German philosopher of unmatched subtlety and depth of thought, influenced Transcendentalism less through his technical contributions to epistemology, ethics, and aesthetics than through some general ideas that the Transcendentalists, with varying degrees of creative misunderstanding, attributed to him, thereby enabling themselves to make him a factor in their efforts at philosophical self-definition or to invoke his authority in support of their own brand of anti-Lockeanism.* Indicative of this rather loose Kantianism is the fact that "transcendental," as understood by most Transcendentalists, has little specific connection with either K's term *transzendental* (which refers to knowledge concerned with our mode of cognition of objects so far as this is possible a priori) or his term *transzendent* (which refers to what lies beyond the limits of possible experience). *Transzendental* was simplified to "intuitive," as R. W. Emerson** makes clear in "The Transcendentalist," when he traces to K's prestige the fact that "whatever belongs to the class of intuitive thought, is popularly called at the present day Transcendental." The limitations inherent in *transzendent* were ignored. K had declared metaphysics to be philosophically unwarrantable; the Transcendentalists, like other post-Kantian idealists,* transformed Kantian concepts in order to make them support their own metaphysical aspirations, in the process granting the Reason, ideas, or intuition a metaphysical reach or content that is decidedly un-Kantian.

F. H. Hedge** and T. Parker** were among the few Transcendentalists who read K carefully in the original. Emerson owned a copy of Francis Haywood, *Critick of Pure Reason* (1838), the first English translation of K's most important work. Authoritative translations of the other major works appeared too late to have had any impact on Transcendentalism. K was chiefly available through English commentaries like F. A. Nitsch, *A General View of K's Principles* (1795) and Anthony Willich, *Elements of K's Philosophy* (1798)—both of which B. Alcott,** for instance, studied carefully in 1833—and D. Stewart,* *A General*

View of the Progress of Metaphysical, Ethical, and Political Philosophy (1822), which young Emerson considered "a beautiful and instructive abridgement" of the works of the major modern philosophers, K among them; and through such creative interpreters as Cousin,** Coleridge,** and Carlyle.** The latter two especially shaped many a Transcendentalist's view of K, and several of their misunderstandings proved immensely stimulating to Transcendentalist thought.

The most significant of these misunderstandings (or creative interpretations) involved the Reason (K's *Vernunft*) and the Understanding (K's *Verstand*). For K, the Understanding is the faculty of conceptualizing; through the imposition of its "categories" (12 in all), the Understanding transforms the "manifold of sensation" into concepts. The Understanding thus provides the conditions that make it possible for sense data to become objects of thought; it does not contain any "innate ideas." The Reason is the source of Ideas, but their role is purely regulative: They guide the Understanding in its use of concepts and direct its conceptual endeavors toward the unconditioned, the absolute, in a word, the transcendent. The Reason makes it possible for us to think about such absolutes as the soul, the universe, and God, but it cannot provide us with any *knowledge* of such absolutes. Though regulatively necessary, the Ideas of the Reason are theoretically empty: We cannot even know whether any actuality corresponds to the Ideas since such actuality (absolute, unconditioned) transcends all possible experience. Hence, K's referring to them as "merely Ideas" and his condemnation of what he considered the speculative arrogance of traditional metaphysics. Kantian Reason attains its apogee in its "practical" role, that is, as source of the moral law. As a product of the Reason, the moral law is absolute (a priori; not a product of experience) and autonomous (it is given to us qua rational beings by our own Reason). K rejected all attempts to derive the moral law from any other source (e.g., God, society, personal desire, moral feeling) as heteronomous. The moral law can be formulated only as a "categorical" imperative, that is, as a formal (without specific, experience-derived content), apodictic, universally binding command. The moral law also involves three postulates: freedom, immortality, and God. The existence of none of these is susceptible to theoretical proof (they are Ideas of the Reason), but the *practical* Reason postulates them not as sources of the moral law (only the Reason itself can be such) but as guarantors of the law's functioning and ultimate efficacy.

Although there were differences among them, Coleridge, Carlyle, and their Transcendentalist followers generally agreed (1) in rejecting the limitations imposed by K on the human mind and (2) in claiming a greater role for nonrational human experience. K's "Copernican revolution" in epistemology, which had transformed the mind from a passive and receptive into an active and constitutive principle (through the role of the categories of the Understanding), was extended so that the mind came to be regarded as inherently and almost limitlessly creative, as virtually creating its own world out of its "innate ideas." We also find a reassertion of the metaphysical claims of the Reason in the form of a new idealism supported by an intuitionism that provided both ontological and moral certainties. For Coleridge, in *Aids to Reflection,* the Reason "is an intuition or *im*mediate beholding, accompanied by a conviction of the necessity and universality of the truth so beholden." Carlyle claims, in "State of German Literature," that "Reason discerns Truth itself, the absolutely and primitively *True*"; it does so "not by logic and argument" but by dwelling "in that holier region, where Poetry, and Virtue and Divinity abide." The Transcendentalists in general held similarly exalted views of the Reason. They also followed Coleridge and Carlyle in rejecting K's supposedly extreme rationalism and formalism, especially as it concerned ethics. The British and American writers alike wanted a more experiential, subjective, affective approach. Coleridge objected, for instance, to K's apparent denial of personal inclination (the affective component of motivation) as morally relevant. For Carlyle the moral law was very much intertwined with the need for belief and the intuitions of the "heart." Emerson's general preference of the term "moral sentiment" to "moral sense" is especially meaningful in this context.

The range of Transcendentalist responses to K is represented by Hedge, Parker, and Emerson. As is evident from his essay on Coleridge in *The Christian Examiner** (14 [March 1833]: 108–29), Hedge came closest to a real understanding of what was distinctive about K's philosophical achievement. Hedge's aim was the scholarly one of trying to clarify K's tenets and method. Parker, looking back on his intellectual development, acknowledged that he had "found most help in the works of IK. . . . If he did not always furnish conclusions I could rest in, he yet . . . put me on the right road" (*Works,* Centenary Ed., 13: 301). Parker put K to the service of his own intellectual and spiritual needs, in the process interpreting K's thought very freely, as when he transformed two of K's postulates of the practical Reason into "the instinctive intuition of the divine . . . [and] the instinctive intuition of the immortal" (ibid.). In a truly creative sense, Emerson was the thinker who engaged Kantianism most significantly. Emerson's views of the mind's constitutive role in our experience of the world, his struggles with solipsistic idealism, his sense of our living in two worlds (in one of which we are free, in the other determined), and his increasing concern with limitation were all, however indirectly, responses to problems defined by K.

REFERENCES: K figures prominently in René Wellek, "The Minor Transcendentalists and German Philosophy," *NEQ* 15 (December 1942): 652–80, and "Emerson and German Philosophy," *NEQ* 16 (March 1943): 41–62. Pochmann (1957) documents in great detail K's presence in Transcendentalist thought. Illuminating discussion of Emerson's Kantianism is provided by David Van Leer, *Emerson's Epistemology* (1986); Stanley Cavell, "Thinking of Emerson," *The Senses of "Walden"* (1981), 123–38, and "Emerson, Coleridge, K," *In Quest of the Ordinary* (1988), 27–49; and Russell B. Goodman, *American Philosophy and the Romantic Tradition* (1991), 44–51.

Gustaaf Van Cromphout

L

LANDSCAPE AESTHETICS became crucial to Transcendentalism because international Romanticism found epistemological and religious meanings in the emotional effect of natural settings. The Transcendentalists' treatment of "nature"* is more abstract than W. C. Bryant's** or Thomas Cole's, and with the partial exception of H. Thoreau's** writings, it should not be called a celebration of the American wilderness. What unites them all is the belief that landscapes must be shown as balanced and organic* wholes that reveal the unity of all things, both outer and inner.

The concept of a nonarchitectural setting having aesthetic value originated in 18th-century English "picturesque" landscape architecture, which featured loose, open, seemingly untouched vistas. Edmund Burke's 1757 invention of "the Sublime" as a quality of landscape painting—wild or desolate vistas that excited the imagination by arousing fear—furthered the idea that a place's most important effects were emotional ones. By 1800, thanks to Burke and to Rousseau's* cult of the "state of nature," the natural vista (genuine or artificial) had acquired primitivist, historical, and pantheistic* associations. By this time Kant* and Fichte* had articulated the idea that, as Coleridge** put it, "our awareness [of nature] was in fact an act of creation." For the German Romantics, looking at nature led to intuition of the correspondences* that existed between the interior self and the exterior world as God's creation.

R. W. Emerson's** *Nature* (1836), which asserted the unity of self and nature (the "NOT ME"),* introduced this landscape aesthetic to America. *Nature* oscillates between several implied definitions for "nature," from the common landscape to the universal Not-Me. It shares the confusion of terms common in the 1830s between (as Barbara Novak puts it) "God's nature" and "God *in* Nature." Like the European Romantics, Emerson redefined the Sublime as a religious attitude that apprehended God through direct, unmediated sense contact with God's creation. Thus, for Emerson, the important features of landscapes are those aspects of the physical world that most encourage looking inward.

The vast spaces and extraordinary light effects that painters and poets had equated with the Sublime's delicious terror now appear as emotional guideposts toward the direct intuition of God, both outside and within the self. In *Nature* the sky and the sense of "infinite space" in the "transparent eye-ball" passage, and the impact of color and light in the dawn vista of chapter 3, "Beauty," not only echo Wordsworth's** poetry but create the same nearly abstract effect of a living entity as D. C. Friedrich's mountain vistas or J.M.W. Turner's glowing seascapes. The similarity comes not from any specific artistic source Emerson knew but from a common search for tokens of correspondence.

In a revision of Burke's definition of the Sublime as wild and frightening, Romantic writers suggested that in more tranquil landscapes the self would have the greatest peace in which to meditate on its correspondence with God's nature. Emerson's intuition of the Ideal* on farmsteads and fields is more characteristic than Thoreau's encounters with Mt. Ktaadn and Cape Cod. Thoreau's preference for semidomesticated Walden Pond* over rougher sites is itself characteristic. Moreover, consciousness of how close the American pastoral landscape was to the wilderness Sublime of forest or sea is a special characteristic of American Romantic aesthetics, which Thoreau's writings convey most subtly.

Thoreau's writings aside, the Transcendentalists' overall landscape attitude is in a broad sense suburban. Emerson remarked that the city "delights the understanding" with its "varieties [and] contrivances," but the country, with its "unbroken horizon, the monotony of an endless road, of vast uniform plains, of distant mountains," where the eye can wander serenely and contemplatively, is "the School of Reason." The workaday Concord* of the Hosmers and Flints is the world of Commodity. The open countryside around it is, for those who do not wrest a living from it, an optical jumping-off place for the Sublime. The relation of the unity of the viewed landscape to the individual objects in it was a complex issue. For Hazlitt, the most transcendent landscape was the most distant one, where details had been refined out into a decorporealized and instantly apprehensible Beauty. Emerson's yearning for an ever-greater and more abstract unity puts him in line with Hazlitt. But for William Blake, and later for J. Ruskin,** the sense of unity could be found in microcosm* in each natural object: The close-up rather than the panoramic view was the gateway into correspondence. This belief encouraged not only Thoreau's intense focus on the particulars of nature but Emerson's more-than-passing interest in geology and other natural sciences. The American followers of Ruskin and the Pre-Raphaelite painters in the 1850s considered themselves Emersonians.

The Transcendentalist landscape aesthetic influenced the landscape architecture of A. J. Downing and Frederick Law Olmsted, but its greatest effect was through the conservation movement inspired by Thoreau's writings at the end of the 19th century. Thanks to J. Muir** and other later interpreters, Thoreau's assertion in "Walking" that "in Wildness is the preservation of the World" became a literal prescription for saving the "wilderness." Behind the ecological and moral imperatives of modern wilderness conservation lies, however reinterpreted, the abstract nature theology of Emerson and the Romantics.

REFERENCES: William Vaughan, *Romantic Art* (1978), and Hugh Honour, *Romanticism* (1979), are accounts of Romantic painting and architecture that firmly locate them in their literary and esp. philosophical contexts. Novak, *Nature and Culture: American Landscape and Painting* (1980), is sometimes speculative but is suggestive on Emerson's responses to contemporary attitudes toward the landscape. Novak builds on literary and intellectual treatments of nature in American Renaissance literature in Leo Marx, *The Machine in the Garden: Technology and the Pastoral Ideal in America* (1964), and Perry Miller, "Thoreau in the Context of International Romanticism," in *Nature's Nation* (1967). The Transcendentalists' stance toward the landscape has usually been analyzed in terms of Romantic aesthetic theory or literary genres. Buell (1973) applies both categories to a valuable consideration of the Transcendentalists' writings on "nature." Vivian Hopkins, *Spires of Form: A Study of Emerson's Aesthetic Theory* (1951), remains essential for Emerson's epistemology, although "nature" is not a central concern of Hopkins's. Among writings specifically on the Transcendentalists' responses to actual places, Robert Gross's provocative "Transcendentalism and Urbanism: Concord, Boston and the Wider World," *JAmS* 18, no. 3 (1984), stands out. Thoreau's impact on the conservation movement is explored in Roderick Nash, *Wilderness and the American Mind* (1967; 3d ed. 1982). Cecelia Tichi, *New World, New Earth: Environmental Reform in American Literature from the Puritans* through Whitman*** (1979), relates Thoreau and Whitman to changes in the built environment but is primarily a literary analysis.

M. David Samson

LANDSCAPE ARCHITECTURE, the art and science of landscape design, became a profession in the mid-19th century United States in response to the needs of a changing society in a changing landscape. Pioneers of the profession—Frederick Law Olmsted (1822–1903), Robert Morris Copeland (1830–1874), and Horace William Shaler Cleveland (1814–1900)—helped change the face of America during the second half of the 19th century. They designed estates, cemeteries, urban and suburban communities, and parks and park systems and helped spur the movement that led to the establishment of national parks. R. W. Emerson** directly called for a new art to guide change in the American landscape. In "The Young American" he viewed landscape art as "the fine art that is left for us, now that sculpture, painting, and . . . architecture have become effete, and have passed into second childhood." Emerson also directly influenced 19th-century landscape architects as they developed an aesthetic vision for the new profession.

Olmsted, often referred to as the father of the profession, in 1858 designed New York's Central Park, the first true public park in America. Before that he lived on Staten Island, where he was a neighbor and friend of Emerson's brother Judge W. Emerson.** Olmsted attended Emerson lectures and was greatly influenced by his writing, particularly by Emerson's ideas about the role of the artist in society. As an artist in the landscape, Olmsted viewed himself as Emer-

son's "seer," capable of higher understanding than the average person but with
a responsibility to communicate the lessons of nature* for public good. In a
number of park and community designs during the second half of the 19th
century—such as Prospect Park in Brooklyn, New York, the Boston Park System, and the suburban community of Riverside, Illinois—Olmsted manipulated
the landscape to make the lessons of nature discernible to the common person
as Emerson suggested.

Copeland and Cleveland knew Emerson personally. Emerson served on the
cemetery board that enlisted their services to design what would become his
final resting place, Sleepy Hollow Cemetery.* Like Olmsted, Copeland and
Cleveland were influenced by Emerson's ideas about the role of the artist and
by his aesthetic of organic form.* Emerson believed that there must be truth in
art and showed a general disdain for unnecessary decoration. In like manner,
Copeland and Cleveland believed that in landscape art it was essential to be true
to the place in which they worked. Those aesthetic principles influenced actual
landscapes designed by Copeland and Cleveland in many parts of the United
States. After Copeland's death, Cleveland continued to emphasize the organic
approach in his work over a career that spanned more than 40 years. Cleveland's
crowning achievement was his design for the Minneapolis Park System in the
1880s. There, as if in answer to Emerson's calling, he left large portions of the
natural environment intact, providing the armature around which that city grew
for decades.

REFERENCES: The most definitive and complete account of Olmsted's life is Laura Wood
Roper, *A Biography of Frederick Law Olmsted* (1973). The most useful description of
Emerson's influence on Olmsted's aesthetic development is Irving D. Fisher, *Frederick
Law Olmsted and the City Planning Movement in the United States* (1976). A good
overview of the life and work of Cleveland is Theodora Kimball Hubbard, "H. W. S.
Cleveland: An Early Pioneer of Landscape Architecture and City Planning," *Landscape
Architecture* 20 (January 1930): 92–111. On Emerson's influence on the aesthetic development of both Cleveland and Copeland, see Daniel Joseph Nadenicek, "Nature in
the City: Horace Cleveland's Aesthetic," *Landscape and Urban Planning* 26 (1993): 5–
15, and "Sleepy Hollow Cemetery: Transcendental Garden and Community Park," *Journal of the New England Garden History Society* 3 (fall 1993): 8–14.

Daniel Joseph Nadenicek

LAVATER, JOHANN KASPAR (1741–1801), was a Swiss artist, teacher, poet,
mystic, and physiognomist whose *Physiognomische Fragmente* (4 vols., 1775–
78) enjoyed widespread popularity as a putative guide to a person's moral or
spiritual character through the study of the facial features and bodily form. The
Transcendentalists believed they found in L's work scientific vindication of their
intuitively held beliefs that each person is an organic and unified entity; his
body is in essential harmony with his soul, spirit, or mental constitution; and
his and the creation's every part reflects in microcosm* the Whole. Fusing as
it did science and religion, parts of *Physiognomische Fragmente* read like an
extended sermon in the tradition of natural religion.*

Upon its publication, *Physiognomische Fragmente*'s popularity was immediate and widespread—55 editions appeared in six different countries in less than 40 years; no literate person could have escaped knowing L's work. How many made systematic use of his system is moot, however, since the innumerable nuances to character L identified resisted codification into distinctive and fixed principles.

Many of the Transcendentalists appear to have had a reading knowledge of L. R. W. Emerson** borrowed *Physiognomy, or The Corresponding Analogy Between the Conformation of the Features and the Ruling Passions of the Mind* (1789) from the Boston Library Society from 8 July to 2 September 1820; B. Alcott** read L's *Physiognomy* during his *Wanderjahre* as a peddler in the South; H. Melville** owned a copy of L's classic that he purchased on his European tour of 1849–50; and N. Hawthorne** borrowed Charles Moore's translation of *Essays on Physiognomy* (1797) from the Salem Athenaeum late in 1828.

Emerson's view of physiognomy constantly wavered. In his retrospective essay "Historic Notes of Life and Letters in New England" (1880) he described L's work as "coarse and odious to scientific men" but sensed it contained "a truth which had not yet been announced." In "Fate" Emerson derided physiognomy's deterministic implications but, in "Behavior," asserted that the "tell-tale body is all tongues. . . . The face and eyes reveal what the spirit is doing."

The fiction writers of this period were similarly familiar with the broad theory of physiognomy and employed it variously: as a useful mode of perception, to enrich symbolic characterization, or, in some instances, to satirize its epistemological pretensions. During the mid-1830s, Hawthorne editorially debunked physiognomy's claim to science and treated it satirically in his notes on "The Science of Noses" in the columns of the *American Magazine*. However, he used physiognomical phenomena in such tales as "Alice Doane's Appeal," "Roger Malvin's Burial," "My Kinsman, Major Molineaux," "The Birthmark," "The Prophetic Pictures," "The Minister's Black Veil," and others to heighten doppelgänger effects and to provide moral and psychological depth to his characters; such techniques are also evident in *The House of the Seven Gables*. His notebooks are also full of physiognomical observations about people he saw.

References to physiognomy punctuate Melville's major fiction—from *Mardi* and *White-Jacket* to *The Confidence-Man* and *Pierre*—though this "semi-science" (in Melville's words) receives its most extended and characteristic treatment in *Moby-Dick*. Here it is employed to underscore Melville's bitterest conclusions about the futility of any attempt to solve the mysteries of existence; despite its subjection to physiognomical examination, the whale, like the world's teleology, remains ambiguous, its meaning obscured by shifting and contradictory symbols. In short, Melville reveals physiognomy merely as a variation of all those other systems man concocts to read the world around him but which do little more than obscure the world in a mist of hypotheses.

E. A. Poe's** references to physiognomy lack an assignable, specific origin. He makes explicit reference to L twice: in his description of Mr. Hunt (of *Merchant's Magazine*) in *The Literati of New York City* (May 1846) and in "Some Passages from the Life of a Lion" (1835), a lightly satirical piece that revolves around one Robert Jones, whose life's focus seems to be "the study of Nosology." Edward W. Pitcher convincingly argues that "The Tell-Tale Heart" is built around symbols and ideas borrowed from physiognomy.

REFERENCES: To my knowledge, no studies of L's reception in this country have been made. Overviews dealing with L in a European intellectual/cultural context include John Graham, *L's* Essays on Physiognomy: *A Study in the History of Ideas* (1979); Michael Shortland, "The Power of a Thousand Eyes: JCL's Science of Physiognomical Perception," *Criticism* 28 (fall 1986): 379–408; and Graeme Tytler, *Physiognomy in the European Novel: Faces and Fortunes* (1982). Studies of individual authors include Taylor Stoehr, "Physiognomy and Phrenology* in Hawthorne," *HLQ* 37 (October 1974): 355–400; Edward W. Pitcher, "The Physiognomical Meaning of Poe's 'The Tell-Tale Heart,'" *SSF* 16 (spring 1979): 231–33; Harold Aspiz, "Phrenologizing the Whale," *NCF* 23 (June 1968): 18–27; and Tyrus Hillway, "Melville's Use of Two Pseudo-Sciences," *MLN* 64 (March 1949): 145–50.

Arthur Wrobel

LAWS OF MANU *(Mānava-dharmásāstra)*, the familiar designation of the oldest and most authoritative legal treatise in the Hindu tradition, was, together with the *Bhagavadgītā*, one of the most influential texts in shaping early knowledge of India among Western Orientalists,* including R. W. Emerson** and H. Thoreau.** Attributed to the figure of "Manu" (transliterated as "Menu" in early renderings), traditionally conceived as the progenitor of the human race as well as its first king and lawgiver, the *Laws of Manu* provide a broad overview of classical Indian society as it would ideally be constituted. Of the 12 chapters contained in the collection, only three are actually devoted specifically to law and government. The rest set out guidelines for the traditional four stages of life and other areas of Hindu society, including education, marriage, economics, diet, and religious observance. The first chapter offers an account of the creation of the world and the ordering of society, while the last contains Manu's teachings on transmigration and final liberation.

First rendered into English by Sir William Jones as the *Institutes of Hindu Law: or, The Ordinances of Menu, According to the Gloss of Culluca* (Calcutta, 1794), the *Laws of Manu* was among the first translations of a classical Hindu text undertaken by members of the Asiatic Society of Bengal. *Manu* owes this distinction almost wholly to political considerations. British colonial policy dictated that while British subjects residing in India were to be governed by British laws, natives should be governed consistently with their own customs and traditions. As an early appointee to Bengal's Supreme Court, Jones assumed responsibility for providing the colonial government with an authentic compendium of Hindu law. Though his motive in translating *Manu* was thus largely pragmatic, as a poet and classicist himself, Jones found much to admire in the text he was preparing for translation. Drawing mainly from cosmogonies he discovered in *Manu* and the *Śrimad Bhagavatam,* in 1785 Jones composed "A Hymn to Narayena," a poem approvingly cited to the young Emerson by his aunt, M. M. Emerson,** in 1822, and much later included among his favorite verses in *Parnassus* (1874), an anthology compiled in old age.

In 1836 Emerson encountered Jones's complete translation of *Manu* in its 1825 edition, thus making it one of the first Hindu classics known in Concord.* Reading it again in the summer of 1840, Emerson recommended it to Thoreau's attention as well. Though obviously appreciative, Emerson's own reception of the *Laws of Manu* seems pale next to Thoreau's. *Manu* struck Thoreau with the force of a revelation, and the next summer his journals* continued to witness its repercussions: "That title—The Laws of Menu—with the Gloss of Culucca—comes to me with such a volume of sound as if it had swept unobstructed over the plains of Hindostan, ... When my imagination travels eastward and backward to those remote years of the gods—I seem to draw near to the habitation of the morning—and the dawn at length has a place. I remember the book as an hour before sunrise." For several years, the *Laws of Manu* was Thoreau's chief source for facts about India and his chief sanction for his developing romantic primitivism. Seeking a wider readership on its behalf, he included selections from *Manu* in the "Ethnical Scriptures" column of the January 1843 number of *The Dial.** And, together with the *Bhagavadgītā, Manu* supplied much of the data for his sustained reflections on the Orient in the "Monday" section of *A Week on the Concord and Merrimack Rivers.*

REFERENCES: For a modern translation and helpful introduction, see Wendy Doniger, *Laws of Manu* (1991). On Thoreau's use of *Manu,* see Sherman Paul, *The Shores of America: Thoreau's Inward Exploration* (1958), esp. 70–75.

Alan D. Hodder

LEIBNIZ, GOTTFRIED WILHELM VON (1646–1716), a philosopher whose writings filtered to the American Transcendentalists through the German Idealists,* was born in Leipzig, the son and grandson of professors. He studied philosophy and law at the University of Leipzig and became secretary of the Rosicrucian Society in Nuremberg, where he met Johann Christian von Boyneburg, a retired statesman, and, through Boyneburg's influence, secured a position with the elector of Mainz. In 1676 he was taken into the service of Johann Friedrich, the duke of Hanover, where he spent the rest of his life. After Friedrich's death in 1679, he served under Ernst August and then under Georg Ludwig, who became king of Great Britain in 1714. He was made president for life of the Berlin Society of Sciences in 1700. Culturally, he is perhaps best known for his work on the Universal Encyclopedia, an ambitious attempt to collect and arrange all human knowledge. Such sweeping aims were also central to his attempts to bring together the common beliefs of all Christian faiths and his promotion of cooperation between all scientists, philosophers, and medical doctors. He is also remembered for his public argument with Sir Isaac Newton, engendered over the primacy of the discovery of the calculus.

L's most important philosophical work, in the context of American Transcendentalism, is his *Monadology,* which stems from his thoughts on the relation between mind and body: The human soul (as with all things, created by God and self-contained) evolves spontaneously and expresses within itself the entire universe. The soul is one example, as are all existing substances, of a monad. The universe is populated with these monads, neither having nor needing communication with one another, acting in a "pre-established harmony." Because the soul is a microcosm* of the universe, any external change in the universe is felt in the soul and either diminishes or increases it.

L's influence on the Transcendentalists is oblique and yet important. R. W. Emerson** appreciated his "nobility of method," but it was Hegel,** who took on the major tenets of L's philosophy, who more directly influenced Emerson. Goethe,** another major influence on Emerson, adopted L's concept of the monad and applied it to the indestructible core of identity with which nature* has endowed each human. The St. Louis Hegelians, such as W. T. Harris,** as well as others of the "Hegelian Left," turned to L for their ideas. L's view of the soul as a monad that possesses the entire universe within itself may be considered a source for Emerson's concept of the Over-Soul. Emerson's insistence on traditional Christian morality (as evidenced by his treatment of I. Kant*) in the face of British empiricism finds justification in L. Emerson's epistemology also suggests points of correspondence with L, for L's understanding that the one thing not first in the senses is the mind itself is utilized by Emerson in his concept of "surprise."

REFERENCES: The definitive edition of L's work, in seven series, was begun in 1923 and is now carried on by the Akademie der Wissenschaften. Less than 10 percent of L's manuscripts exist in any printed edition. The best English edition of his work is *Philosophical Letters and Papers,* trans., ed., and intro. Leroy E. Loemker (1956). *The Monadology and Other Philosophical Writings,* trans. with intro. and notes by Robert Latta (1898), is dated but still a strong source. A fine short work on the man and his system is Nicholas Rescher, *L: An Introduction to His Philosophy* (1986). David Van Leer, *Emerson's Epistemology: The Argument of the Essays* (1986), is an exhaustive, impressive study and makes explicit the debt Emerson owes to L. Gustaaf Van Cromphout, *Emerson's Modernity and the Example of Goethe* (1990), notes the filtering of L's thought to Emerson through Goethe.

Joe Pellegrino

LINNAEUS (CARL VON LINNÉ) (1707–1778), Swedish botanist and physician, was a hero of Enlightenment science and the originator of modern systematic botany. L's lasting contribution to natural science was the system of binomial nomenclature still in use in scientific terminology today, in which a Latin genus name is followed by a species name (e.g., *Viola papilionacea* for the common blue violet). In his own era and during the early decades of the

19th century, L was regarded as the preeminent figure of natural science, one whose classification system ordered living nature* in the same way that Newton's mathematical formulas explained and gave order to the movements of the stars and planets. His classification system was an artificial one, based on a single characteristic (the structure of the sexual organs within flowers), and was gradually superseded during the 19th century by a more natural system that organized the plant kingdom according to overall affinities and relatedness.

Given the American Transcendentalists' interest not only in nature in general but also in the still unexplored and uncataloged riches of American flora and fauna, L remained a major influence on their scientific interests. Both R. W. Emerson's** and H. Thoreau's** journals* are sprinkled with references to L, and Thoreau especially found L's writings indispensable in training himself to be an accurate observer and taxonomist, noting that he "learned in a shorter time & more accurately the meaning of the technical terms used in Botany from a few plates and figures" in L's *Philosophia Botanica* "than a volume of explanations or glossaries could teach."

Still, it was as heroic personality that L most directly spoke to both Emerson and Thoreau. Although they recognized the limitations of his classification system and deplored the mere collection and cataloging of dry facts, they both saw L as a brave and self-sufficient figure who transcended these limitations and took all of nature as his study. "The great man makes the great thing," Emerson said in "The American Scholar": "L makes botany the most alluring of studies and wins it from the farmer and the herb-woman." For this reason, they preferred the more personal L of his travel* writings, especially his account of his tour of Lapland, in which the great botanist's love of his subject is evident. In this work especially, he provided a model of solitary botanizing as heroic activity for Thoreau, who admired the "quiet bravery of the man" and compared him favorably to Napoleon.

REFERENCES: Useful surveys of L's work and significance include *L: The Man and His Work*, ed. Tore Frängsmyr (1983), and Heinz Goerke, *L* (1973). The influence of Linnaean taxonomy on the first generation of American natural scientists is treated in Pamela Regis, *Describing Early America: Bartram, Jefferson, Crèvecoeur, and the Rhetoric of Natural History** (1992). Recent overviews of Emerson's and Thoreau's views toward natural science may be found in essays collected in *American Literature and Science,* ed. Robert J. Scholnick (1992): David Robinson, "Fields of Investigation: Emerson and Natural History," 94–109; and Robert D. Richardson, Jr., "Thoreau and Science," 110–27.

Robert Sattelmeyer

LITERARY REALISM, the predominant mode in American fiction from the end of the Civil War through the early 20th century, would seem to be incongruous with Transcendentalism. Whereas the Transcendentalists emphasized subjective, spiritual investment, the symbolic value of material phenomena, and organic* composition, the realists gave precedence to objectivity, surfaces and social patterns, the material phenomena themselves, and formal structure. Yet the relation between Transcendentalism and realism is not contrasting but evolutionary, for however different they may initially appear, many of the basic values and concepts held by the Transcendentalists still lurk among the guiding principles of American realism. These correspondences may be easily identified and assessed by glancing at representative views of R. W. Emerson** for Transcendentalism and of William Dean Howells (1837–1920) for realism, each writer being a leading exponent of his school.

Briefly stated, Emerson eschewed the distant and romantic in favor of the low and familiar; it was in the commonplace that he found his miracles.* For him, the moral law lies at the center of all and thus unifies all things, an idea later reflected in Howells's doctrine of complicity. Emerson professed, and despite apparent slips to the contrary, steadily held that goodness will ultimately prevail. Finally, he sustained faith in the promise of a free, independent, and democratic America.

After first meeting Emerson and H. Thoreau** on a literary pilgrimage from Ohio to Concord* in 1860, Howells remained under Emerson's influence for the rest of his life, and *Criticism and Fiction* (1891) unmistakably exposes its enduring strength. In that volume, Howells, like Emerson, emphasized the high value he placed on ordinary life, to which he turned for the comedy and tragedy that became the source and substance of American literary realism. In chapter 16, for example, he quoted at length from "The American Scholar" to support this highlighting of "the worth of the vulgar." Although Emerson *read* the details of the commonplace and Howells *described* them as a means of providing a solid, authentic rendering of setting and portraiture, both authors realized the importance of materiality for effective expression and for suggesting meanings that emerged from the surfaces. For Howells, too, "morality penetrates all things," and in realistic fiction, it should lead to poetic justice following immoral or unethical behavior. Moreover, as for Emerson, so too for Howells, at least through the mid-1880s, "the more smiling aspects . . . are the more American," and realism, which celebrates the ordinary, is a literary mode suitable for an equalitarian democratic America. Finally, Howells echoed Emerson's call for American authors to break from antiquated traditions and establish literary independence with an original realistic literature to represent contemporary American life.

Other aspects of the relation between Transcendentalism and realism are less crucial. Instead of philosophical and theoretical, the association may be of a personal or anecdotal nature, it may deal with a particular literary influence, or it may concern a matter of individual praise or criticism. A much-publicized example of the first type is the celebrated J. G. Whittier** birthday dinner on 17 December 1879, at which Mark Twain spoke comically but indiscreetly of and to three intellectual lights of Boston and Concord—O. W. Holmes,** H. W. Longfellow,** and Emerson. His lampoon was evidently not the gross insult that he and Howells assumed it to be, though it may have been received coolly at the dining table. Later Twain's apologies were accepted without rancor; in truth, Emerson, in his midseventies, may not have heard or grasped much of what Twain had said in his humorous address.

With respect to literary influence, Emerson's thought also had a notable impact on H. James,** whom Warner Berthoff characterized as an "heir" to the Transcendentalist's "celebration of concentrated states of mind." Yet James complained in his review of J. E. Cabot's** *Memoir of Ralph Waldo Emerson* (1887) that the sage lacked a deep and true sensitivity to the fine arts. In contrast, although he recognized Thoreau's eccentricity, James praised the natural beauty of his writing. Realist that he was, however, James reduced much of the Transcendentalist effort to *The Dial,** Fruitlands,* and Brook Farm,* which he considered "amusement[s] of the leisure-class."

Perhaps his most notorious characterization of Transcendentalism occurs in his caricature of E. Peabody** as the aged and tireless reformer Miss Birdseye, in *The Bostonians* (1886). Although he adamantly denied that he had modeled her after Peabody, he was not believed, and he was scolded by family and friends alike for treating this venerable idealist* with comic disrespect. James affected shock and embarrassment over the charge, but from the initial installment of *The Bostonians* in the *Atlantic** in February 1885, the resemblance was too pronounced for readers personally acquainted with Peabody to overlook it.

In large ways and small, the realists—and to some extent, the naturalists who followed them—showed an indebtedness to Transcendentalism. As Everett Carter has suggested, Howells found in Emerson a unique combination of force, beauty, and wisdom, a "peculiar blend of idealism and realism" that was fundamental in the evolution of 19th-century American literature. Nearly half a century after the publication of *Criticism and Fiction,* Theodore Dreiser introduced a collection of *The Living Thoughts of Thoreau* (1939), where he acknowledged the Transcendentalist as an inspiring prophet, zealot, and saint. Dreiser was particularly impressed with him as a "fact-seeking researcher who insist[ed] on gathering the evidence and contemplating it himself" before he was willing to trust in God. Although the realists gave closer and more sustained attention to Emersonian fact as "the last issue of spirit" than to spirit itself, virtue and the moral sentiment nonetheless remained in force among them.

REFERENCES: Among the best overviews of American literary realism are Jay Martin, *Harvests of Change: American Literature, 1865–1914* (1967), and Warner Berthoff, *The Ferment of Realism: American Literature, 1884–1919* (1965); both allude copiously to Emerson, suggesting thematic continuity from Romanticism as well as contrasts with realism. Van Wyck Brooks conveys an impressionistic yet detailed panorama in *New England Indian Summer, 1865–1915* (1940); see esp. 55–65 for his charming portrait of Emerson and B. Alcott** in postwar Concord. Valuable for its tracing of moral idealism in relation to eloquence during the age of realism, particularly with respect to Emerson's views on it, see Janet Gabler-Hover, *Truth in American Fiction: The Legacy of Rhetorical Idealism* (1990).

For Howells on Emerson and Thoreau, see his *Literary Friends and Acquaintance*

(1900), 57–64; and for Emerson's impact on Howells, see Everett Carter, *Howells and the Age of Realism* (1954), and Kenneth S. Lynn, *William Dean Howells: An American Life* (1971). Howells's letters are a good source of contemporary insight into Twain's faux pas at Whittier's birthday dinner and its aftermath; see the *Mark Twain–Howells Letters*, 2 vols., ed. Henry Nash Smith and William M. Gibson (1960), 1:210–15. For the controversy over James's satirical portrait of Peabody as Miss Birdseye, see Howells's letter to Edmund W. Gosse (9 March 1885) in his *Selected Letters, Vol. 3: 1882–1891*, ed. Robert C. Leitz III et al. (1980), 118. Additional remarks on the same issue appear in *Letters of Elizabeth Palmer Peabody*, ed. Bruce A. Ronda (1984), 41–42 and 396. James's review of Cabot's *Memoir* is included under the title "Emerson" in *Henry James: The American Essays*, ed. Leon Edel (1956), 51–76.

Sanford E. Marovitz

LOCKE, JOHN (1632–1704), was a well-rounded philosopher against whose theory of the sensory basis of knowledge the Transcendentalists were united in opposition. He held a degree in medicine from Oxford University and served as a diplomatic attaché in the government of Charles II and as commissioner on the British Council of Trade and Plantations. Elected a Fellow of the Royal Society in 1668, he has been called the "Father of Modern Psychology" and the "Father of Modern Empiricism."

L wrote two treatises *On Civil Government*, the second of which contained the famous trilogy of human rights: life, liberty, and property. These rights found their way into the rhetoric of Americans during the Revolution. Thomas Jefferson doctored the trilogy in the Declaration of Independence by replacing "property" as an inalienable right with the Aristotelian "pursuit of happiness." L's *Essay Concerning Human Understanding* (1690), a small book written simply, was a treatise on education in which he denied that the mind has any initial ideas of its own. Ideas, he asserted, find their origin in sensual experiences (which he called the "ideas of sensation") and reflection on experiences (which he called the "ideas of reflexion"). From sensation and reflection, then, all knowledge is derived. L's *Essay* was adopted and studied at most colleges, including Harvard, Yale, Dartmouth, Princeton, Columbia, and William and Mary, well into the 19th century.

The Unitarians* were particularly drawn to L's theory of sensationalism,* since they thought it implied that the only origin of supraempirical knowledge came through divine revelation. But the Rev. J. Marsh,** in his introduction to S. T. Coleridge's** *Aids to Reflection* (1829), called on orthodox Christians to disassociate themselves from L, since a religion that "is essentially spiritual" has no common ground with "a system of philosophy which excludes the very idea of all spiritual power and agency."

When the Transcendental Club* held its first meeting in 1836, there was consensus on their part, too, that a break was needed with the empiricism of L. R. W. Emerson,** G. Ripley,** B. Alcott,** and O. Brownson** all despaired of "the sensuous philosophy of L." Probably their greatest objection was the limits he placed on the extent of knowledge and the soul. J. F. Clarke** wrote in his *Autobiography* (1891), "[S]omething within me revolted at all such attempts to explain soul out of sense, deducing mind from matter, or tracing the origin of ideas to nerves and vibratuncles." Brownson regarded L, a deist, as "a great and good man" but claimed his philosophy was contradictory to "the truths of Christianity . . . [which are] neither objects of the senses nor operations of our own minds." L, however, upheld Christian principles in his *The Reasonableness of Christianity* (1695) and *A Paraphrase and Notes on the Epistle of St. Paul to the Galatians* (1705).

REFERENCES: See Cameron Thompson, "JL and New England Transcendentalism," in *American Transcendentalism: An Anthology of Criticism,* ed. Brian Barbour (1973). A concise overview of L's philosophy of education is in William and Mabel Saharian, *JL* (1975). James Axtell, *The Educational Writings of JL* (1968), contains important letters of L on pedagogy. Maurice Cranston, *JL: A Biography* (1957), is one of the better accounts of L's life. Peter Gay, *JL on Education* (1964), is a classic interpretation of L's *Essay.* Sterling Lamprecht, *The Moral and Political Philosophy of JL* (1918), is still insightful and systematic.

Raymond L. Muncy

The **LORD'S SUPPER** was the focus of R. W. Emerson's** disaffection with his role as minister at the Second Church of Boston in 1832 when he decided to resign the pastorate that he had held since March 1829.

In the summer of 1832, Emerson wrote a letter to the Second Church suggesting a change in the observance of the sacrament. He wrote that since he now saw the Lord's Supper as a simple memorial, not a sacrament required by God, he could not regularly administer it. A committee of seven men, all kindly disposed toward Emerson, evaluated but rejected the proposal. Because the church was closed for repairs, Emerson gained some time to prepare his response. He traveled, first to Maine to visit Aunt M. M. Emerson** and then to New Hampshire. There he finished the sermon that offered both his explanation and resignation. After delays caused by his health, he finally delivered the Lord's Supper sermon on 9 September 1832 before a full church. He then submitted his resignation. Before the church could act on it, Emerson preached three more Sundays at Second Church, including, on 21 October, a sermon on "The Genuine Man"—an attack on the formalism and authority of institutions and traditions. On 28 October the church voted to accept his resignation but to continue his salary temporarily. Seemingly, although Emerson had forced the issue, the congregation was reluctant to lose its preacher. In fact, when illness prevented his presenting a farewell sermon, the church copied Emerson's farewell letter to provide his appreciative parishioners with a final remembrance.

The Lord's Supper sermon has a simple outline and a clear, two-part thesis: "Jesus did not intend to establish an institution for perpetual observance," and "[I]t is not expedient to celebrate [the Lord's Supper] as we do." Emerson then elaborates on those points.

Emerson first argues that the church places too much emphasis on the institution of the Lord's Supper, having misunderstood Christ's words and his symbolic actions. Furthermore, the church relies more on Paul's authority than Christ's even though Paul includes in his argument a mistaken understanding of the imminence of Christ's Second Coming. Emerson concludes that while the Lord's Supper was "an occasion full of solemn and prophetic interest," Jesus did not intend it to be "the foundation of a perpetual institution."

Emerson then lists objections to the expediency of simply practicing the ordinance regardless of its authority. To do so, he says, raises again an aspect of the Trinitarian-Unitarian* dilemma: Are we worshiping God or commemorating Christ? But his most "weighty" objection is that modern Christians no longer think in symbolical actions: "To eat bread is one thing; to love the precepts of Christ and resolve to obey them is quite another." Quite simply, he adds, the rite "is not suitable to me." Finally, the significance placed on the ordinance is not consistent with the spirit of Christianity. Why should God institute a formal ritual to commemorate Jesus who was sent to redeem us from a formal religion?

Emerson concludes: "It is my desire, in the office of a Christian minister, to do nothing which I cannot do with my whole heart. . . . I have no hostility to this institution. I am only stating my want of sympathy with it. Neither should I ever have obtruded this opinion upon other people, had I not been called by my office to administer it. That is the end of my opposition, that I am not interested in it." Since, after considering his view, the church will not endorse it, Emerson announces his intention to resign.

Critics disagree about the relationship between the sermon and Emerson's career and thought. For example, Turpie points out that much of the credit for the argument and design, which critics praise, should go to Thomas Clarkson, whose "portrait" of Quakerism* Emerson borrowed from the Boston Athenaeum* in June 1832. Similarly, although some say that Emerson resigned from his ministry, it is probably more accurate to say that he resigned his pastorate since he continued to preach until 1839.

More important, discussion continues about how the sermon fits into Emerson's developing Transcendentalism. Some see it as central to his career and development. For example, Feidelson notes that the sermon articulated a central theme of Emerson's career: "the fossilization to which every form is subject when it degenerates from a creative force into a static sign." And McAleer points to the sermon's "self-reliant individualism" and concludes that Emerson "was convinced he was leaving his parish so that he could live with his conscience" and not, as some have argued, that "he had contrived an excuse to separate himself from a calling for which his enthusiasm had waned." However, Gura writes that, in reference to Emerson's intellectual development, the sermon was linked "more to the age of Andrews Norton"** than Nature and the Divinity School Address were. And Schweitzer argues that "the doctrinal issue of the Lord's Supper is fundamental to Emerson's vocational crisis" and that the sermon demonstrates an antinomianism through which he "begins to embrace a broadly-based sacramentalism and a doctrine of form that will serve as the basis for his influential moral* and aesthetic philosophy.'' Mott counters by tying Emerson more directly back into his Puritan* heritage. He argues that "the habits of thought that led Emerson to resign his pulpit owe less to Antinomian antiformalism than to orthodox Puritan concepts of the spirit.''

REFERENCES: The best text of the sermon, ed. from manuscript by Wesley T. Mott, is in *Sermons,* 4: 185–94. See Rusk (1949); John McAleer, *Ralph Waldo Emerson: Days of Encounter* (1984); Charles Feidelson, *Symbolism and American Literature* (1953); Philip F. Gura, *The Wisdom of Words* (1981); Wesley T. Mott, "Emerson and Antinomianism: The Legacy of the Sermons,'' *AL* 50 (November 1978): 369–97; Ivy Schweitzer, "Transcendental Sacramentals: 'The Lord's Supper' and Emerson's Doctrine of Form,'' *NEQ* 61 (September 1988): 398–418; and M. C. Turpie, "A Quaker Source for Emerson's Sermon on the Lord's Supper,'' *NEQ* 17 (March 1944): 95–101.

Larry R. Long

LYCEUMS, organizations for literary and scientific education,* helped to disseminate Transcendentalist ideas. Since many figures in the Transcendentalist movement were also lecturers, the speaking platform of the lyceum provided a forum for the development of ideas before refinement into published form.

British "mechanics' institutes" anticipated features of American lyceums. Dr. George Birkbeck, of the Andersonian University (Glasgow), observed a need for the further education of mechanics: craftsmen, machinists, tradesmen, and mill workers. In 1800 he offered a free course of lectures for persons engaged in "the practical exercise of the mechanic arts.'' Illustrated by experiments and delivered with simplicity, these lectures proved immensely popular. By the 1820s the mechanics' course had split off from formal university offerings, and the Glasgow Mechanics' Institution was established. Early in 1824 the London Mechanics' Institution opened.

It did not take long for the practices of the English mechanics' institutes to take root in America. Called "the manifesto of the American lyceum movement,'' an article by Josiah Holbrook appeared in the *American Journal of Education* (1826). He described an association for the diffusion of knowledge, initially called a Society for Mutual Education. Soon to be called the Lyceum, this association initially stressed practical education for apprentices and clerks. Holbrook gave priority to scientific subjects, the branches of science (mechanics, hydrostatics, pneumatics, chemistry, mineralogy, botany) that would play a role in a general education. Fulfilling Holbrook's educational objectives were lectures, demonstrations, and discussions. He also recommended the local purchase of books and technical apparatus.

Holbrook founded the first "American Lyceum" in Millbury, Massachusetts, in 1826. Devoted to the study of natural history,* the lyceum broadened its curricula and enjoyed geographical expansion. It ceased to be purely a New England phenomenon, as settlers moved into northern Ohio, the old Western Reserve. Further migrations and higher literacy rates strengthened an expanding lyceum movement, as did new periodicals like the *Western Messenger,** admired by New England Transcendentalists. In the 1830s proponents worked to form a national lyceum, though the movement remained regional.

By the early 1840s, nearly 4,000 local societies sponsored lectures. By that time, however, the lyceum had passed through its first phase—local education—to an intricately patterned system of public lecturing in which speakers traveled from town to town. Topics were often scientific—R. W. Emerson** offered a tribute to the universal appeal of science—but as audiences broadened, so did subject matter. Common topics included reading, conversation, history, travel,* manners, morals, social institutions. Literary criticism drew lukewarm reactions on the lyceum circuit, as evidenced by the mixed reactions accorded E. A. Poe** for his disquisitions on American poetry, which countered the standard call for didacticism. Lecturers did not necessarily shrink from troubling issues—a typical course might include at least one controversial topic like "the woman question"—but the lyceum officially spurned personal bias and partisan or sectarian discourse. Lecturers received pay for their services, typically $50 plus expenses, and audience members were charged per course or lecture. The respectable public lecturer was distinguished from the itinerant humbug or charlatan who peddled his stores or "parcels of knowledge." The public lecturer, with obligations to a local secretary, sponsoring committee, or other official body, fulfilled a carefully bounded role. The conventions of the lyceum system aimed to immunize lecturers from the perils of the commercial marketplace.

With the emergence of the public lecturing system, economic prosperity in the manufacturing towns allowed the pursuit of culture among all but the poorer inhabitants. The lyceum played a central role, in particular, in the Transcendentalist program of self-culture. Lectures might deal with topics in the public domain—temperance,* slavery, education, reform—but many speakers stressed personal enlightenment rather than grander schemes of social change. One favorite topic, the "ethical" or "spiritual life," was a theme on which Transcendentalist lecturers played multiple variations.

Figures associated with Transcendentalism played roles at every level of lyceum activity: as officers, corresponding secretaries, committee members, sponsors of publications, and lecturers. E. Ripley** founded the Concord* Lyceum, the most intellectually sophisticated of the town bodies, and was its first president. Concord boasted one of the lyceum's most distinguished secretaries (H. Thoreau**), as did the Salem Lyceum (N. Hawthorne**). Scholars of Thoreau have traced the transformation of his "Walden lectures," delivered before audiences in the late 1840s, into chapters of his masterpiece. In the next decade, he used his excursions to Cape Cod and Canada as subjects and tried out a series of nature* essays—"Walking," "Wild Apples," and "Autumnal Tints"—as lectures. His Transcendental essay on "Getting a Living" (i.e., "Life without Principle") and his plea for J. Brown** possess greater resonance if read against the backdrop of the speaking platform.

With the exception of *Essays, First* and *Second Series,* all of Emerson's early essays began as lectures. The subtitle of his *Representative Men,* moreover, reflects its origins in the lyceum: *Seven Lectures.* Advance notices or reviews of his lecture engagements often advertised him as a Transcendentalist, a term sometimes intended as an insult. With considerable frequency, reviewers responded positively to his wit, energy, charm, or demeanor, though many listeners confessed their incomprehension. As a lecturer and essayist, he cultivated a taste for metaphor, paradox, and purposeful discontinuity rather than the more direct address of many of New England's celebrated orators. In decades after the Civil War, he continued to mine materials from lectures for published works. The title of *The Conduct of Life,* for instance, suggests a favorite lyceum topic.

The Civil War, its prelude, and its aftermath had as pronounced an effect on lyceums as on other institutions. As slavery and racial issues occupied speakers on the platform, partisanship increased, and the lyceum ceased to be the force of social cohesion that marked the 1840s and 1850s. After the war, the popular lecture returned in altered form, albeit with greater stress on entertainment rather than instruction, shifts in emphasis Thoreau anticipated two decades earlier. In 1867, the veteran lyceum performer T. W. Higginson** lamented the decline in the quality of public address: Most lectures were "stump speeches," lacking in "enlightenment," "science," or "art" ("A Plea for Culture," *Atlantic Essays,* 5). Mercantile libraries, public schools, and institutions of higher education competed for activities once the exclusive domain of the lyceum. Local groups were supplied with lecturers from central booking agencies, such as J. Redpath's** Boston Lyceum Bureau. By the turn of the century the Chautauqua tent had replaced the lyceum hall, which had devolved into a setting for popular entertainment.

Among notable lyceum speakers were L. Agassiz,** Congregational minister H. W. Beecher, G. W. Curtis,** O. Dewey,** F. Douglass,** C. Dall,** P. Godwin,** temperance advocate John B. Gough, O. W. Holmes,** E. E. Hale,** J. R. Lowell,** W. Phillips,** T. Parker,** travel lecturer and poet Bayard Taylor, and E. P. Whipple.**

REFERENCES: Carl Bode, *The American Lyceum: Town Meeting of the Mind* (1956), can be supplemented by Donald Scott's three essays: "The Popular Lecture and the Creation of a Public in Mid-Nineteenth-Century America," *JAH* 66 (1980): 791–809; "Print and the Public Lecture System, 1840–1860," *Printing and Society in Early America,* ed. John B. Hench, David Hall, and William Joyce (1983), 278–99; and "The Profession that Vanished: Public Lecturing in Mid-Nineteenth-Century America," *Professions and Professional Ideologies in America,* ed. Gerald L. Geison (1983), 12–28. David Mead, *Yankee Eloquence in the Middle West: The Ohio Lyceum 1850–1870* (1951), and Lawrence Buell, *New England Literary Culture* (1986), ch. 6, adopt a regional focus.

Kent P. Ljungquist

M

THE MASSACHUSETTS QUARTERLY REVIEW (1847–1850) was intended to be a mature *Dial**—a "Dial with a Beard" in the words of its founder, chief editor, and principal writer, T. Parker.** When it was first published in 1847, it included articles on reform, biblical scholarship, and other topics that reflected Parker's idiosyncratic interests. R. W. Emerson** reluctantly supplied the "Editor's Address" in the first issue and would be listed for a time as one of the editors. But as neither the responsibility of editing a journal nor the social reform interests of Parker's circle were attractive to him, he soon washed his hands of the project. H. Thoreau,** B. Alcott,** and other distinctive writers from Emerson's *Dial* circle were noticeably absent, as were women writers. Under Parker's direction, the journal promoted liberal democratic thought, often with a loosely Transcendentalist foundation, during its three-year existence. Authors such as W. Phillips** and Samuel Gridley Howe wrote on a range of reform topics including antislavery (the main topic and the real link among the contributors), the Greek revolution, and cheap postage. Although Emerson initially pleaded for a more conspicuous literary character for the journal, literature appeared only marginally in the first volume. Parker eventually filled up to a third of later volumes with literary matter, including some poetry and J. R. Lowell's** review of Thoreau's *A Week on the Concord and Merrimack Rivers.*

Weighted down by heavy seriousness, the *MassQR* never found a wide audience, and when the publisher failed, Parker quietly walked away. Still, the *MassQR* had provided Parker with an outlet for some of his most interesting essays, including his review of Emerson's career, and it had provided a forum for sustaining the Transcendentalist critique of antebellum American society.

REFERENCES: Two useful accounts are Gohdes (1931), 157–93, which includes a listing of articles and known authors; and Mott (1938–57), 1:775–79. Gary L. Collison, *"The MassQR,"* in Chielens (1986), 250–55, concentrates on the evolution of the journal.

Gary L. Collison

MESMERISM emerged in the late 18th century as an alternative to conventional medical treatment. Introducing this remedy, Austrian physician Franz Anton Mesmer (1734–1815) postulated that magnetic currents run through the universe and that extracting them from the ailing individual would effect a cure. To draw forth this energy, Mesmer placed magnets on the patient's ankles and wrists and then laid on hands to bring about healing. In 1775 he presented his theories to the German medical academy, and four years later, he published *Reflections and Discovery of Animal Magnetism*. Mesmer labeled his theory animal magnetism. The Americanized version of this pseudoscience that bears his name resembled more nearly hypnosis, and it made few claims of success as a curative. Rather, thinkers in the United States viewed mesmerism as a gateway to an otherworldliness, a surreal state that heightened the senses and led the person under its influence into new realms of awareness.

Perhaps Charles Caldwell, a midwestern physician and student of Benjamin Rush, assessed most accurately the American version of Mesmer's theory: "It is a well known fact that mesmerism gives striking invigoration and exaltation to the intellectual and moral faculties" (*Facts in Mesmerism and Thoughts on Its Causes & Uses* [1842]). During the heady days of reformist idealism* in the 30 years before the Civil War, the mesmeristic experience meshed with the zeitgeist. Among Transcendentalists, though, the phenomenon received mixed reviews. B. Alcott** was perhaps most drawn to mesmerism. Along the same lines as Caldwell, he found animal magnetism helpful in deciphering the relationship between "spirit and matter." At the other extreme, R. W. Emerson** distrusted mesmerism and the hypnotic state. He went so far as to cast it into the pit with demonology because he saw in it the danger of control of the sacrosanct mind by another.

N. Hawthorne** fell between the Alcott/Emerson poles. As he often did with pure science and the pseudosciences, Hawthorne vacillated between fascination with and disdain for mesmerism. He lost quickly his initial captivation with it when mesmeristic healers gained the reputation as sexual exploiters. Thus, while E. Peabody** encouraged, he discouraged Sophia's** seeking help from such a "professional" to cure her headaches. He questions more than a little the validity of this form of control in *The Blithedale Romance* (1852) when he describes Westervelt's power over Priscilla. Less damning perhaps is his treatment of mesmerism in *The House of the Seven Gables* (1851).

REFERENCES: A good introduction is Robert C. Fuller, *Mesmerism and the American Cure of Souls* (1982), which considers scientific, psychological, and literary aspects. Focused more narrowly, Maria Tator, *Spellbound: Studies in Mesmerism and Literature* (1978), studies a wide range of authors and their use of the subject. Dahlstrand (1982) touches on mesmerism in a section on Fruitlands.* David S. Reynolds, *Beneath the American Renaissance* (1989), makes passing references to mesmerism but is invaluable in placing it within the cultural milieu.

E. Kate Stewart

MICROCOSM appears by name only once each in R. W. Emerson's** *Nature* (1836) and in H. Thoreau's** *Walden* (1854), but it is a significant concept for these Transcendentalists as well as for W. Whitman.** The word is taken from the late Greek, *mikros kosmos* (small world). *The Oxford English Dictionary* explains its meaning as (1) the "little world" of human nature—man viewed as an epitome of the "great world" or universe (the Macrocosm); and (2) in an extended sense, a community or other complex unity regarded as presenting an epitome of the world. It means, in short, a world in miniature, a part of a larger whole. The Transcendentalists use the word, or—more significantly—the concept, to express their Platonic* view that they as individual human souls are part of what Emerson called "the Over-Soul" and that particular natural facts (microcosms) are symbols of the spiritual or ideal* world.

Emerson in the chapter "Discipline" in *Nature* develops this concept in some detail: "[A] leaf, a drop, a crystal, a moment of time is related to the whole, and partakes of the perfection of the whole. Each particle is a microcosm, and faithfully renders the likeness of the world." (Emerson's poem "Each and All" embodies the same view. It lies at the core of his doctrine of "Correspondence."*) As Emerson defines his view of "the Unity of Nature,—the Unity in Variety,—which meets us everywhere," he adds, "All the endless variety of things make a unique, an identical impression." Then he vividly illustrates this concept: "Xenophanes complained in his old age, that, look where he would, all things hastened back to Unity. He was weary of seeing the same entity in the tedious variety of forms."

Thoreau uses the word *microcosm* in *Walden* near the end of the chapter "Economy." In its context Thoreau is describing the illogical projection of a philanthropist—the target of his satire—who because he has an upset stomach therefore thinks the world as a whole must have a similar ailment. In his caustic style Thoreau writes: "If any thing ail a man, so that he does not perform his functions, if he have a pain in his bowels even . . . he forthwith sets about re-forming . . . the world. Being a *microcosm* himself [my emphasis], he discovers . . . that the world has been eating green apples; to his eyes, in fact, the globe itself is a great green apple." Thoreau is taking the obverse view of Emerson, but with the same concept in mind—not that we individual humans are part of the bigger (spiritual) world; rather, that we should *not* project our own selves onto the rest of the world in do-gooder philanthropic or reform efforts.

Whitman, more even than Emerson, employs the concept of himself as a microcosm, an exemplum of the whole creation. Whitman's narrating "I" becomes, progressively and variously, an Everyman, an Everywoman; past, present, and future Humankind. In canto 44 of "Song of Myself" he claims: "I am an acme of things accomplish'd, and I an encloser of things to be." In his fullest expression of evolution, Whitman claims:

> For it [my embryo] the nebula cohered to an orb,
> The long slow strata piled to rest it on,
> Vast vegetables gave it sustenance,

Monstrous sauroids [dinosaurs] transported it in their mouths and deposited it
  with care,
All forces have been steadily employ'd to complete and delight me,
Now on this spot I stand with my robust soul.

Whitman clearly saw himself as a world in himself, a miniature epitome of the
universe. In canto 24 of "Song of Myself" he sings of this microcosm: "Walt
Whitman, a kosmos, of Manhattan the son . . . Divine am I inside and out, and
I make holy whatever I touch or am touch'd from."

REFERENCE: See George Perrigo Conger, *Theories of Macrocosms and Microcosms in the History of Philosophy* (1922).

Reid Huntley

MILLERISM derived from the millennial preachings of William Miller (1782–
1849). Millerites believed in the Second Coming of Christ and the possibility
of projecting the date of the advent. As premillennialists, they trusted that the
appearance of Christ would initiate 1,000 years of paradise on earth and accepted
Miller's prediction that the Second Coming would occur on 22 October 1844.
Like Transcendentalism, Millerite belief was rooted in an expectation of cosmic
unity and balance, the idea of historical recurrence, the good example of the
ideal,* and the embodiment of the absolute good. The early phase of Millerism
coincided with the surge of Transcendentalism in New England and shares the
religious motive that is at its center. The movement was part of a pattern of
fervent religious, utopian, and millenarian movements in New York State and
New England that ignited "the burned-over district" of central New York, extending to Buffalo and into Ohio, a region scorched by revivalist activity of the
Second Great Awakening.

Millerites, more than any adventists of the period, grounded their prophecy
exclusively in the Bible, stayed closest to Calvinism, and extended fundamen-
talist orthodoxy. Miller's predictions were based in a complicated biblical exegesis, an emphasis on a specific date for the advent, and a vision of society as
corrupt. Miller himself was descended from a line of Baptist preachers, although
he strayed from orthodoxy into deism at an early age. Educated in common-
school, he read widely. After a decade of farming in western Vermont, he served
in the military during the War of 1812, from which he returned with an eye on
the last things. His war experiences left him receptive to evangelism, and a local
revival meeting in 1816 led him back to the Baptist Church while his religious
zeal manifested in close study of Scripture. In 1832, Miller was licensed as a
Baptist preacher.

Miller himself was not particularly charismatic, but his predictions and
preaching touched the fears of easterners aroused by evangelical religion and
distressed by economic, social, and natural troubles. Between 1839 and 1843,
Miller's millennial message was spread throughout the Northeast using the organizational skills of the Rev. Joshua V. Himes and "the Great Tent"—55

feet high at the center, with a capacity of 4,000. There were probably at least 50,000 Millerites at the height of the enthusiasm. Most of the followers were simple country people hit by the economic and natural disasters that plagued the Northeast between 1810 and 1844: epidemic disease, floods, crop failures, financial disaster, and social change. Although meetings were sometimes held in urban areas, their proselytizing could not maintain the commitment required in cities, and Millerism remained largely a rural movement. Unlike the community at Brook Farm,* the Millerite camps were not havens for intellectuals, ministers, and writers but a temporary source of succor for the depressed and disaffected class of farmers and artisans.

Millerites attempted to find meaning in the assorted calamities that beset the region, to account for suffering among people of piety and faith. Followers had little interest in the economic and political instability in the rest of the country and less concern for abolition.* Millerites felt the foreboding of difficult times and relied on celestial events and biblical prophecy to counter the distress they felt rather than initiating reform strategies and setting up communities as some Transcendentalists did. Their belief that historical events bore symbolic meanings—the transcendent meanings of signs—sent them searching for confirming portents. Like Transcendentalists, the Millerites romanticized spontaneity and privileged emotional religious experience and believed in individual powers of discernment through the ability to understand cosmic truth by fragments of fact blending with conviction and intuition. Millerism bore the paradox of faith that inspiration came to individuals through their separate consciousnesses but that converting the rest of the world to adventist belief required group effort. In part because of this evangelical impulse, the movement never established a large community but was instead a patchwork of tent meetings and prayer groups loosely linked to Miller himself.

After "the Great Disappointment" of 1844, when Christ failed to appear, a few Millerites held fast, meeting in Albany in 1845 to create an adventist organization called the General Conference of the Second Advent Believers of America, which finally dissolved into splinter groups. Some followers joined the Shakers;* others sought utopian communities or adventist congregations elsewhere; still others quietly returned to the Protestant churches that they had left for Millerism. Miller returned to farming in Low Hampton, New York, until his death in 1849.

REFERENCES: The primary source on Miller is Sylvester Bliss, *Memoirs of William Miller, Generally Known as a Lecturer on the Prophecies and the Second Coming of Christ* (1853). An overview of evangelical religion in New York State, Whitney Cross's classic *The Burned-Over District: The Social and Intellectual History of Enthusiastic Religion in Western New York, 1800–1850* (1950) is most accessible. In *Crucible of the Millennium: The Burned-Over District of New York in the 1840's* (1986), Michael Barkun creates the social context for Millerism and explores the various impulses and processes that give rise to such movements. David L. Rowe takes a regional approach and includes a useful bibliographical essay in his book *Thunder and Trumpets: Millerites and Dis-*

senting Religion in Upstate New York, 1800–1850 (1985). In *The Disappointed: Millerism and Millenarianism in the Nineteenth Century* (1987), editors Ronald L. Numbers and Jonathan M. Butler collected essays that place Millerism in the pattern of American religious history and the major cultural forces of the period.

Kate H. Winter

MILTON, JOHN (1608–1674), was highly regarded in 18th-century America. Because colonial and postcolonial Americans believed that his works addressed the same questions of authority they themselves faced in an age of revolutions, they used him to explore the cultural polarities that underlay those questions— what Keith W. F. Stavely has called "the antinomian and Arminian structures of feeling, . . . the longing for liberation and the requirement of discipline and control." This is why from 1770 to 1800 members of the American elite employed *Paradise Lost* to project their confliction (as members of a hierarchical yet revolutionary bourgeois dominant class) between the claims of order and those of liberty; and it is why, later, members of Boston's Unitarian* ruling class similarly invoked M to justify their ideologically consensualist attempt to bridge these structures of feeling.

This Unitarian critical tradition peaked just after 1826, when the rediscovery of M's *De Doctrina Christiana* prompted contributors to the *North American Review** and *Christian Examiner** to hail the poet as a fellow Arian and precursor in the exercise of elite authority through belles lettres. The most famous of these Unitarian responses to the *De Doctrina* was that of W. E. Channing** (1826). Yet while (like his coreligionists) Channing praised M's poetic genius, resistance to tyranny, and anti-Trinitarian theology in order to make him an ally in reasserting Brahmin hegemony, he differed from them due to his greater awareness of the ideological contradictions of consensualism. His M is, consequently, a more divided figure: one whose opposing tendencies to affirm patriarchalism and egalitarianism are never really resolved.

By contrast, R. W. Emerson's** 1835 lecture "JM" (*EL*, 1:144–63) breaks markedly with the Unitarian tradition, rejecting consensualism and revising Channing's *De Doctrina* review point by point so as to create a new model of poetic authority: one in which the ideal poet affirms both order and liberty, the divine and the satanic, the prophetic and the revolutionary (thereby uniting the Arminian and antinomian impulses in New England culture). However, as Emerson himself realized, his portrayal of his subject in "JM" as just such an ideal poet was not wholly successful. Not until the poem "Uriel" did he adequately resolve these structures of feeling in a Miltonic context—significantly, by drawing upon the poet's own exploration of them in *Paradise Lost.*

Other Transcendentalists also used M to explore poetic and cultural authority, most notably: J. Very** in undergraduate exhibitions and notebooks, the essay "Epic Poetry," and the poem "The Dead"; M. Fuller** in an 1845 review of R. W. Griswold's** edition of M's prose; and T. Parker** in a number of addresses and essays. In addition, *The Dial** contains M criticism or imitations by Fuller, Parker, B. Alcott,** W. H. Channing,** J. F. Clarke,** C. P. Cranch,** F. H. Hedge,** and T. T. Stone.** Yet all of them (even Parker and Fuller) follow earlier Unitarian M criticism in figuring the poet as a consensualist authority figure. The one exception is H. D. Thoreau,** who as an undergraduate began breaking with the Unitarian tradition in "The Speeches of Moloch & the Rest," " 'L'Allegro' & 'Il Penseroso,' " and a theme reviewing Henry Nelson Coleridge's *Introductions to the Study of the Greek Classic Poets* (*EEM*, 50–58, 73–83). Later, his allusions to and imitations of "Lycidas" and *Paradise Lost* in *A Week on the Concord and Merrimack Rivers* and *Walden* follow Emerson in bridging the Arminian and antinomian structures of feeling through a redefinition of poetic authority that is at once prophetic and subversive; similarly, his use of M in the "Ktaadn" section of *The Maine Woods* and "The Humane House" passage in *Cape Cod* bespeak his admission of failure in the face of the intractability of his culture's polarization.

REFERENCES: M's reception before 1800 is discussed in Jay Fliegelman, *Prodigals and Pilgrims: The American Revolution Against Patriarchal Authority, 1750–1800* (1982); George Sensabaugh, *M in Early America* (1964); Lydia Dittler Schulman, *"Paradise Lost" and the Rise of the American Republic* (1992); and Stavely, *"Paradise Lost" and the New England Tradition, 1630–1890* (1987). K. P. Van Anglen, *The New England M: Literary Reception and Cultural Authority in the Early Republic* (1993), is the only book-length study of M and the Transcendentalists, but see also Phyllis Cole, "The Purity of Puritanism:* Transcendentalist Readings of M," *SIR* 17 (1978): 129–48; William M. Wynkoop, *Three Children of the Universe: Emerson's View of Shakespeare, Bacon, and M* (1966), 137–77; and Robin Sandra Grey, " 'A Seraph's Eloquence': Emerson's Inspired Language and M's Apocalyptic Prose," *MP* 92 (August 1994): 36–63. In addition to Channing's 1826 *De Doctrina Christiana* review, noteworthy Unitarian commentators on M include John Quincy Adams, W. C. Bryant,** Sidney Willard, F. W. P. Greenwood, A. H. Everett,** John C. Gray, W. S. Shaw, and S. Osgood** (for bibliographical references and discussion, see Van Anglen, 53–108). On M in *The Dial* and in the works of Very, Fuller, and Parker, see Van Anglen, 161–88.

Kevin P. Van Anglen

The **MIRACLES CONTROVERSY** (otherwise known as the Transcendentalist Controversy) was a public debate between Transcendentalists and conservative Unitarians* that took place mainly from 1836 to 1841. The debate served to define Transcendentalism as a movement and eventually enlisted most of its ablest spokesmen, including G. Ripley,** R. W. Emerson,** T. Parker,** O. A. Brownson,** J. F. Clarke,** C. P. Cranch,** and W. H. Channing** (aided by such temporary allies as W. H. Furness,** S. Osgood,** and R. Hildreth**). The Unitarian opposition included A. Norton,** O. Dewey,** M. L. Hurlbut,** and F. Bowen** (aided by temporary orthodox allies J. W. Alexander, A. Dod,** and C. Hodge,** and the Swedenborgian* S. Reed**). The debate centered on the nature and status of miracles in Christianity but quickly encompassed other fundamental differences over epistemology, human nature, and social and political ideals.

For conservative Unitarians, Christ's miracles were the mainstay and validation of Christianity, and to question them in any way was to impugn Christ's authority as a divine messenger of truth. As ex-dean of the Harvard Divinity School* and the so-called Unitarian Pope, Norton stated in *A Discourse on the Latest Form of Infidelity* (1839), "Nothing is left that can be called Christianity, if its miraculous character be denied." Hence, he pronounced the Transcendentalists atheists. The Transcendentalists believed, however, that the orthodox faith in the historicity of miracles ignored the miraculous nature of creation, a point made by both Furness in *Remarks on the Four Gospels* (1836) and Emerson in the Divinity School Address (1838). According to Emerson, "[T]he very word Miracle, as pronounced by Christian churches, gives a false impression; it is Monster. It is not one with the blowing clover and the falling rain."

At stake in the controversy were diametrically opposed epistemological assumptions. The most conservative Unitarians were, on the one hand, firm adherents of Lockean* sensationalism.* They believed that the truth of Christianity could not be perceived innately; instead, only empirical evidence could attest to its supernatural revelation, and Christ's miracles were their favorite evidence. As Norton declared in *A Discourse on the Latest Form of Infidelity,* "There can be no intuition, no direct perception, of the truth of Christianity, no metaphysical certainty. . . . There is . . . no mode of establishing religious belief, but by the exercise of reason." Norton sought through rigorous scholarship to establish the truth of Christianity in his masterpiece *Evidences of the Genuineness of the Gospels* (3 vols., 1837–44). The Transcendentalists, on the other hand, disparaged rational thinking (which they called the "understanding") in favor of intuition (or "transcendental Reason," a term derived from I. Kant*). As Emerson proclaimed in the Divinity School Address, "There is no doctrine of the Reason that will bear to be taught by the Understanding." Accordingly, the Transcendentalists believed that Lockean empiricism could lead only to skepticism, for nothing could prove that Christ's miracles were authentic except prior faith in Christ. Moreover, Ripley argued in *The Latest Form of Infidelity Examined* (1839) that scholarship neither ensures infallibility nor necessarily enhances the perception of Christian truth, which God "has hid . . . from the wise" yet revealed to the uneducated.

Underlying these epistemological positions were radically different views of human nature. The conservative Unitarians regarded people, although rational, as essentially ignorant and fallible and therefore in need of supernatural revelation. Thus, in *A Discourse on the Latest Form of Infidelity,* Norton described a human being as a mere "creature of a day . . . [who] cannot pretend to attain, by his unassisted powers, any assurance concerning the unseen and the eternal." The Transcendentalists, however, saw people as godlike, self-reliant, and capable of direct apprehension of truth. Thus, Parker argued in *The Previous Question Between Mr. Andrews Norton and His Alumni* (1840) that people are converted not by miracles but rather by appeal to truths inherent in the soul. For Parker, the evidence of miracles was both unreliable and irrelevant.

In addition, the Miracles Controversy entailed diverging social and political views. Norton direly warned in "The New School in Literature and Religion" (Boston *Daily Advertiser,* 27 August 1838) that by controverting established Christian doctrines, Transcendentalism threatened both human society and happiness. He and others also condemned Transcendentalism as un-American because of its presumed genesis in French and German thought, which, they maintained, was obscure, illogical, and deluded. Ripley responded in *The Latest Form of Infidelity Examined* that Transcendentalism was actually a homegrown American movement, although he then defended at length the slighted French and German thinkers. Brownson argued in "Ripley's Specimens" (published in his own journal, *BoQR,** 1838) that French and German thought was needed to combat the predominant English influence on American writers. However, in "Francis Bowen" (1838) and "Norton's Evidence" (1839), Brownson countercharged that it was Norton and his conservative allies who were un-American and undemocratic, for, as Lockeans, they denied the American people's capacity for perceiving truth and thus regarded the masses with suspicion and contempt. Moreover, the Transcendentalists generally observed that doctrinal insistence on the historicity of miracles led merely to dogmatism and uninspired preaching, which could only impair the ministry.

The Miracles Controversy culminated in an open breach between the Transcendentalists and the conservative faction of the Unitarian Church. Although the controversy had no formal resolution, the Transcendentalists, as Charles Crowe has observed, "emerged as a group . . . with greater consciousness of basic aims—intuitional philosophy, antiformalistic religion, and tolerance of all opinions," and their views had a greater lasting influence.

REFERENCES: The major contributions to the Miracles Controversy are reprinted with commentary in Miller (1950). Two excellent critical overviews are Charles Crowe, *George Ripley: Transcendentalist and Utopian Socialist* (1967), 97–123; and William R. Hutchison, "Ripley, Emerson, and the Miracles Question," in *American Transcendentalism: An Anthology of Criticism,* ed. Brian M. Barbour (1973), 179–209. For further information on Ripley, see Henry L. Golemba, *George Ripley* (1977), esp. 26–63; on Emerson, see John McAleer, *Ralph Waldo Emerson: Days of Encounter* (1984), 245–66. Diane Grooters examines Parker's role in the controversy in her unpublished "Theodore Parker and the Miracles Issue" (M.A. Thesis, West Texas State Univ., 1980); John Edward Dirks explains Parker's theology more fully in *The Critical Theology of Theodore Parker* (1948; rpt. 1970), 66–110. Robert D. Habich analyzes Norton's motives in "Emerson's Reluctant Foe: Andrews Norton and the Transcendental Controversy," *NEQ* 65 (1992): 208–37.

                                                                    Terry J. Martin

MONTAIGNE, MICHEL EYQUEM DE (1533–1592), French Renaissance humanist, philosopher, and essayist, was such a favorite author of R. W. Emerson** that he made "M; or, The Skeptic" the central essay of his *Representative Men* (1850). One may see M as Emerson's inspiration for the genre of his own essays or as a philosophical influence on his thought. The two writers reveal similarities in their literary form, humanism, skepticism, and textual self-consciousness. M's assertions of the autonomy of the self could be mistaken for Emerson's. Rhetorically, as well, M's "yes and no" approach to ideas, his famous zigzags or "undulations," seem to prefigure many of Emerson's dialectical strategies; neither writer gets spooked by "foolish consistency."

Emerson read the 1588 *Essays* not in John Florio's first English translation of 1603 but in Charles Cotton's 1685 standard for the 18th and 19th centuries, in its second and third editions (1693 and 1700). "In M; or, The Skeptic" Emerson relates his initial reaction to the French essayist: "It seemed to me as if I had myself written the book in some former life, so sincerely it spoke to my thought and experience."

But Emerson's "M" is less a portrait than a highly selective sketch. Emerson praises M's "independence . . . economy . . . sense . . . probity . . . liberality" and his openness to both sides in the religious civil wars that raged around him. He enjoys the Frenchman's virile extroversion. But considering his often-quoted praise for M's style, "Cut these words, and they would bleed; they are vascular and alive," it is surprising how few of those words Emerson quotes: the *Que sçais je?* motto (twice), two ironic confessions, and one satiric thrust at marriage. Further, Emerson's critical summation may sound tepid: "[M's] writing has no enthusiasms, no aspiration; contented, selfrespecting, and keeping the middle of the road." It is, however, as a "middle of the road" thinker that M's influence on Emerson is most frequently cited in recent scholarship.

REFERENCES: Donald M. Frame, *The Complete Works* (1957), is the current standard edition of M in English, and his is the standard life, *M: A Biography* (1965). Marcel Tetel, *M: Updated Edition* (1990), provides sophisticated analysis of M's thought and art throughout the *Essays*. Charles Lowell Young, *Emerson's M* (1941), dated in approach, still offers sound points of departure. Barbara Packer, *Emerson's Fall: A New Interpretation of the Major Essays* (1982), 199–211, insightfully explores M's "Middle Way" in Emerson's later thought. John Michael, *Emerson and Skepticism: The Cipher of the World* (1988), 105–40, offers new arguments, biographical as well as textual, to support the old influence.

Richard R. O'Keefe

THE MONTHLY ANTHOLOGY, published from 1803 to 1811, was a monthly journal of science, theology, literature, travel, and history. Though its successes were modest, it set a pattern for Boston literary culture of the 19th century and marked the beginning of New England's rise to literary prominence.

Founded in 1803 by David Phineas Adams as *The Monthly Anthology; or Magazine of Polite Literature,* its editorship passed in 1804 to William Emerson, father of R. W. Emerson.** The magazine's title changed as well, to *The Monthly Anthology: or, Massachusetts Magazine,* and then, a few months later, to *The Monthly Anthology, and Boston Review.* Emerson asked a group of friends to help him edit the magazine; this arrangement was formalized in 1805 with the formation of the Anthology Society, a committee of young intellectuals,

most of them Harvard graduates, who together edited and wrote for the magazine. The *Anthology* was eclectic, with articles and reviews on topics ranging
from 18th-century literature to a new algorithm for determining a cube root.

Although the editors were interested in furthering American intellectual culture, their standards were emphatically European. Most were theologically liberal and embraced progress in science, but they lamented the neglect of classical
learning "in this age of innovation" (IV: 1). Noah Webster's grammar and
dictionary were excoriated in the pages of the magazine, whose editors "dep-
recate[d] every instance of diversity between the language of conversation in
England and their country" (VI: 263). Indeed, wrote one reviewer, "we scorn
the notion of an American tongue, or of gaining our idiom from the mouths of
the illiterate, rather than from the pages of Milton,* Dryden, Swift, Addison,
Pope" and a number of lesser British luminaries (V: 277). And John Sylvester
John Gardiner asserted that "all sensible Americans will rely on the great writers
of that [English] nation as authorities, till we can produce equal excellence."

Nevertheless, this belief in the possibility of American excellence qualified
the conservatism of the editors. Despite their neoclassical aesthetic and their
embrace of European standards, Lewis P. Simpson points out that the editors
believed that they were advancing the progress of letters. Aided by *The Monthly
Anthology,* they believed, culture would move westward across the ocean, and
forward in time, and would ultimately redeem society.

The Monthly Anthology itself did not survive to witness this redemption. Editing by committee proved cumbersome, and enthusiasm for the project varied
with the quality of the dinners served at meetings. Moreover, friendships among
the editors sometimes impeded their productivity; minutes of several meetings
describe social gatherings rather than business meetings, with reports that "no
business of any kind was transacted." Following a series of financial disputes
with several different printers, the *Anthology* published its final issue in June
1811.

Nevertheless, *The Monthly Anthology*'s legacy was considerable. In 1805, the
Anthology Society voted to establish a library and reading room. Modeled on
the Liverpool Athenaeum, the library was originally for the use of the society's
members but was opened to other subscribers as well. On 7 April 1807, it was
chartered by the state legislature as the Boston Athenaeum.* Josiah Quincy also
credited the *Anthology* with originating "two independent currents of journalism—one religious but liberal, the other literary and critical." In the first category are Noah Worcester's *Christian Disciple,* which became *The Christian
Examiner,* and the *General Repository and Review,* founded by A. Norton,**
a member of the Anthology Society. The latter category includes both the *North
American Review,* founded by society member William Tudor, and *The Dial.*
Moreover, R. W. Emerson wrote to his brother on 10 February 1850 that his
father's "literary merits" were "really . . . that he fostered the Anthology & the
Athenaeum. These things ripened into Buckminster* [W. E.] Channing** & [E.]
Everett."**

REFERENCES: For history of *The Monthly Anthology* and of the Anthology Society, see the *Journal of the Proceedings of the Anthology Society,* ed. and intro. M. A. DeWolfe Howe (1910); Mott (1938–57); Lewis P. Simpson, *The Federalist Literary Mind* (1962); and Lawrence Buell, *New England Literary Culture: From Revolution through Renaissance* (1986). See also Josiah Quincy, *History of the Boston Athenaeum, with Biographical Notices of Its Deceased Founders* (1851), and Ronald Story, "Class and Culture in Boston: The Athenaeum, 1807–1860," *AQ* 27 (May 1975): 178–99.

Lisa M. Gordis

MORAL PHILOSOPHY, or ethics, is fundamental to New England Transcendentalism. In the 17th and 18th centuries, J. Locke* and D. Hume* iterated developments in the theory of knowledge that were connected to changing beliefs about the relation of God to the world. If morality did not have to be related to a divine source, the logical place to search for the source of morality was in human nature. Thomas Hobbes (1588–1679) had believed that the concepts of good and evil are relative, having meaning only to the persons using them. When people are joined together in a society, the society determines what is good and what is evil. Ultimately, whether personal or societal, morality has only one motive—self-interest. Hobbes believed that if a person's or a society's preservation depends on doing what others call evil, that person or society will pursue it anyway, calling it good. Furthermore, he said, only fear of punishment deters the human being from the practice of evil. In response to Hobbes, Hume and others argued that human nature is not naturally depraved but benevolent. Within each person is a moral sense that allows that person to distinguish between good and evil. This sense and the natural propensity for virtue allow morality to exist. These philosophers did little, however, to counter the charge that morality is relative.

Other philosophers argued that the faculty that allows us to discern right from wrong is Reason or Understanding. They believed morality is unchanging and unchangeable, free from human or divine determination. I. Kant* asserted that morality is Reason in action and said that people have a duty to follow moral law as it is revealed to them through Reason. The moral law is universal and not derived from experience. In the struggle between duty and desire, it is necessary for humans to have the freedom to act according to Reason, to have time in which to carry out the struggle, and to have assurance that the moral struggle is meaningful. Kant's emphasis on duty, moral law, and the primacy of idealism* over utilitarianism played an important part in the Transcendentalists' moral philosophy. They also were influenced by the idealistic German philosophers J. C. Fichte* and F. Schelling** and theologians like Friedrich Schleiermacher,** all of whom were indebted to Kant.

R. W. Emerson's,** G. Ripley's,** and W. H. Channing's** resignations from their pulpits and H. Thoreau's** "resignation from all institutions" were responses to the conflict they perceived between the morality espoused by institutions and morality revealed to them. They believed that having been blessed with something variously called Reason (Intuition), the "inner light," the divine spirit, or the moral sense, each human being had to be responsible for his or her own moral philosophy. Doing good to avoid punishment or because it was required by a religious or governmental institution was ultimately not to do good at all.

The expression of moral philosophy varied from person to person in the Transcendental circle. The reader unfamiliar with the background of Emerson's essay "Self-Reliance" might find the ideas expounded there reprehensible or, at best, advocating a kind of moral relativism. For Emerson, however, being true to his nature means being true to his divine nature, to his Higher Self or the Over-Soul of which he is a part. The moral absolute to which he ascribes will never allow him to err as long as he is true to that nature. When Thoreau castigates benevolent societies, he does not deny social responsibility. He makes a distinction between doing good and being good, between performing charitable acts and being a charitable person. Indeed, he says, those who give the most money to charitable causes are usually those whose way of life keeps people in need of charity.

It was not easy to live by Transcendental principles. Moral reform of the individual had to precede moral reform of the society. One has only to peruse the journals* of Emerson and Thoreau for a while to be impressed with how assiduously they take themselves to task for shortcomings and failures to live up to their moral standards. No Puritan* divine ever examined his soul more diligently. The journals and letters of the Transcendentalists reveal that they were not without the usual human complement of petty jealousies, foibles, and mean spiritedness, but they attempted to live up to the higher laws.*

REFERENCES: Miller (1950) is a convenient resource for the Transcendentalists' statements of moral philosophy. Emerson's "Self-Reliance" and Thoreau's "Civil Disobedience" are essential to an understanding of their moral beliefs. Richard J. Petersen, "Scottish Common Sense* in America, 1768–1850: An Evaluation of Its Influence" (Diss., American Univ., 1964), explores the relationship between the principal philosophy taught in American universities in the 18th and 19th centuries and the moral beliefs of the Transcendentalists. Howe (1970) is indispensable. Paul F. Boller, Jr., *American Transcendentalism* (1974), provides an overview of Transcendentalists' ideas, including moral philosophy.

Mariane Wurst Schaum

N

NATURAL HISTORY would seem to be an oxymoron, given that nature,* Transcendentally speaking, is that which *has* no history. In a typical natural moment, the Indian Summer halcyon that opens "Nature," R. W. Emerson** declared: "The incommunicable trees begin to persuade us to live with them, and quit our life of solemn trifles. Here no history, or church, or state, is interpolated on the divine sky and the immortal year." H. Thoreau,** too, sought in nature a locus of the "real" below the "mud and slush of opinion," intending, as he stated in *Walden,* to burrow downward through the "alluvion" of history and tradition, church and state, to the natural core, "till we come to a hard bottom and rocks in place, which we can call *reality,* and say, This is, and no mistake." Yet during their lifetimes the presumption that nature was timeless and changeless yielded to physical evidence of change and scientific theories of evolutionary transformation. The result is an internal tension that linked Transcendentalism and natural history in productive and complex ways.

The medieval concept of natural history predates the modern separation of natural and human into distinct realms, specifying that zone in which nature intersects with human needs and desires, as in compilations of herbal lore or catalogs of a region's useful natural productions. From it emerged the sciences of geology, biology, botany and zoology, and much later, ecology. In effect, natural history was the empirical side of "natural philosophy," which through theory, experimentation, and mathematical reduction sought the underlying, explanatory scientific laws.

Both natural history and natural philosophy were closely allied to natural theology:* Describing and classifying the productions of nature meant understanding the designful beauty of God's creation. Hence, natural history was familiarly practiced by divines such as W. Paley* and Gilbert White, but it was open to any student of God's creation, from the gentleman amateur (such as Goethe**) to the lady botanist. Yet at the same time, "naturalists" such as

Humboldt,** Lyell,** Gray,** and Darwin** were establishing geophysics, geology, botany, and zoology as separate, specialized fields of research demanding professional training. One result of the professionalization of natural science was the amateurization of natural history, which acquired the status of a harmless, morally uplifting, and instructive popular diversion. Emerson benefited from the widespread interest, but self-taught naturalists like Thoreau were relegated to amateur status.

As the titles of White's *Natural History of Selborne* (1788–89) and Thoreau's *Walden* suggest, natural history is tied to the specificities of place, interpreted by a human observer. By contrast, the goals of science tended toward the formulation of abstract and universal laws, which would be true quite apart from local variations of place. Paradoxically, while such study was dedicated to recovering a timeless, universal nature entirely pure of history, many of the developing natural sciences were demonstrating that nature was characterized by change. Thus, nature was increasingly seen as having its own history quite independent of human concerns. Many scientists resisted the implications; evidence of geological change and catastrophic extinctions challenged one of the guiding metaphors of natural theology, the "balance of nature," which guaranteed a static natural economy, eternally faithful to an ideal divine design. Emerson alludes to this doctrine in his reassurance, in the opening of *Nature*, that all man's operations on nature are so insignificant that "they do not vary the result." But Thoreau, less sanguinely, noticed that man was altering the balance of nature; where in Concord* were the bears and beavers of old? Such observations would ultimately lead Darwin to postulate that nature was constituted by change, writing its own history in every leaf and bone. Everywhere was evidence of adaptation and historical contingency.

The prospect of a historical nature complicated the Transcendental belief in the metaphysical correspondence* of nature and spirit. Though derived from sources as widespread as natural theology, Platonic* essentialism, and Swedenborgian* mysticism, Emerson's key insight came at the Jardin des Plantes in Paris in 1833. In "The Uses of Natural History," delivered soon after to the Boston Society of Natural History, he explained how as he stood there he was "impressed with a singular conviction that not a form so grotesque, so savage, or so beautiful, but is an expression of something in man the observer." He concluded: "I say I will listen to this invitation. I will be a naturalist." While Emerson soon dropped this ambition, he continued to read widely in the natural sciences, seeking the latest information on the "occult relation" between man and nature. "The Naturalist" became his poetic mediator between theory and fact, seeker of "the Idea in the particulars, the Type in the manifold forms," ever open to their beauty and moral truth. Emerson was deeply receptive to the German *Naturphilosophen* such as F.W.J. Schelling** and L. Oken,** in whom he found corroboration for his belief in the harmonious organic* unity of a nature ever striving upward toward the human form.

While Emerson's interest centered on the underlying and unifying law that he knew science would ultimately find, Thoreau turned increasingly toward the particulars of place. In 1842 Emerson directed Thoreau to write a review article, "The Natural History of Massachusetts," in which Thoreau named his own guiding principle: "Let us not underrate the value of a fact; it will one day flower in a truth." The effort to show the universal and absolute truth in the historical and contingent fact governed Thoreau's early work, but over time the transcendentalizing of facts shifted into a different mode, one that sought less to normalize particulars into an a priori framework than to respond to each natural object in its particularity and understand the relatedness of all natural objects and phenomena to each other and to himself. His late natural history writings—"Walking," "Wild Apples," "Succession of Forest Trees," and others—show Thoreau combining traditional natural histories, such as those of the ancient Greeks and the American Indians, with the emerging environmental sciences: the former tracing the history of the association of man and nature, the latter stressing the history of nature apart from man. While natural science in America was turning professional under the auspices of L. Agassiz** at Harvard, Thoreau kept himself on the fringes, joining the Boston Society of Natural History and overworking himself with his private study and research. When he died, the town clerk listed his occupation as "natural historian."

The paradox of Transcendental natural history is illustrated by the careers of Emerson and Thoreau. While both maintained a lively interest in modern science, Emerson's interest was primarily theoretical and metaphysical; he helped popularize "science" as the search for transcendent natural law, privileging the study of nature outside history. Thoreau worked to honor and understand specific natural systems and thus became a practicing natural historian, locally famous in his own time, and afterwards nationally renowned, his essays both model and inspiration for American writing about nature.

REFERENCES: The reader interested in Emerson and natural history should turn first to his four early science lectures, printed in *EL,* 1:1–83; then to David M. Robinson, "Fields of Investigation: Emerson and Natural History," in *American Literature and Science,* ed. Robert J. Scholnick (1992), 94–109. See also Lee Rust Brown, "The Emerson Museum," *Representations* 40 (fall 1992): 57–80; and Elizabeth A. Dant, "Composing the World: Emerson and the Cabinet of Natural History," *NCL* 44 (June 1989): 18–44. A rigorous philosophical introduction is in Leon Chai, *The Romantic Foundations of the American Renaissance* (1987), 141–55. A useful collection of Thoreau's essays is *Natural History Essays,* ed. Robert Sattelmeyer (1980); see also Thoreau, *Faith in a Seed: The Dispersion of Seeds and Other Late Natural History Writings,* ed. Bradley P. Dean (1993). Major works considering Thoreau and natural science include John Hildebidle, *Thoreau: A Naturalist's Liberty* (1983); William Howarth, *The Book of Concord* (1982); and Robert Sattelmeyer, *Thoreau's Reading* (1988). See also Robert D. Richardson, Jr., "Thoreau and Science," in *American Literature and Science,* ed. Robert J. Scholnick (1992), 110–27. Other recent work appears in *Thoreau's World and Ours,* ed. Edmund A. Schofield and Robert C. Baron (1993); a revisionist interpretation is offered by Laura Dassow Walls, *Seeing New Worlds: Thoreau and 19th-Century Natural Science* (1995).

Laura Dassow Walls

NATURAL RELIGION/THEOLOGY is a long-standing and many-sided Christian doctrinal tradition that argues that the unified and lawfully ordered design of nature* proves the existence of a divine Designer. Human reason, by studying nature or "the Book of God's Works," can determine both the existence and attributes of God—though as young R. W. Emerson** warned in sermons, natural religion was "imperfect" without revealed religion.

The rationalistic argument from design was of fundamental importance to Anglo-American religious and scientific traditions and was a basic component of the Unitarian* faith. Generations of Harvard students conned W. Paley's* *Natural Theology* (1802), which Henry Ware, Sr., taught from 1805 to 1838. Emerson's familiarity with the doctrine is everywhere evident; even his arguments with it are defined from within its tolerant and expansive embrace. Only from a later perspective could O. B. Frothingham** write that the Transcendentalist had "small respect for the labored reasonings of 'Natural Religion.' "

The British tradition of natural theology received much of its prestige from Newton's success in describing the universe as a divinely created machine bound by determinative laws. To John Ray (*The Wisdom of God Manifested in the Works of Creation* [1691]), science that studied the marvels of nature could be a form of religious worship—inspiring many a parson-naturalist, in a tradition that included Gilbert White of Selborne (whom H. Thoreau** read and admired), that nearly included C. Darwin,** and that arguably included Emerson.

Paley's *Natural Theology* brought the ancient tradition into the industrial age, synthesizing Newton and Ray by arguing that animals, too, were machines. In Paley's famous analogy, one who stumbled across a watch upon the ground would be compelled to infer "that the watch must have had a maker . . . who comprehended its construction, and designed its use" (ch. 1). Just so must one infer from the marvellous contrivances of the animal body: The eye, for instance, clearly was an instrument for vision designed along the same principles as the telescope. Paley argued that the Divine Designer of these ingenious constructions has a mind commensurate with ours; as Emerson wrote, "[N]ature proceeds from a mind analogous to our own." Moreover, the overall design is beneficial, for the deity has superadded pleasure beyond what was necessary: "It is a happy world after all" (ch. 26). To what end? "It is for the soul of man," Emerson affirms in Sermon XXXIX; "If there were no mind in the Universe, to what purpose this profusion of design? It is adapted to give pleasure to us."

The natural laws described by Newton and celebrated by Paley were the mirror and model for the divinely legislated moral laws of society. As Emerson makes clear, one studies nature not for its own sake but to learn about the place of man in God's creation. It is not the evidence of nature that leads to a belief in God, he observes in Sermon XLIII, but knowledge of the presence of God that explains the evidence of our senses, that throws all things "in a new light as parts of God's agency—nothing is insignificant, for every thing is a part of the mighty whole." God is like the magnet that, once introduced into a pile of steel filings, "the rubbish becomes instantly instinct with life and order. Every particle at once finds its own place." Yet he declared in "Nominalist and Realist," our attention is to rest on neither magnet nor filings but on the ordering force: "The magnetism which arranges tribes and races in one polarity, is alone to be respected; the men are steel-filings. . . . Let us go for universals; for the magnetism, not for the needles." The fault of natural theology lay in its focus on sensual evidence, its endless arguments about contrivances. Where, asked T. Parker,** was God? Natural religion fixes "a great gulf . . . over which there passes, neither God nor man."

The alternative was not to reject natural theology but to redefine it in dynamic, organic* terms. Paley lost favor as mechanistic imagery lost its appeal. During his trip to Europe in 1833, Emerson found displayed before him, in the botanical garden of the Paris Museum of Natural History, the new unity of nature as a dynamic and progressive system: "I am thrilled with delight by the choral harmony of the whole. Design! It is all design. It is all beauty. It is all astonishment." This evidence pointed not to a God beyond us but to the God within us; the lawful unity of nature "corresponds* to this unity in the mind, and makes it available. . . . Hence, the possibility of Science."

Emerson went on to explore the leading edge of a new natural theology that saw design in nature as spirit precipitating itself in matter. Dynamic nature's divine plan was explicated by writers ranging from Coleridge** to the German *Naturphilosophen,* Lyell,** Chambers, Owen, and Agassiz.** Conservatives responded with conventional natural theology; in the 1830s, the "Bridgewater Treatises" were commissioned to update Paley and show authoritatively the "Power, Wisdom, and Goodness of God, as manifested in the Creation." While Emerson owned two of the treatises (Charles Bell's *The Hand* [1835] and Peter Mark Roget's *Animal and Vegetable Physiology* [1836]), the absurdity of the Earl of Bridgewater's gesture earned a dig from Thoreau, who (in *A Week*) found the authors' insistent religion "offensive to the nostrils. . . . There is more religion in men's science than there is science in their religion." Yet what united all these authors, clerics, and scientists was a fundamental belief in the wisdom of divine design, whether evident in the products of nature or in the processes of natural law; science caused not the demise of natural theology but its diversification.

What undid natural theology was the growing irrelevance of both its questions and its working methods. Darwin had used the assumptions of natural theology against itself, turning Paley inside-out to show that design was merely an appearance, an anthropocentric interpretation read onto natural mechanisms— worse, those so-called perfect mechanisms were in reality flawed, inefficient, and redundant. "Harmony" was a cosmic joke. Thermodynamics further undermined providential design, as entropy suggested the eventual and inevitable heat death of the universe.

The fatal weakness of natural theology was that in turning to nature for evidence of God, it had made religion dependent on naturalistic thinking. As Frothingham said, the "labored reasonings" of natural religion did not go far enough: Evidence of the senses could not provide belief in God. The success of evolutionary theory and the collapse of the design argument left two separate and noncommunicating realms of truth, one scientific and one spiritual. Ironically, the bulwarks of natural theology had been erected and buttressed over the course of centuries precisely to avert such a fate, to keep the material and the moral universes coherent.

REFERENCES: Since natural theology united philosophy, science, and religion, much of the literature bears on it. For examples of the argument from design, see Emerson's *Sermons,* 1:296–300; 2:19–24, 138–43. *Nature (CW,* 1:7–45) advances the argument into its dynamic phase; intermediate steps may be found in his early lectures on science (*EL,* 1:1–83; 2:22–40). Parker considers "Naturalism" at length in *A Discourse of Matters Pertaining to Religion* (1842). For a retrospective discussion, see Frothingham (1876), 184–217. For current historical and critical discussions of natural theology, see John Hedley Brooke, *Science and Religion* (1991), passim but esp. 192–224; Robert M. Young, *Darwin's Metaphor* (1985), 126–63; and Neal C. Gillespie, "Divine Design and the Industrial Revolution: William Paley's Abortive Reform of Natural Theology," *Isis* 81 (June 1990): 214–29. Theodore Dwight Bozeman, *Protestants in an Age of Science* (1977), provides a detailed study of natural theology in the American Presbyterian tradition; the maintenance and collapse of natural theology in the United States are traced in James Turner, *Without God, Without Creed* (1985). For Emerson and natural theology, see David M. Robinson, "Emerson's Natural Theology and the Paris Naturalists," *JHI* 41 (January–March 1980): 69–88; and "Emerson and Natural History," in *American Literature and Science,* ed. Robert J. Scholnick (1992), 94–109; also Leon Chai, *The Romantic Foundations of the American Renaissance* (1987), 62–73, 141–55.

                                                                    Laura Dassow Walls

NATURE, as a concept, can be defined by what it is contrasted with. The Transcendentalists tended to contrast it, on the one hand, with the supernatural or miraculous and, on the other, with human society—especially with sophisticated urban life. In both cases, they saw nature as normative. They rejected or downplayed miracles,* arguing that God needed none to accomplish divine ends; God's self-expression required only natural laws. At the same time, the general Transcendentalist belief was that God's will was more directly expressed in nature than in civilization. Thus, nature was the ultimate source of knowledge, inspiration, and originality; to separate oneself, however briefly, from human society and consort with the natural world was held to be good for the development of the soul.

Within these general tendencies the Transcendentalists held a variety of often clashing opinions. R. W. Emerson** stressed the distinction between Nature and Soul; Nature, he writes, is the "NOT ME"* (*Nature*). By contrast, H. Thoreau** wished "to regard man as an inhabitant, or a part and parcel of Nature" ("Walking").

Such disagreements indicate the different ways different Transcendentalists related to the natural world around them—that of antebellum New England.

This environment already had been radically transformed by two centuries of European settlement and was being altered still further by the coming of the railroad and the textile mill. The original Indian inhabitants had been massacred, expelled, or forced into small reservations; some native animals (notably the beaver, deer, and wolf) had been all but exterminated, while new fauna had been introduced, often accidentally (e.g., the rat, housemouse, cockroach, and honeybee); the vast primeval forests of white pine and chestnut oak had been felled for lumber and to make room for European crops and livestock; swamps had been drained, rivers dammed, canals dug. The Transcendentalists lived their lives on tamed, settled land.

Their most ecstatic encounters with "nature" therefore had nothing to do with true wilderness: Emerson (in *Nature*), crossing a bare Concord* common at twilight, feeling the "perfect exhilaration" of a mystic experience; M. Fuller** (in *Summer on the Lakes*), standing on a viewing bridge near Niagara Falls, overcome by emotion at the sight of the tumbling rapids on display before her; Thoreau (in *Walden*) studying the runoff from a railroad embankment and finding evidence of fructifying power in organic* shapes produced by the water in the clay. When the Transcendentalists did encounter wilderness, they did not like it. Even Thoreau, who celebrated "wildness" in the abstract, found such encounters unsettling. In *The Maine Woods,* he describes the desolate summit of Mount Ktaadn as a place hostile to humanity: "Vast, Titanic, inhuman Nature has got [the human beholder] at disadvantage, caught him alone, and pilfers him of some of his divine faculty." Here is the opposite of the effect nature is supposed to have: It makes us not more divine but less so.

With the occasional exception of Thoreau, the Transcendentalists were glad the wilderness had receded. On one level, they wished to balance wilderness with civilization. Their ideal landscape* was pastoral. They frequently extolled agriculture,* or farming, for its closeness to the elements. Sometimes, as at the utopian communes of Brook Farm* or Fruitlands,* or most famously, with Thoreau's beanfield in the Walden Woods,* they actually took up the hoe and plow. On a deeper level, Thoreau suggested that true wildness is within us: "I shall never find in the wilds of Labrador any greater wildness than in some recess of Concord, i.e. than I import into it" (*Journal,* 30 August 1856).

Thoreau was a special case. He was the only one of the Transcendentalists to try, at Walden Pond,* to live apart from human society and "close to nature." He was, too, the Transcendentalists' only genuine naturalist, spending substantial time out in the field, making systematic observations of animals and plants. His later *Journal* is evidence of his industry and insights. His lecture "The Succession of Forest Trees" shows (as does the recently published *Faith in a Seed* [1993]) that he developed in his last years a truly ecological understanding of how nature works. Fittingly, he became a father of the conservation movement with his call, in *The Maine Woods,* for national wildlife preserves.

The Transcendentalists' thoughts on nature appear everywhere in their writings, including their sermons, journals,* and correspondence. The works mentioned above are merely starting points from which to explore the subject.

REFERENCES: Two standard studies of American attitudes toward nature, each containing discussion of Emerson and Thoreau, are Leo Marx, *The Machine in the Garden: Technology and the Pastoral Ideal in America* (1964), and Roderick Nash, *Wilderness and the American Mind* (1967). For the literary associations nature had for the Transcendentalists, see Buell (1973). For discussion of Thoreau's contributions as a naturalist, see Donald Worster, *Nature's Economy: A History of Ecological Ideas* (1985), and selected essays in Edmund A. Schofield and Robert C. Baron, eds., *Thoreau's World and Ours: A Natural Legacy* (1993). William Cronon's *Changes in the Land: Indians, Colonists and the Ecology of Early New England* (1983), although it examines only the 17th and 18th centuries, shows that the Transcendentalists were living in an environment transformed by European settlement; see also Carolyn Merchant, *Ecological Revolutions: Nature, Gender and Science in New England* (1989). John Stilgoe's *Common Landscape in America, 1580–1845* (1982), a study confined neither to New England nor to the Transcendentalist era, nonetheless evokes the landscape the Transcendentalists considered typical.

Dean David Grodzins

NEOPLATONISM is a school of philosophy whose origin is generally ascribed to Plotinus.* Its adherents accepted a modified version of Plato's* doctrines, casting a strong mystic aura over the Greek philosopher's work. In Neoplatonism a mystical system arises out of an idealistic philosophy; the concept of a science based on the knowledge of ideas provides idealism,* truthfully reflecting Plato. The doctrine of an ineffable unity of things above all knowledge necessitates mysticism. The primary tenets of the school, such as the idea of an omniscient One from which all things emanate, appealed to the Transcendentalists, particularly R. W. Emerson.** Other doctrines, for example the concept of the perfectibility of man through self-development, were also congenial to the group.

While Plato's insight into truth stresses a dialectical reasoning, Plotinus's modification of this idea involves occult vision, an attractive concept to the Transcendentalists. Emerson first encountered Neoplatonic literature in V. Cousin's** *Introduction to the History of Philosophy* (1828), then read the Neoplatonists themselves in Thomas Taylor's translations. He was especially enthusiastic about the concept of ecstasy, which results when the individual unites with the One. This idea is treated in detail in Emerson's essay "The Over-Soul."

Other Transcendentalists were also influenced by Neoplatonic concepts. B. Alcott's** doctrine of Genesis or Lapse, which held that the world was an emanation from God by way of man's spirit, descending through animals and finally to atoms, is Neoplatonic. The love of nature* and solitude evidenced in the writings of H. Thoreau,** Emerson, and others reflects the Neoplatonic aim of union with the One through purification of the individual in a prolonged process of contemplative self-development.

REFERENCES: An extensive discussion of Neoplatonic influence on Emerson occurs in John S. Harrison, *The Teachers of Emerson* (1910). Further treatment of Neoplatonism and Transcendentalism is found in Alexander Kern, "The Rise of Transcendentalism, 1815–1860" in Harry Hayden Clark, ed., *Transitions in American Literary History* (1954), 245–314. Also valuable are Donald Koster, *Transcendentalism in America* (1975), and Gay Wilson Allen, *Waldo Emerson: A Biography* (1981).

John D. Cloy

NEW JERUSALEM MAGAZINE (September 1827–December 1893), initially published by a tiny Boston New Church congregation as a missionary journal dedicated to propagating Swedenborgian doctrines, was the primary source through which R. W. Emerson** became acquainted with the doctrines of the Swedish mystic E. Swedenborg.* Emerson's intellectual debt to Swedenborg, albeit secondhand through the magazine's articles, was considerable: the theory of correspondences,* which premised an organic* relation of phenomenal and metaphysical nature* and the correspondence of physical and moral facts; the doctrine of influx from the spiritual to the natural world; and confirmation of his philosophical idealism.*

Emerson's interest in Swedenborgianism dates to his reading of *Observations on the Growth of the Mind* (1826) by S. Reed,** a fellow Harvard graduate and a prolific contributor to *NJM*. Cameron (*Emerson's Workshop* [1965], 1: 40–57) identifies 259 articles in the *NJM* that Emerson read between September 1827 and September 1836; Walter Harding (*Emerson's Library* [1967], 38) lists a bound volume of six tracts issued by the Boston Society of the New Jerusalem, the publishers of the *NJM,* in Emerson's library. The more than 80 references to Swedenborg in Emerson's writings, 40 of them in his journal,* testify to his absorption in the mystic.

So familiar was Emerson with the vocabulary of Swedenborgianism—"influx" and "ultimate"—and its doctrine of correspondences, that many mistook *Nature* (1836) for a New Church document. When a Glasgow New Church minister republished it under the title of "The Religious Philosophy of Nature," the *NJM* set the record straight, taking particularly vigorous exception to Emerson's characterization of Jesus as merely human and his avowal that all religions have equal spiritual value (15 [October 1841]: 49–52). When a similar mistake was made about "The American Scholar" (1837), it was pointedly corrected in Reed's review of the address (*NJM*, 11 [October 1837]: 67). Other Emerson essays clearly echo passages and ideas from his readings in *NJM:* notably, "The Uses of Natural History" (1833), "The Naturalist" (1834), "Demonology" (1839), "The Poet" (1844), and "Swedenborg; or, the Mystic" (1850).

Despite common interests and a mutual curiosity, the Transcendentalists and Swedenborgians ultimately disappointed each other. Both groups shared an interest in many of the "isms" that flitted through midcentury intellectual circles—animal magnetism, Fourierism,** spiritualism,* homeopathy, and phrenology.* Its only sale of any Swedenborgian titles in 1845 (*Heaven and*

Hell, Divine Providence and *Writings of Emanuel Swedenborg*), so the Book Board of the Boston Society reported, was made to the Brook Farm* Library (it netted the board $2.25) (*NJM* 19 [March 1846]: 274). However, writing in Brook Farm's *The Harbinger,** J. S. Dwight** accused the Swedenborgians of being "quietists and exclusivists" and dismissed *NJM* for being "simplistic-spiritual" and "incredulous to any scheme for the political and social regeneration of the race." The Swedenborgians, in turn, regularly faulted the sermons and writings of J. F. Clarke,** W. E. Channing,** W. H. Furness,** and B. Alcott** in *NJM* for their lack of any clear understanding of the concept of the future state, the soul's future existence, and the Incarnation; they dismissed Transcendentalism as spiritually arid, being little more than a well-meaning humanitarian religion (*NJM* ns 1 [December 1878]: 425–26).

REFERENCES: No study has been made of *NJM* per se. A wide-ranging treatment of the history of the New Church on these shores is Marguerite B. Block, *The New Church in the New World* (1932). Emerson's interest in Swedenborgianism is authoritatively treated in the many articles of two scholars: Kenneth W. Cameron, *Emerson the Essayist: An Outline of His Philosophical Development Through 1836* (1945) vol. 1, esp. "Swedenborg in Boston" (228–52) and "Sampson Reed—'My Early Oracle,' " (253–94); and Clarence Hotson, "Sampson Reed, a Teacher of Emerson," *NEQ* 2 (1929): 249–77, and "Emerson and Swedenborg," *NCM* 160 (October 1930): 274–77.

Arthur Wrobel

NOMINALISM is the view that universals or abstract concepts have no real existence but are merely names assigned to some subset of particulars on the basis of perceived resemblance. The term is opposed to "realism,"* the belief that universals do have an absolute, objective, or "real" existence. Transcendentalists rejected nominalism, with its empirical and materialist associations, thus engaging a dispute dating back to medieval theology. As R. W. Emerson** affirms, in "Nominalist and Realist": "In the famous dispute with the Nominalists, the Realists had a good deal of reason. General ideas are essences."

The first well-known name associated with nominalism is William of Ockham (c. 1285–1349), who rejected medieval realism on the basis that only individual and particular things exist. In the 17th century, Hobbes asserted that there is "nothing in the world Universall but Names; for the things named, are every one of them Individuall and Singular" (*Leviathan,* ch. 4). Similarly, Locke,* in a nominalist move, asserts that truth comes only from direct experience with particular things, which are all there really is: "*[G]eneral* and *universal* belong not to the real existence of things; but are the inventions and creatures of the understanding, made by it for its own use" (*Essay,* III.iii.11). Things therefore have no "real" essence, only a "nominal" one that "the mind makes" to rank and distinguish objects and experiences into categories (III.vi.11). For Locke, one of the great abuses of words is to mistake them for the objects they only name, or "*taking them for things*" (III.x.14). H. Thoreau,** in a Harvard class essay, repeats the lesson: Words are "mere signs of ideas." Such a comment points to a nominalist concern with reification, or the tendency of words to take on a life of their own.

Emerson is concerned to reconcile the contradiction between particular and universal by rejecting the implications of nominalism: If we cannot see universals, let us at least "see the parts wisely, and infer the genius of nature* from the best particulars with a becoming charity." For Emerson, the partial and contingent inferences of the understanding, as it "adds, divides, combines, measures" (*Nature*), must finally give way to the revelations of Reason; "Empirical science is apt to cloud the sight, and, by the very knowledge of functions and processes, to bereave the student of the manly contemplation of the whole." Similarly, T. Parker,** in *A Discourse of Matters Pertaining to Religion,* criticizes the limitations of the "Naturalism" associated with Hobbes and Locke: "It makes a *scientific* law a mere generalization from observed facts, which it can never go beyond. . . . It cannot pass from the Particular to the Universal." To some extent, Transcendentalism might even be defined as the rejection of nominalism and the reassertion of medieval realism, under the banner of 19th-century Romanticism.

REFERENCES: The most direct contemporary discussion remains Emerson's essay "Nominalist and Realist," *CW,* 3:131–45. For clear and useful overviews, see A. D. Woozley, "Universals," and Ernest A. Moody, "William of Ockham," both in *EP,* 8:194–206; 307–15, respectively.

Laura Dassow Walls

NONRESISTANCE was a form of Christian anarchism and pacifism, the antipolitical thrust of which exposed divisions within both abolitionism* and Transcendentalism. Originally applied to the practice or principle of not resisting authority, a doctrine held in 17th-century England, the term was taken up by radicals who in 1838 withdrew from the American Peace Society to form the New England Non-Resistance Society. For the nonresistants, *all* wars—even those in defense of property, life, liberty, or religion—were contrary to the spirit of the Gospels. Resting their arguments on Christ's injunctions against violence, the nonresistants extended that opposition to all institutions based on force or coercion, including civil government. Since they denied allegiance to what the nonresistants called "human government," they refused to vote, to hold office, or otherwise to participate in any legislative or judicial body. They were therefore frequently called "no-government men," but the nonresistants rejected that label, placing themselves instead under what they conceived to be the government of God. "We recognize but one KING and LAWGIVER, one JUDGE and RULER of mankind," W. L. Garrison** announced in the Declaration of Principles of the Society, published in *The Liberator* on 28 September 1838. Two years later the American Anti-Slavery Society, of which Garrison was president, split wide open, largely as a result of his radical religious views, his support of the right of women actively to participate in abolitionist agitation, and his embrace of nonresistance, which became the official policy of the society after 1840.

The principles of nonresistance were also embraced by some of the most radical of the Transcendentalists. In a series of essays on the subject of "Voluntary Political Government" published between 1842 and 1844 in the antislavery newspaper the *Herald of Freedom,* a correspondent from Concord* who signed himself "C.L."—apparently B. Alcott's** friend C. Lane**—vigorously protested the government's use of force, arguing that such compulsion in the enforcement of laws infringed upon the individual's natural rights. Unlike the abolitionists, however, Alcott and Lane carried nonresistance a step further, refusing on principle to pay taxes to the State. In 1843 Alcott was arrested for refusing to pay his poll tax, a tax levied on all adult males in Massachusetts. Following Alcott's lead, H. Thoreau** began to withhold payment of his poll tax as early as 1842 or 1843. He was also influenced by the writings and speeches of other nonresistants. He may well have read Lane's essays in the *Herald of Freedom,* which Thoreau reviewed in *The Dial** in 1844; certainly he lavished praise on the editor of the newspaper, N. P. Rogers,** a passionate proponent of nonresistance. In "Wendell Phillips** Before Concord Lyceum,*" published in *The Liberator* the following year, Thoreau praised another eloquent nonresistant, observing that it "was the speaker's aim to show what the state, and above all the church, had to do, and now, alas! have done, with Texas and slavery, and how much, on the other hand, the individual should have to do with church and state."

Like the nonresistants, Thoreau firmly believed that the individual should have nothing whatsoever to do with such corrupt institutions. Consequently, in July 1846 he was arrested and briefly jailed when he once again refused to pay his poll tax. He defended his stand in February 1848, when he delivered a lecture at the Concord Lyceum "on The Rights & Duties of the Individual in relation to Government—much to Mr. Alcott's satisfaction," as Thoreau told R. W. Emerson.** In that lecture—published in 1849 as "Resistance to Civil Government" and now widely known as "Civil Disobedience"*—Thoreau sought to distinguish himself from "those who call themselves no-government men." But his refusal of allegiance to a government that supported war and slavery, his rejection of political means to end such injustices, his protest against the use of force to uphold the law, and his adoption of a form of passive resistance owed a good deal to the arguments developed by the nonresistants during the preceding decade. In fact, Thoreau essentially challenged the Garrisonians to carry nonresistance to its logical conclusion, insisting "that those who call themselves abolitionists should at once effectually withdraw their support, both in person and property, from the government of Massachusetts."

Other Transcendentalists emphasized the futility of such efforts to withdraw from the government. "If you wish to become pure in this way, you must not only come out of the State, but you must go out of the world," J. F. Clarke** told the nonresistants in "The Annexation of Texas," a sermon published in the *Christian World* on 20 April 1844. In a lecture delivered a few weeks earlier and later published as "New England Reformers," Emerson characterized non-resistance as the final stage in "the progress of dissent" in politics, describing with some amusement those "solitary nullifiers, who throw themselves on their reserved rights; nay, who have reserved all their rights; who reply to the assessor, and to the clerk of court, that they do not know the State." Emerson, however, was anything but amused when Thoreau went to jail rather than pay his poll tax. Sharply distinguishing between Thoreau and the abolitionists, who "ought to resist & go to prison in multitudes on their known & described disagreements from the state," Emerson in his journal* challenged both the consistency and utility of Thoreau's refusal to pay the tax to the state, "a poor good beast who means the best." Even after the passage of the Fugitive Slave Law in 1850 generated his own opposition to the State, Emerson responded not by withdrawing from government but by becoming deeply involved in politics, which engaged so much of his attention during the 1850s.

Nonetheless, Emerson remained strongly drawn to the central principle of the nonresistants, their radical pacifism. In a lecture on war—delivered in 1838 and published along with Thoreau's "Resistance to Civil Government" in *Aesthetic Papers** in 1849—Emerson asserted the potential power and ultimate efficacy of "the extreme peace doctrine," which he viewed as a sign that human beings might at last be entering a higher stage of "moral cultivation." Emerson also expressed strong admiration for the doctrines of nonresistance during his tour of Britain in 1847–48. Challenged by some of his English friends to cite "an American idea,—any theory of the right future of that country," Emerson offered "the dogma of no-government and non-resistance." Although he acknowledged that he had "never seen in any country a man of sufficient valor to stand for this truth," Emerson dismissed "the vulgar musket-worship," affirming that it "is certain as God liveth, the gun that does not need another gun, the law of love and justice alone, can effect a clean revolution."

By the time that passage appeared in *English Traits* (1856), however, non-resistance had been subverted by the growing violence generated by opposition to the Fugitive Slave Law, as well as by the emerging struggles between pro-slavery and Free Soil settlers in Kansas. Although few nonresistants actually renounced the doctrines of peace, their growing accommodation to violent means was illustrated by the response to J. Brown's** raid on the Federal Arsenal at Harpers Ferry, Virginia, in 1859. Like Alcott, Thoreau, Emerson, and other Transcendentalists, Garrison and most of the nonresistants strongly defended Brown. Many of the nonresistants also became deeply involved in politics, especially after the outbreak of the Civil War. Indeed, with a few notable exceptions, their devotion to the principles of nonresistance finally proved less deep than their opposition to slavery, which many nonresistants came to believe could be ended only by the force of Union armies directed by the government in Washington.

REFERENCES: The Declaration of Principles of the New England Non-Resistance Society is reprinted in Devere Allen, *The Fight for Peace* (1930), 694–97. Expositions of the doctrine included Adin Ballou, *Christian Non-Resistance, in All Its Important Bearings, Illustrated and Defended* (1846); and Henry Clarke Wright, *Defensive War Proved to Be a Denial of Christianity and of the Government of God* (1846). The fullest discussion of the emergence and ideology of nonresistance is Peter Brock, *Pacifism in the United States: From the Colonial Era to the First World War* (1968), chs. 12–14. Thoreau's debt to the ideas of the abolitionists and nonresistants is explored in Raymond Adams, "Thoreau's Sources for 'Resistance to Civil Government,'" *SP* 42 (1945): 640–53; Wendell Glick, "Thoreau and Radical Abolitionism" (Diss., Northwestern Univ., 1950); John C. Broderick, "Thoreau, Alcott, and the Poll Tax," *SP* 53 (1956): 612–26; and Taylor Stoehr, *Nay-Saying in Concord: Emerson, Alcott, and Thoreau* (1979): 44–66.

Linck C. Johnson

NORTH AMERICAN REVIEW, which began publication in 1815, included both criticism of and some praise for Transcendentalism. In his October 1865 review of H. Thoreau's** *Letters to Various Persons*, J. R. Lowell,** then the editor of the *NAR*, recounted Transcendentalism as being "mental and moral mutiny," a movement that established communities "where everything was to be common but common sense" (101: 597–98). He felt that Thoreau had "so high a conceit of himself that he accepted . . . , and insisted on our accepting, his defects and weaknesses of character as virtues and powers peculiar to himself" (601). However, in the same article, Lowell praised R. W. Emerson** for freeing America from the aesthetic and cultural bonds of England: "[H]e speaks to what always is highest and least selfish in us" (600). Emerson received mixed praise in C. C. Felton's** April 1850 review of *Representative Men*. Felton acknowledged that "some things [Emerson] has published will live as long as the language itself"; however, he also felt that Emerson's poetry and much of his prose "will die out among the short-lived oddities of the day" (70: 520). F. Bowen** found Emerson's poetry indecipherable: "Is the man sane who can deliberately commit to print this fantastic nonsense?" ("Nine New Poets," 64 [April 1847]: 411).

Emerson's opinion of the *NAR*, in his journal* for 1842, echoed that of many other readers of the time: "When I read the North American Review . . . I seem to hear the snore of the muses, not their . . . waking voice." The conservative *NAR* was criticized primarily for not addressing the issues of the day. A Boston-based journal (until it moved to New York in 1878) begun by an association of Cambridge intellectuals, the *NAR* brought the world to Boston. The articles reflected a variety of interests, including anthropology and the exploration of new territories, sociology, politics, biology, philology, history, and biography. Philosophical and theological reviews were not prevalent, but when they did appear, they often were concerned with the debate between natural theology* and the speculative theology of I. Kant* and the Transcendentalists. Bowen had two articles on the subject in 1842 (54: 102–41; 54: 356–97). Specific Transcendentalist works were ignored during the movement's height, however. *Wal-*

den received a scant one-paragraph critical notice in which Andrew Preston Peabody concludes that it should be read because Thoreau says "so many pithy and brilliant things" (79 [October 1854]: 536).

Despite its conservatism, the *NAR* was open to essays by Transcendentalist authors. Commenting on M. Fuller** Ossoli's *At Home and Abroad* in July 1856, F. H. Hedge** explained that Fuller's genius did not appear in her written works because of her varied interests: "[A]uthorship could never have been more than an incident and an episode in her life" (83: 261). Most contributions by Transcendentalists appeared later in the century, however. While Emerson published seven essays in the *NAR*, only two, "Michael Angelo" (44 [January 1837]: 1–16) and "Milton"* (47 [July 1838]: 56–77), appeared before 1866. J. F. Clarke** wrote on the history of the West in 1836 and 1837, with an essay on "Harriet Martineau"** not appearing until 1877 (124: 435–50). Therefore, while Transcendentalists wrote for the *NAR*, most of their essays did not address Transcendentalist issues until after that movement's heyday.

REFERENCES: For a history of the *NAR*, see Mott, esp. his essay in vol. 2. See also [A. H. Everett,*"*] "The Semi-Centenary of the NAR," *NAR* 100 (January 1865): 315–30; and John B. Mason, in Chielens (1986), 289–300. A helpful but sometimes incomplete index to *NAR* articles and authors is Kenneth Walter Cameron, *Research Keys to the American Renaissance* (1967), 83–160.

John P. Samonds

NOT-ME (or Not-I, Not-Self) is a term borrowed from German idealist* philosophy to designate the cultural, social, and material world that appears to exist outside the individual ego or soul. The term stresses a dualism of matter and spirit. In its idealist context, it also denotes that reality starts with the ego or soul and that the outside world exists in and for it, since the world is only an "activity of mind."

The Not-Me has at least three features. It exists as the soul's limit, as that which exists in opposition to the soul. But second, the Not-Me exists as an effect of the "me" or soul; the Not-Me is neither independent of nor superior to the soul, and R. W. Emerson** devotes the early chapters of *Nature* (1836) to showing how objective nature* submits itself to the soul's use. Third, the Not-Me is a symptom of the soul's absolute power to posit itself, for the Not-Me is that which is posited by the soul or absolute ego. This power of self-positing renders the soul's power absolutely independent and autonomous of variable personal efforts, success, or worldly status. Self-positing is absolute, inhering in the ontological constitution of being itself.

New England Transcendentalism tended to adapt the complex metaphysics of its German antecedents into a theory of personal identity. The point of the former was often not the prerequisites so much as the potential effects of consciousness. Although the single most significant German source of the Not-Me terminology, J. G. Fichte,* attempted to distinguish between soul and self, between the absolute conditions of consciousness and consciousness itself, between the positing powers of the transcendental or absolute ego and the powers of the finite, individual self, the American adaptation did not.

The Not-Me has its most renowned American Transcendentalist appearance in Emerson's "Introduction" to *Nature.* Emerson says, "Philosophically considered, the universe is composed of Nature and the Soul. Strictly speaking, therefore, all that is separate from us, all which Philosophy distinguishes as the NOT ME, that is, both nature and art, all other men and my own body, must be ranked under this name, NATURE." Emerson most likely encountered Fichte through *Germany* (1814), by Madame de Staël.* And certainly he encountered the term in T. Carlyle's** *Sartor Resartus* (1833–34), the first book publication of which Emerson himself arranged in 1836.

REFERENCES: An account that remained relatively close to the initial ethos of Transcendentalism is O. B. Frothingham** (1876), which includes a section on Fichte's influence. Convenient English translations of Fichte's major writings are *Science of Knowledge,* ed. and trans. Peter Heath and John Lachs (1970; 1982), and *Fichte: Early Philosophical Writings,* ed. and trans. Daniel Breazeale (1988); the latter title includes "Some Lectures Concerning the Scholar's Vocation," which Emerson added to his library in 1845 and which he may have known directly by the time of *Nature*'s composition.

Christopher Newfield

NOVALIS (1772–1801), pseudonym of Friedrich von Hardenberg, was a German poet, novelist, essayist, and philosopher whose intuitive, pietistic, purposefully philosophical poetry and prose engaged American Transcendentalists swept up in the vogue of German literature. Questions about Goethe's** "morality" always disturbed R. W. Emerson** and others, but N, though his influence was never as great as Goethe's (to say nothing of I. Kant*), was revered because his High Romantic devotion to Idealism* and mysticism made him a more congenial Continental influence for often Puritan*-minded New Englanders.

Among the earliest of German Romantics, one of the so-called Jena Romantics, N was known primarily for two works. *Hymnen an die Nacht* (Hymns to the night, 1800) is a collection of mystical, visionary prose-poems inspired by one of the ur-Romantic subjects: the death of the beloved, who was, in this case, N's 13-year-old fiancée; her swift demise constituted the defining moment in his creative life. *Heinrich von Ofterdingen* (1802) is a philosophical novel wherein will and fate are symbolically characterized. As a meditation on the lost Golden Age, *Ofterdingen* contemplates a reunified universe in which the shortcomings of Enlightenment thinking are rectified. American Transcendentalists were most attracted to N because of his tough-minded and oft-repeated insistence that poetry and philosophy were in fact the same thing, that philosophy was passing over into poetry, and poets would usher in a new age.

N's work was well known and widely available to 19th-century readers. Ten periodical items on him and 18 poems by him appeared in American magazines such as the *Western Messenger,** *The Harbinger,** the *North American Review,** and *The Christian Examiner** between 1830 and 1899. His work was recommended in *The Dial** (July 1842), and his texts were to be found in the libraries of Emerson, B. Alcott,** J. F. Clarke,** T. Parker,** G. Ripley,** F. H. Hedge,** and M. Fuller.** Emerson's initial resistance to German influences is fairly well known, but he did in the end concede his considerable indebtedness to the Germans, "those semi-Greeks," who, to his mind, represented the culmination of European thought. Never a great student of the German language, Emerson first encountered N by way of T. Carlyle,** whose essay "Novalis" appeared in the *Foreign Review** in 1829 and was Emerson's principal early source. Thereafter, numerous brief references to N appear in Emerson's journals;* Emerson records several times N's statement "The division of Philosopher and Poet is only apparent & to the disadvantage of both. It is a sign of disease & of a sickly constitution." Such a sentiment certainly appealed to the author of "The Poet," who yearned for the production of American poetry with a "meter-making argument." Among the last thoughts inscribed in Emerson's journal is a N quotation: "Philosophy is properly home-sickness, the wish to be everywhere at home." Prior to the publication of *Nature* in 1836, Emerson read or reread the writings of N, as well as other German writers including the Schlegels,** Herder,* Fichte,* Tieck, Schiller,* and Schleiermacher.** But of these writers, theologians, and philosophers, N influenced Emerson's construction of *Nature* most directly; indeed, Pochmann argues that "Emerson's *Nature* contains few ideas that have not their counterpart in Carlyle's words on N or in the quotations from N."

Thanks to the efforts of translators of and apologists for German philosophy and literature like Clarke, Hedge, and Ripley, many other Transcendentalists were to come under the sway of N. H. Thoreau** was powerfully moved by the romanticism of *Hymns to the Night*. C. S. Wheeler,** a close associate of Thoreau, reported to *The Dial* from Heidelberg on German books and authors and in *ChEx* praised N specifically for his "religious character" and his "reverence and belief" ("The Religious Poetry of Modern Germany," 1849). W. T. Harris** paid homage to N by appending to his *Journal of Speculative Philosophy* a N quotation as the journal's motto: "Philosophy can bake no bread, but she can procure for us God, Freedom, and Immortality." Even H. Melville** was apparently influenced to some degree by N's work. The flower imagery in Melville's *Mardi* and the rose imagery of his later poetry were derived in part from *Ofterdingen*'s central mystical vision of a blue flower. Like Emerson, Melville was drawn to German writers like N as a possible way of reconciling the intellect and imagination.

Among Transcendentalists, Fuller was by far the most affected by N's work. She was quick to defend his literary reputation against American detractors and worked to promote careful study of him. Fuller candidly acknowledged her preference for Goethe, Tieck, and N rather than for the pure philosophy of Kant and Hegel.** She knew intimately and greatly admired his *Hymns to the Night* and *Ofterdingen,* believing that she had pierced the mysteries of the latter work. Fuller was drawn to N for many reasons, but chiefly he was a source of reassurance to her. She remarked that N was "a relief, after feeling the immense superiority of Goethe"; N was "refreshingly human."

REFERENCES: Useful biographical sketches of N are in Charles E. Passage, ed., *Hymns to the Night and Other Selected Writings* (1980), and Bruno Boesch, ed., *German Literature: A Critical Survey* (1971), 228–36. N's relationship to his fellow German writers is best seen in Oskar Walzel, *German Romanticism* (1932), and J. G. Robertson, *A History of German Literature,* 6th ed. (1970). A recent study is William Arctander O'Brien, *N: Signs of Revolution* (1995). Essential discussions of N and the Transcendentalists are in Stanley M. Vogel, *German Literary Influences on the American Transcendentalists* (1955), and in Pochmann (1957).

Layne Neeper

O

The **OLD MANSE** (built 1770)—a narrow clapboard, spacious, two-story house with attic—stands near the North Bridge on Monument Street in Concord, Massachusetts.* Its long lane, colorful garden, and proximity to the lush river banks, once battlefields of the Revolutionary War, made it an inspiring setting for the composition of N. Hawthorne's** *Mosses from an Old Manse* and R. W. Emerson's** *Nature,* both written in an upstairs corner study. Former inhabitants Sophia Hawthorne** and Emerson left inscriptions—the former on a dining room window, the latter near the fireplace on the wall of an attic room.

The Rev. William Emerson (1743–1776), grandfather of R. W. Emerson, built the Old Manse in 1770 for his wife, Phebe, daughter of Rev. Daniel Bliss. Phebe, tiring of what she referred to as their large block house, a barnlike structure on Concord's Main Street, wanted a house divided into many rooms. William and Phebe had five children: William (Waldo's father), Hannah, Mary Moody,** Phebe, and Rebecca. Phebe remarried the Rev. E. Ripley** in 1780, four years after her first husband's death. Waldo lived with his mother and stepgrandfather from autumn of 1834 until his 14 September 1835 marriage to Lydia Jackson (Lidian Emerson);** at this time he wrote *Nature.*

A year after E. Ripley's death, Hawthorne and his bride rented the house from Ezra's son, the Rev. Samuel Ripley,** and lived there for about three years. The Hawthornes had to vacate it in 1845 when Samuel retired from his Waltham pulpit, and he and his wife, Sarah,** moved into the Old Manse.

Sarah, an unusually accomplished woman in both languages and sciences, occupied the Old Manse until her death in 1867. In his memoirs, her grandson, Edward Simmons (1852–1931), American painter, recollected evenings spent in his grandmother's Old Manse parlor with literary and historical greats like Emerson, F. B. Sanborn,** C. Sumner,** B. Alcott,** and J. Brown.**

Emerson-Ripley descendants lived in the house until its sale to the Trustees of Reservations in 1939. Today the house—with original furniture—features small front parlor with reproduction of French wallpaper hung about 1780; large parlor with rosewood Steinway Square Grand piano; dining room with walnut table, six rush maple chairs, and grandfather clock purchased by William Emerson in 1767; kitchen with large fireplace; and upstairs bedrooms with mahogany beds.

REFERENCES: For references to and descriptions of the Old Manse, see Hawthorne, *Mosses from an Old Manse* and his *American Notebooks;* Edward Simmons, *From Seven to Seventy* (1922), ch. 1; biographies of Emerson; and *JMN.* A pictorial history is "The Old Manse, Concord, Massachusetts," by Paul Brooks and Shirley Eddy Catella, *Antiques* (October 1992). Tours are offered at the Old Manse.

Karen L. Kalinevitch

ORGANIC FORM, or "organicism," makes the formal assumption that the organizing concept of the whole is prior to any of its constituent parts: As R. W. Emerson** says in "The Poet," "[I]n the order of genesis the thought is prior to the form." Thus, the whole is said to be more than the sum of its parts, every part to be instrumental to the whole. In Coleridge's** formulation, the unity of the growing plant could only arise from a preexisting divine principle; hence, the plant came to symbolize the shaping power of the Imagination. Organicism was congenial to New England Transcendentalism, for it joined the latest wave of European Romantic theory with the Anglo-American tradition of natural theology,* in which God was an artist and nature* his material expression. To Emerson, the poet was the earthly avatar of the divine creator: "[I]t is not metres, but a metre-making argument, that makes a poem,—a thought so passionate and alive, that, like the spirit of a plant or an animal, it has an architecture of its own, and adorns nature with a new thing." Organicism itself was a powerful organizing idea, and it extended beyond aesthetics into social theory and natural science.

The idea that the whole preexists and "organizes" the component parts dates to Plato,* whose artist begins with the concept of the whole, disposing the parts accordingly for a creation as harmonious and complete as a living creature—or a machine; Kant,* in *The Critique of Judgement* (1790), tried to clarify the difference. While artworks and machines are creations made to fit a preexisting purpose or design, animals, lacking any prior organizing idea, make themselves according to their own necessary laws. An organism is thus "an organized and self-organizing being" (sect. 63–66). Coleridge elided Kant's distinction, establishing the Romantic idea that organisms are works of God's art, manifestations of his preexisting Idea. Machines are assembled artificially from without, while organisms grow naturally from within—both therefore the organs or instruments of a higher purpose; but machines are constructed by the Understanding, while organisms (and organic works of art) are created by divine Reason working through the Imagination. Nature by itself is dead, but nature animated by spirit, literally the "organizing" idea, is alive or "organic."

The force of the organic metaphor is suggested by Emerson in *Nature:* "We learn that . . . the Supreme Being, does not build up nature around us, but puts it forth through us, as the life of the tree puts forth new branches and leaves through the pores of the old. As a plant upon the earth, so a man rests upon the bosom of God; he is nourished by unfailing fountains, and draws, at his need, inexhaustible power.'' At root (the metaphor has become inescapable) is the fountain of divine power, which once tapped flows through the creating self, from center outward, organizing the world around him: The poet ''unfixes the land and the sea, makes them revolve around the axis of his primary thought, and disposes them anew.'' The growth of the self parallels the growth of organic nature, as man recapitulates the whole of creation, finally through consciousness realizing God in nature: the centering, organizing Idea self-realized in man.

Organicism was fundamentally compatible with socially conservative, hierarchical systems, for in the organic whole, every individual part functions in its preordained place; in Coleridge's ''body politic,'' each individual becomes an ''organ'' or instrument of the state, and ''the integral parts, classes or orders are so balanced or interdependent, as to constitute more or less, a moral unit, an organic whole'' *(On the Constitution of Church and State)*. As Emerson wrote in his journal,* God's Order was ''a harmonious whole, combined & overruled by a sublime Necessity, which embraces in its mighty circle the freedom of the individuals, and without subtracting from any, directs all to their appropriate ends.'' Difficulties emerge with theories of the self-reliant individual. In theory, the God within us would guarantee that the self-trusting individual ultimately coordinated with the social good; but in practice, as Emerson protests in ''Self-Reliance,'' ''Society everywhere is in conspiracy against the manhood of every one of its members''—a corporation feeding on the liberty of its constituents. H. Thoreau,** skeptical of organicist theories, saw the state, in ''Resistance to Civil Government,'' as less a coherent body that integrated the constituent individuals than as a soulless machine that destroyed individuality: ''The mass of men serve the State thus, not as men mainly, but as machines, with their bodies.'' The solution was, ''Let your life be a counter friction to stop the machine.'' While the organicist argues that the whole is prior and determines the parts, the opposition believes in the priority of the individual. To Coleridge it is ''the State that makes men''; Thoreau argues that ''we should be men first, and subjects afterward.''

A second consequence of organicism emerges when it is applied to nature or the natural sciences. Since it presumes that nature itself is dead matter, organicism tends toward instrumental uses of nature: ''Nature is thoroughly mediate,'' Emerson says in *Nature*. ''It is made to serve. It receives the dominion of man as meekly as the ass on which the Saviour rode.'' Organicism played a major role in the scientific controversies of the mid-19th century, for it was the belief in organisms as perfectly designed and integrated wholes that Darwin** had to overthrow, thereby undoing the bedrock assumptions of natural theology and Romantic aesthetics. Yet organicism continues to exert a fascination, both for its great elegance and beauty and for the undeniable power of its controlling idea.

REFERENCES: Explorations into organic form should begin with Raymond Williams, "Organic," in *Keywords* (1983), 227–29. Basic critical, historical, and scientific treatments may be found in G. S. Rousseau, ed., *Organic Form* (1972); and in Frederick Burwick, ed., *Approaches to Organic Form* (1987). For recent treatments of social organicism, see Ben Knights, *The Idea of the Clerisy in the Nineteenth Century* (1978); and Mary Kupiec Cayton, *Emerson's Emergence* (1989), 3–79. Literary organicism is discussed in Buell (1973), 145–65; a classic study is Vivian Constance Hopkins, *Spires of Form: A Study of Emerson's Aesthetic Theory* (1951). See also Richard P. Adams, "Emerson and the Organic Metaphor," *PMLA* 69 (March 1954): 117–30; and Fred Lorch, "Thoreau and the Organic Principle in Poetry," *PMLA* 53 (March 1938): 286–302. A more recent study is Christopher Newfield, "Emerson's Corporate Individualism," *AmLH* 3 (winter 1991): 657–84.

Laura Dassow Walls

ORIENTALISM, in its primary sense, refers to the field of scholarly study developed in Europe and shaped by European interests, attitudes, and preconceptions, whose object has been the peoples and cultures variously associated with "the East." Inspired by early contacts with Asian and other non-European cultures, Western study of the Orient may be traced to the beginnings of Western civilization itself. With the start of its modern phase in the late 18th century, Orientalism received a strong impetus from the deciphering of several Oriental languages, Sanskrit in particular, and the discovery and translation of the mythologies and scriptures of the Eastern world. To late-Enlightenment Europe these discoveries held out promise for what some writers envisioned as an "Oriental Renaissance" and proved a decisive force in shaping the expression of German, French, and English Romanticism. Although American interest in the Orient lagged behind European Orientalism by almost a generation, owing to the unavailability of sources, it became more widespread in New England by the 1840s and 1850s, in large part through the advocacy of several key Transcendentalists. In the work of R. W. Emerson** and H. Thoreau,** in particular, Transcendentalist Orientalism achieved its boldest expressions.

Since classical antiquity, and especially Alexander the Great's Indian campaign (327–325 B.C.E), Europe has appointed "the East" to the role of a mysterious and exotic "Other." During the Middle Ages, when the rise of Islam blocked Western contact with India and the Far East, "the Orient" was identified with the lands of eastern Europe, the eastern Mediterranean, and at times western Asia. During this period, Orientalists were preoccupied with biblical study, Semitic languages, and Islam. Vasco da Gama's arrival in south India in 1498, and the subsequent opening of the spice trade, ended Europe's centuries-long isolation from South and East Asia, and the term "Orient" came to include an array of cultures stretching from Egypt to Japan. With the exception of medieval treatments of India in Arabic, the most instructive contributions to early

Western knowledge of the East, particularly of China, came from Jesuit missionaries. The arrival in India of the French scholar A. H. Anquetil-Duperron (1731–1805) in 1754, however, marked the beginning of an increasingly concerted effort on the part of Europeans to decipher Asian languages and to make Asian scriptures accessible to the West. Though Anquetil did not master Sanskrit, his publication in 1801–02 of the *Oupnek'hat,* a Latin translation of a 17th-century Persian version of the Upaniṣads, had a lasting impact on Western philosophers, including Emerson, and contributed to the growing European sense of India as the homeland of transcendental idealism.*

Notwithstanding the influential work of Anquetil, modern Orientalism may be said to date from 1784 with the founding of the Asiatic Society of Bengal. Established to promote the study of Indian civilization, the Society sponsored the research of several notable British scholars and magistrates who would make a lasting contribution to the study of India in the West. Preeminent among these was Sir William Jones (1746–1794), the Society's first president and a polyglot linguist and scholar of extraordinary erudition, who revolutionized the European study of language with his discovery of the historical relationship of Sanskrit to Latin and Greek; Charles Wilkins (1749–1836), also a magistrate in the Colonial government and Jones's Sanskrit tutor, whose momentous translation of the *Bhagavadgītā** in 1785 constitutes a milestone in the history of modern Indology; Henry Thomas Colebrooke (1765–1837), a mathematician and linguist, who exerted a decisive influence on Western interpretations of India; and Horace Hayman Wilson (1786–1860), who though arriving in Bengal only in 1808 soon became one of the most accomplished Sanskritists and prolific translators of his generation. In the English-speaking world of the 19th century, Wilson's reputation as an Indologist was surpassed only by that of F. Max Müller (1823–1900), Wilson's German-born successor at Oxford and leading architect of the field of comparative mythology.

In 1788 the Society began publishing *Asiatic Researches,* a learned journal appearing till 1839, which became the leading vehicle for information about India. During the next 50 years, the British Orientalists issued a series of translations of Hindu scriptures and classics, as well as scholarly monographs, including: Wilkins's translations of the *Bhagavadgītā* (1785) and *Hitopadeśa* (1787); Jones's translations of Kālidasa's *Śakuntalā* (1789), Jayadeva's *Gītāgovinda* (1792), and, importantly for Emerson and Thoreau, *The Institutes of Hindu Law* (*Laws of Manu,** 1794); Colebrooke's *Essays on the Religion and Philosophy of the Hindus* (1815) and his translation of the *Sāmkhya Kārikas* (1837); and Wilson's translations of Kālidasa's *Megha-dūta* (1813) and the *Viṣṇu Purāṇa** (1840).

News of this rich and previously unsuspected cultural heritage came as a windfall to many European readers. In 1832, the French author Edgar Quinet extolled its discovery as the "Oriental Renaissance," conceiving it along the lines of the rediscovery of the literature of Greece and Rome in the 15th and 16th centuries. With new texts arriving from Bengal year after year, for several decades Orientalists focused principally upon Hindu India. Little was known at this time about Jains, Sikhs, or other Indian communities; indeed, little was known of Buddhism in the West until almost midcentury, due to the relatively late discovery of the Buddhist Sanskrit and Pali canons.

Among the first and most avid consumers of 18th-century reports about the Orient were German philosophers and poets. To the proto-Romantic writer J. G. von Herder,* India represented the "cradle of humanity." For him and his Romantic successors, India was seen as a remnant of Europe's golden age, the home of wisdom and philosophy, in which reason and feeling, art and religion, science and the imagination existed in synthetic harmony. In Germany, Orientalism became inseparable from the Romantic movement itself. "We must seek the supreme romanticism in the Orient," announced F. Schlegel,** the first German to learn Sanskrit.

The repercussions of German Romanticism were slower to be felt in America than in France and Britain, and so it was for Orientalism as well. In contrast to the Europeans, American colonists had fewer missionary reports to rely upon. Until well after the Revolution, most of what American readers understood from the term "Oriental" came to them in the form of the stereotypical "Oriental tale." An exception was the cosmopolitan Benjamin Franklin, who corresponded with Jones and held Chinese thought in great esteem. Also noteworthy are Joseph Priestley, the English Unitarian* and chemist, who, after emigrating to America in 1794, published *A Comparison of the Institutes of Moses with Those of the Hindoos and Other Ancient Nations* (1799), the first study of Eastern religions to be published in America; and John Adams, second president of the United States, who lavished many years in retirement upon the *Asiatic Researches* and other Orientalist works.

Despite these earlier contacts, no one did as much to shape the attitudes of later Americans to Eastern cultures as the Transcendentalists, and Emerson remains a key figure. Though not the first American to study Asian thought, he was the first to extoll its value as a corrective and complement to Western tradition. Evidence from his journals* and letters suggests that his interest in Eastern thought passed through three phases: the first impressions of his youth and college years; a period of gestation between 1830 and 1844, which saw the publication of his major essays and addresses; and finally, his mature and most active interest in the Orient, from 1845 till the end of his life.

Throughout Emerson's boyhood, India Wharf and the Boston Waterfront remained a lively port of call for Asian travel accounts. Emerson's father, William, was interested in Eastern travel* literature, and in *The Monthly Anthology and Boston Review,** which he edited until his death in 1811, he had published items on India as early as 1803. When young Waldo began keeping a journal at Harvard College in 1820, references to Eastern lore occur almost from the start. An opportunity to consolidate extant information on India came a year later when he was assigned the topic of "Indian Superstition" for his Commencement Exhibition project. Although painstakingly researched, the resulting composition reflects the mixture of fascination and aversion common to the popular imagination. However, further information soon prompted him to modify this critical response. Most important was his introduction—through newspaper articles and correspondence from his aunt, M. M. Emerson**—to the life and career of the Hindu theologian and reformer R. Roy.**

With his reading in 1830 of Gérando's** *Histoire comparée des systèmes de philosophie* and Anquetil's *Oupnek'hat,* Emerson's interests in Asian thought were revived, and his attitudes became warmly hospitable, even though his sources remained limited and his knowledge fragmentary. By the mid-1830s, he conceived the Hindu texts, together with Plato,* the Neoplatonists,* and European mystics, as vivid expressions of the *philosophia perennis* and primitive philosophical idealism. At this time Emerson was also drawn to classical Chinese and Persian texts. Early Transcendentalist interest in the Chinese tradition was limited to English and French translations of the works of Confucius and Mencius, including Joshua Marshman's *The Works of Confucius* and David Collie's translation of the Chinese *Four Books.* Although familiar with the Qur'ān by 1840, Emerson's interest in the Islamic tradition confined itself mainly to Sufi poetry, especially to the Persian poets Saadi* and Hafiz.* Exposure to Eastern texts during this period prompted Emerson to look beyond Jewish and Christian scriptures for a universal scriptural anthology or "world bible." This impulse, shared by Thoreau, B. Alcott,** and other Transcendentalists, led in part to the publication of the "Ethnical Scriptures" column of *The Dial** (1842–44), which included excerpts from translations of Hindu, Confucian, Buddhist, Sufi, and other ancient texts.

The period of Emerson's mature Orientalism began in 1845 with the long-awaited arrival in Concord* of Wilkins's translation of the *Bhagavadgītā,* together with Wilson's *Viṣṇu Purāṇa* and Colebrooke's *Essays.* Although Emerson had been acquainted with the *Gītā* for years, this was his first opportunity to read it carefully, and it precipitated a new phase in his knowledge and appreciation of India and the East. Though this exposure came too late to inform his best-known essays, the books of Emerson's middle years and old age—in particular, *Representative Men* (1850), *The Conduct of Life* (1860), and *Society and Solitude* (1870)—draw abundantly upon Eastern ideas, images, and patterns of thought. Several of Emerson's favorite doctrines, including the "Over-Soul," "Compensation,"* "Illusion," and "Fate" have distinct analogues in the Hindu systems with which he was familiar. The most dramatic exhibits of Indian influence, however, are the two poems "Hamatreya" (1847), inspired by his reading of the *Viṣṇu Purāṇa,* and "Brahma" (1857), which consists of a poetic paraphrase and elaboration of a verse that Emerson knew from the *Kaṭha Upaniṣad* and *Bhagavadgītā.*

Though Emerson admired Eastern thought, his appropriation of its sources remained eclectic and idiosyncratic insofar as he wrote, not as a scholar, but as a poet and man of letters. For him, India epitomized an idea, an existential condition, that he contrasted with the West. In his essay "Plato," for example,

India is converted into a type of the eternal feminine, representing passivity but also contemplation, wisdom, and poetry—the land of Unity. Europe, in contrast, is masculine, active, practical, inventive, and "delighted in boundaries." In short, Emerson's Orientalism operated less in the service of objective knowledge than of his own imaginative system. In the end, his greatest contribution to American knowledge of Asia may have been as a catalyst for his younger contemporaries, not least Thoreau.

Throughout his college years, Thoreau's exposure to Orientalist writing was negligible, and his attitudes to India and the Far East were, if anything, conventionally derogatory. This changed dramatically, however, when in August 1840 Emerson loaned him a copy of Jones's translation of the *Laws of Manu*. This first encounter with *Manu* inaugurated a devotion to Hindu texts that would be unmatched by any American of his generation. Having immersed himself in the cosmology and values of Manu, Thoreau pursued his research in the Eastern texts, supplementing those available in Emerson's collection with texts from the Harvard College library.

By the time he moved to Walden Pond* in the summer of 1845, Thoreau had been introduced to Wilkins's translation of the *Gītā*, and by the beginning of the next decade, he was conversant with several other classical Hindu texts as well, including Wilson's translation of the *Viṣṇu Purāṇa*, William Ward's translations of excerpts from the six systems of Indian philosophy, Roy's translations of selected Upaniṣads, and Colebrooke's translation of the *Sāmkhya Kārikas*. Besides English translations, Thoreau studied other European translations, including Langlois's French translation of the *Harivaṇsa*, an appendix to the voluminous Indian epic the *Mahābhārata*, of which Thoreau himself made a partial translation entitled "The Transmigrations of the Seven Brahmans." References in Thoreau's published writings indicate that *Manu*, the *Bhagavadgītā*, and the *Sāmkhya Kārikas* were the most influential.

Although references to Oriental subjects taper off in Thoreau's journals after 1851, throughout the 1840s they were a preoccupation. They also play a central role in *A Week on the Concord and Merrimack Rivers* and *Walden*. These books make clear that Thoreau's fascination with Indian texts lay in their depictions of bodily asceticism, the principles and practice of yoga, philosophical idealism, and a kind of romantic primitivism. One milestone in the history of Transcendentalist Orientalism was the arrival in 1855 of a chest of 44 Oriental books from Thoreau's English friend T. Cholmondeley,** an event more significant for the further transmission of Asian ideas than for their formative impact on Concord's Transcendentalists. Although Thoreau's knowledge of Eastern traditions was more thorough than Emerson's, he also subordinated the Orient to his own imaginative designs. But where Emerson drew upon Asian facts for embellishment, Thoreau often relied upon them for the backbone of his discourse.

By far the most ardent students of the East, Emerson and Thoreau were not the only ones. Alcott was also a convert to the Orientalist faith, and he came to it at about the same time, 1840, and through the same agency, his neighbor Emerson, as Thoreau had. Though familiar with Gérando's *Histoire,* Alcott concentrated on the *Bhagavadgītā,* which he read with admiration in 1846 and continued to praise throughout his life. But there were dissident Transcendentalist voices as well. The most notable was T. Parker.** Though widely informed about Eastern traditions and impressed with their achievements, Parker's views were basically critical. Like Hegel,** he subordinated the Eastern faiths to a lower stage in the evolution of what he conceived as absolute religion.

Idiosyncratic, flawed, and whimsical as it sometimes was, Transcendentalist appropriation of Eastern thought nevertheless established influential precedents for later American encounters with the East. Apart from its popular repercussions in the 20th century, Transcendentalist Orientalism also prepared the way for fuller and more critical treatments of the Eastern religions among second-generation Transcendentalists. After the Civil War Americans were presented with a new wave of Orientalist writings, more scholarly and comprehensive than before, including J. F. Clarke's** *Ten Great Religions* (1871), S. Johnson's** three-volume *Oriental Religions and Their Relation to Universal Religion* (1872–85), and M. D. Conway's** *Sacred Anthology* (1874). Thus, as in Germany, the immediate beneficiaries of the Romantic phase of Orientalism in America were the scholars.

REFERENCES: For the fullest historical reconstruction of the rise of European Orientalism, see Raymond Schwab, *La Renaissance orientale* (1950), trans. Gene Patterson-Black and Victor Reinking as *The Oriental Renaissance: Europe's Discovery of India and the East, 1680–1880* (1984). Building upon Schwab's research is Edward Said's by-now classic *Orientalism* (1978). Though Said's focus is on European representations of Arabs and Islam, his analysis is also relevant to South and East Asia. Though focusing exclusively upon the historical encounters between Europe and India, the most up-to-date treatment is Wilhelm Halbfass, *India and Europe: An Essay in Understanding* (1988). The best survey of early American Orientalism is Carl T. Jackson, *The Oriental Religions and American Thought: Nineteenth Century Explorations* (1981). Older but still helpful is Arthur Christy, *The Orient in American Transcendentalism: A Study of Emerson, Thoreau, and Alcott* (1932). See, too, Roger C. Mueller, "Transcendental Periodicals and the Orient," *ESQ* 57 (4th Q 1969): 52–57; Alan D. Hodder, " 'Ex Oriente Lux': Thoreau's Ecstasies and the Hindu Texts," *HTR* 86.4 (1993): 403–38; and Arthur Versluis, *American Transcendentalism and Asian Religions* (1993).

Alan D. Hodder

P

PALEY, WILLIAM (1743–1805), English theologian and moral philosopher,*
was required reading for Harvard-educated, first-generation American Transcendentalists. But they would eventually turn P into a rhetorical strawman, rejecting
him as a flawed guide to spirituality and morality.

In *Natural Theology** (1802), on which H. Thoreau** wrote a senior essay,
P explained that the world, like a watch, implies a maker, and he extended his
analysis to anatomy and physiology, from which he drew further inferences
about the nature of God. Though the image of God as watchmaker has been
traced to the writings of Robert Boyle (1627–1691) and even to the ancients,
P's "argument from design" in nature* became a standard (and in some circles
the definitive) means to prove the existence of God. P's *A View of the Evidences
of Christianity* (2 vols., 1794) responded to Hume's* skepticism about the ver-
ifiability of miracles,* demonstrating, logically, that miracles are a reliable form
of evidence that confirm revelation. Young R. W. Emerson** was among those
who welcomed P's proofs of the "grounds upon which [Christianity] rests."
But P was a philosophical sensationalist,* not an intuitionist. Coleridge,** in
Aids to Reflection (1825), had already dismissed the evidential school of P and
his ilk as an irrelevant response to Hume. And though Emerson, in a sermon
first preached in 1832, would continue to "quote with pleasure the remarks of
Paley" on the benevolence of God manifested in the " 'pleasures' " of children,
he had begun even in 1829 to find P's rationalism shallow. In a sermon that
year, he worried that P's removed Creator separated the "laws of Nature" from
the active, sustaining "powers" of God; Emerson was already proclaiming a
more dependable and vital innate sense of divinity, the revelation of the "God
within." In "The Over-Soul," Emerson finally spurned P and other philosophers who speak not *"from within,* or from experience" but *"from without, as
spectators merely."*

For P it followed that if God could be known from His creation, morality could be based on His will. In *The Principles of Moral and Political Philosophy* (1785), which both Emerson and Thoreau had read at Harvard, P explained that God's will is perceived not intuitively but on the basis of an action's "tendency to promote or diminish the general happiness." This staple of Unitarian* moral thought began to be questioned even by moderates in the 1820s. In *The Christian Examiner,* Samuel Sewall, still a defender of *Natural Theology,* worried about the dangers of "rest[ing] moral obligation on utility" (6 [July 1829]: 393). In the same journal in 1830, G. Ripley** challenged P's emphasis on "expediency" and "self-interest" (9 [September 1830]: 73). The classic Transcendentalist moral rejection of P is Thoreau's "Civil Disobedience"* (*RP,* 63–90), whose original title, "Resistance to Civil Government," parodies "The Duty of Submission to Civil Government Explained"—Book 6, chapter 3 of P's *Principles.* Decrying the effect of P's "expediency"—to permit injustice in the name of public convenience—Thoreau proposes instead, "It is not so important that many should be as good as you, as that there be some absolute goodness somewhere; for that will leaven the whole lump."

REFERENCES: See Elmer Sprague's entry on P in *EP,* 6:19–20. Emerson's interest in the Christian "evidences" and the Unitarian ambivalence toward P are discussed in Wesley T. Mott, *"The Strains of Eloquence"* (1989), 53–78. See also Edgeley W. Todd, "Philosophical Ideas at Harvard College, 1817–1837," *NEQ* 16 (March 1943): 63–90; Raymond Adams, "Thoreau's Sources for 'Resistance to Civil Government,' " *SP* 42 (July 1945): 640–53; and Wendell Glick, "Bishop P in America," *NEQ* 27 (September 1954): 347–54.

Wesley T. Mott

PANTHEISM became a term associated in the early 19th century with German and American Transcendentalism, and in America it was particularly associated with R. W. Emerson** during the 1830s and early 1840s. For Emerson it meant a divine emanation that permeated the finite universe, a power suffusing the phenomenal world that was consanguineous with one's own nature. One type of pantheism suggests that God is identified with the totality of all things: Creation is represented as a manifestation of the Deity. Another type of pantheism denies reality to anything except God. Emerson was alternately attracted to both kinds. What most attracted Emerson and H. Thoreau** to pantheism was its central assumption of a simple unity that denied the dualist split between spirit and matter most often associated with the Western philosophical tradition. "There is probably not a Pantheist in America who will own the name," according to the Calvinist editors of *The Biblical Repertory and Princeton Review.* Yet B. Alcott,** as recorded in Emerson's journal,* suggested, "Most men are pantheists at heart, say what they may of their theism. No other path is indeed open for them to the One, intellectually at least." In emphasis, Emerson's pantheism tended to focus on consciousness—a mode of pure seeing—which he identified with the divine. This is evident in both the famous "transparent eyeball" passage in *Nature* and an 1835 journal comment: "Our compound nature differences us from God, but our Reason is not to be distinguished from the divine Essence.''

In a moment of exasperation over the fluctuation of moods and powers to which we are liable, Emerson articulated this vacillation in pantheistic terms: ''I am God in nature;* I am a weed by the wall,'' he observed in ''Circles.'' Yet he is not invariably pantheistic: At times expressing himself in more orthodox Christian terms, Emerson reveled in the rare moments of contact with a transcendent Being and designated these the culmination of a life. At other times he was authorized by a belief in his own divine powers—an experience of pure consciousness—which presupposed the immanence* of divinity. Further still, in his essay *Nature,* matter is at times represented as ''the end or last issue of spirit,'' as if, at its furthest extreme, it were not permeated by spirit at all. And at still other times, he suggested that all phenomena, whether the material universe or man's mind, are manifestations of the Deity. In his honesty he acknowledged in his journal: ''A believer in Unity, a seer of Unity, I yet behold two.'' Emerson earnestly desired to put faith in the monist tendencies of pantheism—the belief that everything that exists is the particularization of one substance, the same in kind as God or spirit. Yet some degree of alienation from the material world urged him to give credence to the dualist split between spirit and matter he would have preferred to dissolve.

According to such detractors of Transcendentalism as Unitarians* H. Ware, Jr.,** and A. Norton,** as well as the Calvinist Trinitarians of the *BRPR,* ''pantheism'' was a term of contempt identified with the heresy of an impersonal God, with interpreting the scriptural revelation of a personal God as mere allegory, with denying the supernatural element in Christianity, and ultimately with atheism: ''To call the principles and attributes *God,* is to violate the established use of language. . . . There is a personal God, or there is none,'' insisted Ware. By contrast, Emerson declared in his private journal in 1835 what would become public three years later in his Harvard Divinity School* Address—''It is by magnifying God, that men become Pantheists . . . it is by piously personifying him, that they become idolaters.'' Indeed, with Emerson's tendency toward pantheism in mind, Ware's Unitarian sermon ''The Personality of the Deity'' opposed dispersing the divine personality into principles that govern the universe: ''If the material universe rests on the laws of attraction, affinity, heat, motion, still all of them together are no Deity; if the moral universe is founded on the principles of righteousness, truth, love, neither are these the Deity. There must be some being to put in action these principles, to exercise these attributes.'' ''Consciousness, and the power of will and of action constitute him [God] a person,'' declared Ware. He, moreover, insisted strongly on the moral and spiritual duty of reverence and worship, which obtains only between persons. Responsibility to one's own conscience is effective in promoting virtue, according to Ware, only ''because it is thought to represent and foreshadow decisions of the higher tribunal of God'': ''Let a man believe that [conscience] is ultimate, and he can learn to brave it.''

Norton's "A Discourse on the Latest Form of Infidelity" (1839) was an indignant attack on the Transcendentalists' pantheist tendency to dismiss Judeo-Christian miracles:* Emerson commented in the Divinity School Address that "the very word Miracle . . . is Monster; it is not one with the blowing clover and the falling rain." The conservative guardian of Unitarian values whose *Statement of Reasons* established him as the authority on Harvard Unitarian exegesis, Norton explained that if, as Spinoza* suggested and the Transcendentalists affirmed, God is dispersed or subsumed in the workings of nature, then "the laws of nature are the laws by which God is bound, Nature and God being the same." This pantheist or "infidel" belief denies to God the freedom to reveal his will and his providential engagement with mankind through supernatural and extraordinary means. Indeed, Norton complained that the assumption of a God bound by nature's laws called into question the authenticity of supernatural phenomena and ultimately the revealed and unique status of Christianity.

Entitling a hostile review of Emerson's *Essays, First Series* "Pantheism" (1841), the Calvinist editors of *BRPR* sought to discredit Emersonian Transcendentalism by showing its pantheistic "error" as having a long heritage in ancient and medieval thought. In an earlier review article on "Transcendentalism" (1839) in the same periodical, the Calvinist editors, as well as Norton (who had the review reprinted a year later), signaled their alarm at the Transcendentalists' pantheistic position that "the very essence of God is his creative power; that he is a force that was compelled to act and to pass with all his characteristics into the visible world; and that nothing now exists which has not from eternity existed in God. This necessary transfusion of God into the universe destroys our very idea of God. He is made the substratum, the substance, of all existence; and we are only bubbles thrown up upon the bosom of the mighty ALL, to reflect the rainbow colors, in our brief phenomenal existence, and then be absorbed again into the ocean from which we came." As articulated by the orthodox editors of *BRPR,* pantheistic principles contradict not only the revelation of God's distinct "personality" but also the Christian revelation that God created the universe from nothing (ex nihilo): "They had no conception of an Omnipotence which could pass the gulf between nonentity and existence. Substance, in their view, could not be originated, and all essence was the same essence" ("Pantheism").

Contemporaries of Emerson and Thoreau were, moreover, startled by their exaltation of man—the merging of man's personality in that of the Divinity—as well as by what was perceived as the pantheist's destruction of the moral distinctions between good and evil. According to the Calvinists, pantheists would claim that since "God is revealed by all the phenomena of the world's history, he is partly revealed by moral action, and consequently by sin, no less than by holiness. Sin is therefore a part of the necessary evolution of the divine principle; or rather, in any sense which can affect the conscience, there is no evil in sin—there is no sin" ("Transcendentalism"). Thoreau, too, was charged with pantheistic, pagan beliefs—particularly in his attacks on the Christian church in the "Sunday" chapter of *A Week on the Concord and Merrimack Rivers.*

The sources for Emerson's pantheist ideas—particularly the notion that the all-inclusive unity is divine—are many, both indirect and direct. As was often the case, he read secondary sources first, then later went back to read the original. His reading of the "History of Philosophy" by the French philosopher V. Cousin** accounted for much of his early knowledge of the pantheistic elements in Schelling,** Fichte,* Schleiermacher,** Hegel,** and Spinoza. Coleridge** was undoubtedly another source. Anti-Christian pantheism was available to him in the writings of the heretical Italian philosopher G. Bruno.* Bruno discountenanced miracles and suggested that since God is not distinct from the world, he can have no specific providential intentions. Bruno drew on the writings of the pre-Socratic philosophers Xenophanes (c. 570 B.C.) and Heraclitus (c. 535– c. 475 B.C.), but Emerson seems to have known of both independently of Bruno. Heraclitus's theory—that one substance, a creative fire, underlies all nature, man, and God—provided the later Stoics* (also read by Emerson) with the basis of their cosmology, monist physics, and pantheist tendencies. In his poem "Xenophanes," Emerson assumed the persona of this ancient philosopher to explore imaginatively Xenophanes's assertion, "The All is One and the One is God" (cf. Emerson's poem "Each and All"). Moreover, in the "Discipline" chapter of *Nature,* Emerson embellished his own observations about the relentless unity of nature in the midst of diversity with the comment, "Xenophanes complained in his old age, that, look where he would, all things hastened back to Unity." Another source of pantheistic ideas was J. Böhme,* the Lutheran mystic who recorded illuminations in which he saw nature as entirely the manifestation of spirit.

The Hindu scriptures also supplied Emerson and Thoreau with versions of pantheism. Thoreau announced in "The Pond in Winter" chapter of *Walden,* "In the morning I bathe my intellect in the stupendous and cosmogonal philosophy of the Bhagvat Geeta." In the *Bhagavadgītā,** they would have read about Krishna, the incarnate God, who is introduced as saying: "I am the breath which dwells in the body of the living; I am the beginning, and the midst of the living, and also their end. I am, under the stars, the radiant sun, under the lunar signs, the moon." In Emerson's poem "Woodnotes II," he seems to recall this expression in the praise of "the eternal Pan": "He is the axis of the star; / He is the sparkle of the spar; / He is the heart of every creature; / He is the meaning of each feature; / And his mind is the sky. / Than all it holds more deep, more high." According to the eighth-century Hindu theologian Sankara—an interpreter important to Thoreau's and Emerson's understanding of the *Gītā*—conceptions of a personal God in these scriptures belong to the domain of illusion (maya): The only reality is the impersonal Absolute (Brahma), which is identified with the soul—or in Emerson's terms, the Over-Soul. Emerson's later essays "Illusions," "Works and Days," and "Poetry and Imagination," as well as his poem "Brahma," owe much to this notion, deeply associated with pantheism, "that all is one stuff, cooked and painted under many counterfeit appearances."

REFERENCES: For important responses by contemporaries to Transcendental pantheism, see Ware, "The Personality of the Deity," and Norton, "A Discourse on the Latest Form of Infidelity," both rpt. in Sydney Ahlstrom and Conrad Wright, *An American Reformation: A Documentary History of Unitarian Christianity* (1985), 432–40, and 445–61. The trenchant articles by the Princeton Trinitarians offer useful analyses: "Pantheism," *BRPR* 13 (October 1841): 539–64; and "Transcendentalism," *BRPR* 11 (January 1839): 37–101. Leon Chai presents a modern analysis of Emerson's and Alcott's pantheism in *The Romantic Foundations of the American Renaissance* (1987), 279–93. For the Eastern emphasis, see Frederic Ives Carpenter, *Emerson and Asia* (1930), 103–60.

Robin Sandra Grey

PERFECTIONISM is a social, moral, or religious theory that a perfect and sinless state can be or has been attained by mortals. The Transcendentalists found the doctrine of perfectionism a complement to their belief in the power to master one's own environment and reform society. They identified perfectionism with the possession of such characteristics as timelessness, immutability, and self-sufficiency. G. Ripley** claimed that the more we possess genuine love, the more we resemble God, and love fully developed within us enables us to become "partakers of the Divine nature." He concluded, "[M]an has the power of conceiving of a perfection higher than he has ever reached" (*Discourses on the Philosophy of Religion* [1836]). Perfectionism finds its roots in the New Testament, particularly the writings of St. Paul, who claimed that Jesus had appointed apostles, evangelists, and teachers "for the perfecting of the saints, for the work of the ministry . . . till we all come in the . . . knowledge of the Son of God, unto a perfect man, unto the measure of the stature of the fulness of Christ" (Ephesians 4:11–13).

The Higher Life movement of the 17th century in Germany preached a doctrine of perfectionism in an effort to establish an intimate relation with the perfect Jesus. From the days of his association with the Holy Club at Oxford, John Wesley (1703–1791) preached Christian perfection, although he admitted that he himself had not attained the state. Wesley believed, however, that one could attain a state of grace in which one would be free from sin. He did not regard this as angelic perfection but as the "perfect love" of 1 John 4:18.

Perfectionism in America had its origin at Oberlin College in Ohio during the 1830s. Asa Mahan (1799–1889), chosen the school's first president in 1835, soon became a leading proponent of Perfectionism. The evangelist Charles Grandison Finney (1792–1875) was persuaded to leave his pulpit in New York and accept a faculty appointment at Oberlin, where he helped build a theological seminary that was the first to admit black students. There in 1837 Finney delivered a series of lectures on "Christian Perfection" that were published in the *Oberlin Evangelist,* and thereafter the school was identified as the citadel of Perfectionism. Borrowing the idea of "Universal Benevolence" from Jonathan

Edwards (1703–1758), Finney envisioned America as a nation ruled by God and His laws of benevolence, which obligated Christians to rid society of all evils. Finney was actively involved also in the temperance,* abolition,* and feminist movements.

John Humphrey Noyes (1811–1886) of Putney, Vermont, was an early advocate of Perfectionism, claiming that "as the doctrine of temperance is total abstinence from alcoholic drinks, and the doctrine of anti-slavery is immediate abolition of human bondage, so the doctrine of Perfection is immediate and total cessation from sin." Noyes published *The Perfectionist,* in which he popularized his philosophy, and established the Oneida Community in central New York to test his ideas. Noyes agreed with Rousseau,* who claimed that the present social system limits man's course toward perfection (*The Social Contract* [1762]) and thought that only by forming a community isolated from the ill-conceived and sinful institutions of ordinary society could perfection be realized. Noyes admitted that he became interested in the idea of communal living through reading Fourieristic** literature and by the example of Brook Farm.*

Noyes also found a basis for his peculiar doctrine in biblical chronology. Christian theology generally regards the Second Coming of Jesus and the resurrection of the dead as a future event at which time the "saints" will be delivered to a perfect state and changed into the perfect likeness of Christ. Noyes claimed he discovered the Resurrection as having occurred in A.D. 70 at the time of the destruction of Jerusalem by Titus. Hence, Christians now live in that perfect era when, Jesus said, there would be no marriage, but the resurrected would be "as the angels of God in Heaven" (Matthew 22:30). Consequently, Noyes banned monogamy and instituted what he called "complex marriage" at Oneida, where each woman was married to each man and each man to each woman. Couples were not permitted to cohabit, since he believed that exclusive attachments prevented them from obeying the biblical injunction to "love one another with a pure heart fervently" (1 Peter 1:22). This did not prevent them from having monitored intercourse for an evening, but without sleeping together.

Noyes carried his doctrine to its logical extreme physically by introducing an experiment in eugenics that he called "stirpiculture." If genetic strains in animals could be improved, why not in humans? The present system of random selection in marriage had produced mentally deranged and physically deformed humans—and very few geniuses. A scientific breeding of humans, he thought, may well produce perfect human beings. Since Plato's* *Republic* dealt with eugenics on paper in creating guardians of the perfectly just state, Noyes thought he could accomplish the same in reality at Oneida. Noyes's experiment launched a program of voluntary eugenics that produced 58 children, some of whom were fathered by Noyes, who at the time was in his sixties. No scientific follow-up was made to determine if the children were superior by reasons of select breeding or special attention in their education. The Oneida Community disbanded in 1879, and the members went their separate ways.

REFERENCES: Benjamin Breckinridge Warfield, *Perfectionism* (1958), is a thorough treatment of the Perfectionism of Mahan and Finney, including a history of the German Higher Life movement. Robert Davis Thomas, *The Man Who Would Be Perfect: John Humphrey Noyes and the Utopian Impulse* (1977), is a scholarly analysis. Charles Nordhoff, in *The Communist Societies of the United States, from Personal Visit and Observation* (1875), provides a firsthand account of conversations with Noyes. A. J. MacDonald visited several utopian communities and left a manuscript at Yale University, Microfilm 2116, consisting of 747 pages of observations, letters, questionnaires, brochures, pamphlets, and newspaper and periodical clippings. See also Finney, *Memoirs* (1846); Mahan, *A System of Intellectual Philosophy* (1847); and Noyes, *History of American Socialisms* (1870).

Raymond L. Muncy

PESTALOZZI, JOHANN HEINRICH (1746–1827), was a Swiss educational* reformer whose faith in the innate moral and spiritual capabilities of children accorded well with the Transcendentalists' concern with self-culture. Noted for his kindness, absolute trust, and saintly patience, even among supposedly incorrigible youth, P was celebrated for his schools at Neuhof, Stantz, Burgdorf, and Yverdun, where pupils were expected to assume responsibility for ethical as well as intellectual growth.

New Englanders encountered the doctrines of P through Madame de Staël's* *Germany* (New York, 1814), where the Swiss is compared to Rousseau.* French educator Francis Joseph Nicholas Neef (1770–1854) is generally credited with being the first to practice the master's ideas in America. Author of *Sketch of a Plan and Method of Education* (1808), Neef established schools near Philadelphia (1809–12) and at Village Green (1813–15) before moving to Louisville, Kentucky. He was invited to teach at R. Owen's** New Harmony community (1826–28), where the educational program was run by William Maclure. B. Alcott** read about P and Owen in William Russell's *American Journal of Education* and in 1828 contributed a series of articles to the same journal. Alcott was also familiar with *Hints to Parents*—an anonymous 72-page manual published in Salem, Massachusetts, in 1825 from the third London edition—which included a summary of Pestalozzian principles and practical exercises, sprinkled with quotations from P. The booklet stressed the role of the mother in cultivating intuition and in teaching children with love—the foundation, in P's phrase, of "their first moral sentiments and affections"; the "instructer's MIND" and example were finally more important than books. Popular books on education and moral development by Elizabeth Hamilton (1758–1816), British writer and admirer of P, were also published in Boston and Salem during the 1820s.

One of R. W. Emerson's** Second Church parishioners, I. R. Butts, printed *Letters of P on the Education of Infancy* in Boston in 1830. Indeed, Emerson, whose journals* are filled with allusions to P, avidly read Edward Biber's *Henry P and His Plan of Education* (1831) and discussed his philosophy and reforms in three sermons. Emerson found especially congenial P's microcosmic* principle that "All is in all" and, in a passage used later in the "Introductory

Lecture" to "Lectures on the Times," P's sober reflection after the French Revolution "that the amelioration of outward condition will be the effect, but never can be the means of mental and moral improvement." Inspired by P's experiment of hourly alternating teaching with joining one's students to be taught by another, Emerson wrote in "Uses of Great Men" that "society is a Pestalozzian school: all are teachers and pupils in turn."

In a discerning review of Biber, G. Ripley** observed that, despite his faults, "No man was ever more truly disinterested than P. He literally forgot himself"—and was thus, in an age of superficiality, a true reformer. P's educational theories found application in New England, both in a textbook by E. P. Peabody** and in the experimental schools of Alcott. Indeed Alcott, so often ridiculed for his airy idealism,* left a tangible mark on a Pestalozzian venture on the other side of the Atlantic: Alcott House, established in 1838 by English educator J. P. Greaves.** P's stature among the Transcendentalists is reflected in Emerson's journal comment that Alcott "measures ages by teachers, & reckons history by Pythagoras, Plato,* Jesus, & P."

REFERENCES: Important contemporaneous discussions are Madame de Staël, *Germany*, 3 vols. in 2 (1814), 1:113–20; and Edward Biber, *Henry P and His Plan of Education* (1831). P's influence in New England may be seen in [J. Walker,]** review of *Examples of Questions, Calculated to Excite and Exercise the Minds of the Young*, by Mrs. Elizabeth Hamilton, *ChEx** 6 (July 1829): 287–90; [Peabody,] *First Lessons in Grammar, on the Plan of P* (1830); Emerson's *Sermons*, 3:222, 229–31; 4:96–102; and [Ripley,] "P" [a review of Biber], *ChEx* 11 (January 1832): 347–73. Modern studies include Dorothy McCuskey, *Bronson Alcott, Teacher* (1940); John B. Wilson, "Bronson Alcott, Platonist or Pestalozzian?" *SchS* 81 (February 1955): 49–53; and Dahlstrand (1982). See also Gerald Lee Gutek, *Joseph Neef: The Americanization of Pestalozzianism* (1978), and Gutek, *P and Education* (1968).

Wesley T. Mott

PHRENOLOGY, the 19th-century "science of mind," held that self-knowledge could be imparted by a phrenological examination and that self-knowledge could lead to self-improvement. This affirmative belief conformed with the Transcendental conviction that in this world all things were possible.

Formulated by the Viennese physician Franz Joseph Gall at the end of the 18th century, phrenological concepts were first popularized in the United States during the 1820s and 1830s. Their acceptance owed much to the Boston 1832 lectures of Gall's disciple, Dr. J. Spurzheim,** dubbed by R. W. Emerson** one of the world's greatest minds. Not long after, the phrenologist G. Combe** continued to excite the interest of the American public in phrenology.

Phrenology postulated that since the brain was the organ of the mind and shaped the skull, there was an observable concomitance between the mind (talents, disposition, character) and the shape of the head. To ascertain the former, it was necessary to examine the latter. The brain was, however, not a unitary organ but a congeries of organs or faculties, whose size indicated their functioning power. The size of the faculties (1 for very small to 7 for very large) could be ascertained by a phrenological reading. The reading included measurement of the head, tactile examination of its shape, and assessment of the distances between the organs or faculties, each of which had a specific location. Among the faculties were Amativeness, Philoprogenitiveness, Destructiveness, Benevolence, Combativeness, Acquisitiveness, and Ideality. By sizing those faculties, a phrenological examination provided the subject with self-knowledge. Since phrenology held that the size of the faculties could, if too small, be increased by exercise, or, if too large, be diminished by concentrated effort, it suggested that human beings were literally masters of their minds. The motto of phrenology was "Self-Made or Never Made." The doctrine sat well with the affirmations of Transcendentalism.

Phrenologists held that they could provide a scientific basis for the Transcendental belief in the natural worth and improvability of mankind. They endorsed and broadened the scope of the humanitarian causes embraced by Transcendentalists: antislavery, penal reform, child guidance, woman's rights,* vocational guidance, the humane treatment of criminals and the insane, temperance,* sex education, and marriage counseling.

The most successful practicing phrenologists in 19th-century America were the brothers Orson Squire Fowler (1809–1887) and Lorenzo Niles Fowler (1811–1896), who with their brother-in-law Samuel Roberts Wells (1820–1875) conducted a New York firm that coupled phrenological examinations and lectures with the publication of related books and periodicals.

Among those who endorsed phrenology were Henry Ward Beecher, H. Greeley,** W. Whitman,** Samuel Gridley Howe, and H. Mann,** who looked upon phrenology as "the handmaid to Christianity."

Among the publications of the Fowler firm that advanced Transcendental belief in a God immanent* in man were the firm members' own writings, including Lorenzo Niles Fowler's *The Principles of Phrenology and Physiology Applied to Man's Social Relations* and Orson Fowler's *Self-Culture, and Perfection of Character*. In addition, the firm was involved in publication of Whitman's *Leaves of Grass* (2d ed., 1856) and between 1852 and 1856 issued posthumous reprints of M. Fuller's** *Papers on Literature and Art, Woman in the Nineteenth Century,* and *At Home and Abroad.* Their imprint appeared on books concerned with "Social Harmony": S. P. Andrews's** *The Science of Society,* A. Brisbane's** *Social Destiny,* P. Godwin's** *Popular View of the Theory of Charles Fourier,** Robert Dale Owen's *Labor,* Adin Ballou's *Practical Christian Socialism,* and Greeley's *Hints toward Reforms.* The Fowler list offered also books on the rights of women including *Woman and Her Wishes* by T. W. Higginson** and *Woman and Her Needs* by E. O. Smith.**

By the end of the 19th century, the advancement of technology and the exact sciences cast doubt upon the so-called science of mind, and that border science was finally discredited. The once popular and esteemed phrenological plaster cast of the head was shattered. Nonetheless, especially during the early and mid-

19th century, phrenology had successfully supported the humanitarianism implicit in Transcendentalism and had seemed for a time to provide a scientific basis for its ideology.

REFERENCES: The two most comprehensive works on phrenology are John D. Davies, *Phrenology Fad and Science: A 19th-Century American Crusade* (1955), and Madeleine B. Stern, *Heads & Headlines: The Phrenological Fowlers* (1971). A collection of phrenological examinations of major 19th-century American figures, reprinted mostly from the *Phrenological Journal,* may be found in Stern, ed., *A Phrenological Dictionary of Nineteenth-Century Americans* (1982). The Fowler Family Papers, containing much material of phrenological interest, are deposited in the Collection of Regional History in Cornell University Library.

Madeleine B. Stern

PLATO (427–347 B.C.), a student of Socrates and one of the first philosophers to develop a comprehensive view of the world and man's place in it, was a major influence on the idealism* of the Transcendentalists. He founded his Academy in 388 B.C., for "the prosecution of scientific study," hoping to supply the state with people whose intellects had been developed through the pursuit of truth for its own sake. Unlike Socrates, who did not leave any manuscripts of his ideas, P wrote several letters and more than 20 dialogues in which he positioned his mentor as the protagonist of his own ideas. Like Socrates, however, P believed oral teaching superior to the written word. He thought it better to lead the mind of the inquirer to discover truth individually rather than attempt to impart it dogmatically.

The philosophy of P is grounded on a dualism of materialism and immaterialism in which the latter takes precedence over the former. P's metaphysical dualism poses two fundamental degrees of reality: the material entities observed through the senses and the realm of superior Forms that antecede the material. P called the first the "world of becoming" and the second the "world of being." The sensible world is transient and therefore imperfect. Whatever knowledge one derives from the senses is unsatisfactory and uncertain. The world of the Forms is eternal, therefore more real. The role of the philosopher, according to P, must be to explore the Forms, which are independent of human awareness and can be found only by contemplation. P was concerned about human conduct within this dualism since man is both a material and a contemplative being. He believed that through a knowledge of the Forms one could find the perfect standard of human conduct, or the "good." Each person must make the discovery personally, as he illustrated in his famous "Allegory of the Cave." P claimed he had never found the absolute good, but even were he to do so, he could not describe it to another. In *Timaeus,* P posited the theory of a cosmic design of the universe by a divine craftsman. He did not believe in a creator god but in one who took the materials of the universe and assigned them a teleological role. Man also must become a craftsman in ordering the microcosm* of his own life.

Transcendentalists found in P a kindred spirit, since he exalted intuition as a source of knowledge superior to sense experience. John S. Harrison, in *The Teachers of Emerson* (1910), speaks of R. W. Emerson's** fascination with the dialogues of P. B. Alcott** positioned a bust of P on a bookcase in his classroom. Although the Transcendentalists had no unified system of beliefs, they generally conceded that there are ideas that are not derived through the senses or the sheer power of human reasoning but are intuitive. They believed that man has the inborn knowledge of what is right, beautiful, and true and with proper inner direction may attain perfection. The Transcendentalists had faith in ordinary people to order their lives in accordance with truth and beauty. G. Bancroft,** in "On the Progress of Civilization, or Reasons Why the Natural Association of Men of Letters Is with the Democracy" (*BoQR* [October 1838]), claimed that P was a thoroughgoing democrat, since he too believed that "reason exists within every breast" and that there was "no difference between one mind and another"; indeed, "there was no faculty given, no intellectual function conceded, which did not belong to the meanest of their countrymen."

The Transcendentalists were more closely aligned with the Neoplatonists* than the Platonists,* since they generally had a more mystical vision of truth than the process of P's dialectical reasoning. Neoplatonism affirmed that the highest good lies beyond empirical experience, leading to the conclusion that all earthly things are vain.

REFERENCES: See Emerson's "Plato, or the Philosopher," *CW*, 4: 21–44. For a thorough study of the Forms, one must read the entirety of P's dialogues and letters. R. G. Bury, *P with An English Translation* (1929), is still standard. A. E. Taylor provides a perceptive and comprehensive overview of P's philosophy in his popular *P: The Man and His Work* (1926). Walter Pater delivered an excellent series of lectures for young students of philosophy, published in *P and Platonism* (1949). For an in-depth examination of the Forms of P, see I. M. Crombie, *An Examination of P's Doctrines,* 2 vols. (1963).

Raymond L. Muncy

PLATONISM, the philosophy of Plato,* was one of the three or four major influences on R. W. Emerson,** some think the most significant one. B. Alcott** and M. Fuller** were intrigued with certain aspects of Plato and Platonism, which had much less impact on H. Thoreau.** Platonism may be defined by four of its primary concepts: (1) Plato believed that the supreme values—the Good, the Beautiful, and the True—were ultimately One, but it was the Good that concerned him most frequently—especially the practical application of philosophy to personal, family, and social problems; (2) Plato's theory of ideas led him to view the created world as an imperfect imitation of a divine archetype; (3) poets must be moved by a divine power speaking through them—there can be no genuine poetry except by inspiration (*furor poeticus* was the suprahuman state during which the poet glimpsed the ultimate nature of things, the divine archetypes); and (4) Plato used myths, images, and symbols as the best vehicles to express ideas.

Emerson read Plato while in college and as a young pastor; in 1820 he wrote a college composition on "The Character of Socrates." Extensive references to Plato may be found in *EL, L,* and *JMN,* and Plato represents "the Philosopher" in *Representative Men* (1850). Why did Emerson lecture and write in the first place? A clue lies in the timeless analogy of the cave in Plato's *Republic.* The philosopher there struggles to free himself from the chains of ignorance and superstition, making his way to the light outside the cave. He sees truth. Loving its clarity, he might bask in its light. But the thought of the chained multitude still in the cave gives him no rest, and he understands, as Platonic seekers of truth must, that he cannot fail to carry glimmerings of light to the poorer minds who inhabit the cave still.

Especially attractive to Emerson was Plato's theory of the eternal Ideals, or Forms. In describing the Beauty in nature* in *Nature* (1836), he reiterated Plato's Doctrine of Forms, for physical beauty was at best only preliminary, "the herald of inward and eternal beauty." He repeatedly reiterated both the matter-of-factness and the otherworldliness of the physical world. Particular facts of nature are symbolic of the spiritual world. Emerson's concept of the Over-Soul owes much to Plato's view of the existence of a spiritual or intelligible reality that is independent of, or reflected in, the world of physical things and is the ultimate origin of both existence and values. Emerson's "Love" is one of his most Platonic essays, with its sublimation of physical passion into spiritual love. As Rusk (1949) says, "Emerson climbed, with Plato's Socrates, the ladder of love, asserting that by physical love we are 'put in training for a love which knows not sex, nor person, nor partiality, but which seeks virtue and wisdom everywhere, to the end of increasing virtue and wisdom.' " Emerson thus exalted the image of his first wife, Ellen, which remained in his mind after she died: He said he saw her as "an Ideal that, if I were a Platonist, I should believe to have been one of the Forms of Beauty in the Universal Mind." Emerson early in life took a Platonic attitude toward the form of the afterlife. In his Sermon CVII, said Arthur C. McGiffert, he "adheres to the Platonic theory of disembodied spirit rather than to the Hebraic and Aristotelian theory of some form of corporeality in the future life."

Alcott read Plato beginning in 1833 and continued his interest in Platonism and Neoplatonism* throughout his life, giving talks and meeting with midwestern Plato clubs through the 1870s. Odell Shepard says that Alcott could not have given a clear outline of Plato's philosophy but did make the Platonic world of pure idealism* seem to Emerson "as solid as Massachusetts." His mind had a Neoplatonic, more than a Platonic, slant; that is, he found "reality not in matter and its forms but in Mind and Its Ideas. 'I set out,' he wrote in 1835, in words that Emerson had before him while writing *Nature,* 'from the wide ground of Spirit, that *IS.* All else is manifestation.' " Dahlstrand comments, "Plato's ideas helped Alcott establish a definite relationship between spirit and matter. Now he saw spirit as the ultimate reality and matter as only the form and shadow of spirit. . . . Material things, including the human body, were merely types or symbols of ideas. . . . The universe was but an imperfect symbol of the spirit which pervaded it. Clearly matter was subordinate to spirit.'' Fuller also read Plato and discussed his philosophy often with Emerson, and in *Woman in the Nineteenth Century,* she invokes Plato three times.

The influence of Plato on Thoreau is another matter. Allegory-of-the-cave imagery has been detected in *Walden;* in the ''Visitors'' chapter, Thoreau refers to Plato's humorous definition of man as ''a biped without feathers''; and in the chapter ''Reading'' he refers to Plato as someone any serious student should have read: ''We should be as good as the worthies of antiquity . . . and soar . . . higher in our intellectual flights than the columns of the daily paper.'' However, Thoreau in the first version of *Walden* wrote that Plato's ''Dialogues, which contain what was immortal to him, lie on the next shelf, and yet I never read them. *I describe my own case here''* (Thoreau's emphasis). And in his journal* on 27 July 1840 he wrote, ''The wood thrush is more modern than Plato and Aristotle. They are a dogma, but he preaches the doctrine of this hour.'' This is typical Thoreau satire, with Plato the foil for the more relevant contemporary philosopher, singing in the forest for the modern ear.

In conclusion, we return to Emerson, the fountainhead of American Transcendentalism. He first seriously encountered Plato, argues Vivian C. Hopkins, through R. Cudworth,* the Cambridge Platonist, and his anthology embracing Plato, Aristotle, and the Neoplatonists. ''Emerson's reading in Cudworth,'' Hopkins observes, ''formed the mold for his apprehension of Neoplatonic thought.'' ''The clear distinction expressed by Cudworth between material and Spiritual nature,'' she concludes, ''became in a sense the foundation-stone for Emerson's theory of art.'' The long-standing war between the material and the Spiritual worlds, given definition by many interpreters of Plato, has itself been brought to a peaceful settlement by Ray Benoit, who claims that Emerson, like Plato, did not see matter and spirit as opposites in a dualistic combat. Rather, they are both aspects of a ground of being higher than both. In his ''Plato, or the Philosopher,'' Emerson finds Plato a monistic dualist, finds him believing that spirit and matter have an existence independent of each other: That is, one is not a refinement of the other but hints at a higher ground in which they are reconciled into a bipolar unity.

Finally, we might rephrase Keats's insight in ''Ode on a Grecian Urn'': Emerson—and before him Plato—might have said, ''Matter is Spirit, spirit matter—that is all ye know on earth, and all ye need to know.'' For one like Emerson who sought to see unity in all things, this is the ultimate vision, that of the mystic. Put in Hindu terms, Atman (the individual self) is Brahman (the Invisible Universal Self); the material self IS the spiritual self. And behind even Brahman is the unknowable source of all, what Benoit calls ''the fire's center.''

REFERENCES: Perhaps the place to start is Emerson's own essay ''Plato, or the Philosopher,'' *CW,* 4:23–50. Floyd Stovall in his bibliographic study of Emerson in *Eight American Authors* (1963) traces the book-length studies of Emerson's sources. J. S. Harrison, *The Teachers of Emerson* (1910), highlights ''the essentially Platonic quality of Emerson's thought.'' Harrison says Emerson derived his Platonism chiefly from Thomas Taylor's translations of Plato and the Neoplatonists, from Cudworth's *True Intellectual System of the Universe* (4-vol. 1820 ed.), and from Coleridge's** *Aids to Reflection* and *The Friend,* which Emerson read as early as 1829. Harrison should be supplemented by such later studies as F. I. Carpenter, *Emerson and Asia* (1930), which plays down the Platonism and Neoplatonism in Emerson's thought to make room for the influence of Oriental* philosophy. S. G. Brown agrees with Harrison that the essence of Emerson's thinking is Platonic, though disguised in the cloak of German idealism and Oriental mysticism (''Emerson's Platonism,'' *NEQ* 18 [September 1945]: 325–45). See also Hopkins, ''Emerson and Cudworth: Plastic Nature and Transcendental Art,'' *AL* (1951; rpt. in *On Emerson: The Best from "American Literature,"* ed. Edwin H. Cady and Louis J. Budd [1988], 62–80); Benoit, ''Emerson on Plato: The Fire's Center,'' *AL* (1963; rpt. in Benoit, *Single Nature's Double Vision* [1973], 57–67, and in *On Emerson,* 127–38); and George Mills Harper, ''Thomas Taylor in America,'' in *Thomas Taylor the Platonist,* ed. Kathleen Raine and Harper (1969), 49–102. McGiffert's assessment is in *Young Emerson Speaks: Unpublished Discourses on Many Subjects* (1938), 244 (McGiffert's selected edition has been superseded by *Sermons*). And see Joseph R. Millichap, ''Plato's Allegory of the Cave and the Vision of *Walden,''* *ELN* 7 (June 1970): 274–82; J. Lyndon Shanley, *The Making of Walden* (1957), 150; Shepard, *Pedlar's Progress: The Life of Bronson Alcott* (1937); and Dahlstrand (1982).

Reid Huntley

PLOTINUS (205–270), probably born in Egypt, is generally considered the founder of the Neoplatonic* school of philosophy. His mystical interpretation of the doctrines of Plato* attracted the Transcendentalists. R. W. Emerson** was particularly intrigued with P's idea of the One, the source from which all goodness, truth, and beauty flows. This outpouring from the One is termed ''emanation'' by P and accounts for the existence of the sensate world, which is a reflection of the ideal residing in the One, remaining undiminished by continual issuances. P perceived the universe as intrinsically positive; he viewed evil as failure of the soul to harness the senses and the negative influences of matter, concepts largely adopted by Emerson.

P's mysticism, which stresses as ultimate goal an ecstatic union with the One, suggests the intuitive certainty that the highest good lies beyond empirical experience. Emerson's careful study of Platonic scholarship (after finding Neoplatonic writings summarized in V. Cousin's** *Introduction to the History of Philosophy* [1828]) came through Thomas Taylor's translation of Plato (1804), which was heavily tinged with the Neoplatonic doctrine of P. He later examined other translations that disavowed Taylor's bias, particularly that of Bohn (1848), but remained essentially committed to his earlier convictions.

Many of Emerson's central ideas, such as the concept of the Over-Soul, mystic union with God, and the perfectibility of man through developmental stages, are drawn directly from P. Indeed, the first edition of Emerson's *Nature* (1836) bore an epigraph from P on the title page: ''Nature* is but an image or imitation of wisdom, the last thing of the soul; nature being a thing which doth only do, but not know.''

REFERENCES: One of the best studies of P's influence on the key figure of the Transcendental movement is John S. Harrison, *The Teachers of Emerson* (1910). Gay Wilson Allen, *Waldo Emerson: A Biography* (1981), contains extensive discussion of Emerson's involvement in the philosophy of P. The chapter "Major Influences" in Donald N. Koster, *Transcendentalism in America* (1975), is also helpful in tracing P's impact on the movement.

John D. Cloy

PLUTARCH (46?–120?), Greek biographer and moralist, furnished classically trained Transcendentalists with useful anecdotes of ethical conduct and heroism as well as important models of biography. P's appeal is a reminder that Transcendentalists were interested not simply in mystical influxes of divinity and rapture in nature* but also in behavior and character—what R. W. Emerson** called the "moral sublime."

Emerson borrowed volumes from the *Œuvres de Plutarque,* translated by Jacques Amyot (22 vols., (1783–87), from the Harvard College Library from 1826 to 1828. He also owned the *Lives,* translated by John Langhorne and William Langhorne (8 vols., 1822), and the *Morals* (5th ed., 5 vols., 1718). According to Edmund G. Berry, "Emerson, Montaigne,* and P all admire the same type of great man. . . . He is humble, reasonable, simple, self-reliant, self-denying, devoted to principle." In his early journals* and sermons, which are sprinkled with illustrations from the *Lives,* Emerson strives to reconcile the balance and wisdom he finds in both Stoicism* and Christianity. His essays reflect a growing preference for the *Morals.* The method of Plutarchan moral biography is inherent in his 1835 lecture series on Biography, in which he celebrates, says Gustaaf Van Cromphout, the "greatness or uniqueness" of his subjects. By the 1845–46 lecture series that became *Representative Men* (1850), however, Emerson's practice had become influenced, according to Van Cromphout, by the example of Herder* and Goethe,** with his six "representative" figures drawn against the backdrop of history, ideas, and cultures from which they emerged.

The Fruitlands* library had the *Morals* and *Lives,* and ten-year-old L. M. Alcott** noted in her journal on 12 October 1843, "I read in P"; nine years later she included the *Lives* on her "List of books I like." B. Alcott,** like Emerson, measured perception and delineation of character against P's example. He accounted H. Thoreau,** for example, "the purest of our moralists, and the best republican in the Republic—viz., the republican at home. . . . [T]here is about him a nobleness and integrity of bearing that make possible and actual the virtues of Rome and Sparta. . . . P would have made him an immortal, had he known him" (Journal, 9 June 1851). Alcott found the *Morals,* moreover, strikingly contemporary as anticipating the lyceum,* the modern version of which he thought distinctly Emersonian: P's "fair fragments were briefs of discourses made by the philosopher to assembled companies, Athenian and Roman, and since collected for our entertainment in good learning. But besides these we have nothing reminding us of Emerson's utterances'' (Journal, 2 February 1856). The aging Emerson himself contributed to a revival of interest in P, as author of the widely praised introduction to *P's Morals,* edited by William W. Goodwin (5 vols., 1870).

REFERENCES: The most complete study remains Edmund G. Berry, *Emerson's P* (1961). Gustaaf Van Cromphout explores Emerson's shift from Plutarchan to Goethean methods of biography in *Emerson's Modernity and the Example of Goethe* (1990), 98–115. Broadly vocational implications of Emerson as biographer are discussed penetratingly by Merton M. Sealts, Jr., in *Emerson on the Scholar* (1992)—esp. 46–59 and 155–72.

Wesley T. Mott

THE PRESENT, founded and published in New York by W. H. Channing,** was a short-lived periodical, appearing from September 1843 until April 1844. Channing's editorial column titled "Signs of the Times" dealt with a variety of topics of interest to reformers, and particularly to Transcendentalists, with its announcements of progress being made at Fruitlands* and Brook Farm.* Contributions by many important Transcendentalists appeared: several articles by C. Lane;** 25 "Orphic Sayings" by B. Alcott** (170, 261); the Conversation* titled "The Two Herberts" by M. Fuller;** early poems of T. W. Higginson;** and translations of Goethe** by T. Carlyle.**

When Channing began *The Present,* it was similar in content to *The Dial* and competed with it directly. *The Dial* reviewed it in January 1844 as a "valiant and vivacious journal, [which] has no superior in the purity and elevation of its tone, and in the courage of its criticism." Channing stated in his prospectus to the first issue that it was "designed to reflect the Signs of the Times. Its aim will be to aid all movements which seem fitted to produce union and growth in Religion, Science and Society." The journal also reviewed both American and foreign books and published essays on a variety of subjects, as well as fiction and poetry. Channing frankly solicited submissions from "friendly contributors." By the end, the subject matter had shifted, says Clarence Gohdes, to "matters of special consequence," including capital punishment, labor, and slavery. Channing's selections developed a decidedly Fourieristic** slant, although Gohdes contends that "at no time did the journal manifest an uncompromising attitude."

Already in financial difficulties by the beginning of 1844, *The Present*'s February issue never appeared, though issues for March and April did. A total of seven issues were published. The failure of *The Present* to thrive in the reform-minded Transcendentalist era was caused largely by Channing's poor management.

REFERENCES: See Gohdes (1931); Mott (1938–57); Myerson (1984); Paul F. Boller, *American Transcendentalism, 1830–1860: An Intellectual Inquiry* (1974); and Donald N. Koster, *Transcendentalism in America* (1975).

Suzanne D. Green

PROCLUS (410–485) was the last major Greek philosopher and the last great representative of Neoplatonism.* Both R. W. Emerson** and B. Alcott** read P, originally in Thomas Taylor's translations, and derived considerable inspiration from P's writings: Alcott especially in 1833, Emerson in the 1830s and again especially in the spring of 1843. Although P does not rival Plato,* or even Plotinus,* nevertheless P is often included along with Plato and his Neoplatonic successors as one of the philosophers who influenced some of the American Transcendentalists, especially Emerson.

P codified later Platonism,* combining his own views with those of his teachers (Plutarch,* Syrianus, Porphyry, and Iamblichus). In *The Elements of Theology* (trans. E. R. Dodds, 2nd ed., 1963), P offered a concise exposition of Neoplatonic metaphysics, in 211 propositions. In his *Platonic Theology* P aspired to a complete, coherent metaphysical system. He explicated Plato's metaphysics but also offered a complete pagan theology. P helped Neoplatonic ideas to spread throughout the Byzantine, Islamic, and Roman worlds. He opposed Christianity, passionately defending paganism. (Thomas Taylor, whose translation of P the American Transcendentalists read, was himself militant in his own pagan Platonism.) As a Platonic idealist,* P held that thoughts comprise reality, while concrete "things" are mere appearances. Ultimate reality, the "one," is both God and Good.

M. Fuller** makes one reference to P in *Woman in the Nineteenth Century:* "Proclus teaches that every life has in its sphere a totality of wholeness of the animating powers of the other spheres, having only as its own characteristic a predominance of some one power." Such was the appealing unity and diversity she found in P. She also discussed Plato, Plotinus, and P with Emerson in their close years when she was editing *The Dial.**

Alcott, according to Odell Shepard, when he read Plato, Plotinus, and P "filled his thoughts with majestic and cloudy conjectures." Shepard's introduction to Alcott's *Journals** and his *Pedlar's Progress: The Life of Bronson Alcott* play down Alcott's intellectual abilities, and he suggests that Alcott had few, but nevertheless strongly propelling, ideas.

Emerson had two of P's books in his personal library and gave two additional identical copies in 1873 to the Concord* Free Public Library. Emerson's letters and journals make occasional references to P. Two stand out. After finishing his *Essays* in 1841, Emerson had a period of time to reread his favorite authors, including Plato, Plotinus, and P. He wrote that in reading those authors he was present "at the sowing of the seed of the world." Sometime in the spring of 1843, Emerson expressed his most profound enthusiasm for this Neoplatonist: "I read P for my opium, it excites my imagination to let sail before me the pleasing & grand figures of gods & daemons & demoniacal men. . . . By all these & so many 'rare & brave words' I am filled with hilarity & spring, my heart dances, my sight is quickened, I behold shining relations between all beings, and am impelled to write and almost to sing. I think one would grow handsome who read P much & well. . . . This is inspiration." This reference to how he read P illustrates supremely Emerson's own view of why one should read books, the same as he advocates in "The American Scholar"—that is, as inspiration.

REFERENCES: *The Philosophy of P,* a biography by P's successor in the Athenian Academy, was trans. Laurence J. Rosan (1949).

                                                                    Reid Huntley

PURITANISM, often called Calvinism because of the influence of French divine John Calvin (1509–1564) on Protestant Reformed theology, was the broad name for the religious culture that dominated New England from the founding of the Massachusetts Bay Colony in 1628 until the late 18th century. The Puritanism that found its way to Boston arose as a religious and political movement during the reign of Elizabeth I, seeking to extend the principles of the Reformation by purifying the Church of England. Its fundamental doctrines included human depravity and original sin, the sovereignty of God (expressed through predestination, and His redemption of the elect through His offer of free, irresistible grace), and the consequent partial ability of the saints to discern God's will as revealed in the Bible. These tenets underwent transformations in America throughout the 18th century and were finally challenged head-on in the early 19th century by Unitarianism* (early known also as "liberal Christianity"), which promoted a theology of self-culture stressing a benign God interested in fostering human growth. In important ways, Transcendentalism draws this liberal theology to its logical conclusion, emphasizing divine immanence* in the creation, intuitive experience of that divinity, and the potential moral perfectibility of all people. The nature of the relation of Transcendentalism to Puritanism, however, remains a matter of dispute.

The terms *Calvinism* and *Puritanism* are both problematic. Calvin's *Institutes of the Christian Religion* (1536) helped to codify the doctrines of strict Reformed theology, but these had been shaped by earlier leaders of the Reformation, notably Martin Luther (1483–1546) in Germany and Ulrich Zwingli (1484–1531) in Switzerland. Premedieval principles of original sin and redemptive grace already had been articulated by St. Augustine (354–430). Moreover, the sinful Paul's seizure on the road to Damascus by a sovereign God (Acts 9:3–18) was cited by many Puritans—literal readers of Scripture— as the archetypal conversion. But Puritanism in America, no less than Transcendentalism later, was a diverse movement, with conflicting views of ecclesiastical and doctrinal matters, including the crucial order of salvation.

In New England the dominant model of conversion—which had been allowed even by Calvin—held that human response to God's call was an important preliminary to grace. To varying degrees, most Puritans accepted the paradox that God, though sovereign, covenanted with the saints, enabling them to discern their spiritual estate for signs of assurance lest they be paralyzed by anxiety. "Puritanism," notes David Robinson, "sustained a sense of dynamism through its doctrines of 'preparation for grace,' a theological stance that carried the seed of later liberal doctrines of character formation. The Arminians stressed moral development, [W. E.] Channing** preached self-culture, and [R. W.] Emerson** described the expanding circle as the emblem of the growing soul.'' Puritan radicals such as Anne Hutchinson heretically asserted the rigid Reformed view that God's sovereignty is absolute, that human faculties are bypassed, or ''destroyed,'' in conversion, and that by virtue of their spiritual status the elect are immune from the moral law. The charge of Antinomianism thus implied fear of ecclesiastical and social, as well as spiritual, anarchy.

The Transcendentalists were open to charges that their ''newness'' was the new Antinomianism. They rejected Lockean* sensationalism* in the name of intuition, a stance that seemed to many conventional minds the equivalent of Antinomian spiritual seizure. They challenged institutional authority in the name of the ''higher law.''* Emerson's ''apostasy'' in his Divinity School Address in 1838 was, according to A. Norton,** ''the latest form of infidelity.'' Emerson acknowledged, in his 1841 lecture ''The Transcendentalist,''that ''In action, [the Transcendentalist] easily incurs the charge of antinomianism by his avowal that he, who has the Lawgiver, may with safety not only neglect, but even contravene every written commandment.'' But even in this lecture Emerson finds the Transcendentalist unrealized: ''[W]e have yet no man who has leaned entirely on his character, and eaten angels' food.'' On 19 July 1842, T. Carlyle** put the question of cultural continuity to Emerson: ''The disease of Puritanism was *Antinomianism;*—very strange, does that still affect the *ghost* of Puritanism?'' Carlyle had just met B. Alcott,** whose enthusiasms seemed zany and unworldly. Emerson had similar reservations about his beloved neighbor. And his own lifelong concerns with the paradoxes of experience, the complexity of human faculties, and the moral imperative of social action make it difficult indeed to label him an Antinomian in any meaningful sense.

Transcendentalists, like most of their contemporaries—and many Americans today—were deeply ambivalent about the Puritan legacy. The Puritans seemed paradoxically both stern witch-hunters and the founders of democracy. Transcendentalists who had emerged from Unitarianism recalled the struggle of liberal Christianity against orthodox dogma, and in turn they were only too eager to dismiss anything smacking of restraint on personal growth and self-culture as a vestige of Puritanism. ''Our age is retrospective. It builds the sepulchres of the fathers,'' declared Emerson at the start of *Nature*. But if Transcendentalists prided themselves on rebelling against dead forms and conventions, they were equally capable of invoking the Puritans as models of belief and purpose, in contrast to the reckless expansionism of the materialistic, rudderless 19th century. Proud of his ancestor Peter Bulkeley, a founder of Concord* in 1635, Emerson in his Historical Discourse for the town's bicentennial had praised the Puritans' ''ideal social compact'' and found that this communal spirit had animated the Revolution. In ''The Transcendentalist'' he went so far as to declare Transcendentalism an *extension* of the nonconformist tradition, the latest version of ''the Saturnalia or excess of Faith''; ''This way of thinking,'' he went on, "falling . . . on popish times, made protestants and ascetic monks, preachers of Faith against the preachers of Works; on prelatical times, made Puritans and Quakers;* and falling on Unitarian and commercial times, makes the peculiar shades of Idealism* which we know."

This rhetorical strategy, grounded in a mythic appropriation of the past, was useful in Transcendentalist critiques of both the individual soul and national politics. Morally, the 19th century seemed a Puritan world in ruins. Emerson redeployed Christian concepts of fall and redemption (in a simplified Puritan order of salvation) in "Self-Reliance": He lashes us as "timid and apologetic" and exhorts us to an "isolation" that is "elevation" but reminds us that "the law of consciousness" is "stern." And H. Thoreau** used Puritan righteousness as a touchstone in defining J. Brown** as a genuine hero—a Puritan and a Transcendentalist—who in an age of moral cowardice and expediency stood for principle. Transcendentalist calls for better preaching, better men and women, and a better society could elicit nostalgia for Puritanism, even in an age that had long since spurned the tenets of Reformed theology.

REFERENCES: Excellent introductions to Puritanism are William Haller, *The Rise of Puritanism* (1938), and Alan Simpson, *Puritanism in Old and New England* (1955). Perry Miller did most to establish American Puritanism as a field of scholarship, in such works as *Orthodoxy in Massachusetts, 1630–1650* (1933; rpt. 1970) and the 2-volume *The New England Mind* (*The Seventeenth Century* [1939] and *From Colony to Province* [1953]). Miller has been challenged and refined, esp. by scholars who stress the diversity of Puritanism in America. Important studies include Edmund S. Morgan, *Visible Saints: The History of a Puritan Idea* (1963); Philip F. Gura, *A Glimpse of Sion's Glory: Puritan Radicalism in New England, 1620–1660* (1984), which in emphasizing 17th-century dissent takes issue with Miller's depiction of a monolithic Puritan "mind"; and Norman Pettit, *The Heart Prepared: Grace and Conversion in Puritan Spiritual Life* (1966), the definitive study of preparationism. Perry Miller's influential "From Edwards to Emerson," *NEQ* 13 (December 1940): 589–617, placed Emerson in a tradition of Puritan mysticism, piety, and antiauthoritarianism. Miller has been challenged by two studies that in different ways are indebted to Pettit's account of the legacy of preparationism: Wesley T. Mott, *"The Strains of Eloquence": Emerson and His Sermons* (1989), 143–67, argues that Emerson's complex view of the spirit and human experience, and his dialectical habits of thought, made him distrust Antinomianism in any meaningful doctrinal sense. And David Robinson, "The Road Not Taken: From Edwards, Through Chauncy, to Emerson," *ArQ* 48 (spring 1992): 45–61, shows that the missing link between Edwards and Emerson, which Miller ignored, is Arminianism. Sacvan Bercovitch explores symbolic and mythic continuities in *The Puritan Origins of the American Self* (1975), esp. 157–86.

Wesley T. Mott

PUTNAM'S MONTHLY MAGAZINE OF AMERICAN LITERATURE, SCIENCE, AND ART was begun in 1853 and failed after four and a half years, during the Panic of 1857. A second series, less interesting to students of Transcendentalism, ran from 1868 to 1870, and a third, from 1906 to 1910. The original *Putnam's* was the outstanding literary serial of its time in the United States, surpassing its rival, *Harper's Monthly,* in the quantity of material by American writers. Its moving spirit was the novelist and magazinist Charles F. Briggs, who in 1852 interested the book publisher George Palmer Putnam in undertaking a review-cum-literary magazine of high quality—a domestic equivalent of *Blackwood's.* Briggs's coeditors would be G. W. Curtis** and P. Godwin.**

The publisher cast a wide net for potential contributors and received promises from, among others, N. Hawthorne** and R. W. Emerson.** Although Hawthorne sent nothing, and Emerson only a brief memorial item on Samuel Hoar,** two long narratives by H. Thoreau,** *An Excursion to Canada* and *Cape Cod,* were accepted and partially published. Other figures associated with the Transcendental movement who contributed to *Putnam's* were J. R. Lowell** (a good friend of Briggs's), H. Greeley,** W. C. Bryant,** H. W. Longfellow,** C. E. Norton,** G. Ripley,** the abolitionist* and editor Francis H. Underwood, and C. A. Dana.** Melville** was able to serialize *Israel Potter* and to place the best of his tales and sketches in its columns—only "The Two Temples" was rejected by Briggs, on the score of offensive religious content—and he collected five of those pieces in *The Piazza Tales* (1856), published by the partnership of Dix & Edwards, which acquired *Putnam's* in March 1855.

The magazine's staff and many of its contributors had ties to New York and the metropolitan daily press, but it succeeded in attracting talent from the various sections, even the South (John Pendleton Kennedy, Mrs. R. B. Hicks, and Francis Lieber, for example). Curtis supplied a great deal of copy, including his satirical series *The Potiphar Papers* and the more genial, sentimental *Prue and I* sketches. Godwin, the political editor, provided cutting and sometimes vituperative liberal commentary on party politics, politicians (starting with President Franklin Pierce), and public issues such as the explosive question of whether Kansas would be a free or slave territory. With the change of ownership, Briggs withdrew from the editorial triumvirate. Curtis and Godwin recruited to their aid as managing editor Frederick Law Olmsted, a young man of talent, convictions, and means, who in fact became a coinvestor with Joshua A. Dix and Arthur Edwards. Olmsted—later distinguished as America's foremost designer of city parks—had recently printed serially in the *New York Times* an investigation of the economic and social aspects of slavery, based on personal travels. His current interest in Kansas took the concrete though necessarily surreptitious form of providing the antislavery settlers in Lawrence with weapons to resist the Border Ruffians.

Although the chief excellence of *Putnam's* lay in its fiction, poetry, literary criticism, and book reviews, it also featured pieces on travel* and the West, art and music, urban architecture, history, biography, current world events, nature,* and technology. Thoreau's Canadian piece ran in three installments, beginning with the maiden issue of January 1853, before his disagreement with Curtis over the bowdlerization of an anticlerical passage caused Thoreau to reclaim the remainder. Putnam and his sophisticated editors were free from the prejudices and prudery that constrained most of the contemporary press; but Curtis felt justified in toning down Thoreau's "heresies" and "defiant Pantheism,"* particularly since the policy of anonymous publication made all *Putnam's* contents "(so to speak) *editorial*" (Greeley to Thoreau, 2 January 1853). The serialization of *Cape Cod* was also suspended after the third installment (August 1855), though this time Curtis made the decision.

In 1856, Curtis invested his own resources—cash and copyrights—in Dix & Edwards; unbeknown to him, one or both of the named partners mismanaged the firm's finances. They slipped away in April 1857, Olmsted withdrawing at a heavy loss soon afterward. Curtis remained as the general partner responsible to the creditors; seeking to save *Putnam's,* he went into business with the printer, a Mr. Miller, and compounded his woes by accepting a very large investment by his father-in-law, F. G. Shaw.** (Curtis lectured for years in order to repay this debt.) Miller & Company failed in August 1857, selling *Putnam's* to the owners of *Emerson's United States Magazine.* The last issue under the original title was that of September, and the new, merged magazine lasted only a year longer. The second *Putnam's* was begun by G. P. Putnam, his son George Haven Putnam, and Briggs in 1868. Those of its contributors with Transcendental associations were W. Whitman's** admirer W. D. O'Connor, J. Burroughs,** and William Dean Howells.

REFERENCES: Mott (1938–57) contains the authoritative summary treatment, 2:419–31. H. E. Scudder, *James Russell Lowell* (1901), 1:348–54, describes the origins of *Putnam's* and Lowell's part in the publication. For Curtis's extensive role, see Gordon Milne, *George William Curtis & the Genteel Tradition* (1956), 64–96 passim. A detailed account of Thoreau's contributor experiences appears in the historical introduction to *Cape Cod,* ed. J. J. Moldenhauer (1988), 258–78.

Joseph J. Moldenhauer

Q

QUAKERISM, emphasizing each individual's immediate access to God and a consequent responsibility for social justice, paralleled—and in important cases helped shape—Transcendentalist concepts of spirit and ethical action. G. Bancroft,** in his *History of the United States,* was one of the first to observe similarities to the Quaker Inner Light in the philosophy of I. Kant* and the vision of European Romantics.

Founded in England about 1650 by George Fox (1624–1691), the Society of Friends, or Quakers, believe that Christ's spirit—an Inner Light—is available to each person without external means such as creeds, sacraments, or professional clergy. This indwelling presence radically transforms the individual conscience; and because divinity resides in all, it follows, believers ought to resist institutional barriers to equality, whether theological, moral, social, or political. Though a quietist strain runs through the sect, Quakers since the earliest days have been at the forefront of reform, and Fox was particularly noted for his brave witness to the truth and his endurance of persecution and frequent imprisonment for that stance.

Quakerism directly influenced the course of American Transcendentalism through R. W. Emerson's** vocational struggle with the Unitarian* ministry. Returning from his southern journey in 1827, he met Edward Stabler, a Quaker from Alexandria, who apparently helped inspire his important notion of compensation.* During his ministry at Second Church in Boston, he read William Sewel's *The History of the . . . Quakers* (3d ed., 2 vols., 1823) and *The Select Works of William Penn* (3d ed., 5 vols., 1782). The definitive theme of Emerson's sermons—the "God Within"—may be found in sources as diverse as Marcus Aurelius, the New Testament (e.g., Luke 17:21), Fénelon,* and Böhme*—but its resemblance to the Quaker concept of the Inner Light is striking. As Emerson considered resigning his Boston pulpit, Quaker sources provided inspiring examples of Fox's moral courage as well as useful doctrinal rationale. On 11 June 1832 he withdrew volumes 1 and 2 of Thomas Clarkson's *A Portraiture of Quakerism* (1806) from the Boston Athenaeum* and took volume 2—with Sewel's *History*—on his retreat to the White Mountains to reflect on his decision. His famous sermon on the Lord's Supper* (*Sermons*, 4:185–94), preached on 9 September to explain his pending resignation, was buttressed by the example of Quaker antiformalism: The Quakers, he declared, "denied the authority of the supper altogether and gave good reasons for disusing it."

Not all Transcendentalists found Quakerism so indispensable. E. P. Peabody,** in a letter to Emerson on 24 September 1838, compared Quakerism to the spiritual enthusiasm, or delusions, of J. Very** (who read Fox in the 1840s): "*These impulses* from above I think are never sound minded—the insanity of Quakers—(which is very frequent under my observation) always grows out of it—or rather begins in it.—" H. Thoreau** in his journal* scorned the Quaker meetinghouse near New Bedford—an "ugly shed" "altogether repulsive to me, like a powder-house or grave"—and the "doubt and narrowness" of one Quaker minister.

The Quaker influence on Transcendentalism, nevertheless, was pervasive. B. Alcott** had encountered Quakers by 1822 in North Carolina, and in Philadelphia in the early 1830s he was drawn to the Quakers' commitment to abolition* and education reform.* His wife, Abba, befriended Quaker reformer Lucretia Mott (1793–1880). Emerson and Mott were mutual admirers over many years, and even Thoreau, having heard her preach, wrote his sister, "It was a good speech,—Transcendentalism in its mildest form." Long after resigning his pulpit, Emerson continued to be engaged by Quakerism. In the winter of 1833–34 he supplied his relative O. Dewey's** pulpit in New Bedford, a Unitarian parish with a substantial Quaker presence. There Quaker Mary Rotch's capacity to "acquiesce" may have helped him conceive his emerging doctrine of self-reliance as fundamentally *selfless,* a quality he later called "a voluntary obedience, a necessitated freedom." His 1835 lecture "George Fox" (*EL*, 1:164–82) depicted the Quaker virtually as an early "representative man"—the embodiment of the living "Religious sentiment." As had Bancroft, Emerson regarded the Quakers as like-minded truth-seekers: "[T]he books and tracts written to announce and defend their faith are a string of citations from all the sages, such as one would expect to find in the lecture of Kant or Fichte* on the Transcendental Philosophy." Fox combined courage with the "self renouncement" necessary to real faith. And the legacy of Quaker reform, Emerson observed in the lecture, included modern peace, abolition, and temperance* movements. Thoreau invoked the Quakers as examples of Christ-like moral "indignation" in "A Plea for Captain John Brown."** And both Emerson and Thoreau were attracted to Fox's organic* metaphor of rebirth: "Geo. Fox's chosen expression for the God manifest in the mind," Emerson noted, "is the Seed"; for Thoreau, the image (which he could have found in his Quaker grandmother's copy of Sewel's *History*) reflected his impulse, as a Transcendental natural historian,* to discover unity between spirit and nature.*

In "The Transcendentalist" (1841), Emerson posited Quakerism as an important stand for Idealism* in the evolving but eternal struggle with materialism. Quaker ideas run throughout his own essays. Fox, who is quoted in *Nature,* is included in "The Over-Soul" with ancient and modern representatives of "the opening of the religious sense." But Emerson pays Fox and the others perhaps the highest tribute by refusing to canonize them. "We are all," he insists, "discerners of spirits"; and "Jesus speaks always from within." As he put it in the Divinity School Address, "Once leave your own knowledge of God, your own sentiment, and take secondary knowledge, as St. Paul's, or George Fox's, or Swedenborg's,* and you get wide from God with every year this secondary form lasts."

Asked once about his religious stance, Emerson is variously reported to have declared, "I am more of a Quaker than anything else," or "If I am anything, I am a Quaker." Given Emerson's remarkable eclecticism, a claim for affiliation with any party may be suspected as a momentary effusion. Yet the example— for Emerson and other Transcendentalists—of Quaker adherence to truth can hardly be overstated.

REFERENCES: The best study remains Frederick B. Tolles, "Emerson and Quakerism," *AL* (1938; rpt. in *On Emerson: The Best from "American Literature,"* ed. Edwin H. Cady and Louis J. Budd [1988], 19–42). Mary C. Turpie carefully traced Emerson's use of Clarkson in "A Quaker Source for Emerson's Sermon on the Lord's Supper," *NEQ* 17 (March 1944): 95–101. Yukio Irie finds Quaker echoes throughout Emerson's sermons, in *Emerson and Quakerism* (1967). Bancroft's comparison of Quakerism and Transcendentalism is noted by O. B. Frothingham** (1876), 117–20, who accepts the analogy—with the caveat that the Quaker Inner Light is "supernatural," the Transcendentalist equivalent, natural. For Thoreau's use of Fox's seed image, see Robert D. Richardson, Jr., introduction to *Faith in a Seed,* ed. Bradley P. Dean (1993), 16.

Wesley T. Mott

R

THE RADICAL (September 1865–June 1872), a liberal-Unitarian* monthly publication edited by the Rev. Sydney H. Morse, was conceived as "[a] monthly magazine devoted to religion," hence the subtitle of the first issue. Gradually, *The Radical* became more inclusive, with some articles on secular topics, though it never strayed from its original purpose. As an open forum for the free discussion of religion, it was attractive to Transcendentalists.

Operating out of his office on Bromfield Street in Boston, Morse provided a lively vehicle for expressing controversial views. The principal contributors to the early issues were among the most eloquent second-generation Transcendentalists: S. Johnson,** D. A. Wasson,** and J. Weiss.** *The Radical* did not feature standard departments or columns, instead allowing its contributors substantial latitude in topics and format. Weiss, for example, discussed "The Essential Jesus," and Johnson equated the voice of nature* with the voice of God in "Discourses Concerning the Foundation of Religious Belief," which ran for the first six issues.

On 30 May 1867, O. B. Frothingham** chaired the organizational meeting of the Free Religious Association* (FRA) and sought the use of *The Radical* as its voice. Sympathetic to the cause, Morse agreed, and the result was an increase in his pool of authors. Frothingham, C. Bartol,** M. D. Conway,** T. W. Higginson,** and S. Longfellow** were among frequent contributors to the later issues.

Ultimately, Morse's decision to affiliate with the FRA resulted in the decline of *The Radical,* as its already limited audience became alienated by the views expressed by the new wave of contributors. In the spring of 1872, the Radical Publishing Company was formed by five members of the Radical Association, and stocks were issued in an attempt to save the dying magazine. The company issued $50,000 in stock at $100 per share, but only 93 shares were sold, most of them to the magazine's contributors. The attempt failed, and *The Radical* died, but the magazine had served its purpose of providing an open forum for the discussion of liberal religion.

REFERENCES: The best source for information on *The Radical* is E. Bruce Kirkham's entry in Chielens (1986). Also of value is Mott (1938–57), 3:78. Brief references are scattered throughout Myerson (1984).

Nathaniel T. Mott

The **RADICAL CLUB** was an outgrowth of the Free Religious Association* that was founded by the more radical wing of Unitarians* who broke from the main body of the denomination following the second national convention in Syracuse, New York, in 1866. Also known as the Chestnut Street Club because it met at the Chestnut Street home of the Rev. John T. Sargent, the club was first organized by C. A. Bartol** in February 1867 as a forum for the promotion, G. W. Cooke** reports, of "free discussion of subjects of interest to free thinkers." The club had no formal organizational structure, and its "membership" consisted solely of those who wished to attend. Many of those who attended most regularly were Transcendentalists such as R. W. Emerson,** A. B. Alcott,** F. H. Hedge,** E. P. Peabody,** C. P. Cranch,** and J. F. Clarke.** Emerson, in fact, was invited to present the first paper at the May 1867 meeting on the subject of religion.

Within months of its founding, the club had begun to attract considerable publicity (in part because one member, Louisa Chandler Moulton, regularly reported the activities of the club to the New York *Tribune*). Emerson, who thought the publicity detracted from the members' ability to speak with complete candor, withdrew not long after becoming involved with the club. Other members of the Transcendentalist circle remained for several years until the club finally folded in 1880. One of the most significant contributions of the club was the fact that it included both men and women, "placing them on a plane of intellectual equality," says Cooke. J. W. Howe** noted, "It was a glad surprise to me when I was first invited to read a paper before this august assemblage."

REFERENCES: Mary E. Sargent, *Sketches and Reminiscences of the Radical Club* (1880), provides the only account of selected meetings. Cooke, "The Free Religious Association," *NEMag* n.s. 28 (June 1903): 484–99, provides a better historical sketch of the club and its origins, though it does not contain detailed information about individual meetings. Howe, *Reminiscences, 1819–1899* (1899), provides a chapter on "The Boston Radical Club" (281–303), and O. B. Frothingham,** *Recollections and Impressions* (1891), includes his reminiscences about the club's activities. Finally, Stowe Persons, *Free Religion* (1947), chronicles the history of the FRA and discusses the Radical Club and the spread of other radical clubs throughout the Midwest in the late 19th century.

Alfred G. Litton

REALISM in general asserts the "real," objective, or absolute existence of some object or entity. Since the entities under dispute can range from abstract universals to material objects, the exact referent of "realism" can be confusing.

In Transcendental usage, it refers to the medieval doctrine that the human mind can apprehend in the particulars of the world a preexisting order of abstract universals. Thus, the categories of human thought are discoveries by the reason of what is "really" there, preexisting human perception—not arbitrary constructions by the understanding based on mere sense perception (see "Nominalism"*). R. W. Emerson** expresses a typical realist position when he writes in "The Transcendentalist," "Mind is the only reality, of which men and all other natures are better or worse reflectors." Similarly, A. B. Alcott** writes: "God is the one type, which the soul strives to incarnate in all organizations" (Orphic Sayings #48, "Beauty").

Realism traces back to Plato's* theory of ideal forms; as Emerson says in "Plato," "His definition of Ideas as what is simple, permanent, uniform, and selfexistent . . . marks an era in the world." As Emerson elaborates in "The Transcendentalist" (along Augustinian lines): "Everything real is self-existent. Everything divine shares the self-existence of Deity. All that you call the world is the shadow of that substance which you are." Aristotle modified Plato's realism by arguing that universals are not substances after all but essences common to particular objects. Emerson argues an Aristotelian version of realism in "Nominalist and Realist," where he writes, "In the famous dispute with the Nominalists, the Realists had a good deal of reason. General ideas are essences." Though no one individual attains to universality, every individual contains part of the universal essence, and so from the collectivity of the parts, "Nature* keeps herself whole, and her representation complete in the experience of each mind."

In *Nature* (1836), realism (ironically, for a modern audience) leads to idealism:* "[M]aterial forms . . . preëxist in necessary Ideas in the mind of God," and their true usefulness is to lead us back to God, to "the universal spirit." True science fastens the attention not on matter but "upon immortal necessary uncreated natures, that is, upon Ideas; and in their beautiful and majestic presence, we feel that our outward being is a dream and a shade." G. Ripley,** in *Discourses on the Philosophy of Religion* (1836), also suspects that visible objects are finally less real than those that are invisible: "What if the things that are not seen, should turn out to be enduring realities, while the things that appear, are only transitory appearances?" The unseen possesses "the only independent reality," hence should be "the chief object of our attention. In so doing, we become conversant with the primal source of reality." Or, as Emerson says, "[W]hen the fact is seen under the light of an idea, the gaudy fable fades and shrivels. We behold the real higher law.*" Transcendentalism centers on this belief in a preexisting and even predetermining absolute; such realism was the basis of their idealist faith.

REFERENCES: Most discussions of realism focus on modern concepts of perceptual, natural, or scientific realism, not on the Platonic realism favored by the Transcendentalists. The confusion is elegantly untangled by Raymond Williams in "Realism," *Keywords* (rev. ed. 1985), 257–62; see also A. D. Woozley, "Universals," *EP,* 8:194–206, and

Ray Bhaskar, "Realism," *Dictionary of the History of Science,* ed. W. F. Bynum et al. (1981), 362–63.

Laura Dassow Walls

REID, THOMAS (1710–1796), was the originator of the Scottish philosophy of Common Sense,* popular in antebellum America and especially at Harvard University during R. W. Emerson's** undergraduate education there. Although M. Fuller's** letters of 1825 and 1836 suggest her familiarity with these philosophers, it was Emerson who most consistently engaged in assessing the importance of their work.

R's notion of "Common Sense" refers to principles in the consciousness that organize data gained by experience; these innate principles yield conceptions, which in turn are self-evident convictions. R's ethical ideas were particularly appealing to the undergraduate Emerson. R's insistence on a faculty of moral perception inherent in the structure of the human mind, as well as the objective nature of moral discrimination, attracted Emerson. Emerson sketched the "leading characteristics of ethical science as it is represented by . . . R, Paley,* Stewart"* in his 1821 Bowdoin Prize essay, "The Present State of Ethical Philosophy," written at Harvard. Emerson implicitly approved of R's objective morality: "The truths of morality," writes the young Emerson in this essay, "must in all ages be the same. . . . Its fundamental principles are taught by the moral sense, and no advancement of time or knowledge can improve them." Emerson characterized the Common Sense philosopher's ideas on morality: "The object of these reasonings is to confirm the decision of the moral faculty, which is recognized as an original principle of our nature,—an intuition by which we directly determine the merit or demerit of an action." Here, Emerson has paraphrased a rendition of R's idea by his student D. Stewart. (Emerson may have known R at this point only through Stewart.) R, however, claimed that this moral faculty is developed by the practice of exercising judgment within the context of circumstances: It is neither fully developed at birth, nor does it have an immediate perception of an action's moral worth.

R's theories about knowledge, elaborated in his *An Inquiry into the Human Mind on the Principles of Common Sense* (1764), were also appealing to the young Emerson insofar as R's method, following Francis Bacon's, emphasized empirical observation as the basis for knowledge and eschewed philosophical subtlety. R frequently criticized theories about epistemology by comparing them with information gained through actual practice.

Emerson also found attractive R's attempt to rescue from both skepticism and idealism* the notion that the world really exists, that the system of morals is true and absolute, and that one could rely on sensory data for objective knowledge. Thus, R provided Emerson with an appealing critique of the "ideal philosophy" that, particularly in the Stewart rendition of R's writings used at Harvard, linked the skepticism of D. Hume* with Berkeley's* idealism. Hume's philosophy asserted that all we can know is a stream of sense impressions without certainty of their reference to an external world, their causal relations, or even the integrity of the individual identity perceiving them. Berkeley's philosophy was often used by later philosophers to refute the extreme subjectivity and uncertainty of Hume's philosophy. Berkeley had posited that God projects the world into each individual consciousness, thereby giving the world the semblance of a separate existence by painting it "in the firmament of the soul," as Emerson says in *Nature*. In his *Essays on the Intellectual Powers,* R summarized Berkeley's and Hume's positions as suggesting that "there is no such thing as matter in the universe—the sun, moon, and stars, the earth which we inhabit, our own bodies, and those of our friends, are only ideas in our minds, and have no existence but in thought; . . . we find the latter [Hume] maintaining that there is neither body nor mind—nothing in nature* but ideas and impressions, without any substance on which they are impressed—that there is no certainty, nor indeed probability, even in mathematical axioms." Thus, while the "ideal theory" of Berkeley entailed the notion that the immediate object of thought is always an "idea" or impression rather than the object itself, at Harvard this was interpreted, in light of Hume's skepticism, as the assumption that the verification of sensory data about the material world is not possible. And this latter is the form Berkeley's "ideal" philosophy takes in Emerson's chapter "Idealism" in *Nature:* "In my utter impotence to test the authenticity of the report of my senses, to know whether the impressions they make on me correspond* with outlying objects, what difference does it make, whether Orion is up there in heaven, or some god paints the image in the firmament of the soul?"

In *An Inquiry into the Human Mind on the Principles of Common Sense*, R assaulted the premise that the only possible objects of human knowledge were mediating ideas (mental representations of things), rather than the sensible things themselves. This mediation led inevitably, R believed, to Hume's skepticism. That matter should be composed merely of sensations, and mind or spirit be constituted entirely of a collection of ideas, were repellent notions to R, who was also a pious minister. Emerson no less than R believed Hume's skepticism assailed the very basis of moral discernment. Moreover, Emerson, the rhapsodist of nature, did not want nature to disappear altogether under the "visionary schemes" of Hume or Berkeley, nor did he wish the moral lessons nature could teach vitiated or doubted. R at least partially restored to Emerson the foundation that Hume had undermined.

REFERENCES: The standard edition is *The Works of TR,* ed. Sir William Hamilton, 2 vols. (1863). For both an introduction to R's philosophy and a detailed study of his major works, see Keith Lehrer, *TR* (1989); see also Terence Martin, *The Instructed Vision: Scottish Common Sense Philosophy and the Origins of American Fiction* (1961). A useful discussion focusing on Emerson's interest in R and Hume is offered in John Michael, *Emerson and Skepticism: The Cipher of the World* (1988), 38–42.

Robin Sandra Grey

RICHTER, JEAN PAUL FRIEDRICH (1763–1825), a German Romantic novelist and humorist, was the author of *Quintus Fixlein* (1796), which was trans-

lated by T. Carlyle** in 1827; *The Invisible Lodge* (1793), his first literary success; and the romances *Titan* (1800–03), *Wild Oats* (1804–05), and *Schmeltzle's Journey to Flätz* (1809), which was also translated by Carlyle in 1827. An admirer of J. J. Rousseau,* R adopted the pseudonym "Jean Paul." Bridging the gap between neoclassical formalism and early Romanticism, his works helped establish the 19th-century German novel as a literary form.

R was known to the Transcendentalists initially through Carlyle, who published essays on R and other German writers in the English periodicals that were available in Boston. R. W. Emerson** recommended Carlyle's essay on R in *The Edinburgh Review** to his brother in 1827 and later quoted R in "Love," *Essays: First Series* (1841).

When M. Fuller** began to study and read German writers in 1832, she included R, probably through the encouragement of F. H. Hedge,** who loaned her copies of several works, including *Titan*. Finding R's penchant for coining words hard going for a newcomer to the German language, Fuller wrote to Hedge that she was not certain that she was in a position to judge his works. Nonetheless, she observed, "I think he and I shall not be intimate. I prefer wit to humour, and daring imagination to the richest fancy, his infinitely variegated and I confess most exquisitely coloured web fatigues my attention. I like widely extended plan, but the details more distinc[t.] Besides his philosophy and religion seem to be of the sighing sort, and having some tendency that way myself I want opposing forces in a favorite author." Later, Fuller included the first volume of *Titan* in the curriculum for a class at Hiram Fuller's Greene Street School in Providence, Rhode Island, where she taught German and Italian language and literature in 1837. In *The Dial,* Fuller published two poems about R, "Richter," and "Some Murmur at the 'Want of System,' " as well as a review of *Life of JPFR* (1842). She published a review of R's *Walt und Vult* in the *New-York Daily Tribune* (3 March 1846, 1:1).

REFERENCES: A modern treatment of R and the Transcendentalists is Edward V. Brewer, "The New England Interest in JPFR," *UCPMP* 27 (1943): 1–25. For references to R and the Transcendentalists, see *NET*Dial; and Joseph Slater, ed., *The Correspondence of Emerson and Carlyle* (1964). On German sources of Transcendentalism, see Stanley M. Vogel, *German Literary Influences on the American Transcendentalists* (1955), and Pochmann (1957).

Susan Belasco Smith

ROUSSEAU, JEAN-JACQUES (1712–1778), Swiss-French philosopher and prose writer, was no metaphysician or logician, but he was a sharp analyst "of man, society, and politics." He had widespread influence on Western culture, whether accepted or rejected. R wrote not only works of philosophical importance but also an epistolary novel, *Julie, ou La Nouvelle Héloïse* (1761; Julia, or the new Heloise), which was very popular in its day, and a famous autobiography, *Les Confessions* (wr. c. 1764–76; pub. 1782/89; The confessions). R's important works of philosophy are as follows: *Discours sur l'origine et les fondemens de l'inégalité parmi les hommes* (1755; Discourse on the origin and basis of inequality among men), in which men in a primal state are viewed as both equal and good, their inequality and immorality beginning as soon as they organize society into a civilized state. *Émile, ou de l'Education* (1762; Emil, or on education) lays out his "natural plan" for the education of the common people. Believing in the rights of the child as an offspring of nature,* R would have it spend its first 12 years close to nature in a rural environment. Then would come a three-year period in learning survival techniques (from Defoe's *Robinson Crusoe*), geography, natural science, and a *trade*. The last five years would be devoted to the study of history and to socialization. In *Émile*—which is edited in the form of a novel—R discloses his religious thought in a short section, "The Profession of Faith of the Savoyard Vicar." Filtered through the words of the vicar, R's doctrine amounts to a mild *deism* that allows him—or anyone—to follow the predominant religious custom of one's locale, as he does with his Roman Catholicism. *Du Contrat social* (1762; The social contract) contains his most profound political theory and has a chapter "On Civil Religion" in which R holds that "natural religion"* supports the state and affirms "the sacredness of the social contract."

New England Transcendentalists were more German than French minded. *The Confessions,* however, strongly impressed R. W. Emerson,** as he noted in his journals.* Though R declares at the beginning his wish to show himself "*dans toute la vérite de la nature*" (in every way true to nature), this is not an entirely reliable account of his life. Nevertheless, like Emerson in the United States, Goethe** in Germany and Hazlitt and George Eliot in England were mightily impressed by *The Confessions.* Emerson noted also reading *Émile* and *The Social Contract*—French as well as English versions. Although a certain parallelism can be observed between the philosophies of Emerson and H. Thoreau** and R's philosophy, no direct influence is detectable. Even in the field of child education,* B. Alcott** and E. Peabody** were directly influenced by German educator Friedrich Froebel (1782–1852) and the Swiss J. Pestalozzi* rather than by R.

R did not want to be called a philosopher. Indeed, he was in revolt against the tribe of Parisian *philosophes:* Diderot, d'Alembert, Voltaire, Holbach, La Mettrie, whose rationalism, skepticism, and materialism he scorned. Although he agreed with the Enlightenment effort to encourage a kind of "rugged individualism," he differed in admonishing men to look deeply within themselves to discover the "natural man." In this policy R has been misread as a primitivist who saw the savage as a "noble savage" (a term he never mentions). He never thought that a modern man could go "native" in any literal sense. R recognized that a natural man in the primordial state was a being quite different from a natural man in the civilized state. He seriously contended, however, that in his primeval state man was naturally disposed to goodness and compassion and that he was largely controlled by instinct rather than by doubt. He also contended that society and civilization promoted immorality and alienation among men. He believed that given education and discipline a man could learn to keep faith with his primeval self and could thus perfect himself. Here is a kind of antici-pation of the social criticism of Marx and of Nietzsche's** dream of human perfectibility in the *Übermensch* (Overman).

R insisted on the primacy of feeling and sentiment over thinking and ideas, privileging the "heart" over the "head"—instinct and intuition over reflection and calculation. To him the most basic feelings are (1) *amour de soi* (love of self), the seat of all emotions—the natural feeling in animals and humans of self-preservation; and (2) *amour propre* (self-love), of major importance in con-nection with society and politics, for in human relationships it prompts the competitive urge to best other people and thus gain power over them while acquiring prestige. This process divides people into superior and inferior rank-ings, thus accounting for the existence of social classes. Thus, R's philosophical method was to look into himself to discover basic principles as felt things.

If R believed in the possibility of the civilized adult to deliberately recover his original nature by willpower and self-cultivation, the ideal also was to for-mally educate the young from infancy to adulthood. In *Émile* R broaches the idea of "negative education"—what the teacher ought not do. First, the teacher ought not neglect taking into account the student's age and naturally ordered stages of physical and psychological development; second, the teacher ought not overly control, direct, or correct the student. This ideal man of the future should live, preferably, in an ideal state, which R describes in *The Social Contract.* In such a state, the "sovereign" is made up of persons who have voluntarily trans-ferred their individual rights to the community. Therefore, all who have agreed to the social contract must obey the *general will* of the state's citizens. Fur-thermore, if the ideal citizen lives in an ideal society governed by an ideal government, then, according to R, there is an ideal natural religion ready made for the new natural man—R's light deism. Every citizen of this ideal state must subscribe to this view because it is requisite for the maintenance of law and order, without which no state can long exist. In all this critique of civilization, R anticipates Freud's *Das Umbehagen in der Kultur* (1930; Civilization and its discontents).

REFERENCES: The modern standard French edition of R's works is *Oeuvres completes,* ed. B. Gagnebin and M. Raymond, 4 vols. (1959–69). The modern approved English edition is *The Collected Writings of R,* trans. J. R. Bush, C. Kelley, and R. D. Masters, ed. Masters and Kelley, vol. 1 (1990). A valuable key to R's writings is N. J. H. Dent, *A R Dictionary* (1992). Biographies and special studies include Jean Guehenno, *J-JR,* trans. from the French (1966); Ronald Grimsley, *J JR, A Study in Self-Awareness* (1961); Ernst Cassirer, *The Question of J-JR,* trans. from the German (1956); Harold Höffding, *J-JR and His Philosophy,* trans. from the Danish (1930; rpt. 1934); Mark J. Temmer, *Art and Influence of J-JR* (1973); and Penny A. Weiss, *Gendered Community: R, Sex, and Politics* (1993).

Richard P. Benton

S

SAADI (SHEIKH MUSLIH-UDDIN SA'DI SHIRAZI) (c. 1193–c. 1291) was a Persian lyric poet best known for his ethical works the *Gulistan* (The rose garden, 1258) and the *Bustan* (The orchard, 1257). S's poetry is inextricably connected to the Islamic form of mysticism called Sufism. According to Arthur Christy, the poetry of Sufism is one of the three major Oriental* influences on the Transcendentalists (behind the Indian and Chinese).

Sufism evolved an elaborate poetic symbolism used extensively by S. The fundamental principle in Sufi poetry is that divine love lives within everyone, but the manifestation of this love is dependent on externals, whether the love of woman or appropriate surroundings. Furthermore, in Sufi poetry, the human soul is subject to change. Ideally, it is attuned to God, who plays upon it through those externals, reminding it of its true nature. S's poetry aimed at attuning the soul to God. This idea was often communicated through the sensual metaphor of a man's union with his beloved, whose lips, for example, were the opening to the inscrutable mysteries of God's essence, or whose eyebrow was often compared to the domed or arched recesses of a mosque where prayers were offered with the face toward Mecca.

R. W. Emerson** read and admired S and other poets from the Sufi tradition and experimented widely with Persian forms after 1841, after he was exposed to Joseph von Hammer-Purgstall's German translations of Persian verse published in 1818. Emerson coined the name *Seyd,* a kind of anagram from S, for his ideal poet.

Emerson's enthusiasm for S resulted in the request that he write the preface to Francis Gladwin's translation of S's *Gulistan* (1865). In that preface, he writes: "S . . . has wit, practical sense, and just moral sentiments. He has the instinct to teach, and from every occurrence must draw the moral, like Franklin. He is the poet of friendship, love, self-devotion, and serenity. There is a uniform force in his page, and, conspicuously, a tone of cheerfulness, which has almost made his name a synonyme [sic] for this grace."

H. Thoreau** also felt an affinity to S, about whom he wrote in his journal:* "I can find no essential difference between S and myself. He is not Persian, he is not ancient, he is not strange to me. By the identity of his thoughts with mine he still survives."

M. D. Conway,** spending time with Emerson and Thoreau in Concord* during the summer of 1853, read the *Gulistan* on Emerson's recommendation. Conway included the writings of S in his collection *The Sacred Anthology: A Book of Ethnical Scriptures* (1874).

REFERENCES: See Joseph von Hammer-Purgstall, *Geschichte der schönen Redekunste Persiens, mit einer Bluthenlese aus Zwehhundert Persischen Dichtern, Wien, Heubner und Wolfe* (1818); and S, *The Gulistan or Rose Garden,* trans. Francis Gladwin, preface by R. W. Emerson (1865). Sir Richard Burton's introduction to his trans. *Tales from the Gulistan or Rose Garden of the Sheik Sa'di of Shirâz* (1888) is helpful on S's life. Modern studies include Frederic Ives Carpenter, *Emerson and Asia* (1930); Arthur Christy, *The Orient in American Transcendentalism* (1932); Stanley M. Vogel, *German Literary Influences on the American Transcendentalists* (1955); and Arthur Versluis, *American Transcendentalism and Asian Religions* (1993).

Moumin Manzoor Quazi

SAINT-SIMON, CLAUDE-HENRI DE ROUVROY, COMTE DE (1760–

1825), was a French soldier, eccentric, and visionary whose social philosophy has had widespread influence in industrialized countries and deeply interested R. W. Emerson** and O. Brownson.** (He should not be confused with his distant relative, the Duc de Saint-Simon, famous author of court memoirs.) A captain of artillery in the French forces at the seige of Yorktown (1781) in the American War of Independence, S declined to pursue an army career after returning to France, henceforth always being a man of peace. Having to renounce his title and imprisoned during the Reign of Terror, S nevertheless made a fortune investing in the nationalized landed estates of the Gallican Church, enabling him to lead a life of luxury and license. But he also had a passion for learning. He published his first work of social philosophy, *Lettres d'un habitant de Genève* (Letters from an inhabitant of Geneva), in 1804. Soon he had spent himself into bankruptcy, but in 1808, to continue his study of the new industrial society, he enrolled at the distinguished École Polytechnique.

To fully understand S's ideas, one must imagine certain coterminous historical events as if painted on a mural: Enlightenment (reason, empiricism, materialism); French Revolution (heads rolling, immense public debt; feudal medieval social structure plopped); and looming industrial age with a new technology, factory system, expanding bourgeoisie, and city proletariat. Indeed, S witnessed a society in chaos: The government was a headless horseman; the economy seemed a system devised by property owners to exploit the working class; and the idea that personal interest promoted by laissez-faire always harmonized with the public interest seemed false if not mad. S felt it essential that contemporary morals, politics, and religion—indeed, the whole system of ideas—be completely reorganized. S took the same position Alexander Hamilton had taken in *Report on Manufactures* (1791)—that the future power and prosperity of France, as of the United States, depended on an industrial rather than on an agricultural* economy, with the creation of a strong central government headed by a strong leader.

S sought to develop a "positive science" of society. In the *Letters* he showed concern for the character of the leadership of the new industrial society on a class basis. Of the three "estates" (social classes) that had exercised political power during the *Ancien Régime,* the "Lords Temporal" (heredity-titled nobility) were no longer a factor. The "Lords Spiritual" (Gallican priests) were too ignorant to be permitted to exercise power. There remained the "Commons" (middle-class property owners and artisans, or the bourgeoisie), the most rapidly rising class. But a new class was afoot, with thousands more outlined on the horizon marching toward urban centers as potentially propertyless factory workers. S argued that property owners could not hope to maintain their power against this onslaught unless they subsidized the education of these workers. Although the propertied class owned the means of production, it lacked the knowledge and skill to operate the new technology. S recommended that scientists and engineers as well as artisans and mathematicians be chosen for a "Council of Newton" to replace the "Lords Spiritual." The only equality he believed in was that of opportunity.

Taking a technocratic view, S saw the leadership of economic affairs in terms of *industriels, artistes,* and *savants* (those with knowledge). He believed that this elite corps could through economic planning and efficient production solve all of society's problems. He considered the "producers"—*la classe industrielle*—the basis of economic well-being. He respected property owners as such but insisted that they be under state control. He made a sharp distinction between the *producers* and the *idle,* or leisure class. S's designation "producers" included *workers* of all kinds from farmhand to wheelwright, from engineer to banker. Indeed, in his producer hierarchy the banker was number one. He further insisted that it was the duty of the state to care for the poor. Some have seen S's thought as socialistic, but such elements are minimal; his thought has more in common with the corporate state of fascism—but S was in no way racist or militarist. He suggested an international organization to promote world peace.

S was dissatisfied, moreover, with the failure of Christianity. He recognized the social value of spiritual power, however, and asked if a new Christianity might be formulated that would meet the needs of the new industrial age—an issue discussed in his last published, unfinished work, *Nouveau Christianisme* (1825; The new Christianity). He had already—with Augustin Thierry in *De la réorganization de la societé Européene* (1814; The reorganization of European society)—denied the validity of the Fall of Man because it placed the Garden of Eden at the beginning of human life on earth. He maintained that "the age of gold is not behind us; it lies ahead of us; it consists in the perfection of the social order." After S's death, two of his disciples, Barthélemy-Prosper Enfantin and St. Armand Bazard, glorified him by declaring him the founder of a new church—the Saint-Simonian Church, which proposed a new and feminist theology. It proclaimed the emancipation of women, the demortification of the flesh, and the eventual coming of a female Messiah who would complement the male Jesus.

S influenced Thierry, the Romantic historian, and Auguste Comte, the philosophical sociologist, in France; the Russian social philosopher Alexander Herzen; the Scottish writer T. Carlyle;** and Friedrich Engels, German economist and collaborator with Karl Marx. Emerson's journals* show that he read *De la réorganization,* from which he copied out in English the "age of gold theory." Evidence supports that he read *Doctrine de Saint-Simon. Exposition. Première année, 1828–29* (1831). Emerson also notes that while visiting Paris in May 1848 he purchased two busts of S for his friend E. P. Clark, cashier in the New England Bank, Boston. Brownson took special interest in S's religious view and in the Saint-Simonian Church. Brownson's "transcendental manifesto" *New Views of Christianity, Society and the Church* (1836—the same year as Emerson's *Nature* but opposed in view) owes something to S's *The New Christianity,* an English version having been published in London in 1834. Brownson continually searched for a religious faith he could stand on but did not find it until he was converted to Roman Catholicism in 1844.

REFERENCES: The standard French edition is *Oeuvres de S & d'Enfantin . . .,* 47 vols. (1865–78). A modern edition is *Oeuvres de C-H de S,* 6 vols. (1966). The few translations include *The New Christianity,* trans. Rev. J. E. Smith (1834); *The Doctrine of S. An Exposition. First year, 1828–1829,* trans. George G. Iggers (1958); *Selected Writings,* ed. and trans. F. M. H. Markham (1952) [contains nearly all of *New Christianity*]; rpt. as *Social Organization, the Science of Man and Other Writings* (1964); *Selected Writings,* trans. and ed. Keith Taylor (1975). Biographical studies are Mathurin M. Dando, *The French Faust: H de S* (1955); F. E. Manuel, *The New World of H de S* (1956); Manuel, *The Prophets of Paris* (1962); and A. J. Booth, *S and Saint-Simonism* (1871). See also Chita Ionescu, ed., *The Political Thought of S* (1976); Iggers, *The Cult of Authority: The Political Philosophy of the Saint-Simonians* (1958); David B. Cofer, *Saint-Simonism in the Radicalism of Thomas Carlyle* (1931); and Hill Shine, *Carlyle and the Saint-Simonians of Historical Periodicity* (1941).

Richard P. Benton

The **SATURDAY CLUB** was, arguably, the leading literary and intellectual club in Boston in the latter half of the 19th century. The club took definite form late in 1854, growing out of a series of dinners held by individuals formerly associated with the Transcendental Club* and the Town and Country Club.* The group met at the Parker House on the last Saturday of each month, tradition has it, because that was the day of R. W. Emerson's** regular visits to the Old

Corner Bookstore in Boston. At its height, the club boasted some of the most prominent Bostonians as its members, including Emerson, H. W. Longfellow,** H. James, Sr.,** N. Hawthorne,** O. W. Holmes,** and C. E. Norton.**

While Hawthorne's failing health and shy temperament kept him from a lengthy association with the club, Emerson remained a regular member for more than 20 years. In fact, of all the clubs to which Emerson belonged, he seems to have been fondest of his monthly meetings with "The Mutual Admiration Society," as some called it. Shortly after the club's formation, an inner circle of members ventured forth to the Adirondacks for a series of "wild camping-out journeys." Emerson, J. R. Lowell,** L. Agassiz,** and others formed an "Adirondack Club"* in 1858, and some of the members returned the following two years.

The Saturday Club has often been confused with the Atlantic Club, a group of editors and contributors to the *Atlantic Monthly*.* Though many of the Saturday Club's members (Lowell, James T. Fields, Longfellow, and others) were also members of the Atlantic Club, the two groups were, says G. W. Cooke,** "quite distinct from each other." Nevertheless, the Saturday Club's regular meetings, which most often involved the presentation of a paper and a subsequent discussion, provided *Atl's* associates with an important circle of writers from which to draw contributions.

REFERENCES: Many years after its founding, Holmes lamented that the club had no Boswell to record the minutes of its earlier meetings. Thus, the best sources on the club's history often consist of fragmentary reminiscences or incomplete accounts of selected meetings. Long considered the definitive works on the "transcendental years" of the Saturday Club are E. W. Emerson,** *The Early Years of the Saturday Club, 1855–1870* (1918), and M. A. DeWolfe Howe, *Later Years of the Saturday Club, 1870–1920* (1927). A much more concise history is Cooke, "The Saturday Club," *NEMag* n.s. 19 (September 1898): 24–34. The best discussion of Emerson's involvement is Rusk (1949), 392–401. Because J. E. Cabot** and Holmes were also members of the club, their works (*A Memoir of Ralph Waldo Emerson* [1887] and *Ralph Waldo Emerson* [1884], respectively) contain personal reminiscences and anecdotes. Paul Jamieson, "Emerson in the Adirondacks," *NYH* 39 (July 1958): 215–27, discusses how the Adirondack Club grew out of the Saturday Club's inner circle.

                                                                    Alfred G. Litton

SCHILLER, JOHANN CHRISTOPH FRIEDRICH VON (1759–1805), a German dramatist, lyric poet, and historian, was the author of a variety of works admired by the Transcendentalists, who were deeply engaged by his recurring theme of liberty and dignity for all. Next to Goethe,** S was the German literary figure who most interested the major New England writers, many of whom were introduced to S through Carlyle's** *Life of S* (1825).

M. Fuller** admired the verse trilogy about the Thirty Years' War, the *Wallenstein* (1796–99), comprising *Wallensteins Lager, Die Piccolomini,* and *Wallensteins Tod*. H. D. Thoreau** owned copies of the drama *Maria Stuart* (1800) and S's history of the Thirty Years' War, *Geschichte des dreissigjährigen Kriegs* (1791–93). J. F. Clarke** wrote to Fuller in 1833 that he was translating S's drama about Joan of Arc, *Die Jungfrau von Orleans* (1801). R. W. Emerson,** musing in his journal* in 1832 about what he might read, observed: "I propose to myself to read S of whom I hear much. What shall I read? His Robbers? Oh no, for that was the crude fruit of his immature mind. He thought little of it himself. What then: his Aesthetics? Oh no, for he was a poet only by study. His histories? & so with all his productions, they were the fermentations by which his mind was working itself clear, they were the experiments by which he got his skill & the fruit, the pure bright gold of all was—S himself."

Fuller used two of S's dramas in the private German classes she offered in Boston in 1836. She later taught *Don Carlos* (1787) and lectured on S's works in her German class at Hiram Fuller's Greene Street School in Providence, Rhode Island, in 1837. In that same year, she exchanged letters about the difficulties of German translation with J. S. Dwight,** who was working on a translation of S's *Lied von der Glocke* (1799). Later she reviewed George H. Calvert's translation, *Correspondence Between S and Goethe,* for the *New-York Daily Tribune* (14 March 1845, 1:1–2).

Other New Englanders who were interested in German Romanticism found S's works useful in articulating the tenets of Transcendentalism. F. H. Hedge** wrote articles on German writers, including S, for *The Christian Examiner,* and C. T. Brooks** translated *Wilhelm Tell* (1804) in 1838.

REFERENCES: For references to S and the Transcendentalists, see *NET*Dial and Myerson (1984). For treatments of German sources of Transcendentalism, see Thomas L. Buckley, "The Bostonian Cult of Classicism: The Reception of Goethe and S in the Literary Reviews of the *North American Review,* *Christian Examiner,* and the *Dial,*" 1817–1865," in Wolfgang Elfe, James Hardin, and Gunther Holst, eds., *The Fortunes of German Writers in America: Studies in Literary Reception* (1992), 27–40; Stanley M. Vogel, *German Literary Influences on the American Transcendentalists* (1955); and Pochmann (1957). For Clarke's comment, see *The Letters of James Freeman Clarke to Margaret Fuller,* ed. John Wesley Thomas (1957), 39.

Susan Belasco Smith

SENSATIONALISM refers to the empirical tradition that posits that knowledge and experience come through sensory perception. J. Locke,* the father of British empiricism, and the Scottish Common Sense* philosophers, who both employed and modified Locke's positions, formed the strongest arguments for sensationalism. I. Kant's* assaults on the dependence on rational understanding helped erode Lockean psychology and epistemology in the 19th century. Lawrence Buell explains that in "epistemology, Transcendentalism marked the first American manifestation of an international reaction against the constraints of John Locke's theory of the human mind, according to which the individual can know only what he or she learns empirically through sense experience—a position that, according to Locke's detractors, led to skepticism and atheism." Locke's antiidealist and materialist philosophy stood in opposition to the Transcendental emphasis on intuitive idealism* and the apprehension of reality beyond the scope of the logical, sensory faculties of the mind. If Locke privileged the mind in the apprehension of truth, then the Transcendentalists privileged the spirit as the mode of apprehension. Transcendentalists saw Lockean psychology, with its depiction of the mind as a clean slate (tabula rasa) waiting to be engraved by the experiences of the senses, as preempting the possibility of innate ideas and subsequently discounting the possibility of transcending what the senses could discern. Sensationalism was also associated with materialism, a notion rejected by the Transcendentalist assumption that sensory perception was not a final fact.

Locke's *An Essay Concerning Human Understanding* (1690) was a discussion point for many Unitarians* who relied on Locke's philosophy for their positions on miracles,* biblical interpretation, and other theological matters. Unitarian and Transcendentalist discussions of sensationalism include A. H. Everett,** *History of Intellectual Philosophy* (1829); F. Bowen,** "Locke and the Transcendentalists" (1837); and O. Brownson,** "Norton's** Evidence" (1839)—all reprinted in Miller (1950). Writers like Brownson complained that Locke's reliance on sensory perception denied "the reality of [the] inner light; he denies the teachings and the authority of the universal reason." Miller's anthology has several more important remarks on sensationalism, including works by W. E. Channing** (who objected to Locke's overreliance on rationalism), F. H. Hedge,** J. Walker,** W. H. Furness,** G. Ripley,** and T. Parker.** R. W. Emerson** discusses the function of the senses in "The Transcendentalist" (*CW*, 1:206–7).

REFERENCES: Buell's comments are in Myerson (1984), 2. See Cameron Thompson, "John Locke and New England Transcendentalism," *NEQ* 35 (December 1962): 435–57; Merrell R. Davis, "Emerson's 'Reason' and the Scottish Philosophers," *NEQ* 17 (June 1944): 209–28; Edgeley Woodman Todd, "Philosophical Ideas at Harvard College, 1817–1837," *NEQ* 16 (March 1943): 63–90; Terrence Martin, *The Instructed Vision: Scottish Common Sense Philosophy and the Origins of American Fiction* (1961); William Charvat, *The Origins of American Critical Thought, 1810–1835* (1936); Sydney E. Ahlstrom, "The Scottish Philosophy and American Theology," *ChH* 24 (September 1955): 257–72; Merle Curti, "The Great Mr. Locke: America's Philosopher, 1783–1861," *HuLB*, no. 11 (April 1937): 107–51; and Richard J. Peterson, "Scottish Common Sense Philosophy in America, 1768–1850" (Diss., American Univ., 1963). See, too, Sheldon W. Liebman, "Origins of Emerson's Early Poetics: His Reading of the Scottish Common Sense Critics," *AL* 45 (March 1973): 23–33; and on assumptions of sensationalism and Transcendentalist uses and theories of language, Philip F. Gura, "The Transcendentalists and Language: The Unitarian Exegetical Background," *SAR* 1979: 1–16. On the importance of sensationalism to Unitarianism, see Howe (1970). For the role of sensationalism in forming Transcendentalist beliefs, see Alexander Kern, "The Rise of Transcendentalism, 1815–1860," in *Transitions in American Literary History,* ed. Harry Hayden Clark (1954), 245–314.

Doni M. Wilson

SHAKERS are a celibate religious sect that flourished in 19th-century America. Formally called The United Society of Believers in Christ's Second Appearing, they originated in England as an off-shoot of the Quaker* sect. Their religious exercises were characterized by ecstatic trances during which members would tremble or shake—hence, the name ''Shaking Quakers,'' which quickly became shortened to ''Shakers.'' Believing that they were called to a Christ-like life, they were led by an illiterate woman named Ann Lee, whom her followers believed was the embodiment of the Christ-spirit in female form. To escape persecution in England, Mother Ann and a group of ten Shakers left for New York in 1774. Despite lack of money, and suspicions that they were Tory sympathizers, they were able to purchase property near Albany and there established their first community, Niskeyuna.

Mother Ann and the Shakers proclaimed the Second Coming of Christ and heralded the beginning of the millennium in America. Capitalizing on the frontier waves of religious revivalism known as the Great Awakening, the Shakers were successful at winning converts. At the same time, they were often persecuted for their unorthodox religious beliefs and practices and were charged with offenses from lascivious dancing to ecstatic spirit possession and even witchcraft. After Mother Ann's death in 1784, her successors as leaders of the faith organized the scattered groups of Believers into communities concentrated in eastern New York, Massachusetts, New Hampshire, and Maine. In 1805, missionaries were sent to the West, establishing Shaker societies in Ohio, Indiana, and Kentucky. Many of these villages persisted into the 20th century. Central to the faith of the Shakers is the communal, celibate life. They believed in the dual nature of God as embodying both the male and female, and in equality of the sexes and of all races. Confession of sin, and dancing and singing in worship were part of their religious ritual. One of the sayings of Mother Ann has become the Shaker hallmark: ''Put your hands to work and your hearts to God.''

Shaker villages attracted many curious visitors in the 19th century. Many came out of a bizarre fascination with the celibate life and to see the trancelike dances that were part of the worship services. Others came to inspect and admire the Shakers' well-kept fields, orchards, and vineyards or to buy their well-made products such as furniture, herbs, or baskets. All respectful visitors were welcomed, for as celibates, the Shakers had to rely on converts to sustain themselves.

In the first half of the 19th century, the Shakers were the focus of much interest in what they called the World. Reformers such as S. Graham,** utopians such as the Brook Farm* community, and writers all visited the Shakers and commented on their peculiar beliefs and lifestyle. Many found much to admire in the Shaker example. The general air of prosperity in their villages, the spacious and well-kept aspect of their buildings, and their progressive agricultural* techniques were eloquent testimony to their success. Yet Shakerism was not without its detractors, and frequently visitors' accounts contained both admiration and disbelief, respect and ridicule. In 1842, N. Hawthorne** and R. W. Emerson** visited the community at Harvard, 35 miles west of Boston. Emerson in his 30 September journal* concluded that "they are in many ways an interesting society, but at present have an additional importance as an experiment of socialism which so falls in with the temper of the times. . . . Moreover, this settlement is of great value in the heart of the country as a model-farm." A cousin of his, after being widowed, joined the Shakers for a time with her young daughter. B. Alcott's** wife, Abigail, was less charitable. "Visited the Shakers. I gain but little from their domestic or internal arrangements. There is a servitude somewhere, I have no doubt. There is a fat sleek comfortable look about the men, and among the women there is a stiff awkward reserve that belongs neither to sublime resignation or divine hope" (26 Aug. 1843). Hawthorne found in the Shakers a rich backdrop for two stories, "A Shaker Bridal" and "The Canterbury Pilgrims." Other literary uses of Shaker settings included Catherine Sedgwick's *Redwood,* Kate Douglas Wiggin's *Susanna and Sue,* and William Dean Howells's articles in the *Atlantic Monthly** and the books *Three Villages* and *The Undiscovered Country.* Woodcuts and engravings of Shaker villages illustrated numerous magazine articles, and prints of their religious dancing were widely circulated by such well-known lithographers as Nathaniel Currier and Daniel Pendleton.

The population of Shaker communities began to decline after the 1840s, when the eastern villages were at their peak. Even then, many had joined more for economic security than from religious conviction. Throughout the second half of the 19th century, the Shakers continued to profit from their industries and agricultural products, but interest in the millennium and in personal salvation was waning, and the attractions of Shaker life could not compete with the new wages and freedom promised in the mills along the eastern rivers. Beginning in 1876, Shaker villages were closed and consolidated, until only three survived into the 1950s. Today, there are seven remaining Shakers at one community, Sabbathday Lake, in Poland Spring, Maine.

REFERENCES: The largest collection of Shaker manuscript material is held at the Western Reserve Historical Society in Cleveland, Ohio, and is available as part of University Microfilms Series. Stephen J. Stein, *The Shaker Experience in America* (1992), is the definitive history. Abba Alcott's journal is in *The Journals of Bronson Alcott,* ed. Odell Shepard (1938). See also Priscilla J. Brewer, "Emerson, Lane,** and the Shakers: A Case of Converging Ideologies," *NEQ* 55 (June 1982): 254–75. Mary L. Richmond, *Shaker Literature* (1977), is a comprehensive two-volume bibliography of writings by and about the Shakers.

Maggie Stier

SHAKESPEARE, WILLIAM (1564–1616), Elizabethan dramatist and poet, is the most widely acclaimed, thoroughly studied author in English; since his death, each generation has found new perspectives from which to explore his art. In antebellum America, S's plays were more abundantly performed than those of any other dramatist, both in the cities and on the frontier. Children became acquainted with his words through school texts in which major soliloquies and other suitable passages were published to be memorized and recited as exercises in elocution. For lecturers such as Richard Henry Dana, Sr., and Henry Norman Hudson, S's work was a leading subject at lyceums* across the country, and R. W. Emerson** himself delivered three different lectures on S between 1835 and 1846.

Nevertheless, like the writing of any other author whose work gains wide popular acclaim, S's plays generated controversy in the new American Republic, even among such enthusiastic admirers as W. Whitman,** who believed that because of their feudal background they were detrimental to the democratic culture of the United States. Especially the comedies, he felt, though "exquisite," were written merely to amuse the aristocrats of Elizabethan England, and the characters consequently were unacceptable for America.

Although he was far more effusive in his praise, Emerson, too, expressed reservations, though his were based on S's apparent moral detachment in writing the plays. In concluding his most widely known essay on the poet-dramatist, "S; or, the Poet," in *Representative Men* (1850), he disparaged S as "master of the revels to mankind." This conclusion, however, contradicts nearly everything else that Emerson wrote before and after the essay; moreover, that conclusion served more to illustrate his democratic, humanistic thesis in *Representative Men* than to expose an apparently superficial appreciation for S's art. Influenced strongly at first by the views of his youngest brother, Charles,** and soon afterward by those of Coleridge** and the German Romantic S critics, Emerson nevertheless incorporated enough of his own Transcendental moral vision into his assessment to distinguish it from those of his predecessors.

His first two lectures on S were delivered in Boston in December 1835. Whereas the first one is an attempt to analyze the poet's imagination at work, the second constitutes a general examination of the plays, especially with respect to S's dramatic method of *composition*, the putting together of reading and experience to create art. Emerson emphasized this word in his admiration of the poet's natural use of language, which for him indicated S's remarkable ability to fuse diversified elements for holistic representation. Later in the decade the fanatical J. Very** inspired Emerson to consider the plays from a more religious point of view, an influence that becomes strikingly apparent several years afterward in "S; or, the Poet." However, even in that lecture Emerson devoted at least three times as much attention to praising the Elizabethan as to criticizing him for his apparently amoral perspective as author of the plays. Ultimately, Emerson seems never to have tired of praising the "all-wise music" of his "King of men."

Among other authors directly associated with Transcendentalism, only Very approaches Emerson in the extent of critical thought given to S. In his two essays on the dramatist—one broadly on S and the other on *Hamlet*—he regarded the Elizabethan as a moral innocent whose plays lack the necessary core of Christian truth that he himself could have provided by identifying with both S and Hamlet, allegedly the dramatist's persona, and rewriting the plays under the inspiration of the Holy Spirit. Very was introduced to Emerson by E. Peabody,** who had been deeply impressed upon hearing the young poet speak in Boston on the epic; she hoped that Emerson would be able to "channel Very's divine madness into creative effort." He could not.

Peabody's childhood affection for S was initiated by her mother. Many years later, she sympathized with D. Bacon** and tried to help her, but eventually Bacon lost her mind in a vain attempt to prove that Francis Bacon had led several collaborators in writing the works attributed to S. By then, however, she was no longer responsive to Peabody's attention.

Like Peabody, M. Fuller** was attracted to S's plays at an early age, and as she matured, she often returned to them, for she found that reading the plays counterbalanced the pedagogical emphasis of her father on Roman concepts of authority, austerity, and duty. Although her devotion to S waned later, in writing "The Great Lawsuit" (1843), she mentioned Cordelia to illustrate the beauty of virtue and alluded in passing to others of S's heroines. Still, she noted, virtuous as they are, S's heroines lack the authority of predominant women in the plays of certain other early dramatists and Spenser.

Similarly qualified but for a different reason was H. Thoreau's** appreciation for S, which wanted the warmth and intimacy that such empathic admirers as Emerson enjoyed. Moreover, Thoreau complained that not only Shakespeare but English literature as a whole misses the "wild strain" that would give it true vitality.

In short, Thoreau exemplifies the fact that if S's writing was broadly admired among the Transcendentalists and their associates, their praise was sometimes reserved. Nevertheless, as Emerson's may be regarded as the leading voice among the Transcendentalists, so also was his admiration for S the most enthusiastic. By the end of his life, Emerson seems to have recognized him as the ideal "poet-priest" he had envisioned, though not exactly an avatar of *the* Poet for whom he had said America was waiting back in 1841.

REFERENCES: The best general source for S and the Transcendentalists, now dated but still the place to begin, is Esther Cloudman Dunn, *S in America* (1939). Beyond that comprehensive resource, one must turn to individual essays, journals,* and letters written by the Transcendentalists themselves and, for all but Emerson, to occasional references in biographies and critical studies. For Emerson, see Robert P. Falk, "Emerson and S," *PMLA* 56 (June 1941): 532–43; William M. Wynkoop, *Three Children of the Universe: Emerson's View of S, Bacon, and Milton** (1966); and Sanford E. Marovitz, "Emerson's S: From Scorn to Apotheosis," in *Emerson Centenary Essays,* ed. Joel Myerson (1982), 122–55, 205–9. Also helpful are Vivian C. Hopkins, *Spires of Form: A Study of Emerson's Aesthetic Theory* (1951); and Merton M. Sealts, Jr., *Emerson on the Scholar* (1992). For Peabody, see the *Letters,* ed. Bruce A. Ronda (1984); and for Whitman, see Dunn, 271–72, and Gay Wilson Allen, *The Solitary Singer* (1967). The best secondary source for Very on S is Marvin Gittleman, *Jones Very: The Effective Years, 1833–1840* (1967).

Sanford E. Marovitz

SLEEPY HOLLOW CEMETERY in Concord, Massachusetts,* is the final resting place of R. W. Emerson,** H. Thoreau,** the Alcotts,** E. P. Peabody,**
and other Transcendentalists. The cemetery was designed in 1855 by pioneer
landscape architects* Robert Morris Copeland (1830–1874) and Horace William
Shaler Cleveland (1814–1900). It is also a built reflection of many of Emerson's
ideas about aesthetics and the landscape.* On 29 September 1855, Emerson
delivered "An Address to the Inhabitants of Concord at the Consecration of
Sleepy Hollow," in which he laid out the aesthetic vision and the design intent
for the cemetery. Sleepy Hollow was to serve the Concord community as a
place given to the dead but "for the reaction" and "benefit on the living."

The plot known as Sleepy Hollow had been a favorite haunt of Concordians
for many years and was likely named for Washington Irving's picturesque musings in the "Legend of Sleepy Hollow." Emerson, M. Fuller,** N. Hawthorne,** and others walked in that landscape on a regular basis. By the 1850s
Concord was in need of more burial space, and the site known as Sleepy Hollow
seemed the perfect location for a new cemetery. It was Emerson, with others
on the cemetery board, who hired Copeland and Cleveland to do the design. In
keeping with Emerson's organic* aesthetic—truth in design and a disdain for
unnecessary decoration—the cemetery was gracefully set into a natural amphi-
theater, and native plantings were used. In his "Consecration Address" Emerson
said that the cemetery was meant to communicate the relationship of humans to
nature.* There visitors might be reminded that they were part of the processes
of the natural environment and that they would one day die. However, from the
landscape they would also learn that they were part of the "vast circulations of
nature" where the individual is never spared and the race never dies.

Sleepy Hollow was also meant to fit the immediate needs of the Concord
community as a park. It was designed as a place of recreation and entertainment
for civic functions, for games for schoolchildren, and for education.* Emerson
spoke of Sleepy Hollow as part of a system of public open space since it was
connected "to the Agricultural Society's ground, to the New Burial ground, to
the Court House and Town House." In their later careers, both Copeland and
Cleveland worked with connected systems of public open space, but their first
encounter with the idea came in 1855 with the design of Sleepy Hollow. Today
Sleepy Hollow is visited annually by hundreds of people who wish somehow
to connect with the Transcendentalists who are interred there, to "read the dates
of their lives," as Emerson put it. But Sleepy Hollow is more than a collection
of monuments. It is a place of contemplation and recreation, a place where
nature allows the just "relation between the Past and the Present."

REFERENCES: Emerson's manuscript "Address to the Inhabitants of Concord at the Consecration of Sleepy Hollow" is housed at Harvard's Houghton Library; it is published
in *W*, 11: 427–36. A number of primary documents related to the history of the cemetery
itself are deposited at the Concord Free Public Library. Emerson's aesthetic influence
and a discussion of the design intent for Sleepy Hollow can be found in Daniel Joseph
Nadenicek, "Nature in the City: Horace Cleveland's Aesthetic," *Landscape and Urban*

Planning 26 (1993): 5–15, and "Sleepy Hollow Cemetery: Transcendental Garden and Community Park," *Journal of the New England Garden History Society* 3 (fall 1993): 8–14.

Daniel Joseph Nadenicek

The **SOCIAL CIRCLE OF CONCORD** was a club of farmers, villagers, and respected members of the town that met regularly to discuss local and national issues of the day. R. W. Emerson** was elected to the Social Circle in 1839, within five years of settling in Concord;* the Emerson family entertained the Social Circle at home, and Emerson would lecture for them in later years. He held the club in high esteem, once boasting that Harvard was but a "wafer" compared to the solid land that his friends in the Social Circle represented; and he rarely missed a Tuesday-night meeting.

The Social Circle grew out of the town's old Committee of Safety (headed by John Hancock), formed in 1774 to cope with potential trouble from Tories and to direct and organize the "minute men." In the next decade it adapted to fairer times in order to "promote the social affections and disseminate useful communications among its members." The original group, its 25 members (including David Brown, Jonas Heywood, Joseph Hosmer, and Ephraim Wood) nearly all wealthy and engaged in trade, met every Tuesday from October to March at a member's parlor. Few concerns at town meetings passed without first having had an airing at the club. This evolved a few decades later to the club of which Emerson was so proud to be a member; but however solid these Concordians were, Emerson probably preferred the intellectual exchanges of the Boston-based Town and Country* (later "Saturday"*) Club. Only a month before his death in 1882 he attended, and was honored at, the Social Circle's Centennial meeting. When he was buried, some village friends from the Social Circle went before the hearse on the way to Sleepy Hollow Cemetery.*

REFERENCES: Townsend Scudder, *Concord: American Town* (1947), 285–86, 346–47, documents the early years of the club, as does Robert A. Gross, *The Minutemen and Their World* (1976), 174–80. Interesting is *JMN*, 11:329. For details of the legendary Centennial meeting, see *The Centennial of the Social Circle of Concord, March 21, 1882* (1882), 49–62. Other accounts of the Social Circle's role in Emerson's life are found in Gay Wilson Allen, *Waldo Emerson* (1981), 526, 623; and Rusk (1949), 506–7.

David Hicks

SPECIMENS OF FOREIGN STANDARD LITERATURE, a 14-volume series of translations of European, primarily German and French, philosophical writings, was edited by G. Ripley** from 1838 to 1842. A year prior to the publication of volumes I and II, Ripley wrote C. Francis** about the intended project: "We have a plenty of true scholars, studious men, men of taste & skill, in different parts of the United States, who might do a great service to our own literature, by combining to enrich it with some of the most valuable foreign products. . . . If each of these would undertake the translation of some work of truly classical reputation, accompanied with original notes & dissertations, in which the reading & study of years could be embodied, we should have a Library, which would do honor to our land and enlarge the cultivation of our people.''

In order of their publication, the volumes were: I–II. *Philosophical Miscellanies, Translated from the French of Cousin,*** *Jouffroy,*** *and Benjamin Constant*** (1838); III. *Select Minor Poems, Translated from the German of Goethe*** *and Schiller** (1839); IV. *Conversations with Goethe in the Last Years of His Life. Translated from the German of Eckermann*** (1839); V–VI. *Introduction to Ethics, Including a Critical Survey of Moral Systems, Translated from the French of Jouffroy* (1840); VII–IX. *German Literature, Translated from the German of Wolfgang Menzel* (1840); X–XI. *Theodore; or The Mystic's Conversion. History of the Culture of a Protestant Clergyman, from the German of De Wette*** (1841); XII–XIII. *Human Life, or Practical Ethics, from the German of De Wette* (1842); XIV. *Songs and Ballads. Translated from Uhland, Korner, Burger, and Other German Lyric Poets* (1842). Those who contributed translations to the series included J. S. Dwight,** N. Frothingham,** G. Bancroft,** F. H. Hedge,** W. H. Channing,** M. Fuller,** C. C. Felton,** J. F. Clarke,** C. P. Cranch,** S. Osgood,** and C. T. Brooks.** In his biography *George Ripley* (1967), Charles Crowe suggests that the publication of *Specimens* was the ''first and perhaps most important group project'' undertaken by members of the Transcendental Club.*

REFERENCES: Ripley's plans for the series and his negotiations with contributing translators are best seen in Mathew David Fisher, ''A Selected, Annotated Edition of the Letters of George Ripley, 1828–1841'' (Diss., Ball State Univ., 1992). For discussion of *Specimens'* impact on American Transcendental philosophy and letters, see Pochmann (1957).

Mathew David Fisher

SPINOZA, BENEDICTUS DE (1632–1677), was an objective, impersonal thinker who attempted a level of systematic thought that is little matched in the entire Western tradition. Born in Amsterdam, where he lived until 1660, he earned his living as a lens grinder, an appropriate occupation for one so concerned with truth and clarity. A Jew, he was expelled from the synagogue for heresy in 1656. He turned down a chair of philosophy at the University of Heidelberg in 1673 and died of consumption in Voorburg.

S's main philosophical goal was the search for a good that would ''so fill the mind that all dependence on contingent circumstance and uncertainty would end.'' Like Descartes,* he used a geometrical method in this quest. He believed that there is only one substance in the universe—and therefore only one cause or ultimate explanation for all existence. His most famous phrasing of this concept was *deus sive natura,* ''God or Nature,''* because for him the two were interchangeable. He greatly influenced German Idealists* such as Goethe,** who placed heavy emphasis on S's theological content. S's attacks against the Car-

tesian mind/body dichotomy and Scholastic theology's god/created-world dichotomy are for him necessary arguments arising from the first principles of the
universe. His recognition of humanity as part of nature, or part of God, enjoined
him to take a Stoic* ethical approach, wherein the greatest joy is a human nature
that is perfectly aware and accepting of its place in and unity with the universe.

S's work, as it was filtered through the German Idealists, greatly influenced
the American Transcendentalists. Van Cromphout rightly claims that R. W. Emerson** came to know S's *deus sive natura* primarily through "the age's most
eminent literary exponent of pantheism,* Goethe." Emerson's idea of the Over-
Soul as a final incorporation of Soul and Nature is indebted to S's idea of nature
or God in that it recognizes the existence of only one substance in the universe.
S's stoical view of human nature can be seen in H. Thoreau's** thoughts on
the human community in *Walden* and Emerson's in "Self-Reliance."

S's life and thought also became tangentially involved in the Divinity School
Address debate. He was brought into the argument by A. Norton,** who made
disparaging remarks about S's religious sentiments. G. Ripley** responded, defending S as a truly religious man. At the end of his life, T. Parker** affirmed
Ripley's defense by poking fun at Norton's charges. Emerson made perhaps the
best comment on S's influence on the American Transcendentalists when he
noted in his journal* in 1868, "In my youth S was a hobgoblin; now he is a
saint."

REFERENCES: The denseness of S's system makes a good commentator necessary. Among
the best overall are R. H. M. Elwes's edition, *The Chief Works of Benedict de S* (1951),
and Edwin Curley, *A S Reader:* The Ethics *and Other Works* (1994). The best one-
volume introductions to S's works are R. J. Delahunty, *S* (1985); Gilles Deleuze, *S:
Practical Philosophy* (1988); Alan Donagan, *S* (1989); and Roger Scruton, *S* (1986).
Albert Goodheir, *Founded on a Rock: The Philosophy of S After Three Centuries* (1978),
is one of the finest looks at S's influence on later philosophers. S's part in the Divinity
School Address debate can be seen in Norton's *A Discourse on the Latest Form of
Infidelity* (1839), Ripley's *The Latest Form of Infidelity Examined* (1839), and Parker's
Theodore Parker's Experience as a Minister (1859). All are excerpted in Miller (1950).
His influence on Emerson is masterfully demonstrated in Gustaaf Van Cromphout, *Emer-
son's Modernity and the Example of Goethe* (1990).

                                                                    Joe Pellegrino

SPIRIT OF THE AGE (July 1849–April 1850), a New York weekly edited by
W. H. Channing,** had both personal and ideological ties to Transcendentalism.
Channing and his assistant G. Ripley** had been connected with the Brook
Farm* experiment and were active in Transcendentalist and reformist circles
generally; moreover, the paper addressed issues that concerned many Transcendentalists, including prison reform, abolition,* and woman's rights,* with
particular attention to the promotion of Associationism and Christian Socialism.
The *Spirit of the Age* defined as its goal "the Peaceful Transformation of human
societies from competitive to co-operative industry, from disunity to unity" (I,

8). As editor, Channing pursued what he called a "mediatorial" attitude, avoiding partisanship and vituperative controversy within the paper and promoting peaceful socialist reform of society rather than violent revolution. With clear reference to the tumultuous events of 1848 in Europe, Channing sought to promote a "social reorganization" that would steer a middle course between "Revolution" and "Reaction" (II, 8).

The *Spirit of the Age* reprinted extensively from other periodicals and published English translations of Indian religious and philosophical works, as well as tracts by European social thinkers. Poems, "News of the Week," and "Town and Country Items" helped to break up the long columns of prose, as did (in the second volume) a sprinkling of book reviews and a weekly report on the progress of various reform movements. The bulk of the paper, though, consisted of long essays on socialist and reformist topics by Channing himself and by such contributors as A. Brisbane,** C. Lane,** C. A. Dana,** and J. K. Ingalls.

Channing admitted that the paper's title was "high and comprehensive" but assured readers that it was "assumed without presumption, for it signifies a prayer rather than a promise, and . . . marks the hope with which this periodical is undertaken" (I, 8). The title had a bit too much currency, though, as at least three other contemporary periodicals, and a Boston temperance* weekly from the 1830s, bore the same name. After *The Liberator* pilloried another *Spirit of the Age* in its "Refuge of Oppression" column, Channing sought to avoid similar embarrassments by asking that reprints or quotations from his paper be identified as coming from the (New York) *Spirit of the Age.*

Surviving less than a year, the paper was beset by difficulties from the beginning. Channing wrote in the 29 December 1849 issue that a cholera epidemic had prevented his going to New York to "superintend" the publication of the first issue and admitted that he had written several articles in the early weeks of publication while he was ill with the disease. He continued to lecture widely throughout his tenure as editor and was often absent from New York, leaving much of the responsibility of producing the paper to Ripley. Financially, the paper never flourished, despite a plea to loyal readers in the 15 September 1849 issue "to procure for us twelve, seven, five, assuredly one additional subscriber" (I, 169). In the final issue (27 April 1850), Channing wrote that he was discontinuing publication because "in brief, I am brain-sick—and it does not pay," adding that his regret "in cutting short this publication is lessened by the assurance, [sic] that its readers can find their wants supplied elsewhere" (II, 264–65). While Clarence Gohdes has surmised that the paper failed (and no other Transcendentalist publication took its place) because of "the growing interest in abolition, which gradually absorbed the activity of the reformers in America," it is possible that Channing's list of other publications where his readers might "supply their wants" speaks to a surplus of reformist journalism that the market could not bear. In any case, the *Spirit of the Age,* despite its occasional ponderousness and early demise, is valuable as a record of American socialist thought in the mid-19th century.

REFERENCES: Although Gohdes (1931) sees the *Spirit of the Age* primarily as the heir of *The Harbinger** (Brook Farm's publication), it more immediately superseded a weekly called the *Univercœlum and Spiritual Philosopher*. Whatever its precise genealogy, the paper took over the subscription rolls of both earlier periodicals. (See Channing's account of taking on the editorship [I, 406].) The Newberry Library has Channing's own copy of the *Spirit of the Age* with his marginalia. Gohdes's treatment of the periodical (132–42) is thorough (if at times dismissive). See also A. G. Thacher, Jr., "William Henry Channing and the *Spirit of the Age*" (M.A. thesis, Columbia Univ., 1941). On specific aspects of the paper, see Roger Chester Mueller, "The Orient* in American Transcendental Periodicals (1835–1886)" (Diss., Univ. of Minnesota, 1968); Barbara Gans Gallant, "The New England Transcendentalists and the European Revolutions of 1848" (M.A. thesis, Univ. of Florida, 1966); and Irving Lowens, "Writings About Music in the Periodicals of American Transcendentalism (1835–50)," *JAMS* 10 (1957): 71–85. Mott (1938–57) mentions the paper briefly, 2:207, 210.

Susan M. Ryan

SPIRITUALISM is a term that has been applied with varying degrees of accuracy and consistency to the beliefs and practices of a number of movements in 19th-century America. With respect to Transcendentalism, the most appropriate use of *spiritualism* is as a descriptive term for the varieties of Platonism* practiced among Transcendentalists and for the metaphysical position, invariably traced to Plato,* that accepts the reality of a nonmaterial or spiritual world and identifies the facts and language of the physical world as symbols of that spiritual world. Belief in the reality of a spiritual world was a central conviction of New England Transcendentalism. While the intellectual and aesthetic unity between subject and nature* in H. Thoreau's** journals* or the oracular quality of B. Alcott's** prose and poetry may serve as literary illustrations of spiritualism, the implications of this use of the term for Transcendentalism are most clearly set forth in R. W. Emerson's** *Nature* and his essays "The Method of Nature," "History," "Circles," "Nominalist* and Realist,*" and "Poetry and Imagination."

In contrast, the term *spiritualism* has also been invoked to describe practices current among 19th-century individuals and institutions that emphasized communication with the deceased—communication with, literally, the world of spirits. Although some linguists have urged the adoption of "spiritism" to distinguish movements concerned with communication with spirits from the more metaphysical emphases of movements such as Transcendentalism, their efforts have been unsuccessful.

Spiritualism, then, was a popular and widely held belief not only in 19th-century America but also in England and on the Continent. Usually requiring the agency of a medium who served as intermediary between the living and the spirits of those "on the other side," this brand of spiritualism encompassed a great variety of practices and of physical as well as psychic phenomena. Practitioners often enacted communication with spirits through prophecy and the interpretation of dreams, crystal gazing, trances, and mesmerism* or hypnotism, and they authenticated their communications through an array of physical manifestations that included table rappings and table tippings; spirit writings and drawings made involuntarily by the medium; spontaneous movements of large material objects such as tables and pianos without any physical explanation; apparitions of the dead; spirit music—sometimes provided with instruments, sometimes without; human levitation; and possession.

The modern practice of spiritualism in America is often dated from 31 March 1848, when young Margaret (1833 or 1834–1893) and Kate (1836–1892) Fox of Hydesville, New York, reported that they could communicate with spirits who made their presence known to them by knocks or rappings throughout the house. By the summer of 1850 their story had become so well known, and their credibility so well established, that the sisters could easily command $100 a night for seances in New York City, their first stop in a cross-country tour.

In the early 1850s, spiritualist circles were formed in the large cities of New York and Massachusetts; they quickly spread through the northeastern, mid-Atlantic, and midwestern states, and eventually through most states, their message transmitted and reinforced by spiritualist newspapers and journals such as the Springfield (Mass.) *Spiritual Messenger,* the St. Louis *Light from the Spirit World,* the Auburn (N.Y.) *Spiritual and Moral Instructor,* and *Heat and Light, Spirit World,* and *New Era*—all published in Boston. Abroad, the progress of the spiritualist movement, especially within intellectual circles in England and on the Continent, was astonishing. In the Anglo-American community of literary and artistic expatriates in Florence, Italy, during the mid-1850s, Elizabeth Barrett Browning, H. Martineau,** and the American sculptor H. Powers,** among many others, became early converts to spiritualism and disciples of Daniel Dunglas Home (1833–1886). Home, a British subject, was possibly the century's most famous medium; besides charming members of Italy's several Anglo-American communities to accept spiritualism, he conducted séances and orchestrated a variety of psychic phenomena before receptive audiences of European and Russian nobles, and he persuaded several prominent British scientists to accept spiritualism, among them Robert Chambers (1802–1871), whose theories of evolution prepared the way for Darwin** and commanded Emerson's respect.

Although the spiritualist movement progressed with the rapidity of a new religion, and although many of its practitioners enjoyed financial success and some degree of temporary renown, it was invariably the object of intense public scrutiny and the target of severe criticism, if not outright ridicule, from both the press and the pulpit. In America, along with enthusiasts, it met doubters and detractors everywhere—sometimes even in the same household. The Hawthornes were just such a case. Sophia** accepted most popular practices of phrenology* and eagerly participated in spirit-rapping and spirit-summoning experiments with Powers and Browning, when the Hawthornes sojourned in Italy in the late 1850s. Nathaniel** was far more cautious from the outset. On 24 July 1851 he wrote old family friend William Baker Pike, thanking him for his testimony in favor of spiritualism but acknowledging that he was incapable of embracing the movement: "I have heard and read much on the subject, and it appears to me to be the strangest and most bewildering affair I ever heard of." Besides doubt, however genuine, Hawthorne kept his distance from the movement out of concern for his literary reputation. Allen Putnam (1802–1887), farmer, preacher, spiritualist, and author of the popular *Mesmerism, Spiritualism, Witchcraft, and Miracle* . . . (1858), had written to ask his help in preparing for publication his manuscript of *Witchcraft in New England Explained by Modern Spiritualism* (not published until 1888); in his 19 October 1851 response, Hawthorne complimented Putnam on the quality of his research but confessed his "reluctance to connect myself with a work of the mystic character of the one proposed. My reputation (what little there is of it) has already too much fog and mist diffused through it; and if the public find me setting myself up as a sponsor of other people's books of dream craft and witchery, I shall get a very bad name." In *The Blithedale Romance,* he expressed reasonable concern for the viability of will and the loss of independent consciousness during mesmeric trances, but in the privacy of his notebooks, he remained as skeptical as ever.

In the otherwise progressive Concord, Massachusetts,* spiritualism elicited uncharacteristic invective. Writing to his sister Sophia on 13 July 1852, Thoreau expressed exasperation—bordering on contempt—with his neighbors who, like most Americans, were caught up in the latest news of mediums and spirit encounters: "Concord is just as idiotic as ever in relation to the spirits and their knockings. . . . If I could be brought to believe in the things which they believe—I should make haste to get rid of my certificate of stock in this & the next world's enterprises, and buy a share in the first Immediate Annihilation Company that offered." Over the course of his career, Emerson, whose distrust of spiritualists and disgust with spiritualism is as pointed as Thoreau's, moved from modest satire of the popular spiritualists to broadside attacks on the corruptive influence of spiritualism. He ridiculed as self-serving the Fox Sisters and other imagined "adepts," and in his journals and lectures he began to characterize the movement as faddish "*Pseudo-Spiritualism,*" the latest in "a series of conspiracies to win from nature some advantage without paying for it."

Emerson's aversion to spiritualists' peeping and prying into the spirit world, his conviction that those who did so for profit were only charlatans, and his belief that spiritualism was undermining the moral fabric of society are collectively represented in *The Conduct of Life* (1860); "Success," a title under which he lectured in the 1860s and under which he published an essay in *Society and Solitude* (1870); and "Demonology," a title under which he lectured in the late 1830s and under which he published an essay in the *North American Review** in 1877. In *The Conduct of Life,* he observed that the spiritualist phenomenon was not only a confusing, faddish nuisance but also one among several factors contributing to the decline in faith in the intellectual component of spirit, of moral conduct in personal affairs, and of progress in political economy as well as in the arts and sciences—all evidenced in "the squalor of Mesmerism, the deliration of rappings, . . . thumps in table-drawers, and black art.'' Because we have lost hold of the guidance of basic values, ''we ape our ancestors . . . [and] stagger backward to the mummeries of the Dark Ages.'' In ''Demonology''— the essay form of which bears passages from as early as 1838–39, when Emerson lectured on the sudden popularity of persons successfully trading as mesmerists and clairvoyants in and around Boston, as well as passages improved over several decades as he refined his belief in the authority of dreams to convey fleeting knowledge of ourselves and our relation to the spiritual world—Emerson reprised the image of spiritualism as a step backward for the human race. ''These adepts,'' he wrote, ''have mistaken flatulency for inspiration.''

Apart from Emerson's and other Transcendentalists' genuine concern for the movement's impact on the moral culture of America, Emerson may also have been weary of caustic and damaging associations in the popular imagination between spiritualism and Transcendentalism, a tendency that C. P. Cranch's** caricatures of Emersonian idealism* might best represent. Also, despite Emerson's railing at the seeming newness of the spiritualist movement and its practices, he and virtually all of his literary contemporaries had to recognize something inherently American in spiritualism and in the speed with which it captured the public's attention and approval. From the defenses by long-gone Puritans* Increase and Cotton Mather of ''the wonders of the invisible world,'' to the witchcraft hysteria at Salem in 1692, to the excesses of revivalist movements during the 18th century, to Swedenborgianism's* rise to respectability in America (in part through Emerson's championing of the merits of its Swedish mystic-founder), to the bizarre and ''other worldly'' encounters through which Washington Irving, E. A. Poe,** H. Melville,** and of course Hawthorne entertained 19th-century readers of their tales, America had been, after all, a culture that always kept at least one eye fixed on ''the other side.''

REFERENCES: Hawthorne's extensive observations on spiritualism are scattered throughout *The French and Italian Notebooks,* ed. Thomas Woodson (1980), vol. 14 of *The Centenary Edition of the Works of Nathaniel Hawthorne.* The most comprehensive public statement of a position by a Transcendentalist is Emerson, ''Demonology,'' *W,* 10:1–28. Most of the numerous books and articles on 19th-century American authors and their attitudes toward dreams also comment on spiritualism; the most thorough is Rita K. Gollin, *Nathaniel Hawthorne and the Truth of Dreams* (1979). See Geoffrey K. Nelson, *Spiritualism and Society* (1969); Earl Wesley Fornell, *The Unhappy Medium: Spiritualism and the Life of Margaret Fox* (1964); and Horace Wyndham, *Mr. Sludge, the Medium: Being the Life and Adventures of Daniel Dunglas Home* (1937). Katherine H. Porter, *Through a Glass Darkly: Spiritualism in the Browning Circle* (1972), and Ronald A. Bosco, ''The Brownings and Mrs. Kinney: A Record of Their Friendship,'' *Browning Institute Studies* 4 (1976): 57–124, treat spiritualism in Italy's Anglo-American communities in the 1850s.

Ronald A. Bosco

STAËL-HOLSTEIN, ANNE-LOUISE-GERMAINE NECKER, BARONNE DE (1766–1817), nurtured in the Enlightenment, became a theorist of Roman-

ticism and significant agent for introducing the ideas of German Romanticism
to French and English readers. She was born in Paris to Swiss parents, Jacques
Necker, a banker who later was Louis XVI's finance minister, and Suzanne
Curchod, who established a famous salon. Her marriage to the Swedish ambassador to France, Baron Erik de Staël-Holstein, was short-lived, although there
were three children (the youngest allegedly fathered by B. Constant**). Her wit,
intelligence, and intellectual curiosity supported her own brilliant career as a
salonnière and writer of novels, essays, memoirs, and history. Although a supporter of the French Revolution, her difficulties with Napoleon led her to travel
throughout Italy, Germany, and England, often drawing upon her experience for
her writing. Her friendships with Constant, A. W. Schlegel,** Simonde di Sis-
mondi, and Lord Byron offered intellectual support. She wrote plays before she
was 21 and published *Lettres sur . . . J. J. Rousseau** in 1788, but her first
influential work was probably *De l'influence des passions sur le bonheur des
individus et des nations* (1796). This was followed in 1800 by *De la littérature
considérée dans ses rapports avec les institutions sociales* and by the novels
Delphine (1802) and *Corinne* (1807). Her *De l'Allemagne* (1810) introduced a
generation to the contemporary art, literature, and philosophy of Germany and,
along with *Corinne,* was probably her most widely read book. Her *Considéra-
tions sur la Révolution française* (1818) and *Dix Années d'exil* (1821) appeared
posthumously, the first a memoir, the second a recommendation of the merits
of the British political system for France. After the restoration of the French
monarchy, she spent the summer of 1816 in Coppet with Lord Byron and returned that winter to Paris, where she held her salon for the last time. The first
generation of Transcendentalists early on made her one of their favorite writers,
but by the early 1840s her popularity waned, although her name was still cited
as the type of the woman of intellect. In the 1820s and 1830s her books found
a wide readership, but they seemed most often regarded as introductions to new
ideas and subjects rather than as definitive statements. M. Fuller** in her youth
wrote to a friend about reading the novels but after the late 1830s seldom refers
to her in letters. T. Parker** and G. Ripley** read her in the early 1830s, but
they read more thoroughly the writers she introduced. R. W. Emerson** was
one of her earliest and most faithful readers among the group, starting *Germany*
in 1822 and checking out *Dix Années d'exil* from the Boston Athenaeum* as
late as 1845. William Girard in his study of French influences on Transcendentalism claimed that de Staël's *Germany* was almost a family textbook in America
for continental Romanticism, and her character Corinne, an Italian *improvisatrice* who enchanted rationalist northern Europeans, demonstrated the ability to
arrive at truth through intuition and feeling. If her power to influence Transcendentalist thinkers waned after about 1840, her *Germany* and *Corinne* remained
almost continuously in print for the rest of the century.

   In New England, as elsewhere, the figure of de Staël and her fictional creation,
Corinne, merged in the popular imagination and became a type for women of
passion and intellect. She demonstrated an intelligence equaling that of any man

of her age without surrendering what the age regarded as her womanliness. Emerson, for example, variously included de Staël with M. M. Emerson,** George Sand, and George Eliot in lists of admirable or notable women. Above all, Fuller, the conductor of the Boston Conversations* and editor of *The Dial,** was associated with the type almost as a commonplace. Parker noted after a party, "Miss Fuller resembles Mme. de Staël more than any woman I know," and W. H. Channing** described her as "a Yankee Corinna."

REFERENCES: Madame de Staël's works were available individually in French and in translation, but several of the Transcendentalists read volumes from her 17-volume *Oeuvres complètes* (1820–21). L. M. Child's** *Biographies of Madame de Staël and Madame Roland* (1832) was reprinted under this title and as *The Memoirs of Madame de Staël and Madame Roland.* A good recent biography is J. Christopher Herold, *Mistress to an Age* (1958). Richmond Laurin Hawkins, *Madame de Staël and the United States* (1930), discusses her extensive influence; and Girard, "Du transcendentalism consideré essentiallement dans sa définition et ses origines françaises," *UCPMP* 4 (18 October 1916): 351–498, notes her importance.

Frank Shuffelton

STEWART, DUGALD (1753–1828), was a Scottish Common Sense* philosopher whose "intuitive philosophy" influenced the early development of the ideals of many Transcendentalists, especially R. W. Emerson** and H. Thoreau.** For S, humankind's most important faculty is "reason," which he believed has an affinity to intuition. Like his contemporaries in the Scottish Common Sense school, S reacted against the materialism of Locke* and the skepticism of Hume.* He argued that all human beings possess an innate "moral sense" that cannot be taught and that is an original and universal principle of the mind that apprehends the distinction between right and wrong to be absolute. This "moral sense," he argues in *Outlines of Moral Philosophy,** is intuitive and an "essential part of the human constitution."

Emerson and Thoreau became familiar with S's work while students at Harvard. During the 1820s and 1830s, the faculty at Harvard and other eastern universities emphasized the works of the Scottish Common Sense school in their philosophy classes. Emerson first studied S's *Elements of the Philosophy of the Human Mind* during his junior year in 1819 and also during his senior year and read his *Outlines of Moral Philosophy* outside the curriculum in 1820 and 1821. Thoreau also read S's *Elements* during his junior year.

Although Emerson, like other Transcendentalists, was to grow beyond S's philosophies, his influence is evident in Emerson's early writing and in his mature ideology. While Emerson's knowledge of the terms *reason* and *understanding* was attained through his reading of Coleridge,** Emerson was familiar with the ideas behind these terms in the 1820s. In both his college writing and journals* during this period, Emerson wrote of a moral law, which he argued "is the Moral Sense; a rule coextensive and coeval with Mind." This "moral sense" is intuitive and is derived "from a Mind, of which it is the essence. That Mind is God."

Thoreau, like Emerson, was initially attracted to S's philosophy. Many of Thoreau's college essays reflect S's ideology, especially in aesthetic and ethical matters. S's principle of intuition helped to prepare the way for young Thoreau to accept the doctrines that Emerson set forth in *Nature* in 1836.

Other Transcendentalists, such as O. Brownson,** subscribed to S's work early in their development, eventually to discard it. Although S rebelled against the school of Locke, the Transcendentalists believed he did not revise Locke's works enough and labeled him as another sensationalist.* Yet S's philosophy is important in the development of Transcendentalism, for like the work of others of the Scottish Common Sense school, it helped prepare the transition from the materialism of Locke and the utilitarianism of Paley* to the idealism* of the Germans, Coleridge, and others.

REFERENCES: The standard edition is *The Collected Works of DS*, ed. Sir William Hamilton, 11 vols. (1971). On the influence of Stewart and the Scottish Common Sense school on American thought, see William Charvat, *The Origins of American Critical Thought, 1810–1835* (1961), and Terence Martin, *The Instructed Vision* (1961). On Common Sense philosophy at Harvard, see Edgeley Woodman Todd, "Philosophical Ideas at Harvard College, 1817–1837," *NEQ* 16 (March 1943): 63–90. Cameron Thompson examines the Transcendentalists' reaction to Locke and the Scottish Common Sense school in "John Locke and New England Transcendentalism," *NEQ* 25 (December 1962): 435–57. On S's specific influence, see Merrell R. Davis, "Emerson's 'Reason' and the Scottish Philosophers," *NEQ* 17 (June 1944): 209–28; J. Edward Schamberger, "The Influence of DS and Richard Price on Emerson's Concept of the 'Reason': A Reassessment," *ESQ* 18 (3d Q 1972): 179–83: and Joseph J. Kwiat, "Thoreau's Philosophical Apprenticeship," *NEQ* 18 (March 1945): 51–69.

Kathleen M. Healey

STOICISM, in its early Greek and later Roman renditions, offered the Transcendentalists both a cosmology appealing in its pantheism* (the belief that all of creation is a manifestation of the divine fire, a spark of the Deity) and ethical values attractive in their emphases upon virtue, duty, benevolence, and brotherhood, as well as upon self-reliance and calm endurance. Although ancient philosophy was notably absent from the Harvard curriculum, R. W. Emerson** took notes from his own reading in 1820 and in 1830 on the speculative theories and cosmic ideas of the early Greeks. His interest in the later Roman Stoics was based upon their practical moral precepts and proverbs emphasizing individual autonomy: "[I]f one [were to] reduce the doctrine of Zeno & the Stoic sect," he noted in an 1855 journal* entry, "you will not find many thoughts, but a few thoughts; one thought, perhaps;—self-reliance." The crisp, epigrammatic styles of Seneca and Aurelius were, moreover, appealing to Emerson and H. Thoreau,** who were often experimenting with their own prose styles.

As emphasized by Seneca and Epictetus,* the inherent rewards of virtue were especially attractive to Emerson, whose Harvard training focused heavily on moral duties. Associated with the virtuous life, the asceticism of some of the

Stoics appealed not only to Emerson and Thoreau as a discipline for an inspired, scholarly life but also to M. Fuller,** who revered the Romans' lives as examples of noble discipline for civic duty. In an 1833 journal entry Emerson asserted: "I believe that virtue purges the eye, that the abstinent, meek, benevolent, industrious man is in a better state for the fine influences of the great universe to act upon than the cold, idle, eating disputant." In his address "The Man of Letters," Emerson also describes the ideal training of a scholar in terms of Stoic discipline and military prowess: "So let his habits be formed . . . no spoiled child, no drone, no epicure, but a stoic, formidable, athletic, knowing how to be poor, loving labor. . . . I wish the youth to be an armed and complete man; no helpless angel to be slapped in the face, but a man dipped in the Styx of human experience, and made invulnerable so,—self-helping."

In the writings of ancient pagan Stoics, moreover, the three Transcendentalists found viable challenges to the uniqueness of Christian revelations about morality, as well as an alternative to the ritual-ridden theology involved with Christian morality. In "Character," for example, Emerson explained: "This charm in the Pagan moralists, of suggestion, the charm of poetry of mere truth . . . the New Testament loses by its connection with a church. . . . [T]he office of this age is to put all these writings on the eternal footing of equality of origin in the instincts of the human mind."

As early as 1820 and 1821 Emerson listed in his journals and lauded in his Bowdoin Prize essays the early Greek founder of Stoicism, Zeno of Citium, and the high-minded moral wisdom of later Roman Stoics Lucius Seneca and Marcus Aurelius Antoninus. As an epigraph and motto to his 1822 commonplace book, Emerson quotes Aurelius's earnest and serene meditation: "For I seek the truth, whereby no one was ever harmed" (*Meditations*, Book VI. no. 21). Emerson's early acquaintance with Stoic writings was based on excerpts and summaries, such as Joseph Priestley's *The Doctrines of Heathen Philosophy Compared with Those of Revelation* (U.S. ed., 1804); intermediate ancient sources, such as Plutarch's* *Lives* and *Moralia,* and Montaigne's* essays; and some of the original sources of Aurelius and Epictetus. Thoreau's knowledge was probably gleaned from Cicero's *De Officiis,* as well as from F. Fénelon's* summary of their lives (1822).

Since the cosmology and physics of the Stoics were the bases of their ethics and were also influential in Transcendental conceptions, a brief discussion of them will be useful here. The Stoics took up and developed, many centuries later, Pythagoras's theory of the orderly nature of the universe. The writings of Pythagoras (c. 582 B.C.–c. 507 B.C.), which came to Emerson by way of Plutarch's *Moralia,* suggested that "Pythagoras was the first philosopher that gave the name of *kosmos* to the world, from the order and beauty of it" (*Moralia,* 3:132). The importance of beauty in Emerson's exposition of *Nature* probably owes much to this notion of the synonymity of *kosmos,* beauty, and order. According to the Stoics, also borrowing from and revising Heraclitus (c. 535 B.C.–c. 475 B.C.), the eternal course of the universe is cyclical, with each cycle

initiated by the *logos spermatikos,* or creative fire, which informs man, nature,*
and the universe as a whole. (Compare this notion of *logos spermatikos* with
Emerson's demand: "Give me initiative, spermatic, prophesying man-making
words" [*JMN,* 8:148; used again in "Inspiration"]). Each cycle, which involves
the organization of creation into the four elements, is identical in every aspect
with every other cycle, and ends in a return to the originating fire. Thus, there
is both eternal flux (Heraclitus's doctrine *panta rei*—"all things flow") and an
eternal recurrence of all things, a fundamental uniformity. In fact, according to
"the flowing philosopher," as Emerson terms him, transition is the only true
state, since all things carry within them their opposites, both being and not being.
Indeed, to highlight the inevitability of flux, Emerson cites in "The Method of
Nature" Heraclitus's apothegm: "You cannot bathe twice in the same river."
This philosopher's notion of flux, moreover, figures significantly in Emerson's
"Experience," "Poetry and Imagination," "Illusions," "Woodnotes II," and
"Quotation and Originality," where Emerson cites the Greek of Heraclitus and
translates it as "all things are in flux."

While Heraclitus highlighted relentless transition, the Stoics' adaptation of his
doctrine emphasized the orderliness of change: Change is subject to the un-
swerving "law of nature." Indeed, in Emerson's 1830 summary of Heraclitus's
doctrine, which he read in de Gérando's** *Histoire comparée des systèmes de
philosophie,* there are elements of both the Greek and later Stoic revision:
"[Wisdom] consisted in discovering the law which governs all things. All nature
is governed by constant laws. The phenomena themselves, which appear dis-
cordant, concur in the harmony of the whole. . . . Meanwhile all change. Attraction, Repulsion." Since the *logos spermatikos* or "life-giving" word fulfills its
own agenda and exerts its own powers, change is autonomous—neither affected
nor limited by circumstances. And since change is already immanent* in God,
it is unchanging in its laws. What may appear as "chance" is actually initiated
by unseen causes, some of which are revealed to mankind by daemons through
dreams and prophecies.

Stoic physics emphasizing the eternal and universal "law of nature" led to
a significant degree of determinism, the belief in the inflexible control of Fate,
particularly among some Roman Stoics like Seneca. This fatalism led in turn to
the "indifference to circumstances" and "tranquil endurance in the face of
adversity" usually associated with Roman Stoicism. But put another way—one
more appealing to Emerson, who admitted the efficacy of free will—this conception of the universe led to the fundamental Stoic injunction to live according
to the universal law of nature. Indeed, at the end of "Fate," Emerson exhorts,
"Let us build altars to the beautiful Necessity" that teaches that "Law rules
throughout the universe." Through the exercise of a virtuous attitude as well as
willed virtuous actions—emphasized by Epictetus, Arrian, Seneca, Panaetius,
and Aurelius—a wise individual could live in conformity with the orderly and
beautiful law of nature, and so achieve the same autonomy and uniformity as
the divine fire that informs her. As Emerson avowed in the Divinity School

Address: "The sublime is excited in me by the great stoical doctrine, Obey thyself. That which shows God in me, fortifies me." This self-reliance, pursuit of virtue for its own sake, or strength of character, as Zeno (c. 336 B.C.–c. 264 B.C.) expressed it, enabled the individual not so much to resign to Fate's dicta as to conform nobly with those laws not subject to the accidents of circumstances. Indeed, Thoreau, writing in his journal in 1838, was most struck by Zeno's self-possession: "[S]till the fleshly Zeno sails on, shipwrecked, buffetted, tempest-tost—but the true Zeno sails ever a placid sea. . . . Himself Truth's unconcerned help-mate." At the end of the "Economy" chapter of *Walden,* Thoreau exhorts his audience to a similar poise and undeflected pursuit of truth.

Such a position of equanimity, according to Epictetus—a favorite of Aurelius—was made possible by distinguishing what was within one's power and what was not. And according to Lucius Annaeus Seneca (c. 3 B.C.–A.D. 65), this self-possession is a product of both knowing what to value (virtue) and how to achieve self-control—knowing how to harmonize our will with that of the universe, which involves knowing that passions and emotions are mistaken judgments to be suppressed or modified. In 1834, Emerson tasked himself with exactly this Senecan requirement: "[T]o govern my passions with absolute sway is the work I have to do." The apparent ruthlessness or indifference in Emerson's notions of friendship and love (e.g., in *Nature,* "Self-Reliance," "Circles," and "Experience") owe much to this Stoical desire to harmonize his will with that of the universe. The encumbrances of relationships and the desire for autonomy became explicit in his essay "Friendship": "Let us even bid our dearest friends farewell, and defy them, saying 'Who are you? Unhand me: I will be dependent no more.' " On more than one occasion, he copied into his journal of the 1820s the self-dependent proverb from Aurelius (paraphrasing Epictetus): "If you must die, saith Marcus Antoninus, let it be as those who have suffered nothing. If the smoke be troublesome, I leave it." Yet such an individual is immediately compensated* by an inward reward, for, as Emerson notes in his journal in 1830, "you cannot do [the good man] any harm."

In the *Meditations* of Marcus Aurelius Antoninus (A.D. 121–A.D. 180), Emerson found not only the desire to live life well as an individual but also a sense of duty to others in a larger brotherhood. Since, according to Stoic physics, each individual is informed and sustained by the same spark or fire, a parity exists between all, regardless of nationality or race. Given the Transcendentalists' focus on the soul as a spark of the divine fire, the Stoics' enfranchisement of that spark in the human mind may have underwritten the egalitarianism of Fuller's feminist agenda in *Woman in the Nineteenth Century* and the other Transcendentalists' abolitionist* activities. Indeed, Emerson cites Aurelius on the powers of the mind: " 'It traverses the whole world & what surrounds it. It contemplates its form & looking forward into eternity, it considers the renovation of the universe at certain intervals.' " It is no surprise then that in "The Sovereignty of Ethics" Emerson lamented that Stoicism "has now no temples, no academy, no commanding Zeno or Antoninus. It accuses us that it has none."

REFERENCES: For a detailed history-of-ideas survey of the Stoic strain in Plutarch and its relation to similar concepts in Emerson's writings, see Edmund G. Berry, *Emerson's Plutarch* (1961); see also *The Stoic Strain in American Literature,* essays ed. Duane J. Macmillan (1979).

Robin Sandra Grey

SWEDENBORG, EMANUEL (1688–1772), Swedish scientist and mystic, was "a pervasive influence upon New England Transcendentalism," declared Perry Miller, "as fundamental as Coleridge** and Carlyle."** R. W. Emerson** acknowledged this impact by choosing S to exemplify "the Mystic" in *Representative Men* (1850).

Educated at Uppsala, where his father (later bishop at Skara) was a professor, S also studied Newtonian science in England. Appointed assessor in Sweden's Board of Mines, he wrote prolifically on subjects as diverse as anatomy, astronomy, chemistry, mechanics, natural history,* metallurgy, and psychology; his contributions to technological theory included design of a flying machine, and his inventions ranged from an improved ear trumpet and stove to a sophisticated dry dock. The turning point in his life came in 1745 in the form of a vision, or illumination. Thereafter, S claimed to converse with spirits and dedicated his life to explaining the correspondence* between spiritual and natural realms, the basis of his mystical reinterpretation of Scripture. This exegetical calling, he believed, would help establish a New Jerusalem made evident in a New Church, though he had no intention of starting a new sect. The Neoplatonic* concept of "correspondence," which he had articulated even before his vision, held that "the living body" and all of nature* are "purely symbolical of the spiritual world." S thought that words, restored to their true meaning, can decode the emblematic world, converting "natural truth" into "spiritual truth, or theological dogma." Emerson came to think S's linguistic formula too rigid; but the concepts of nature as "picture-language" (as Emerson called it in his lecture on S) and of language as a vehicle for spiritual truth were liberating for Transcendentalists rebelling against Lockean* notions of reality and knowledge.

Before S was widely read in New England, his views on spirit, nature, mind, ethics, and language were introduced (without using his name) by American followers such as S. Reed,** whose "Oration on Genius" (1821) and *Observations on the Growth of the Mind* (1826) were avidly read by Emerson. Emerson also encountered S's ideas and life through the *New Jerusalem Magazine** (published by the Swedenborgian New Church in Boston), beginning with the first volume (1827–28). Transcendentalists were soon enthusiastically reading his works, translated into English from the Latin, and Emerson acquired many volumes for his own library. F. H. Hedge,** however, wrote a dissenting review of S's *The True Christian Religion* in *The Christian Examiner** (15 [November 1833]: 193–218). He defined S ambivalently as a "mystic"; more damagingly, while Hedge praised the New Church's "progressive spirit," he rejected "that idolatry which can embrace a human tradition as if it were a revelation from God." At about the same time, B. Alcott** began to read S, who, he told Emerson in 1839, "should be in the hands of every earnest student of the Soul." Alcott's journal* notes his reading and rereading S over decades and discussing him with H. James, Sr.** as well as Emerson. Emerson's own antiformalism and philosophical idealism* led many to associate him with Swedenborgianism, and this reputation was reinforced following publication of *Nature* (1836) with its correspondential theory of language. Throughout the mid-1830s S appears in Emerson's journal, grouped with men of "genius" like Carlyle and Alcott, or "religious enthusiasts" like Guyon, Fox, Luther, Böhme* (even Jesus), and throughout the great essays he is quoted or invoked in the company of Coleridge, Kant,* and St. Paul.

Emerson's lecture "S, or the Mystic," first given on 25 December 1845 and eventually published in *Representative Men,* offers a more nuanced assessment; Emerson not only adopts the tag "mystic" suggested by Hedge 12 years earlier—he shares his friend's reservations. The lecture draws on such sources as S's own writings and biographical work by English surgeon and S translator James John Garth Wilkinson (1812–1899), who became Emerson's friend. Emerson sketches the life of S and credits him with bravely tackling "the problem of Essence . . . the questions of Whence? and What? and Whither?" S's "systematic" mind embraced vast knowledge, yet he wholly lacked "egotism." Though derivative as a scientist in an age of great scientists, he "put science and the soul, long estranged from each other, at one again," comprehending the universe through microcosm* and correspondence—a living "symbolism" that provided the basis of language and led him to speak "in parable." Yet S was too "exclusively theologic" in his reading of nature and Scripture: "The slippery Proteus," thought Emerson, "is not so easily caught." In a famous criticism, Emerson finds that "S's system of the world wants central spontaneity" because attached "to the Christian symbol, instead of to the moral sentiment." As a result, S was "disagreeably wise" and "repels" with his "entire want of poetry." Still, Emerson grants him "a merit sublime beyond praise."

Emerson's "S" immediately generated controversy that is still felt. Attending his Boston lecture was Professor George Bush (1796–1859), a Swedenborgian who was so offended by Emerson's mixed judgment that he answered Emerson point by point in a widely publicized lecture of his own, the transcription of which Emerson read in the newspaper. The most thorough 20th-century scholar of Emerson and S—Clarence P. Hotson—declared Emerson's lecture "a piece of play-acting or buffoonery, as one prefers." Hotson maintained that Emerson, reluctant to admit his full debt to Swedenborgianism and embarrassed to be identified with the sect, used the occasion as part of a larger attack on Christianity and all religion. According to Hotson (himself a Swedenborgian), Emerson was so stung by counterattacks by Bush and others that he projected his annoyance onto S in "progressively more derogatory" subsequent lectures and in the

published version, where his "ignominious performance" took its "most vin-
dictive form."

Emerson's enthusiasm for S had been qualified, however, almost from his
first encounter with his work. As early as Sermon CXI, Emerson cautioned that
no doctrine, including those of the New Jerusalem Church, is "truth itself, but
only as proceeding from truth." Accordingly, Emerson almost always distinguished S from the church that bore his name; in his journal for 22 June 1838
he put all sectarianism on equal footing: "[Y]ou must treat the men & women
of one idea, the Abolitionist,* the Phrenologist,* the Swedenborgian, as insane
persons." "Each owes all," he had written in his journal on 7 January 1835,
"to the discovery that God must be sought within, not without." In the moment
of insight, the messenger of such wisdom, even a great seer or prophet, becomes
secondhand and dispensable. This high but still mediate role Emerson assigns
alike, in the Divinity School Address, to St. Paul, George Fox—and S.

REFERENCES: See Miller (1950), 49. The S Foundation maintains a 30-volume "Standard
Edition" of S's theological works. Nearly two dozen volumes of his scientific and philosophical writings are also in print. A good introduction, with annotated bibliography,
is Inge Jonsson, ES (1971); Jonsson also outlines S's ideas in EP, 8:48–51. Emerson's
"S, or the Mystic" is in CW, 4:53–81. From the beginning, commentary on Emerson
and S has been tainted by partisanship. Hotson's many valuable articles, based on his
1929 Harvard diss., are listed in B&M. Though published by The Academy of the New
Church, S and His Influence, Erland J. Brock, Gen. Ed. (1988), is more balanced; see
esp. Anders Hallengren, "The Importance of S to Emerson's Ethics," 229–50. A useful
introduction is Kenneth W. Cameron, "Emerson and Swedenborgism: A Study Outline
and Analysis," ESQ, no. 10 (1st Q 1958): 14–20. Philip F. Gura discusses Swedenborgian influences on language theory in The Wisdom of Words (1981), 75–88.

                                                                    Wesley T. Mott

T
___

TEMPERANCE was a movement dedicated to controlling Americans' alcohol consumption and not, primarily, a call for total abstinence. Often associated with Grahamism* and other health reforms, temperance activists usually emphasized the physical effects of drink, sometimes with a lofty moral tone and sometimes with a gruesome relish. R. W. Emerson** recognized the movement but did not banish alcohol from his festive board. Claiming, in 1841, that friends such as W. L. Garrison** were creatures of "isms," he grumbled: "[N]ow we must become temperance watersops."

Historians have traditionally dated American temperance activities from the 1810s, but recent scholarship suggests that calls for moderate use of alcohol arose among colonial Quakers* and Methodists. During the early national period, Benjamin Rush helped spread the secular gospel, and soon Presbyterians and Congregationalists eagerly advocated moderate consumption of spirituous liquors. Lyman Beecher's *Six Lectures on Intemperance* (1826) mark the beginning of widespread national interest in alcohol reform.

By 1834, more than 1 million Americans had climbed on the temperance bandwagon, many of them Calvinists and the majority from New England. Unitarians* were not central to the crusade, though a few, such as H. Ware, Jr.,** and John Pierpont, became embroiled in temperance agitation. Later in the century, the Midwest was the scene of action, as temperance became associated with "civilizing" frontier towns. After the 1870s, women's groups orchestrated the reform campaign until it culminated, or imploded, in the era of Prohibition.

At one time, scholars understood calls for temperance as a middle-class attempt to increase productivity and cut down on the amounts employers had to pay toward their workers' grog. This school of thought points out that calls for temperance coincided with a rise in industrial patterns that required workers to adhere to increasingly rigid schedules. More recently, temperance activity has been explained as a social marker that "respectable" Americans could utilize as a behavioral status symbol. Advocacy of temperance, in this light, was a way to distance one's own mores from those of immigrants and the unwashed. This was not a view antebellum Americans would have proffered. They were more likely to present temperance as evidence of self-determination, or a resolute will, crucial to moral uplift. Temperance lecturers who followed this line linked overindulgence to a host of crimes and sins.

Ministers dominated temperance activity, but doctors and health reformers joined the outcry. So did a number of canny hacks. W. Whitman's** temperance novel, *Franklin Evans* (1842), was not canny enough: It languished on forgotten shelves. But Timothy Shay Arthur scored a huge hit with *Ten Nights in a Barroom* (1854), now remembered for its sensational scenes of low dives, delirium tremens, and children left hungry while parents drank. In a gentler vein, N. Hawthorne** won praise for "A Rill from the Town Pump," which was reprinted in a children's temperance reader.

In the early 1830s, Emerson expressed some guilt about spending money for alcohol instead of saving up to buy Plato.* But he did not stop buying liquor, and he soon stopped expressing guilt. Brook Farm* followed the same general line: Drunkenness was of course taboo, but a taste for alcohol was permitted. At Fruitlands,* on the other hand, total abstinence was the norm, since B. Alcott** and C. Lane** thought bodily purity prepared the way for spiritual cleansing.

But the Massachusetts legislature probably had other aims in mind when, in 1838, it passed a short-lived "Fifteen Gallon Law" that prohibited the sale of liquor by the glass. Emerson found this mandated morality cold and smug. He wrote, in 1841, impersonating a Simon Pure: "I fight in my fashion but you, o paddies & roarers, must not fight in yours. I drink my tea & coffee, but as for you & your cups, here is the pledge." The more significant reaction to complacent authority was a working-class groundswell of opposition. Emerson may, in fact, have been reacting to the "Washingtonians," a group that upheld temperance goals but rejected genteel lecturers' self-appointment as moral guides. Arguing that suasion relied on shared backgrounds more than know-all models, the Washingtonians helped convince American laborers to decrease their use of alcohol. Their successors, the Sons of Temperance, learned from the Washingtonians and downplayed class bias when preaching prudent use of liquor.

REFERENCES: Histories of the temperance agitations include Joseph J. Rumbarger, *Profits, Power, and Prohibition: Alcohol Reform and the Industrializing of America, 1800–1930* (1989), Robert L. Hampel, *Temperance and Prohibition in Massachusetts 1813–1852* (1982), and Joseph Gusfield, *Symbolic Crusade: Status Politics and the American Temperance Movement* (1963). See also Anne C. Rose, *Transcendentalism as a Social Movement, 1830–1850* (1981), and, on temperance literature, David Reynolds, *Beneath the American Renaissance: The Subversive Imagination in the Age of Emerson and Melville** (1988).

Barbara Ryan

TEMPLE SCHOOL, the most important educational* experiment undertaken by any of the Transcendentalists, was operated by A. B. Alcott** in Boston from 1834 to 1838. Having previously taught with varying degrees of success in rural Connecticut and the Philadelphia area, Alcott believed that his radical ideas about children could be realized best in Boston, which he believed to be the most enlightened place in America and where just before moving to Pennsylvania in the early 1830s he had conducted an infant school.

While in Pennsylvania he became immersed in Idealist* philosophy, especially the writings of Plato,* Proclus,* Plotinus,* Berkeley,* Goethe,** and French philosopher V. Cousin,** who was popularizing such German thinkers as Kant,* Fichte,* and Schelling.** Above all, he was influenced by Coleridge.** Combined with his earlier study of the great Swiss educator Pestalozzi* and his long-standing faith in the innate goodness of children, this reading provided Alcott with the intellectual foundation that underpinned the theory and practice of his innovative "School for Human Culture."

During the summer of 1834 he was able to gather a school with the help of his friend and onetime mentor, the Rev. W. E. Channing,** and E. P. Peabody,** Channing's former amanuensis who became Alcott's principal assistant. In September, having rented several spacious, well-lit rooms in the Masonic Temple on Tremont Street, Alcott opened his school with 30 pupils. No expense was spared to make the environment as conducive to learning as possible. The central classroom was carefully furnished with books, individual blackboards, comfortable chairs, pictures, paintings, and busts, including ones of Socrates and Christ, his two favorite teachers. Patrons of the school included prominent business, civic, and social leaders. His pupils came from a variety of religious backgrounds—Unitarian,* Calvinist, Baptist, Swedenborgian,* Episcopalian, Methodist, Universalist, and even Free Inquirer. Wanting as diverse a mix as could be enrolled from the area, he hoped to add a Quaker* and a Catholic. During its first years of operation, enrollment ranged as high as 40; even at that, though, he could not pay off his startup costs or even pay Peabody a salary.

Alcott's overarching aim was to cultivate his students' mental, moral, and spiritual faculties. He believed that children needed to realize the divinity within themselves and that teachers must facilitate this recognition without driving or coercing their charges. Contrary to the established practice of the day, Alcott avoided corporal punishment. Typically, he excluded unruly pupils from the group until their conscience showed them the error of their ways; in unusual instances, he had students who misbehaved strike him, causing them to break into tears. While the curriculum included the standard subjects—reading, grammar, spelling, arithmetic, geography, Latin, and at one time, French—he did not rely on rote learning or believe that the imparting of information was the central goal of education. The ability to think, to show connections, to discuss rather than memorize was of paramount concern.

To nurture his pupils' thought and expression, he also made journal* writing part of their lessons. To cultivate the imagination, he frequently used fables, parables, allegories, and emblems. In all instances, his method was Socratic, inductive. To show society Alcott's successes, Peabody kept daily accounts that she published in *Record of a School: Exemplifying the General Principles of Spiritual Culture* (1835; rev. ed. 1836). Peabody's book seemed to help realize Alcott's hope that his students would become missionaries to their parents and other adults.

By far the boldest experiment that Alcott tried was conducting a series of wide-ranging Conversations* on the New Testament during 1835–36. Ranging in age from 6 to 13, his pupils, females as well as males, openly discussed such topics as birth and the pain of Christ's circumcision. As Alcott prepared the 50 Conversations for press, Peabody resigned her position in the summer of 1836, correctly sensing the controversy that would erupt and unhappy that she had never been paid. Stubborn to the end, Alcott hired a new assistant, M. Fuller,** and began collecting material for another volume, which was never published. Though defended in print by Peabody herself, R. W. Emerson,** J. F. Clarke,** and other Transcendentalists, the two-volume *Conversations with Children on the Gospels* (1836–37) outraged the community and many patrons and support- ers of the school. Even Channing disapproved. The most vicious attacks came from the *Boston Daily Advertiser* and the *Boston Courier,* the city's two leading dailies. James T. Buckingham, editor of the *Courier,* called Alcott a corrupter of youth (29 March 1837, 2) and later printed the hearsay remarks of a local clergyman, identified by Alcott as "Unitarian Pope" A. Norton** of Harvard Divinity School,* who said of the book that *"one third was absurd, one third was blasphemous, and one third obscene.* And such, we apprehend, will be the deliberate opinion of those who diligently read and soberly reflect" (9 May, 2).

Alcott's patrons agreed. Despite resorting to advertising his school, a desper- ate measure he loathed on principle, enrollment steadily declined to six. He even moved to less expensive rooms in the Masonic Temple and sold his treasured school library to help ward off the duns. In June 1838, several thousand dollars in debt, he had no choice but to close the school. Another attempt to start a similar school in 1838–39, this time at his own home, also failed when parents withdrew their children because Alcott refused to dismiss an African-American student he had enrolled.

Ironically, even as the Temple School was being attacked in Boston, the "American Pestalozzi" Alcott had disciples elsewhere who had either visited or read about his innovative experiment in self-culture. In Providence, Rhode Island, Hiram Fuller began a school modeled directly on the Temple School and in which M. Fuller (no relation) taught after leaving Alcott. Cousin, at the time engaged in education reform, and Dr. Nicholaus Heinrich Julius of Prussia wished to integrate Alcott's practices into their own countries' school systems. Most impressive was the homage paid to Alcott by J. P. Greaves,** a disciple of Pestalozzi who established near London a school called the Alcott House.

REFERENCES: The clearest statement by Alcott of his beliefs about education is *The Doctrine and Discipline of Human Culture* (1836), which also served as the introduction to the *Conversations*. Examples of his students' journal keeping are found in Alfred G. Litton and Joel Myerson, "The Temple School Journals of George and Martha Kuhn," *SAR* 1993: 55–145. Of the many contemporary responses to the Temple School and the *Conversations*, perhaps the most perceptive is [O. A. Brownson],** "Alcott on Human Culture," *BoQR* 1 (October 1838): 417–32. Revealing are Alcott's journals of the period, parts of which have been published in *The Journals of Bronson Alcott*, ed. Odell Shepard (1938). In its entirety Joel Myerson has published "Bronson Alcott's 'Journal for 1836,' " *SAR* 1978: 17–104. Larry A. Carlson's two-part edition of the complete 1837 journal appears in the 1981 and 1982 volumes of *SAR,* 27–132 and 53–167, respectively. Carlson has also published a two-part edition of the complete 1838 journal in the 1993 and 1994 volumes of *SAR,* 161–244 and 123–93, respectively. Important modern studies include George E. Haefner, *A Critical Estimate of the Educational Theories and Practices of A. Bronson Alcott* (1937); Odell Shepard, *Pedlar's Progress: The Life of Bronson Alcott* (1937); Dorothy McCuskey, *Bronson Alcott, Teacher* (1940); and Dahlstrand (1982). Arno Press rpt. the *Conversations* (1972), and Lindisfarne Press issued the book under the title *How Like an Angel Came I Down* (1991). For a sympathetic reading of the *Conversations* by fellow Transcendentalist W. H. Furness,** see Carlson, " 'Those Pure Pages of Yours': Bronson Alcott's *Conversations with Children on the Gospels,*" *AL* 60 (October 1988): 451–60.

Larry A. Carlson

TICKNOR AND FIELDS developed in the 1840s into the leading literary publishing house of Boston and then in the several succeeding decades into that of the entire nation. Operating out of Boston's famed Old Corner Bookstore at the intersection of Washington and School Streets, the firm successfully cultivated itself as the chief address for American writers, many of whom were of New England origin and a fair number of whom were associated with Transcendentalism.

The partners in the firm were William Ticknor (1810–1864) and James T. Fields (1817–1881). Ticknor, the senior partner until his death, was chiefly responsible for the financial management of the firm; Fields, an amateur man of letters and shrewd reader of public taste, primarily for dealings with authors and the press. Together, their divergent styles and talents blended into a formidable partnership, one well positioned and intelligently managed to take advantage of the flowering of letters in New England and the rapid expansion of print culture in the United States.

The beginnings of the house were modest. Ticknor had made the crossover from banking to bookselling in his early twenties, when he went into partnership with John Allen at the Old Corner Bookstore. He took over from Allen in 1834 after a few years as its sole proprietor, by which time the teenage Fields was serving a clerkship in the store. By the time Fields had worked himself up to a junior partnership in 1843, the firm, in large part due to Fields's prodding, had begun to devote a larger portion of its resources to publishing, especially in the field of the belles lettres. Once begun, that process accelerated, as Ticknor and Fields (the official name of the firm only between 1854 and 1864) gradually gathered into its well-coordinated publishing list many of the leading creative writers not only of the United States but also of Britain.

By midcentury, the firm enjoyed a period of fast growth in which its offices at 135 Washington Street became the premier literary gathering place in Boston, a welcome space for such writers as R. W. Emerson,** J. R. Lowell,** H. W. Longfellow,** and N. Hawthorne.** Not only did Ticknor and Fields attract to the house the finest assemblage of writers in the country, but Fields moved to ensure that an inner corps of his authors would "permanently" remain attached to the house by purchasing rights to their collected works, as well as to their future books. With the sea change affecting American letters, as Boston for a generation outcompeted New York to become the publishing center of American letters, Ticknor and Fields maneuvered itself into an unprecedented situation of literary publishing centrality.

Though neither Fields nor Ticknor was personally attracted to Transcendentalism, the momentum of their expanding operations drove them to become the publishers of numerous of the leading figures in the movement, most notably Emerson and H. D. Thoreau.** Then after the death of Ticknor in 1864 and the retirement of Fields in 1871, the literary property of the firm, which included the works of numerous leading writers of midcentury (and, among them, those of some of the Transcendentalists), passed into (and through) the hands of his successor James Osgood and finally into those of Houghton Mifflin.

REFERENCES: The archive of Ticknor and Fields, on deposit at the Houghton Library, Harvard University, is one of the most comprehensive and best preserved American publishing archives still in existence. The most comprehensive study of Ticknor and Fields is Michael Winship, *American Literary Publishing in the Mid-Nineteenth Century: The Business of Ticknor and Fields* (1995). Also useful are W. S. Tryon, *Parnassus Corner: A Life of James T. Fields* (1963), and William Charvat and W. S. Tryon, eds., *The Cost Books of Ticknor and Fields* (1949).

Ezra Greenspan

The TOWN AND COUNTRY CLUB

The **TOWN AND COUNTRY CLUB** was organized early in 1849 by A. B. Alcott,** with the help of R. W. Emerson,** "to establish better acquaintance between men of scientific, literary, and philanthropic pursuits." The club, which held weekly conversations and monthly, quarterly, and annual meetings, lasted only a little more than a year but managed to attract more than 100 of Boston's leading intellectuals, businessmen, and artists including T. Parker,** J. F. Clarke,** E. P. Whipple,** J. S. Dwight,** and even H. D. Thoreau** (though he attended only the first meeting on 20 March 1849). Alcott's chief object in organizing the club seems to have been the desire to promote his Conversations,* and Emerson (who almost certainly is responsible for naming the club) seems to have wished greater contact with the "Town" members he otherwise would not have regularly seen.

Unlike its informal predecessor the Transcendental Club,* the Town and Country Club had a constitution and formal rules for membership, and it was the question over membership that contributed, at least to some extent, to the club's undoing. Members such as T. W. Higginson** and W. L. Garrison** wanted women included, but other members (including Emerson) protested that such a move would make the club "a saloon for ladies." Alcott quickly realized as well that the large number of members actually constrained rather than promoted discussion, and he grew disappointed that the meetings began to resemble social gatherings for the literati rather than philosophical discussions. Even more disappointing was the fact that the club could not remain financially solvent, given the large expense of renting club rooms and feeding large numbers of members. Though the club was forced to dissolve in May 1850, during the group's brief existence, a number of members gave papers at the meetings, including Emerson's paper on "Books and Reading," Parker on "The Scholar's Relation to his Age," and H. James, Sr.'s** address on "Socialism and Individualism."

REFERENCES: The most important documents relating to the club's history are the Town and Country Club records, which have been edited by K. W. Cameron ("Emerson, Thoreau, and the Town and Country Club," *ESQ,* no. 8 [3d Q 1957]: 2–17). Cameron reproduces the membership list and the club's constitution. The best discussion of Alcott's organization of the club is in Dahlstrand (1982), 220–22. Also of use is F. B. Sanborn,** *Recollections of Seventy Years,* 2 vols. (1909), though Sanborn was notorious for altering the historical and textual records. Also of interest is Thomas Wortham, "Did Emerson Blackball Frederick Douglass** from Membership in the Town and Country Club?" *NEQ* 64 (June 1992): 295–98.

Alfred G. Litton

The **TRANSCENDENTAL CLUB** and *The Dial** were the two focal points of Transcendentalism, places where the members of the "new school" of literature, philosophy, and religion could meet and discuss their views with sympathetic minds. The Club had its origins in June 1836, when F. H. Hedge,** a minister in Bangor, Maine, mailed R. W. Emerson** a letter proposing the formation of a "symposium" to discuss the mood of the times. Hedge and two Boston ministers, George Putnam and G. Ripley,** wished to assemble "certain likeminded persons of our acquaintance for the free discussion of theological & moral subjects." Emerson agreed, and they used the Harvard College bicentennial celebration in September as the occasion for their first meeting. On 8 September they gathered at Willard's Hotel in Cambridge and agreed that the present state of philosophy and theology was "very unsatisfactory"; they wished to discuss what, if anything, could be done "in the way of protest and introduction of deeper and broader views." The tone of the discussion was encouraging, and Ripley volunteered his home for the next meeting on 19 September, when 11 people gathered. During the four years that followed, the Club met nearly 30 times, discussing matters of mutual religious and philosophical interest. Among those who attended the Club's meetings were A. B. Alcott,** G. Bancroft,** C. A. Bartol,** O. A. Brownson,** W. E. Channing,** W. H. Channing,** J. F. Clarke,** C. P. Cranch,** J. S. Dwight,** C. Francis,** M. Fuller,** T. Parker,** E. P. Peabody,** H. D. Thoreau,** and C. S. Wheeler.** After the meeting in September 1840, the Club disbanded. What had originally been organized for informal discussion among a small but somewhat influential group of dissidents now found itself containing some very important members who wielded real power. With other forums and careers to occupy its members, who were beginning to differ sharply and often harshly among themselves, the Club wisely and silently drifted apart. The contemporary impact cannot be denied. In an era of "Conversations,"* such as those made by Alcott and Fuller, the opportunity to freely discuss and exchange ideas was important. In addition, the Club was a major force behind the founding of *The Dial.*

REFERENCES: See Joel Myerson, "A Calendar of Transcendental Club Meetings," *AL* 44 (May 1972): 197–207; and Myerson, "A History of the Transcendental Club," *ESQ* 23 (1st Q 1977): 27–35.

Joel Myerson

TRANSCENDENTALISM, a movement of theological innovation and literary experiment arising within New England Unitarianism* in the 1830s and 1840s, has had a significant impact on later developments in American religious, educational, literary, and political culture. Despite visible leading figures (such as R. W. Emerson,** M. Fuller,** T. Parker,** and H. D. Thoreau**), galvanizing events, and a variety of tangible expressions such as periodicals, clubs, and utopian communities, Transcendentalism in the United States was never a codified set of beliefs, a formal philosophy, or a monolithic social movement. So elusive is the term, and so diverse the people, writings, and institutional forms with which it is associated, that many scholars despair of adequate definition. Certainly the technical theological usage of the word *transcendental* is confusing, even misleading, in discussions of Transcendentalism in America: Theologically, *transcendent* refers to a divinity that is above or apart from the world; but for Emerson, Thoreau, and most leading American Transcendentalists, God is immanent* in the creation.

In the American context, *transcendental* more accurately relates to epistemological issues—to assertions about the grounds of knowledge and the apprehension of truth—that is, to *how* we know reality. In his lecture "The Transcendentalist" (1841), Emerson explained that "the Idealism* of the present day acquired the name of Transcendental, from the use of that term by Immanuel Kant,*" freely interpreting the German philosopher to mean "whatever belongs to the class of intuitive thought." Transcendentalism is perhaps most usefully approached as a "spirit of the age," embodying a widespread belief in the dignity and potential of human nature, a desire for institutional reform to sweep away impediments to self-culture, and a call for freedom of creative expression—all arising among the generation that came of age in the late 1820s and 1830s.

What came to be called Transcendentalism in the United States emerged in New England intellectual life in 1836, the "Annus Mirabilis" of the movement, as Perry Miller termed it. This year saw publication of Emerson's *Nature,* generally regarded as the "manifesto" of Transcendentalism, and several other works of revisionist theology and educational experiment: O. Brownson's** *New Views of Christianity, Society, and the Church;* W. H. Furness's** *Remarks on the Four Gospels;* G. Ripley's** *Discourses on the Philosophy of Religion;* E. P. Peabody's** *Record of a School;* and A. B. Alcott's** *Conversations* with Children on the Gospels. Together these works challenged institutional approaches to truth and argued against the prevailing belief that religious certitude must be grounded in institutional authority or the historical verification of the biblical miracles.* Divinity, these new voices declared, is at hand, immediately available to the pure in spirit. Transcendentalism was, in this sense, originally fueled by the desire for religious reformation, and such reform brought with it the revision of key theological concepts. Revelation may be said to have been supplanted by Intuition, Soul by Self, and God by the Over-Soul (Emerson's term) or more broadly by Nature* (as both physical presence and abstract conception of the realm of human experience).

Despite celebration of self-reliance and innovation, "the newness," as it was called, had a long social, intellectual, and theological foreground. Native sources and issues provided much of the impetus for the emergence of what became known as "Transcendentalism." Assertion of the worth of the individual is in part a cultural logical conclusion of the political independence established in the American Revolution. Many of the leading Transcendentalists had been Unitarian ministers, and "Liberal Christianity," as the denomination was often called, had itself been in large part a reaction against Calvinist (or Puritan*) concepts of human depravity and God's sovereignty, doctrines that seemed to limit human agency. The liberals within the New England Congregational churches had begun to revise, or simply ignore, Calvinist dogma in the late 18th century. In the early decades of the 19th century, the tension between the Calvinist "Orthodox" and the Liberals broke into the more open schism of the Unitarian Controversy, with the Unitarians espousing a theology of self-culture that affirmed human potential and human means against what they perceived as the deterministic disposition of Calvinism.

The chief intellectual influence on Transcendentalism can be found very close to home in the work of the Unitarian leader W. E. Channing,** whose rhetorical eloquence and generosity of spirit served as a crucial example to Emerson and others. But Unitarian theology was for the most part premised on the empiricist epistemology of Locke,* which explained truth in terms of the mind's apprehension of external facts and stimuli. By the early 1830s this view of knowledge had become stale for Emerson, Parker, Ripley, and others, and they responded with real eagerness to alternative theories of knowledge and intuition, originating in the work of Kant and later German idealists. This epistemological revolution was transmitted first by Coleridge** and Carlyle** through their commentaries and responses to German philosophical and literary trends. It was reinforced by the powerful example of Goethe's** range of intellectual and aesthetic sympathies and the stimulation of Wordsworth's** poetic revelation of the inner and spiritual life.

Traditional figures such as the French cleric and mystic Fénelon* and the speculative theologian Swedenborg* were rediscovered. German higher criticism* taught the relativity of scriptural truth, making other secular and more contemporary texts valid sources of inspiration. The sacred scriptures of the East, then in the process of being translated and disseminated in the West (a pursuit termed Orientalism*), also had an invigorating impact. Though a mystical strain characterizes certain prominent Transcendentalists and "the newness" emphasized the immediate and the prospective, many Transcendentalists, educated in a curriculum based heavily on the classics at Harvard, still found living models of myth, heroism, or character in Greek and Roman literature. Stoicism* held special appeal for Emerson and Thoreau.

The social and cultural manifestations of Transcendentalism were diverse. The 1840s were the "Age of Reform." Several of the most prominent Transcendentalists remained within the Unitarian denomination and devoted themselves to reform of the church and using the church as a tool of reform. Others struggled to free the human spirit through antislavery or abolitionism,* or agitation for temperance,* woman's rights,* education reform,* and humane treatment of prisoners and the mentally ill. Some sought more fundamental change in social organization and established utopian communities such as Brook Farm* and Fruitlands* as experiments in alternative economic and social relations. An important strain of Transcendentalism—that favored by Emerson and Thoreau—emphasized spiritual reform of the individual as prerequisite for real and lasting social reform. Fuller, a close friend of Emerson's and the first editor of *The Dial,** recognized the feminist implications of the strand of self-reliant individualism preached by Emerson and drew on his doctrine as one of the bases for her *Woman in the Nineteenth Century* (1845), one of the most important early articulations of the need for social equality and intellectual freedom for women. Parallel to these social and political aspects, literary Transcendentalists declared independence from inherited modes of expression, insisting on a more "natural," organic form,* and pushing the boundaries of established genres such as the sermon, essay, and travel* excursion. Emerson's essays and Thoreau's *Walden; or, Life in the Woods* (1854) best realized the movement's artistic possibilities; E. Dickinson** and W. Whitman** are the best-known examples of the continuing impact of Transcendentalist experiment in letters.

Not everyone, of course, shared the Transcendentalists' enthusiasm for reform, experiment, and "newness." It was variously depicted as an impious threat to orthodoxy or the silly self-indulgence of oddball intellectuals. On 15 July 1838, Emerson, in his Divinity School Address, tried to inspire graduating divinity students to remember the sacredness of their calling, particularly the "inestimable advantage" of preaching. But his criticism of the dull formalism of "historical Christianity" so offended former professor A. Norton** that he attacked Emerson's views as "The Latest Form of Infidelity," pulling Emerson's supporters Ripley and Parker into an acrimonious controversy over the worth of the new movement. The vaguely mystical reputation of the movement was often ridiculed in popular circles. "What is transcendentalism . . . ?" asked Boston's leading newspaper, the *Daily Evening Transcript,* on 23 September 1840. The *Transcript* answered its own question by ridiculing *The Dial* as a product of "this crazy sect," concluding that "we do not believe the world will be made much wiser by these infatuated zanies than it was before the lofty discoveries of this sect of demented infuriates and visionary unintelligible crazy sophists." The historical reputation of the movement has continued to be disparaged in some quarters by those who are dismissive of speculative thought, social experiment, or unconventional forms of literary or religious expression.

Emerson, generally regarded as the leader of the movement—drawing pilgrims to his home in Concord, Massachusetts*—acknowledged the problem of defining just what Transcendentalism was. He wrote with bemusement to his mother from Providence, Rhode Island, on 28 March 1840: "You must know I am reckoned here a Transcendentalist, and what that beast is, all persons in Providence have a great appetite to know. . . . They have various definitions of the word current here. One man, of whom I have been told, in good earnest defined it as 'Operations on the Teeth'; A young man named Rodman, answered an inquiry by saying 'It was a nickname which those who stayed behind, gave to those who went ahead.' " More seriously, but still provisionally, he observed in his lecture "The Transcendentalist" (published in *The Dial* in January 1843) that the Transcendentalist "believes in inspiration, and in ecstasy" but that "there is no such thing as a Transcendental *party.*" Moreover, the modern Transcendentalist, despite noble principles, is presently misunderstood and has yet to exercise genuine power. He portrayed the Transcendentalists as a class of young intellectuals alienated from the ordinary paths of work and daily life but unable to devise any satisfying and sustaining alternatives. For Emerson, the prospective nature of our aspirations—the impossibility of finally realizing intuitions in a world of mutability and organic growth—would paradoxically engender both hope and anxiety. Other writers of the time with a darker view of human nature—notably N. Hawthorne,** H. Melville,** and E. A. Poe**— would be attracted to the heroic aspirations of Transcendentalism, especially as exemplified by Emerson, but would stress its tragic implications.

Though 1836 has widely been cited as the more or less official beginning of Transcendentalism, scholars disagree over when it ended. Several classic works were published early in the 1850s, giving rise to F. O. Matthiessen's characterization of the age as the "American Renaissance": Emerson's *Representative Men* (1850), Thoreau's *Walden* (1854), Whitman's *Leaves of Grass* (1855)— and works that in various ways engage with Transcendentalism—Hawthorne's

The Scarlet Letter (1850) and *The Blithedale Romance* (1852) and Melville's *Moby-Dick* (1851). In many ways the Civil War (1861–65) culminated the reform impulse of the 1830s and 1840s. But the Civil War also conveniently signals the effective end of Transcendentalism. Fuller had died in 1850, Parker in 1860, Thoreau in 1862, and Emerson, though intellectually active throughout the 1850s and 1860s, was increasingly less associated with any "movement" he may have inadvertently founded. The spirit of America changed with the war as well. The world of the Transcendentalists was predominantly rural, the nation's economy still based largely on agriculture.* And if it meant anything, Transcendentalism meant confidence and hope—confidence in human potential, hope in a future that would realize our best aspirations. The Civil War held the Union and freed the slaves. But it introduced wholesale slaughter, industrial growth, and eventually political and economic corruption and public cynicism on a scale the United States had never known.

After the Civil War the idealism, introspection, and enthusiasms of Transcendentalism began to be described by historians, and even some participants in the movement, as a quaint bucolic interlude that could be either enjoyed for its nostalgia or dismissed as irrelevant. Several attempts to keep alive the spirit of Transcendentalism persisted after the war: The Free Religious Association* arose as a radical alternative within postwar Unitarianism; a second, even a third, "generation" wrote biographies of the leading figures; A. B. Alcott's Concord School of Philosophy,* often depicted as the "twilight" of the movement, briefly revived both the ideas and the forum of Transcendentalist Conversation. But among 20th-century American literary and intellectual historians, the importance of the movement has been increasingly noted, and its influence has come to seem pervasive. Emerson, whose work has undergone a major revival of interest in the 1970s and 1980s, is widely regarded as a central and widely influential figure in American culture. Thoreau, admired for his tough-minded prose, has had an enormous impact as a prophet of social justice and the American originator of ecological awareness. Fuller joined shrewd journalistic gifts with a passionate commitment to political activism and is recognized as a founding voice in the history of American feminism. And Whitman's expansive, sensual celebration of the representative self exemplifies the rich possibilities of American verse. The forces of history may have altered the climate in which the Transcendentalists flourished. But the issues of human dignity, natural beauty, social and political justice, and national purpose that they so eloquently espoused continue to resonate in American culture.

REFERENCES: The first book-length study of Transcendentalism, by a member of the "second generation," was O. B. Frothingham** (1876); available in a paperback facsimile edition, this is still a useful introduction to the sources and figures of Transcendentalism. Miller (1950), available in paperback, is an excellent sourcebook of the diverse contexts and manifestations of Transcendentalism. Modern surveys include Paul F. Boller, Jr., *American Transcendentalism, 1830–1860: An Intellectual Inquiry* (1974), and Donald N. Koster, *Transcendentalism in America* (1975). Most of the scholarly work on

Transcendentalism has focused on individual figures such as Emerson, Thoreau, and Fuller, but works on the Transcendentalist movement that are of particular interest include Matthiessen (1941); Pochmann (1957); Hutchison (1959); Howe (1970); Buell (1973); and Richardson (1978). Joel Myerson's annual *SAR* (1977–96) publishes textual, bibliographical, historical, and biographical studies and primary texts significant for the study of Transcendentalism.

Brief bibliographical notes are appended to each entry in this encyclopedia. An indispensable bibliographical guide to major and minor figures, contemporaneous reactions, and important topics is Myerson (1984). Ongoing editions and critical books and articles on Transcendentalism are cited in the annual *American Literary Scholarship* (published by the American Literature Section of the Modern Language Association of America) and in the annual MLA *Bibliography*. Specialized bibliographies also appear annually in *ESP* and quarterly in the *TSB*.

Wesley T. Mott and David M. Robinson

TRAVEL provided Transcendentalists with important tropes, and travel writing, or the excursion, became a characteristic Transcendentalist genre. The ancient motive of wonder enhanced by motives of economics and empire made the 19th century a great age of travel writing. Many Transcendentalists avidly read travel accounts, themselves dreamed of travel to distant places, and eventually produced their own travel writing. Although figures such as J. F. Clarke,** his sister Sarah, and G. and S. Ripley** enjoyed reading about travel, R. W. Emerson,** H. Thoreau,** and M. Fuller** among all the Transcendentalists were the most notable writers about it.

They did not view traveling as an unalloyed good, however, and did not think it permitted easy escape from boredom or trouble. Emerson, for example, wrote in "Self-Reliance," "Travelling is a fool's paradise. Our first journeys discover to us the indifference of places. At home I dream that at Naples, at Rome, I can be intoxicated with beauty, and lose my sadness. I pack my trunk, embrace my friends, embark on the sea, and at last wake up in Naples, and there beside me is the stern fact, the sad self, unrelenting, identical, that I fled from." Nevertheless, he went to Europe the first time while grieving the death of his wife Ellen, and its impact on him was significant, particularly his visit to the Jardin des Plantes that occasioned his decision to become a "naturalist." His second trip to England, responding to an invitation to lecture, was a desirable "change and a tonic." If "one use of travel," he later wrote, was "to recommend the books and works of home," it remained true that "of the six or seven teachers whom each man wants among his contemporaries, it often happens that one or two of them live on the other side of the world." Similarly, Thoreau, the greatest travel writer of all the Transcendentalists, commented in his journal,* "I am afraid to travel much or to famous places, lest it might completely dissipate my mind. Then I am sure that what we observe at home, if we observe anything, is of more importance than what we observe abroad. The far-fetched is of the least value." Yet he, too, would later record in the same journal, "A traveler.

I love his title. A traveler is to be reverenced as such. His profession is the best symbol of our life. Going from—toward; it is the history of every one of us.''

Transcendentalist travel writers pursued several strategies to deal with their ambivalent feelings about travel. Thoreau made traveling a process of figuration, a troping of life and of the world. ''The question,'' he wrote, ''is not where did the traveler go, what places did he see?—it would be difficult to choose between places—but who was the traveler? how did he travel? how genuine an experience did he get?'' His *A Week on the Concord and Merrimack Rivers,* as John Aldrich Christie has pointed out, ''converted the obvious activity of travel and voyaging into a structural metaphor for self-exploration.'' If Emerson feared that the inescapable self might negate travel, the very presence of self made it possible for Thoreau to familiarize the strange and make the homely wondrous. When he boasted in *Walden,* ''I have travelled a good deal in Concord,''* he affirmed that self-exploration, the key to travel writing, could be done anywhere, that Concord could be represented as ''a distant land to me'' even as Baffin's Bay could be as near as Flint's Pond covered with snow. Travel became one of Thoreau's central metaphors, strategically organizing his writing as he plumbed the genuineness of his experience. Posthumously published volumes, like *Cape Cod* and *The Maine Woods,* kept a steadier gaze on perceived facts of the world, but along with the essays contained in *Excursions,* they ultimately troped Thoreau's own life under the code of travel writing.

Thoughtful travel writers recognized that self-discovery was one of the purposes of travel, but equally important was self-culture, the acquisition of broadening experience and fresh perspectives on the world. Fuller's *Summer on the Lakes, in 1843* presents itself less as a discovery of the genuine self than as ''footnotes . . . made on the pages of my life.'' Fuller's account of her trip to Wisconsin and Illinois taken in the company of Sarah Clarke attends to people in different situations, to Native Americans or the wives of frontier settlers, with greater sympathy for the ''heartsickness and weariness'' of their lives than symbolizing Thoreau ever displayed. After making her journey, Fuller recognized that she needed more knowledge in order to work her notes up into a published book, so she spent six months in the Harvard library reading about the American West. (Thus becoming the first woman reader admitted to the Harvard libraries.) Susan Belasco Smith describes *Summer on the Lakes* as ''at least in part, an intensely personal account of Fuller's own inner life during the summer of 1843,'' but in revealing that personal life in terms of its emotional relations to a complexly presented external world, Fuller tapped different possibilities for travel writing than Thoreau did. Also, by contextualizing her work in terms of writers like James Adair, Alexander Henry, and Thomas L. McKenney, she participated in the nationalist concerns of the ''Young America'' of the 1840s.

The question of America, in fact, drove a great deal of the travel writing of the period, and the contemporary interest in travel writing responded to the critical accounts of English travelers such as Basil Hall, Frances Trollope, Frederick Marryat, and Charles Dickens. Emerson turned the tables on British sneers at American crudity by criticizing in his *English Traits* the "cramp limitation in their habit of thought, . . . a drag of inertia which resists reform in every shape." His version of travel writing, however, demonstrates some of the dangers that he warned against. Written after his second trip to England in 1847–48, *English Traits* advances a theory about the relationship between England and America that he had worked out in a lecture series five years earlier. New England, he suggested in 1843, inherited a vital Anglo-Saxon materialism but possessed an elasticity missing in England. America in his eyes, as Phyllis Cole has pointed out, "was both a new England and an anti-England." Claiming that he was intent upon "a faithful seeing of England," he thus arrived with a scheme already in mind to account for whatever he might see. To his credit, he looked widely and wrote thoughtfully in order to answer his question, "Why England is England?" Emerson as a travel writer turned out to be less interested in self-discovery or self-culture than in the question of national character, both England's and America's. Granting England its virtues, he was ready to see the compensating limitations of this "best of actual nations" that was yet "no ideal framework." Emerson as traveler, more than either Thoreau or Fuller, was a "naturalist" of society; not content to write a mere travel guide, he sought to comprehend England's inner principle of order.

REFERENCES: John Aldrich Christie, *Thoreau as World Traveler* (1965), provides a valuable account of Thoreau as reader and writer of travel literature. He includes a list of travel works read by Thoreau whose catholicity suggests the range of material available to Transcendentalist readers. The literature on Thoreau's writing about his travels is enormous, but notable is Sherman Paul, *The Shores of America: Thoreau's Inward Exploration* (1958), esp. its concluding chapter. Susan Belasco Smith's introduction to her edition of *Summer on the Lakes* (1991) is useful, as is Stephen Adams, " 'That Tidiness We Always Look for in Women': Margaret Fuller's *Summer on the Lakes* and Romantic Aesthetics," *SAR* 1987: 247–64. Phyllis Cole, "Emerson, England, and Fate," in *Emerson: Prophecy, Metamorphosis, and Influence,* ed. David Levin (1975), 83–105, puts *English Traits* into the context of Emerson's travels there, his earlier comments on England, and the later *Conduct of Life.* James B. Thayer, *A Western Journey with Mr. Emerson* (1884), gives a charming account of Emerson as traveler.

Frank Shuffelton

U

UNITARIANISM in America, championing "free inquiry" in the service of "rational religion," acknowledged its debt to 18th-century rationalism and laid the foundation for 19th-century Transcendentalism. Under the guidance of ministers J. S. Buckminster,* the H. Wares, father and son,** and W. E. Channing,** churchgoers in early 19th-century Boston subscribed to a faith based on the moral perfection of God and the moral perfectibility of man. Rejecting the theological legacy left by their Puritan* forebears, Unitarians argued strenuously for revised versions of both human and divine nature.

Initially preferring the phrase "liberal Christianity" to the at that time pejorative term *Unitarianism,* ministers stressed the reasonable nature of their faith. They borrowed the methods of higher criticism* to frame their own scriptural interpretations. Against charges that liberality meant license, they defended their claim to Christianity by maintaining the singular importance of revelation as recorded in the Bible. Theirs was a revealed religion grounded in history, dependent upon its particular past. It remained a religion of persons—a fatherly God and a brotherly Christ whose exemplary life mediated between humanity and divinity. The miracles attributed to the historical Jesus became its most-debated aspect. They were problematic for a rational religion yet seemingly indispensable to a revealed one. Conflicting claims led to the highly charged miracles controversy* of the 1830s with its unsettling questions about religious and individual authority. What had been Liberal Christianity's earlier defense against critics became the complicated border between Unitarianism and Transcendentalism.

In the 1820s, however, such divisions were a decade away. From the pulpit and in the periodical press, Channing and his colleagues celebrated the capacity of the human mind and created a moral imperative for self-development. Privileging the "active mind," ministers championed formation of character as the only acceptable means of salvation. Channing termed the process "self-culture," and his colleagues left no doubt about its difficulty. The individual followed a demanding discipline in which rigorous self-control regulated the "animal appetites" and freed the "higher nature" to cultivate a far-reaching development.

Few areas of interest were excluded; the individual was encouraged to study history, biography, poetry, biblical criticism, the arts, and the fledgling sciences. The ministers' work yielded an ample harvest. The first years of Liberal Christianity saw the publication of the literary magazine *The Monthly Anthology** (1803–11), the formation of Boston's Anthology Society (1805), and the founding, under its auspices, of the Boston Athenaeum* (1807). In subsequent decades, parishioners were offered a growing number of educational opportunities: lectures on biblical history, biblical geography, or scriptural interpretation structured by higher criticism. Ministers encouraged their parishioners to participate in weekly reading groups, counseled parents on their sons' and daughters' educations, and supported the first of many exhibitions sponsored by the Athenaeum. Through their periodicals, *The Christian Examiner,** *The Scriptural Interpreter, The Christian Register,* and later, the *Western Messenger,** they offered readers running commentary on the pivotal issues of the day.

Ranked prominently among the means for self-improvement, sermons epitomized the moral aesthetic supported by the Unitarians. Maintaining an integral connection between art and morality, ministers prized a pulpit eloquence based upon the innate beauty of "moral ideas." Expanding the function of the sermon, Unitarian congregations sought "inspiration" from the pulpit in addition to, and often in place of, explication. Sermons, Channing commented, should "quicken and exalt" their listeners. The function of the essay, in Transcendentalist terms, was anticipated and defined by the voice from the pulpit.

Unitarian influence was also felt in social reform. Ministers and parishioners actively involved themselves in benevolent work, defining their duty through social action; yet in the early 19th century, Unitarianism publicly distanced itself from reform movements. Subscribing to a morally charged version of cause and effect, the official position upheld the "primacy of principle." According to this model, attempts to force change would invariably fail. Individuals targeted for reform would respond with short-lived virtue; the reformers themselves hardly fared better. By focusing exclusively on particular social ills, they fragmented their characters, compromising the "Good" in their efforts to accomplish some "good." Little wonder, then, at R. W. Emerson's** ambivalence toward the reform movements of the day.

Championing human capability, interested in public utterance (whether oral or written), Liberal Christianity offered its audience the frame within which individuals could experiment with their own versions of self-culture. In many cases, what began as Unitarianism ended in Transcendentalism. The members of the Transcendental Club,* the individuals who attended M. Fuller's** Conversations,* the contributors to *The Dial,** the participants and visitors to Brook Farm:* The names reappear in Boston's Unitarian churches—J. F. Clarke,** E. P. Peabody,** J. S. Dwight,** G. Ripley,** T. Parker,** F. H. Hedge,** Fuller,

Emerson. Ministers, poets, teachers, lecturers, music critics, journalists: As Channing had argued in his 1838 lecture "Self-Culture," "[S]elf-culture must vary with the individual."

These individuals clearly took Channing at his word. Some, like Clarke and Peabody, engineered a working relationship that allowed them to remain closely affiliated with Unitarianism throughout their lives. Others found it impossible to pursue their work within its frame. In an 1841 ordination sermon, "A Discourse of the Transient and Permanent in Christianity," Parker advocated a "pure religion" based on the "divine life of the soul" and met with active opposition for relegating doctrine, forms of worship, and scriptural revelation to his category of the "transient." In response to the sermon, his fellow Unitarian ministers refused him their time-honored practice of pulpit exchange. His colleague Ripley had resigned his pulpit a few months earlier and moved to West Roxbury to head the utopian experiment at Brook Farm. In a letter to his congregation at the Purchase Street Church, Ripley charged Liberal Christianity with betraying its own principles. "Liberal churches," he commented, "began to fear liberality." With fear came varying forms of censure, and with censure, Liberal Christianity no longer supported "the unlimited freedom of the human mind." Embracing Transcendentalism as the organic expansion of Unitarianism, Ripley applauded its preference of "soul" over "tradition" and "history."

His comments sounded a familiar note. Three years earlier in 1838, one of Unitarianism's favorite sons had affirmed the same position and met with unequivocal resistance from the Unitarian establishment. When he delivered his address at the Harvard Divinity School,* Emerson added his voice to the increasingly divisive debate about "true religion" and the nature of its authority. He questioned every element of Unitarian belief: the role of Jesus, the meaning of the miracles, the nature of God, the definition of revelation.

For Emerson, the Unitarian ministry initially offered a vocation in eloquence, in which sermons served as the vehicle for free-ranging exploration. At his 1829 ordination, he dedicated himself to free inquiry in the form of ongoing, relentless thought. He was already the "endless seeker, with no Past at my back" ("Circles"). Equally interested in exploring the nature of humanity and of divinity, Emerson found it increasingly difficult to separate them. He preached the "absolute sovereignty" of the "inward nature." The individual required no mediator. Emerson told his congregation in 1832, "This voice of your own mind is the voice of God" (Sermon CLXIV). Six years later at the Divinity School, he set aside the Unitarian concept of a fatherly God and a necessary Christ, urging his listeners "to go alone; to refuse the good models. . . . [B]e to them a divine man." Three years later in 1841, the disciplined self-control essential to Unitarian self-culture was relegated to the past. The carefully regulated procedure had been replaced by spontaneity, instinct, and intuition. "The soul's advance," he wrote in his First Series essay "The Over-Soul," was not linear but "metamorphic." Its image was most aptly figured as the circle, and its method was most evocatively described in the essay "Circles" as "abandonment."

Like his colleagues Ripley and Parker, Emerson extended Unitarianism beyond its limits. With Ripley, he argued that Unitarianism no longer supported the full development of the individual. From his perspective, the "formation of Christian character" had become a one-way street to an all-too-predictable exemplar. What the new age required, and what Unitarianism could not produce, was a "new form of character." With its adherence to particular doctrines and traditional forms of worship, Unitarianism would only yield poor imitations of a onetime original. Emerson dismissed what the Unitarians endorsed, and the Harvard Divinity School professors returned the favor.

What once met with rejection, however, won a revisionary acceptance in the late 19th century. "Parkerism" became synonymous with the reform element within Unitarianism. "Emerson Clubs" were formed by a number of Unitarian congregations. In the 1870s, minister William Channing Gannett claimed ministers like Emerson and Parker were path-breaking pioneers whose work was essential to the development of Unitarianism. The 20th century has continued to question the distinctions between Unitarian self-culture and Transcendental self-trust, drawing and redrawing the blurred line that separates them.

REFERENCES: For early commentary on the relationship between Unitarianism and Transcendentalism, see William Dexter Wilson, "The Unitarian Movement in New England," *The Dial* 1, no. 4 (April 1841): 409–43. For 20th-century assessments, see Hutchison (1959); Conrad Wright's bibliographic essay "Unitarianism and Transcendentalism," in Myerson (1984), 45–55; and essays by Daniel Walker Howe, David Robinson, Robert Hudspeth, and Lawrence Buell in *American Unitarianism, 1805–1865,* ed. Conrad Edick Wright (1989). Miller (1950) remains the best primary source chronicle of Unitarianism's position and Transcendentalism's dissent from it. For histories of Unitarianism in America, see Wright, *The Beginnings of Unitarianism in America* (1955); *Liberal Christians: Essays on American Unitarian History* (1970); Wright, ed., *A Stream of Light: A Sesquicentennial History of American Unitarianism* (1975); and Robinson (1985). Unitarianism's sociocultural context is discussed in Howe (1970), and its influence on literary expression in Buell (1973). For Emerson's relation to the Unitarian Church, see *Sermons;* David Robinson, *Apostle of Culture: Emerson as Preacher and Lecturer* (1982); and Wesley T. Mott, *"The Strains of Eloquence": Emerson and His Sermons* (1989).

Sarah Ann Wider

V

VIRGIL, or Vergil (Publius Vergilius Maro, 70–19 B.C.), was the great Roman epic poet. Although C. P. Cranch** produced an excellent translation of V's *Aeneid* that has been admired by Allen Mandelbaum, the modern translator of the poem, the *Aeneid* was not a major text for most of the Transcendentalists. H. Thoreau** says in "A Walk to Wachusett" that he lost interest in the *Aeneid* at line 7 and the reference to "the walls of high Rome." V's *Eclogues* (37 B.C.E.) and *Georgics* (29 B.C.E.) were, however, important texts for Thoreau. Reading the *Eclogues* in 1840, he declared V valuable because he showed "the identity of human nature in all ages." Thoreau was even more impressed by the *Georgics*, the great four-part poem on farming that Dryden considered "the best poem by the best poet."

V spent seven years on the poem, and it has been called "the most carefully finished product of Roman literature." The four parts of the *Georgics* cover tillage, plowing, cattle raising, and beekeeping. Thoreau found it the great poem of the earth, practical enough to use as a handbook, and the best poem in praise of country life. The *Georgics* are practical and beautiful at the same time. V so exalts labor—the world of work—that we may speak of a Virgilian work ethic, to which Thoreau subscribed. And Thoreau's much-quoted assertion "Surely joy is the condition of life" may well have its earliest root in the opening line of the *Georgics*, where V undertakes to tell *Quid faciat laetas segetes*, What makes the crops joyous. Thoreau rated V first among the Roman agricultural* writers (others are Cato, Varro, Columella, and Palladius) and hoped that his own work would one day have a place among the classics of country living.

REFERENCES: For Thoreau's interest in V, see Ethel Seybold, *Thoreau: The Quest and the Classics* (1951); Robert Sattelmeyer, *Thoreau's Reading* (1988); and Robert D. Richardson, Jr., *Henry Thoreau: A Life of the Mind* (1986).

Robert D. Richardson, Jr.

VIṢṆU PURĀṆA is one of 18 *Purāṇas,* or "old traditional stories," in the Vedic tradition of Hindu sacred literature. The Transcendentalists were heavily influenced by the dialogical questions found in the five-volume 1840 English translation from the original Sanskrit by H. H. Wilson.

The *Viṣṇu Purāṇa* is primarily concerned with Viṣṇu, the second deity in the Trimurti, or Hindu trinity, who represents the preserving and protecting aspect of the godhead. The theology of the *Viṣṇu Purāṇa* is largely inspired by earlier Vedic writings. The subjects discussed include the creation of the universe, the division of time, the institutions of the law and religion, the genealogy of patriarchal families, and the dynasties of kings.

Authorship is unknown, but tradition holds that the *Purāṇas* were written by a generous sage who simplified the Vedic doctrines. The specific dates for the *Viṣṇu Purāṇa* are also unknown. Wilson writes that "the Vishnu Purana has kept very clear of particulars from which an approximation to its date may be conjectured"; contemporary scholar Leyla Goren believes, however, that the *Purāṇas* were written in A.D. 500.

The first major Transcendentalist to be heavily influenced by Oriental* writings like the *Viṣṇu Purāṇa* was R. W. Emerson.** Early on in his career, he showed a slight interest in them. On 10 June 1822, a year after his graduation from college, Emerson wrote to his aunt M. M. Emerson,** "I am curious to read your Hindoo mythologies." In 1834, Emerson began seriously browsing Oriental writings. It was not until his mature years, though, that Emerson became an Orientalist in earnest, and the *Viṣṇu Purāṇa* was probably as important to Emerson as the *Bhagavadgītā.** In 1845, "Vishnu Purana" first appears in his journal.*

H. D. Thoreau** and A. B. Alcott,** according to Christy, both "caught the Oriental contagion" from Emerson. All three men had read Oriental literature before they had published a single book. In 1849, Alcott compiled a list of Oriental writings, including the *Viṣṇu Purāṇa,* which he intended to borrow from the library of the Boston Athenaeum.* In 1850, Thoreau first drew the *Viṣṇu Purāṇa* from the Harvard College Library, and again in 1854. During this time, Thoreau copied about 30 pages of extracts for future reference. In 1855, Thoreau's English friend T. Cholmondeley** sent him a gift of 44 Oriental books, including the *Viṣṇu Purāṇa.* Robert Sattelmeyer claims that while Thoreau responded gratefully, he did not seem to have been "inspired to read or reread the books themselves to any significant extent." Other Transcendentalists who borrowed the *Viṣṇu Purāṇa* from either the Athenaeum or Harvard include J. F. Clarke** and T. Parker.**

In 1845, passages from the *Viṣṇu Purāṇa* inspired Emerson's poems "Hamatreya" and "Brahma." For example, the underlying idea of "Hamatreya" is that "words *I* and *mine* constitute ignorance." Later, Emerson versified specific passages from the *Viṣṇu Purāṇa.* For instance, the Hindu text says, "What living creature slays or is slain? What living creature preserves or is preserved?

Each is his own destroyer, as he follows evil or good." Emerson's journal version looks like this: "What creature slayeth or is slain? / What creature saves or saved is? / His life will either lose or gain, / As he shall follow harm or bliss."

Thoreau's thought and writings likewise demonstrate an interpenetration of East and West. For example, he writes in *Walden*, "[T]he pure Walden water is mingled with the sacred water of the Ganges." Thoreau tended to quote the *Viṣṇu Purāṇa*, however, more as a springboard into his own commentary or as a punctuation mark for his own narrative. For example, in the "Former Inhabitants; and Winter Visitors" chapter of *Walden*, he writes:

There too, as every where, I sometimes expected the Visitor who never comes. The Vishnu Purana says, "The house-holder is to remain at eventide in his court-yard as long as it takes to milk a cow, or longer if he pleases, to await the arrival of a guest." I often performed this duty of hospitality, waited long enough to milk a whole herd of cows, but did not see the man approaching from the town.

In his *A Week on the Concord and Merrimack Rivers*, Thoreau wrote this regarding friendship:

My friend is not of some other race or family of men, but flesh of my flesh, bone of my bone. . . . We do not live far apart. . . . Have not the fates associated us in many ways? It says, in the Vishnu Purana: "Seven paces together is sufficient for the friendship of the virtuous, but thou and I have dwelt together."

REFERENCES: See Kenneth Walter Cameron, *Transcendental Reading Patterns* (1970); Frederic Ives Carpenter, *Emerson and Asia* (1930); Arthur Christy, *The Orient in American Transcendentalism* (1932); Leyla Goren, *Elements of Brahmanism in the Transcendentalism of Emerson*, ed. Kenneth Walter Cameron (1977), esp. part one; Umesa Patri, *Hindu Scriptures and American Transcendentalists* (1987); Robert Sattelmeyer, *Thoreau's Reading* (1988); Philip Van Doren Stern, *The Annotated* Walden (1970); and *The Vishnu Purana: A System of Hindu Mythology and Tradition*, trans. H. H. Wilson (1840), in *Works by the Late Horace Hayman Wilson*, ed. Fitzedward Hall (1864). The last is available as part of the Garland Publishing, Inc. Series on Oriental Religions (1981).

Moumin Manzoor Quazi

W

WALDEN POND, a small glacial kettle lake located about a mile and a half from Concord* Village, became, arguably, the geographic symbol of the Transcendental movement. The favorite terminus for R. W. Emerson's** Sunday walks and the site of H. Thoreau's** cabin, Walden Pond was immortalized in Thoreau's *Walden* (1854).

Up to the last month of his life, Emerson enjoyed walking toward and around Walden, which he considered Concord's "chief ornament." Among those whom he took to the pond were J. Very,** C. P. Cranch,** N. Hawthorne** (who on his first visit was not impressed by the size but appreciated the clarity of the water after having seen the murky Concord River behind the Old Manse*), M. Fuller,** A. H. Clough** (who called it "a prettyish pool"), M. D. Conway,** and Fredrika Bremer, a Swedish author whom Emerson entreated to extend her visit to Concord by one day so that she could see Walden. F. B. Sanborn** saw so much interest in these walks to Walden, especially on Sunday mornings, that he named the walkers the Walden Pond Society and considered them an important religious society in Concord.

Emerson purchased land around the pond throughout his life. In the fall of 1844, ostensibly to keep the trees from being cut for firewood and, possibly, as the site of a study for himself or a house for the Alcotts,** he bought the Wyman field on the village side of the pond. The next year he allowed Thoreau to build his cabin there and to raise beans in the field behind the cabin. Emerson so identified that parcel of land with Thoreau that in 1845 he assigned it to Henry in his will (although that provision was later removed). In 1846 Emerson went so far as to commission Thoreau to pick a house site for him on the south side of Walden on what came to be called Emerson's Cliff. After Thoreau surveyed the land and picked a site, nothing more came from the project.

If Emerson valued Walden Pond, Thoreau immortalized it. In a journal* entry from the summer of 1845, Thoreau recalls his first memory of Walden:

Twenty three years since when I was 5 years old, I was brought from Boston to this pond, away in the county . . . one of the most ancient scenes stamped on the tablets of my memory—the oriental* asiatic valley of my world—whence so many races and inventions have gone forth in recent times. That woodland vision for a long time made the drapery of my dreams. That sweet solitude my spirit seemed so early to require that I might have room to entertain my thronging guests, and that speaking silence that my ears might distinguish the significant sounds. Some how or other it at once gave the preference to this recess among the pines where almost sunshine & shadow were the only inhabitants that varied the scene, over that tumultuous and varied city—as if it had found its proper nursery.

Seeking solitude to recover from the death of his brother, John,** and to write about their trip on the Concord and Merrimack Rivers, Thoreau moved to the shore of Walden on 4 July 1845, Independence Day. He was following the lead of others whom he knew, including his college roommate C. S. Wheeler,** who had lived in a cabin at Sandy Pond. Another friend, Ellery Channing,** wrote to Thoreau on 5 March 1845, suggesting that he build a hut and live at Walden in order to "devour himself."

In *Walden*, Thoreau described the site of his new home as "a small pond, about a mile and a half south of the village of Concord and somewhat higher than it, in the midst of an extensive wood . . . about two miles south of that our only field known to fame, Concord Battle Ground." Later in the book he added: "This pond is so remarkable for its depth and purity as to merit a particular description. It is a clear and deep green well, half a mile long and a mile and three quarters in circumference, and contains about sixty-one and a half acres; a perennial spring in the midst of pine and oak woods, without any visible inlet or outlet except by the clouds and evaporation." These characteristics, especially the pond's depth and purity, provided Thoreau with the controlling symbolism for *Walden*. For Thoreau, Walden represented the divine in nature,* and through an identification with the pond, he and anyone who appropriated its powers could revitalize their lives, just as the pond manifested the rebirth of nature each spring. Walden was, in his words, "God's Drop." And Thoreau went on to describe his elaborate efforts at plumbing its mythical depths. Since its publication in 1854, *Walden* has inspired spiritual and personal reform as well as pilgrimages to the shores of Walden Pond. Many come to place a stone on the cairn begun in 1872 to memorialize the site of Thoreau's sojourn. Others come to see the place that served both Emerson and Thoreau as the symbol of all that is good in nature.

Since the mid-1950s Walden Pond has been the center of controversy. Long one of the most popular fishing and swimming places in the Northeast, Walden Pond has been threatened by overuse and environmental abuse with as many as a half million annual visitors being documented in the late 1970s. Having been deeded by Edith Emerson Forbes to the Commonwealth of Massachusetts in 1922, Walden was named the first Registered National Literary Landmark in

1965. Control of the pond has shifted from the county to the state. But debate still rages over its use. Walden Forever Wild, an organization incorporated in 1981, advocates that the park's use be changed from recreation to an educational-historical-ecological sanctuary and refuge. In 1988 the state limited the carrying capacity, or maximum number of people who could use the pond at one time, to 1,000, a far cry from the reported 15,000 to 20,000 who previously might be found fishing or swimming at Walden. Despite these actions, many contend that, ironically, the purity of the pond that meant so much to Thoreau remains in jeopardy.

REFERENCES: In addition to *Walden* (Princeton Univ. Press edition, 1971), good sources about the importance of Walden Pond to the Transcendentalists include such biographies as Harding (1965); and John McAleer, *Ralph Waldo Emerson: Days of Encounter* (1984). The controversy over the pond's use is summarized in "Walden Pond: A Place to Think, or Swim?" in *The Christian Science Monitor,* 6 June 1983, B1–2. Lawrence Buell, "The Thoreauvian Pilgrimage: The Structure of an American Cult," *AL* 61 (May 1989): 175–99, discusses the development of Walden as a major site for literary pilgrimages. A special issue of *CS* (20, nos. 1 & 2 [December 1988]), devoted to Walden Woods,* contains more background on Walden and the Transcendentalists.

Larry R. Long

WALDEN WOODS is an ecologically and historically distinct 2,680–acre glacial feature extending from southern Concord* to northern Lincoln, Massachusetts, with profound ties to the Concord Transcendentalists. Long obscured by its famous component the Walden Pond State Reservation, the larger identity of Walden Woods was reasserted in the late 1980s by Thoreauvians and environmentalists working to protect sites associated with H. D. Thoreau** from commercial development.

Walden Woods is most famous as the site of Thoreau's 1845–47 experiment in Transcendental economy, immortalized in *Walden; or, Life in the Woods* (1854). Though Walden Pond* is the symbolic center of this classic, Thoreau is explicit that he "went to the woods . . . to live deliberately," and the saunterings, descriptions, encounters, and meditations of the book indeed range throughout Walden Woods. Walden Woods was also a favorite walking place of Concordians N. Hawthorne,** Ellery Channing,** and the Alcotts.** R. W. Emerson,** who owned the site of Thoreau's house and the ledge on the opposite side of Walden Pond, called Walden Woods his "sacred grove."

Traditionally associated by the Concord establishment with freed slaves, Irish laborers, drunkards, and other "unseemly" types, Walden Woods was rarely held in the esteem accorded such landmarks as the North Bridge and Concord's literary homes; its identity was further diminished when in the 1930s it was bisected by the construction of Route 2. Even among Thoreau scholars and enthusiasts, concern usually focused on preserving Walden Pond and its fragile shores and banks. Thus, it came as a surprise when in 1989 the Thoreau Country Conservation Alliance (TCCA)—originally consisting of Thomas Blanding,

Jack Borden, Walter Brain, Vidar Jorgensen, and Edmund Schofield—called urgent attention to two threats of imminent development within Walden Woods: A 139-unit condominium project was proposed on Bear Garden Hill, a favorite spot for Thoreau's huckleberrying and moonlight walks, 1,400 yards from Walden Pond; and trees had already been cleared for a three-story office complex only 700 yards from the pond on Brister's Hill—the location, ironically, of Thoreau's pioneering ecological study of forest succession.

Land-use patterns within Walden Woods for over three centuries have reflected Concordians' practical sense of the area's surficial geology. The porous sands and gravels deposited in Glacial Lake Sudbury are not conducive to farming, which is why Walden Woods has remained largely forested throughout Concord's history. The ecological coherence of Walden Woods was scientifically established in the 1980s. TCCA research into letters, journals,* literature, legal deeds, town reports, and maps demonstrated that "Walden Woods" was a historical and cultural entity as well—confirming Thoreau's use of the term. The scope of Walden Woods as established by TCCA was validated in a newly uncovered 1895 map by Albert Wood. In the spring of 1990—in the nick of time—recording artist Don Henley founded the Walden Woods Project (WWP) to raise the millions of dollars needed to successfully acquire Bear Garden Hill (1990) and Brister's Hill (1993). Concerts, walks, and other fundraising efforts continued as Henley and the WWP remained committed to preserving sites associated with Thoreau and other Concord authors. Thoreau, who had begun to formulate a conservation ethic in his later years, would have been pleased. As he wrote in his unfinished lecture "Huckleberries," "All Walden wood might have been reserved, with Walden in the midst of it."

REFERENCES: Thomas Blanding authoritatively presents the cultural background and significance of "Historic Walden Woods"—with testimony by Thoreau, Channing, Hawthorne, Emerson, Alcott, and other Concordians—in a special issue of *CS* (20, nos. 1 & 2 [December 1988], 86 pp.). The natural history* and ecology of Walden Woods are explored in 13 essays composing Part VI of *Thoreau's World and Ours: A Natural Legacy,* ed. Edmund A. Schofield and Robert C. Baron (1993), 153–297, part of the proceedings of the 50th anniversary Jubilee of the Thoreau Society. *Heaven Is Under Our Feet: A Book for Walden Woods* (1991), ed. Don Henley and Dave Marsh—a bestselling collection of essays by writers, performing artists, environmentalists, political leaders, and scholars—was published to support the work of the Walden Woods Project. The TCCA and WWP produced a "Map of Walden Woods" (1991) showing over 100 natural and cultural features within Walden Woods.

Wesley T. Mott

WALKER, FULLER AND COMPANY was the firm of James P. Walker (1829–1868) and Horace B. Fuller (1836–1899), minor Boston publishers whose books reflected and catered to the interests of the later Transcendentalists. The firm's beginnings may be traced to 1859 when, with Daniel W. Wise, Walker organized Walker, Wise and Company, Boston, as "a depot and headquarters" for Unitarianism* and liberal Christianity. Its imprints included tracts on antislavery, works on the advancement of women, and books of instruction for the young. In 1864 Fuller, having clerked with a firm specializing in dictionaries and schoolbooks, was employed by Walker, Wise. With the departure of Wise in 1865, Fuller became a partner, and the name was altered to Walker, Fuller and Company.

During its brief existence, the firm made an impact, publishing books that asserted "the inalienable worth of man." Among its authors were J. F. Clarke,** O. B. Frothingham,** F. H. Hedge,** T. Parker,** W. E. Channing.** Its imprints supported woman's rights* in works by C. H. Dall,** Dr. Marie Zakrzewska, and Virginia Penny; it championed abolition* and condemned slavery by issuing Augustin Cochin's *The Results of Slavery* and *The Results of Emancipation,* M. D. Conway's** *Rejected Stone,* W. Phillips's** *Speeches, Lectures, and Letters,* and D. A. Wasson's** *Radical Creed.* Through the works it distributed, the firm evinced its advocacy of Transcendental ideology, a God immanent* in man, the purposes of humanitarianism.

In 1866, when the American Unitarian Association withdrew its support, resuming its own publishing, the firm failed and the partners separated. Between 1867 and 1873, Horace B. Fuller, "successor to Walker, Fuller and Company," continued to serve later Transcendental Boston by publishing the works of Parker and H. Mann.** One of his last imprints was—appropriately enough—Alphonse Daudet's *The New Don Quixote* (1873).

The output of Walker, Fuller championed the causes and reflected the affirmations of Transcendentalism, and the partners themselves, having experienced a kind of success in failure, demonstrated the idealism* of New England's renaissance. Despite its short life, the firm distributed to an appreciative readership works on liberal Christianity and antislavery, the advancement of women and the enlightenment of children, works that released the liberated conscience of man to do its work in the world.

REFERENCES: For the careers of Walker and Fuller, the fullest account is Madeleine B. Stern, *Imprints on History: Book Publishers and American Frontiers* (1956), 45–59, 401–5. Other sources include the obituary notice of Fuller in *Publisher's Weekly* 55 (21 January 1899): 56, and [Thomas B. Fox, ed.,] *Memoir of James P. Walker* (1869), where Walker's early career and character are discussed. For the firm's imprints, their *Catalogue of Standard Books Chiefly by Eminent Unitarian Divines, for Sale by Walker, Wise, & Co.* (n.d.) is useful, along with the advertisements of Walker, Fuller in *American Literary Gazette* 5 (15 May 1865): 33; 5 (15 September 1865): 221; 6 (1 November 1865): 29; 6 (1 December 1865): 101; 6 (2 April 1866): 302, 316.

Madeleine B. Stern

WESTERN MESSENGER, a monthly magazine of religion and literature, was published in Louisville and Cincinnati from 1835 to 1841 by a group of New England expatriates closely associated with the Transcendental circle. Originally planned as part of the Unitarian* missionary effort in the Ohio Valley, where antisectarian preaching and cultural indefiniteness augured well for liberal religion, the magazine early on asserted its independence. As one of the editors, William Greenleaf Eliot (1811–1887), said in the preface to the first volume, "[O]ur object is not to build up a sect, but to establish the truth" (*WM*, 1:2). In its continuing adherence to this "living and always new *spirit* of truth" (*WM*, 8:407), the *WM* is justifiably considered the first periodical of American Transcendentalism.

Under Ephraim Peabody (1807–1856), its first editor, the *WM* offered readers a mixture of practical theology and articles on Western affairs and literature. With the third volume in 1836, under the new supervision of J. F. Clarke** in Louisville, its focus was broadened to include discussions of antislavery, labor relations, German literature, and contemporary poets such as Tennyson, Shelley, and Wordsworth.** A "living mirror of its times" (*WM*, 3:853), its policy of avoiding "ultraism" progressively alienated those readers interested in partisanship, while at the same time its defenses of the Transcendentalists cost it support among moderate Unitarians. Clarke repeatedly chastised the American Unitarian Association for its lukewarm support of the magazine. In 1838, a month before R. W. Emerson's** Divinity School Address, Clarke anticipated the criticism of his denomination's "coldness" and later that year defended "R. W. Emerson and the New School" (*WM*, 6:37–47) against the "orthodoxism" of A. Norton**—a position Norton and others found subversive and in bad taste.

In 1839 Clarke turned the editorship over to James Handasyd Perkins (1810–1849) and W. H. Channing,** who had come to Cincinnati more interested in social reform than theological debate. The magazine turned away from doctrinal matters—Channing dismissed Unitarianism as a "mere scholastic title" (*WM*, 8:6)—and toward social and economic critiques, including a positive review of O. Brownson's** "Labouring Classes." Flagging interest among subscribers, Channing's crisis of spirit, and the appearance of *The Dial** all contributed to the magazine's demise in 1841.

REFERENCES: For a full study of the magazine and its editors, see Robert D. Habich, *Transcendentalism and the "WM": A History of the Magazine and Its Contributors, 1835–1841* (1985). Habich indexes the *WM*'s contents in "An Annotated List of Contributions to the *WM*," *SAR* 1984: 93–179.

Robert D. Habich

The **WOMAN'S RIGHTS MOVEMENT** was nurtured by Transcendentalism, which was a protest against a social system as well as traditional religious and intellectual doctrines, all of which subjugated women. The Transcendentalist revolt against narrow Christianity, based in a belief in intuitive revelation, included women and turned the "feminine" values of domesticity into a new social ethic. Transcendentalism taught the liberation and fulfillment of human potential for all people including women. Placing intuition at the pinnacle of perceptual categories, the movement relegated rationalism to second position, raising women's perceived abilities to the highest level and reordering the conventional hierarchy. M. Fuller's** idea that a woman had an identity beyond her sex was grounded in her belief that each woman had an independent relationship with God. Transcendentalist women emphasized education* as not merely the acquisition of knowledge but the exercise of the intellect and consciousness. Evangelical Unitarianism* moved religion out of church and into voluntary associations and reform activities—women's sphere—thereby including women in the enterprise while maintaining the role of spiritual missionary sanctified by the cult of domesticity. In the social reform movements, women found not only an outlet for their altruistic, benevolent impulses but the strength and inspiration for their future collective action.

In the realms of marriage and family, economic, legal, and social issues converged. The Transcendentalist view of marriage was based in the Swedenborgian* ideal of marriage as the symbol for universal order, a balance of divine attributes that defined women and men as separate and distinct creatures. The concept of marriage as a union of equal and complementary souls, a joining beyond legal sanction, made anything less an abomination to the divine spirit and thereby suggested that divorce was possible and even necessary. There were obvious tensions between the doctrine of maximum individual growth and the constraints of domestic arrangements. Although this new vision contradicted social reality, it framed a world in which presumably all social injustice would disappear when the male hegemony gave way to the harmony of both sexes mutually evolving.

Seeing a reformed society as an extended family, the Transcendentalists considered the familial group as the essential unit of change, making this a domestic rather than institutional movement. Both Brook Farm* and Fruitlands,* for example, were conceived of as family arrangements. The social orientation of the movement led them to try to live according to their convictions about human nature and need, reconstructing ideas of family relationships, community relations, and work. While it maintained the domestic ideal of women, it gave them a larger sphere of influence by their rights to vote, to choose an occupation, and to speak in public. Transcendentalist Fourierists** could gauge progress toward the utopian ideal by examining the position of women in their society.

Fourierism's socialist critique advocated the economic liberation of women, and within the ranks of the Transcendentalists, there was some economic equality and autonomy. Sophia Ripley's** financial investment in Brook Farm brought her voting rights and an official position. E. P. Peabody,** a charter member of the Transcendental Club,* owned the bookstore where Fuller offered her Conversations.* She became perhaps the first woman book publisher in America and remained financially independent. However, the economic liberation of Transcendentalist theory did not necessarily free women from financial burdens imposed by families. B. Alcott's** refusal to labor for hire forced his wife, Abigail, to work outside the home and his daughter Louisa** to write for a living in order to ensure the family's economic survival.

Beyond issues of economic equality lay the responsibility for the work of the movement. The choice of Fuller as editor of *The Dial** signified the inclusion of women as trusted sharers in the intellectual work. Peabody's bookshop created a place where women joined with men in intellectual conversation and planned social reform. Women's engagement in Transcendental endeavors resulted in a sensitivity to issues concerning women and family.

The Transcendentalists' radical social vision aroused controversies that effectively excluded these women and men from conventional society. This separateness and their convictions encouraged them to consider both social and intimate relationships in revisionist ways. Their social circumstances and Transcendental conscience also encouraged crossing the boundaries of conventional male and female spheres through friendship: Fuller and R. W. Emerson,** C. S. Tappan** and Emerson, E. Peabody and W. E. Channing,** Peabody and H. Mann,** Lidian Emerson** and H. Thoreau.** The relaxed codes of dress and easy association of unmarried young people at Brook Farm, for example, led to—among other things—companionable relationships across conventional barriers. In addition, the close bonds of female friendship that women formed provided a basis for self-awareness and sisterly solidarity that later propelled the woman's rights movement.

The emergence of a feminist consciousness coincided with the surge of organizations that spread it, such as abolitionist* groups, millenarianism, and utopian communities. For some women, the imperative to individual freedom became self-conscious feminism, although Fuller's *Woman in the Nineteenth Century* (1845) was the only major feminist statement produced by the Transcendentalist movement. If Fuller had not met her death on her return to America, the course of the woman's rights movement might have been somewhat different. Her legacy was her intellectual framing of the questions and women insisting on answers, women like C. W. H. Dall,** who participated in Fuller's Conversations when she was 19 and became corresponding editor of Pauline Wright Davis's woman's rights monthly, *Una.*

The May 1847 formation of the Women's Associative Union in Boston was an attempt to maintain the bonds formed at Brook Farm and assert women's unity. Recognizing the right to economic security at the core of their agenda, the group opened a store to sell needlework and to assure employment for women. Although their resolution was not as radical as the "Declaration of Sentiments" framed in Seneca Falls, New York, that same year, it marked a parallel moment in the history of the woman's rights movement, one when women realized their hope lay in collective action. Among Transcendentalists, debate often centered on the matter of voting rights rather than more substantive issues. Emerson, for example, recoiled from the idea of women voting but advocated woman's rights in principle. When the Women's Rights Convention met, the participants were familiar with Mary Wollstonecraft's *Vindication of the Rights of Woman* (1792), Sarah Grimké's *Letters on the Equality of the Sexes* (1838), and Fuller's *Woman in the Nineteenth Century.* Unlike their eloquent foremothers, the women in Seneca Falls forged a simple list of grievances.

It was a moment that linked the idealism* and short history of Transcendentalism with the feminists of the future.

REFERENCES: The most wide-ranging and useful work on the relationship between Transcendentalism and the woman's rights movement is Anne C. Rose, *Transcendentalism as a Social Movement, 1830–1850* (1981). For an overview of the movement, Eleanor Flexner, *Century of Struggle: The Woman's Rights Movement in the United States* (1975), is valuable. Nancy F. Cott, *The Grounding of Modern Feminism* (1987), is less focused on the period but explores the strands of feminist ideology that emerged in the 19th century. Susan P. Conrad, *Perish the Thought: Intellectual Women in Romantic America 1830–1860* (1976), addresses the relationship between the intellectual pursuits of women such as Fuller and the woman's movement.

Kate H. Winter and Elaine Handley

Bibliography

Following is a selected list of recent and historically important book-length studies treating major facets of Transcendentalism in the United States. Consult entry references for specialized studies.

GENERAL STUDIES

Barbour, Brian M., ed. *American Transcendentalism: An Anthology of Criticism.* Notre Dame, Ind.: Univ. of Notre Dame Press, 1973.

Boller, Paul F., Jr. *American Transcendentalism, 1830–1860: An Intellectual Inquiry.* New York: Putnam's, 1974.

Brooks, Van Wyck. *The Flowering of New England 1815–1865.* New York: E. P. Dutton, 1936.

Cameron, Kenneth W. *Transcendental Climate.* 3 vols. Hartford: Transcendental Books, 1963.

Carafiol, Peter. *The American Ideal: Literary History as a Worldly Activity.* New York: Oxford Univ. Press, 1991.

Frothingham, Octavius Brooks. *Transcendentalism in New England: A History.* New York: G. P. Putnam's, 1876.

Goddard, Harold Clarke. *Studies in New England Transcendentalism.* New York: Columbia Univ. Press, 1908.

Gura, Philip F., and Joel Myerson, eds. *Critical Essays on American Transcendentalism.* Boston: G. K. Hall, 1982.

Koster, Donald N. *Transcendentalism in America.* Boston: Twayne, 1975.

Matthiessen, F. O. *American Renaissance: Art and Expression in the Age of Emerson and Whitman.* New York: Oxford Univ. Press, 1941.

Miller, Perry. *Nature's Nation.* Cambridge: Harvard Univ. Press, 1967.

———. *The Transcendentalists: An Anthology.* Cambridge: Harvard Univ. Press, 1950.

Myerson, Joel, ed. *The American Renaissance in New England (Dictionary of Literary Biography,* vol. 1). Detroit: Gale, 1978.

Packer, Barbara L. "The Transcendentalists." In Sacvan Bercovitch, ed., *The Cambridge*

History of American Literature, vol. 2, *Prose Writing—1820–1865.* New York: Cambridge Univ. Press, 1994.

INFLUENCES, SOURCES, APPROPRIATIONS

Bercovitch, Sacvan. *The American Jeremiad.* Madison: Univ. of Wisconsin Press, 1978.
———. *The Puritan Origins of the American Self.* New Haven: Yale Univ. Press, 1975.
Cameron, Kenneth Walter. *Ralph Waldo Emerson's Reading.* Raleigh, N.C.: Thistle Press, 1941.
———. *Transcendental Reading Patterns: Library Charging Lists for the Alcotts, James Freeman Clarke, Frederic Henry Hedge, Theodore Parker.* Hartford: Transcendental Books, 1970.
Christy, Arthur. *The Orient in American Transcendentalism: A Study of Emerson, Thoreau, and Alcott.* New York: Columbia Univ. Press, 1932.
Grey, Robin S. *The Complicity of Imagination: The American Renaissance, Contests of Authority, and Seventeenth-Century English Culture.* New York: Cambridge Univ. Press, 1995.
Harding, Walter. *Emerson's Library.* Charlottesville: Univ. Press of Virginia, 1967.
———. *Thoreau's Library.* Charlottesville: Univ. of Virginia Press, 1957.
Leighton, Walter L. *French Philosophers and New-England Transcendentalism.* Charlottesville: Univ. of Virginia, 1908.
New, Elisa. *The Regenerate Lyric: Theology and Innovation in American Poetry.* New York: Cambridge Univ. Press, 1993.
Pochmann, Henry A. *German Culture in America: Philosophical and Literary Influences, 1600–1900.* Madison: Univ. of Wisconsin Press, 1957.
Poirier, Richard. *Poetry and Pragmatism.* Cambridge: Harvard Univ. Press, 1992.
Sattelmeyer, Robert. *Thoreau's Reading: A Study in Intellectual History.* Princeton, N.J.: Princeton Univ. Press, 1988.
Sealts, Merton M., Jr. *Emerson on the Scholar.* Columbia: Univ. of Missouri Press, 1992.
Seybold, Ethel. *Thoreau: The Quest and the Classics.* New Haven: Yale Univ. Press, 1951.
Van Anglen, Kevin P. *The New England Milton: Literary Reception and Cultural Authority in the Early Republic.* University Park: Pennsylvania State Univ. Press, 1993.
Van Cromphout, Gustaaf. *Emerson's Modernity and the Example of Goethe.* Columbia: Univ. of Missouri Press, 1990.
Versluis, Arthur. *American Transcendentalism and Asian Religions.* New York: Oxford Univ. Press, 1993.
Vogel, Stanley M. *German Literary Influences on the American Transcendentalists.* New Haven: Yale Univ. Press, 1955.

LITERATURE AND LANGUAGE

Buell, Lawrence. *Literary Transcendentalism: Style and Vision in the American Renaissance.* Ithaca: Cornell Univ. Press, 1973.
———. *New England Literary Culture: From Revolution Through Renaissance.* Cambridge, England: Cambridge Univ. Press, 1986.

Gura, Philip F. *The Wisdom of Words: Language, Theology, and Literature in the New England Renaissance.* Middletown, Conn.: Wesleyan Univ. Press, 1981.

Gustafson, Thomas. *Representative Words: Politics, Literature, and the American Language, 1776–1865.* New York: Cambridge Univ. Press, 1992.

Loving, Jerome. *Emerson, Whitman, and the American Muse.* Chapel Hill: Univ. of North Carolina Press, 1982.

Myerson, Joel, ed. *Studies in the American Renaissance: An Annual.* Boston: Twayne, 1977–82; Charlottesville: Univ. Press of Virginia, 1983–96.

Porte, Joel. *Emerson and Thoreau: Transcendentalists in Conflict.* Middletown, Conn.: Wesleyan Univ. Press, 1966.

Richardson, Robert D., Jr. *Myth and Literature in the American Renaissance.* Bloomington: Indiana Univ. Press, 1978.

Simpson, David. *The Politics of American English, 1776–1850.* New York: Oxford Univ. Press, 1986.

Waggoner, Hyatt H. *American Poets from the Puritans to the Present.* Boston: Houghton Mifflin, 1968.

THEOLOGY

Albanese, Catherine L. *Corresponding Motion: Transcendental Religion and the New America.* Philadelphia: Temple Univ. Press, 1977.

Brown, Jerry Wayne. *The Rise of Biblical Criticism in America, 1800–1870: The New England Scholars.* Middletown, Conn.: Wesleyan Univ. Press, 1969.

Howe, Daniel Walker. *The Unitarian Conscience: Harvard Moral Philosophy, 1805–1861.* Cambridge: Harvard Univ. Press, 1970.

Hutchison, William R. *The Transcendentalist Ministers: Church Reform in the New England Renaissance.* New Haven: Yale Univ. Press, 1959.

Mott, Wesley T. *"The Strains of Eloquence": Emerson and His Sermons.* University Park: Pennsylvania State Univ. Press, 1989.

Robinson, David M. *Apostle of Culture: Emerson as Preacher and Lecturer.* Philadelphia: Univ. of Pennsylvania Press, 1982.

———. *The Unitarians and the Universalists.* Westport, Conn.: Greenwood Press, 1985.

NATURE, PHILOSOPHY, AND SCIENCE

Buell, Lawrence. *The Environmental Imagination: Thoreau, Nature Writing, and the Formation of American Culture.* Cambridge: Harvard Univ. Press, 1995.

Goodman, Russell B. *American Philosophy and the Romantic Tradition.* New York: Cambridge Univ. Press, 1991.

Henley, Don, and Dave Marsh, eds. *Heaven Is Under Our Feet: A Book for Walden Woods.* Stamford, Conn.: Longmeadow Press, 1991.

Horwitz, Howard. *By the Law of Nature: Form and Value in Nineteenth-Century America.* New York: Oxford Univ. Press, 1991.

McIntosh, James. *Thoreau as Romantic Naturalist: His Shifting Stance toward Nature.* Ithaca: Cornell Univ. Press, 1974.

Marx, Leo. *The Machine in the Garden: Technology and the Pastoral Ideal in America.* New York: Oxford Univ. Press, 1964.

Nash, Roderick. *Wilderness and the American Mind.* New Haven: Yale Univ. Press, 1967.

Oelschlaeger, Max. *The Idea of Wilderness from Prehistory to the Age of Ecology.* New
    Haven: Yale Univ. Press, 1991.
Sealts, Merton M., Jr., and Alfred R. Ferguson, eds. *Emerson's* Nature: *Origin, Growth,
    Meaning* (1969). Revised and enlarged edition. Carbondale: Southern Illinois
    Univ. Press, 1979.
Walls, Laura Dassow. *Seeing New Worlds: Henry David Thoreau and Nineteenth-
    Century Natural Science.* Madison: Univ. of Wisconsin Press, 1995.

REFORM

Codman, John Thomas. *Brook Farm: Historic and Personal Memoirs.* Boston: Arena,
    1894.
Delano, Sterling F. *Brook Farm: A Retrospective and Celebration.* Exhibition catalog.
    Villanova, Pa.: Villanova Univ., 1991.
Gougeon, Len. *Virtue's Hero: Emerson, Antislavery, and Reform.* Athens: Univ. of Geor-
    gia Press, 1990.
Guarneri, Carl J. *The Utopian Alternative: Fourierism in Nineteenth-Century America.*
    Ithaca: Cornell Univ. Press, 1991.
Myerson, Joel. *Brook Farm: An Annotated Bibliography and Resources Guide.* New
    York: Garland, 1978.
————. *The Brook Farm Book: A Collection of First-Hand Accounts of the Community.*
    New York: Garland, 1987.
Rose, Anne C. *Transcendentalism as a Social Movement, 1830–1850.* New Haven: Yale
    Univ. Press, 1981.
Sears, Clara Endicott. *Bronson Alcott's Fruitlands.* Boston: Houghton Mifflin, 1915.
Stange, Douglas C. *Patterns of Antislavery among American Unitarians, 1831–1860.*
    Rutherford, N.J.: Fairleigh Dickinson Univ. Press, 1977.
Swift, Lindsay. *Brook Farm: Its Members, Scholars, and Visitors.* New York: Macmillan,
    1900.

TRANSCENDENTALIST PERIODICALS

Chielens, Edward E., ed. *American Literary Magazines: The Eighteenth and Nineteenth
    Centuries.* Westport, Conn.: Greenwood Press, 1986.
Cooke, George Willis. *An Historical and Biographical Introduction to Accompany* The
    Dial. 2 vols. Cleveland: Rowfant, 1902.
Delano, Sterling F. The Harbinger *and New England Transcendentalism: A Portrait of
    Associationism in America.* Rutherford, N.J.: Fairleigh Dickinson Univ. Press,
    1983.
Gohdes, Clarence L. F. *The Periodicals of American Transcendentalism.* Durham: Duke
    Univ. Press, 1931.
Habich, Robert D. *Transcendentalism and the* Western Messenger: *A History of the
    Magazine and Its Contributors, 1835–1841.* Rutherford, N.J.: Fairleigh Dickinson
    Univ. Press, 1985.
Mott, Frank Luther. *A History of American Magazines.* 4 vols. Cambridge: Harvard Univ.
    Press, 1938–57.
Myerson, Joel. *The New England Transcendentalists and the* Dial: *A History of the*

Magazine and Its Contributors. Rutherford, N.J.: Fairleigh Dickinson Univ. Press, 1980.

BIBLIOGRAPHY

American Literary Scholarship: An Annual. Durham: Duke Univ. Press (since 1965). Bibliographical chapters on "Emerson, Thoreau, Fuller, and Transcendentalism" (Fuller added to chapter title in 1992) and on "Whitman and Dickinson."
Emerson Society Papers. Published by the Ralph Waldo Emerson Society. Includes annual Emerson bibliography.
MLA International Bibliography. New York: Modern Language Association of America. Published annually.
Myerson, Joel, ed. *The Transcendentalists: A Review of Research and Criticism.* New York: Modern Language Association of America, 1984.
Thoreau Society Bulletin. Published by the Thoreau Society. Includes quarterly Thoreau bibliography.

Index

Italicized numbers indicate a main entry

About the Editor and Contributors

Richard P. Benton is Associate Professor Emeritus of English and comparative literature, Trinity College, Hartford, Connecticut.

Elisa E. Beshero is a graduate student at the Pennsylvania State University, University Park.

Ronald A. Bosco is Distinguished Service Professor of American literature at the University at Albany, State University of New York, and an editor of the Emerson Papers at the Houghton Library, Harvard University.

Robert E. Burkholder is Associate Professor of English at the Pennsylvania State University, University Park, and past president of the Ralph Waldo Emerson Society.

Larry A. Carlson, Professor and Director of the Graduate Program in English, teaches American literature and American Studies at the College of Charleston.

John D. Cloy is bibliographer for the humanities at the J. D. Williams Library of the University of Mississippi.

Gary L. Collison, Associate Professor of English at Penn State at York, teaches courses in American literature and culture.

Sterling F. Delano is Professor of American literature at Villanova University.

Mathew David Fisher is Assistant Professor at Ball State University and Director of the College of Architecture and Planning's Writing in the Design Curriculum program.

Lisa M. Gordis is Assistant Professor of English at Barnard College.

Len Gougeon is Professor of American literature at the University of Scranton.

Suzanne D. Green is a Ph.D. candidate at the University of North Texas, specializing in modern American literature and feminist studies.

Ezra Greenspan is Associate Professor of English at the University of South Carolina.

Robin Sandra Grey is Associate Professor of English at the University of Illinois at Chicago.

Dean David Grodzins is a lecturer in history and literature at Harvard University and editor of the *Journal of Unitarian Universalist History.*

Robert D. Habich is Professor of English and Director of Graduate Programs at Ball State University.

Elaine Handley is on the faculty at Empire State College and also teaches writing at Great Meadow Correctional Facility.

Kathleen M. Healey is a doctoral candidate at the Pennsylvania State University, University Park.

David Hicks is Associate Professor and Assistant Chair of literature and communications at Pace University, Pleasantville, New York.

Alan D. Hodder is a member of the faculty of the School of Humanities and Arts at Hampshire College.

Reid Huntley is Associate Professor of English at Ohio University in Athens.

Linck C. Johnson is Professor of English at Colgate University.

Karen L. Kalinevitch is Professor of English at St. Louis Community College.

Alfred G. Litton is Assistant Professor of English at Texas Woman's University.

Kent P. Ljungquist is Professor of English at Worcester Polytechnic Institute and edits the *Poe Studies Association Newsletter.*

Larry R. Long is Professor of English and Director of Honors at Harding University.

Mark J. Madigan teaches in the English Department at the University of Vermont.

Sanford E. Marovitz is Professor of English at Kent State University.

Terry J. Martin is Associate Professor of English at Baldwin-Wallace College.

Charles Mitchell is Assistant Professor of American Studies at Elmira College, Elmira, New York.

Joseph J. Moldenhauer is Mody C. Boatright Regents Professor at the University of Texas, Austin.

Nathaniel T. Mott, a graduate of Gettysburg College, is a freelance writer.

Wesley T. Mott, the editor of this volume, is Professor of English at Worcester Polytechnic Institute, secretary of the Ralph Waldo Emerson Society, which he organized in 1989, and managing editor of *Emerson Society Papers.*

Raymond L. Muncy, who died in January 1994, was Distinguished Professor and former Chair of the Department of History and Social Science at Harding University.

Joel Myerson is Carolina Research Professor of American literature at the University of South Carolina and editor of the annual *Studies in the American Renaissance.*

Daniel Joseph Nadenicek is Assistant Professor of Landscape Architecture at Pennsylvania State University.

Layne Neeper is Assistant Professor of English at Morehead State University.

Christopher Newfield is Assistant Professor of English at the University of California at Santa Barbara.

Julie M. Norko is a doctoral student at the University of North Carolina at Chapel Hill.

Richard R. O'Keefe is Assistant Professor of English at Lock Haven University, Pennsylvania.

Ralph H. Orth is Corse Professor of English language and literature at the University of Vermont.

Joe Pellegrino is a doctoral candidate at the University of North Carolina at Chapel Hill.

D'Ann Pletcher-George, a doctoral candidate in American literature and composition and rhetoric at the University of North Carolina at Chapel Hill, also teaches writing at Towson State University.

Moumin Manzoor Quazi is a doctoral candidate in English literature at the University of North Texas, and a freelance writer and poet.

Robert D. Richardson, Jr., is an independent scholar living in Middletown, Connecticut, and has taught at various universities including Wesleyan, Harvard, University of Denver, and University of Colorado.

Susan L. Roberson is instructor of English at Auburn University.

David M. Robinson is Distinguished Professor of American literature at Oregon State University.

Bruce A. Ronda is Associate Professor of English and Director of the American Studies Program at Colorado State University.

Barbara Ryan is a junior member of the Michigan Society of Fellows and Assistant Professor in the University of Michigan's Program in American Culture.

Susan M. Ryan is a doctoral student in American literature at the University of North Carolina at Chapel Hill.

John P. Samonds is a doctoral student at the University of North Carolina at Chapel Hill.

M. David Samson is Assistant Professor of art history in the Department of Humanities and Arts, Worcester Polytechnic Institute.

Robert Sattelmeyer is Professor of English at Georgia State University and general editor for the *Journal* in THE WRITINGS OF HENRY D. THOREAU.

Mariane Wurst Schaum is a Ph.D. candidate at Georgia State University and an editorial assistant for the *Journal* in THE WRITINGS OF HENRY D. THOREAU and teaches American literature and creative writing at The Lovett School in Atlanta.

Heidi M. Schultz is a Ph.D. candidate and Director of the Writing Center at the University of North Carolina at Chapel Hill.

Frank Shuffelton is Professor of English at the University of Rochester, where he commutes between early American literature and the Transcendentalists.

Susan Belasco Smith is Associate Professor of English at the University of Tulsa.

David J. Sorrells is a Ph.D. candidate in American literature at the University of North Texas.

Madeleine B. Stern, partner, Leona Rostenberg & Madeleine Stern—Rare Books, has written numerous books on 19th-century feminism, publishing history, and biography.

E. Kate Stewart is Associate Professor of English at the University of Arkansas at Monticello.

Maggie Stier, formerly curator at Fruitlands Museums, is a freelance writer, museum consultant, and educator.

Kevin P. Van Anglen has taught English at the University of Pennsylvania, Boston College, and Harvard.

Gustaaf Van Cromphout is Professor of English at Northern Illinois University.

Laura Dassow Walls is Assistant Professor of English at Lafayette College.

Daniel A. Wells is Professor of American literature at the University of South Florida in St. Petersburg.

Jonathan Wells is a graduate student in history at the University of Michigan, specializing in 19th-century American political and intellectual history.

Sarah Ann Wider is Associate Professor of English at Colgate University.

Doni M. Wilson is a Ph.D. candidate in American literature and a teaching fellow at the University of North Carolina at Chapel Hill.

Kate H. Winter is Lecturer in English at the University at Albany, SUNY.

Arthur Wrobel is Associate Professor of English at the University of Kentucky and editor of *ANQ: A Quarterly Journal of Short Articles, Notes, and Reviews.*